Structured Programming in COBOL

B. J. HOLMES, B.Sc., M.Sc., Cert.Ed.

Barry Holmes *is a Senior Lecturer in Computer Studies at Oxford Polytechnic. He has taught computer programming for a number of different examinations, and has used the COBOL language extensively with a wide range of computers, applications and college courses.*

D.P. PUBLICATIONS LTD
Grand Union Industrial Estate
Unit 6, Abbey Road
London NW10 7UL
Telephone 01-965 8898
1986

First Edition 1984

First Impression 1985

Second Impression 1986

British Library Cataloguing in Publication Data

Holmes, B.J. (Barry J.)
    Structured programming in COBOL.
    1. COBOL (Computer program language)
    I. Title
    001.64'24   QA76.73.C25

ISBN 0-905435-41-9
Copyright B.J. HOLMES © 1984
Reprinted 1988

Printed in Great Britain by
Benham & Co. Ltd.,
Colchester, Essex.

ACKNOWLEDGEMENTS

The author wishes to express his thanks to the following:

The Technical Committee X3J4 for permission to use extracts from the Draft Proposed Revised X3.23 American National Standard Programming Language COBOL in Appendix III.

Norma King, software consultant, for advice on software design methods.

My degree and HND Computer Studies students, past and present, who have contributed to the evolution of this book.

Any organization interested in reproducing the COBOL report and specifications in whole or in part, using ideas taken from this report as the basis for an instruction manual or for any other purpose is free to do so. However, all such organizations are requested to reproduce this section as part of the introduction to the document. Those using a short passage, as in a book review, are requested to mention 'COBOL' in acknowledgement of the source, but need not quote this entire section.

COBOL is an industry language and is not the property of any company or group of companies, or of any organization or group of organizations.

No warranty, expressed or implied, is made by any contributor or by the COBOL Committee as to the accuracy and functioning of the programming system and language. Moreover, no responsibility is assumed by any contributor, or by the committee, in connection therewith.

Procedures have been established for the maintenance of COBOL. Inquiries concerning the procedures for proposing changes should be directed to the Executive Committee of the Conference on Data System Languages.

The authors and copyright holders of the copyrighted material used herein

FLOW-MATIC (Trademark of Sperry Rand Corporation, Programming for the UNIVAC (R) I and II, Data Automation Systems copyrighted 1958, 1959, by Sperry Rand Corporation; IBM Commercial Translator, Form No. F23-8013, copyrighted 1959 by IBM; FACT, DSI 27A5260-2760, copyrighted 1960 by Minneapolis-Honeywell

have specifically authorized the use of this material in whole or in part, in the COBOL specification in programming manuals or similar publications.

--from the ANSI COBOL Standard

(X3.23-1974)

Preface

Currently there are many books published on the COBOL language that claim to offer a structured approach to programming. Sadly many of these books fall short of the mark since they offer no more than modular programming. Such books tend to describe coding methods in COBOL with little emphasis on the design of computer programs.

Structured Programming in COBOL adopts a different approach. The author has written the book around two themes; the design of structured computer programs based on the techniques of M.A. Jackson, and the methods available for coding these structured designs in the COBOL language. Throughout, the two themes are shown to complement each other, with programming solutions to problems being designed using Jackson Structured programming (JSP), and the designs then translated into COBOL code.

The JSP methodology of program design has been chosen by the author for the following reasons.

> The techniques of JSP are rapidly becoming adopted as a commercial program design standard. For example it is now specified, under the name of Structured Design Method – SDM, as a Central Government Mandatory Standard for use by civil servants.

> The technique uses a well defined and teachable approach that produces structured program designs.

> The method produces a complete documentation for all programs.

> Program testing and program maintenance is made easier.

> The amount of coding can be reduced to a minimum if the program design is implemented using a JSP COBOL pre-processor. (A JSP COBOL pre-processor is a software package that translates JSP designs into COBOL code).

With a new standard for the COBOL language being proposed at the time of writing this book it has been necessary to include many of the features of the new language that help to enhance structured coding. Three methods of coding computer programs are used. Throughout the book both in-line coding and hierarchical coding methods based on the 1974 Standard for COBOL are used and compared with computer programs, in Appendix II, written using statements from the Draft Proposed Standard.

The depth to which the topics are treated is sufficient for students requiring a knowledge of commercial programming for the following courses.

> First degree courses in Computer Studies or Business Studies with a computing content.

> The BTEC Higher National Diploma, Higher National Certificate and National Certificate in Computer Studies.

> The City & Guilds 746 and 747 examinations.

> Industrial and commercial short courses in programming.

Structured Programming in COBOL familiarises the reader with the fundamentals of the methodologies quickly and uses that foundation to develop more complex programming ideas and skills. The book contains many fully documented worked examples and is packed with well tried and tested exercises, with answers to selected questions, covering a wide variety of data processing applications. A separate answer supplement is available to teachers and lecturers giving the answers to questions not included in Appendix I.

Such questions are denoted by the question numbers being prefixed by the symbol †.

In writing this book the author has assumed that the reader will already have a foundation knowledge of computer terminology used in data processing and will probably have programmed at an elementary level in a language other than COBOL. This is a very realistic assumption since many readers will have met with some form of computer education whilst at school or college and may possibly own a micro-computer and be familiar with some of the concepts of programming. *Structured Programming in COBOL* can be regarded as the next step up from that knowledge!

B.J.H.
Jan. 1984

BIBLIOGRAPHY

Principles of Program Design, M.A. Jackson, Academic Press, 1975.

Structured Design Method – Central Government Mandatory Standard 18: parts 1, 2 and 3, Central Computer and Telecommunications Agency, 1983.

Structured Design Method – Central Computer and Telecommunications Agency, 1978.

Draft Proposed Revised X3.23 American National Standard Programming Language COBOL, Technical Committee X3J4, 1981.

COBOL Programming – a structured approach, P. Abel, Reston, 1980.

COBOL: An introduction to structured logic and modular program design, W.S. Davis, R.H. Fisher, Addison-Wesley, 1979.

Structured COBOL for Data Processing, N. Lyons, Glencoe, 1980.

A guide to COBOL programming, D.D. McCraken, U. Garbassi, Wiley, 1970.

PR1ME – The COBOL Programmer's Guide PDR3056, PR1ME Computer Inc, 1978.

Contents

	Page
Acknowledgements	iii
Preface	iv
Bibliography	vi

CHAPTER 1 ELEMENTS OF COBOL

1.1	Introduction	1
1.2	The structure of a COBOL program: Identification Division, Environment Division, Data Division, Procedure Division	1
1.3	Elements of the Procedure Division: Paragraph names, sentences, statements, reserved words, variables, literals	3
1.4	The COBOL character set	7
1.5	The COBOL program sheet	7
1.6	Questions	9

CHAPTER 2 PROCEDURE DIVISION VERBS

2.1	Introduction	10
	COBOL Standards, notation	
2.2	Data movement – MOVE	11
2.3	Arithmetic – ADD, SUBTRACT, MULTIPLY, DIVIDE, COMPUTE	12
2.4	Input and Output – ACCEPT, DISPLAY	15
2.5	Conditional branching – IF....ELSE...., EVALUATE	16
2.6	Unconditional branching – GO TO, STOP	19
2.7	Procedural control – PERFORM	19
2.8	Questions	21

CHAPTER 3 PROCEDURE DIVISION CODING

3.1	Introduction – coding methods	25
3.2	The constructs – sequence, selection, repetition	26
3.3	Multiple selection	34
3.4	Worked example	36
3.5	Questions	38

CHAPTER 4 THE COMPLETE PROGRAM

4.1	Introduction	44
4.2	The Picture clause – PICTURE	44
4.3	The Data Division – level 77	46
4.4	The Identification Division	46
4.5	The program	47
4.6	Worked example	47
4.7	Program implementation: storing a program, compilation, loading and running	51
4.8	The complete program compiled source code, results	56
4.9	Comments – ON SIZE ERROR, ROUNDED	60
4.10	Questions	62

CHAPTER 5 PICTURE EDITING   Page

5.1	Introduction	66
5.2	The purpose of picture editing	66
5.3	Edited pictures	67
5.4	The effects of data movement	69
5.5	Worked example	71
5.6	Questions	74

CHAPTER 6 CODING DATA FILES AND REPORTS

6.1	Introduction	76
6.2	Elements of a computer file	76
6.3	Coding records in the Data Division – levels 01-49	77
6.4	Coding reports FILLER, VALUE	78
6.5	The File Section: format, physical and logical records, BLOCK clause, RECORD clause, LABEL clause, VALUE OF clause, DATA RECORD clause	82
6.6	Environment Division: format, Configuration Section, Input-Output Section	84
6.7	Worked Examples	86
6.8	Questions	89

CHAPTER 7 INTRODUCTION TO FILE PROCESSING

7.1	Introduction	95
7.2	File processing verbs OPEN, CLOSE, READ, WRITE	96
7.3	Creating a serial file	99
7.4	Report generation	103
7.5	Serial files to sequential files – SORT	107
7.6	Questions	112

CHAPTER 8 PROGRAM STRUCTURES FROM DATA STRUCTURES

8.1	Introduction	117
8.2	The constructs – sequence, selection, repetition	117
8.3	Worked example	124
8.4	Worked example	133
8.5	Questions	139

CHAPTER 9 WORKED EXAMPLES OF COMPLETE COBOL PROGRAMS

9.1	Introduction	144
9.2	Problem	144
9.3	Problem	144
9.4	Questions	156

CHAPTER 10 FILE MAINTENANCE
10.1	Introduction	160
10.2	Merging	160
10.3	Design of merging algorithm	161
10.4	Implementation	163
10.5	The terminology of file updating	164
10.6	Design of simple update algorithm	166
10.7	Implementation – optimisation	169
10.8	Design of an update algorithm with validation	172
10.9	Implementation	183
10.10	Questions	187

CHAPTER 11 TABLES
11.1	Introduction	189
11.2	The concept of a table	189
11.3	Methods of defining tables – OCCURS clause	192
11.4	Initialisation of tables – REDEFINES clause	194
11.5	Indices – SET	202
11.6	SEARCH, SEARCH ALL	204
11.7	Questions	205

CHAPTER 12 TABLE PROCESSING – WORKED EXAMPLES
12.1	Problem	210
12.2	Problem	217
12.3	Problem	225
12.4	Questions	230

CHAPTER 13 RANDOM ACCESS FILES
13.1	Introduction	234
13.2	Description of indexed sequential files	234
13.3	COBOL statements – OPEN, CLOSE, READ, START WRITE, REWRITE, DELETE	236
13.4	Worked example	241
13.5	Worked example	251
13.6	Description of Relative Files	263
13.7	COBOL statements	264
13.8	Worked Example	264
13.9	Worked Example – level 66	267
13.10	Questions	274

CHAPTER 14 DATA VALIDATION
14.1	Introduction	276
14.2	Definition of good and error data	276
14.3	Classification of errors	276
14.4	Features of COBOL that aid data validation Class conditions, condition names – level 88, INSPECT	278
14.5	Worked example	280
14.6	Worked example	284
14.7	Questions	292

CHAPTER 15 PROGRAM IMPLEMENTATION TECHNIQUES

15.1	Introduction	294
15.2	Structure clashes – ordering clash, boundary clash	294
15.3	Program Inversion	297
15.4	Worked example	299
15.5	Subprograms – CALL, EXIT PROGRAM	304
15.6	Recognition problems – backtracking, multiple read ahead, processing file twice, redesigning the system	309
15.7	Questions	315

CHAPTER 16 MISCELLANEOUS FEATURES

16.1	Introduction	317
16.2	Internal storage of numbers – DISPLAY, COMPUTATIONAL, COMPUTATIONAL-3, SYNCHRONIZED	317
16.3	Duplicate identifiers – qualification, CORRESPONDING	320
16.4	String processing – STRING, UNSTRING	322
16.5	INITIALIZE	324
16.6	COPY	324
16.7	Declaratives Section – USE statement	325

APPENDIX I	Answers to selected questions	327
APPENDIX II	Procedure Division coding based on the Draft Proposed Standard	360
APPENDIX III	Procedure Division verbs from the Nucleus module as defined in the Draft Proposed Standard	366
INDEX		381

x

1 Elements of COBOL

1.1 INTRODUCTION

Within this chapter the reader is given an initial overview of the structure of a COBOL program and an introduction to the PROCEDURE DIVISION.

1.2 THE STRUCTURE OF A COBOL PROGRAM

A COBOL program normally consists of up to four Divisions, in the order presented below, and with the following names.

IDENTIFICATION DIVISION.
ENVIRONMENT DIVISION.
DATA DIVISION.
PROCEDURE DIVISION.

The last three Divisions can be subdivided into *sections*. Figure 1.1 illustrates a typical structure of a COBOL program.

The reader should note that it is possible to write a somewhat restricted COBOL program using a minimum of two Divisions – IDENTIFICATION DIVISION and PROCEDURE DIVISION.

The four Divisions and their respective sections have the following functions.

1.2.1 Identification Division.

This allows the programmer to give a name to the program and provide useful comments such as the name of the author of the program, the date the program was written and compiled and remarks relating to the security of the program.

1.2.2 Environment Division.

The CONFIGURATION SECTION is used to describe the make and model of computer used to compile and run the COBOL program.

The INPUT–OUTPUT SECTION has the primary function of describing the relationship between hardware devices and the attributes of the files that use those devices.

1.2.3 Data Division.

All DATA DIVISION statements relate to the format in which data is either input, stored or output.

The FILE SECTION describes the format of records and data held on computer files.

The WORKING–STORAGE SECTION is used to describe data that is local to the computer program.

The LINKAGE SECTION describes data that is to be passed between COBOL programs when several programs are used for one particular application.

1

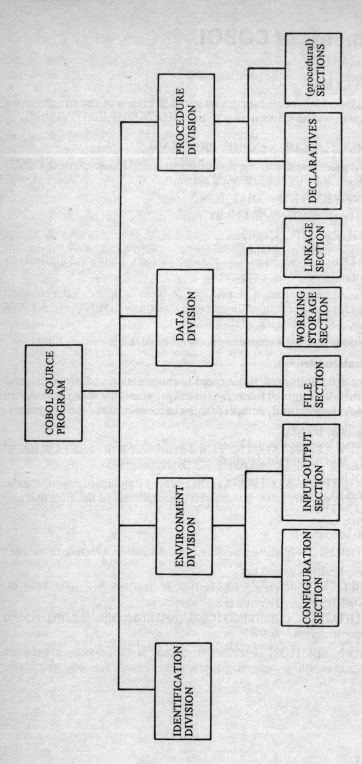

note: the DATA DIVISION can have up to five sections, however, such detail is not covered in this book.

Figure 1.1

1.2.4 Procedure Division.

The DECLARATIVE sections provide a method for including procedures which are invoked when a condition occurs which cannot be tested by the programmer. These sections are optional and a PROCEDURE DIVISION normally consists of procedural sections. These contain instructions that form the coded algorithm of the solution to a problem.

The last four paragraphs serve only as an introduction to the Divisions. Each Division will be written about in detail, in context, later in the book. The first Division to receive a more rigorous treatment is the PROCEDURE DIVISION since it is through this Division that the logical solution to a problem is expressed.

1.3 ELEMENTS OF THE PROCEDURE DIVISION

The PROCEDURE DIVISION has a hierarchical structure. PROCEDURE DIVISION code can be **optionally** subdivided into *sections;* sections are subdivided into *paragraphs;* paragraphs are subdivided into *sentences;* and sentences are subdivided into one or more COBOL *statements*.

Sections and paragraphs must be given a name according to the following convention. Some compilers will allow paragraphs to be empty, that is, the paragraph is given a name but does not contain any sentences. The use of such a technique would be for documentation purposes.

1.3.1 Paragraph Names.

A paragraph can contain zero, one or more sentences and is referenced by a paragraph name. A paragraph name can contain up to 30 characters taken from the characters A through to Z, 0 through to 9 or a combination of the two types, and the name may contain single embedded hyphens.

Paragraph names must **not** be taken from the list of COBOL *reserved words* (see table 1.1 – taken from the Draft Proposal).

An example of legal paragraph names would be:

> TAX–SEQ
> CALC–ITER
> CODE–SEL
> A
> B3

Illegal paragraph names would be:

START	(reserved word)
ANSWERS?	(? not a legal character)
–END–POINT	(only embedded hyphens are legal the first hyphen is not)
E O F	(embedded spaces are not allowed)

COBOL RESERVED WORDS

In the following list of COBOL reserved words, the appearance of [1] indicates a reserved word appearing only within the Debug module; the appearance of [2] indicates a reserved word appearing only within the Report Writer module; the appearance of [3] indicates a reserved word appearing only within the Communication module.

ACCEPT	DEBUG–NAME[1]	GENERATE[2]	OFF
ACCESS	DEBUG–NUMERIC–CONTENTS[1]	GIVING	OMITTED
ADD	DEBUG–SIZE[1]	GLOBAL	ON
ADVANCING	DEBUG–START[1]	GO	OPEN
AFTER	DEBUG–SUB[1]	GREATER	OPTIONAL
ALL	DEBUG–SUB–ITEM[1]	GROUP[2]	OR
ALPHABET	DEBUG–SUB–N[1]		ORDER
ALPHABETIC	DEBUG–SUB–NUM[1]	HEADING[2]	ORGANIZATION
ALPHABETIC–LOWER	DEBUGGING	HIGH–VALUE	OTHER
ALPHABETIC–UPPER	DECIMAL–POINT	HIGH–VALUES	OUTPUT
ALPHANUMERIC	DECLARATIVES		OVERFLOW
ALPHANUMERIC–EDITED	DELETE	I–O	
ALSO	DELIMITED	I–O–CONTROL	PADDING
ALTERNATE	DELIMITER	IDENTIFICATION	PAGE
AND	DEPENDING	IF	PAGE–COUNTER[2]
ANY	DESCENDING	IN	PERFORM
ARE	DESTINATION[3]	INDEX	PF[2]
AREA	DETAIL[2]	INDEXED	PH[2]
AREAS	DISABLE[3]	INDICATE[2]	PIC
ASCENDING	DISPLAY	INITIAL	PICTURE
ASSIGN	DIVIDE	INITIALIZE	PLUS[2]
AT	DIVISION	INITIATE[2]	POINTER
AUTHOR	DOWN	INPUT	POSITION
	DUPLICATES	INPUT–OUTPUT	POSITIVE
BEFORE	DYNAMIC	INSPECT	PRINTING[2]
BLANK		INSTALLATION	PROCEDURE
BLOCK	EGI[3]	INTO	PROCEDURES[1]
BOTTOM	ELSE	INVALID	PROGRAM
BY	EMI[3]	IS	PROGRAM–ID
	ENABLE[3]		PURGE[3]
CALL	END	JUST	
CANCEL	END–ADD	JUSTIFIED	QUEUE[3]
CD[3]	END–CALL		QUOTE
CF[2]	END–COMPUTE	KEY	QUOTES
CH[2]	END–DELETE		
CHARACTER	END–DIVIDE	LABEL	RANDOM
CHARACTERS	END–EVALUATE	LAST[2]	RD[2]
CLOSE	END–IF	LEADING	READ
CODE[2]	END–MULTIPLY	LEFT	RECEIVE[3]
CODE–SET	END–OF–PAGE	LENGTH[3]	RECORD
COLLATING	END–PERFORM	LESS	RECORDS
COLUMN[2]	END–READ	LIMIT[2]	REDEFINES
COMMA	END–RECEIVE[3]	LIMITS[2]	REEL
COMMON	END–RETURN	LINAGE	REFERENCE
COMMUNICATION[3]	END–REWRITE	LINAGE–COUNTER	REFERENCE–MODIFIER[1]
COMP	END–SEARCH	LINE	REFERENCES[1]
COMPUTATIONAL	END–START	LINE–COUNTER[2]	RELATIVE
COMPUTE	END–STRING	LINES	RELEASE
CONFIGURATION	END–SUBTRACT	LINKAGE	REMAINDER
CONTAINS	END–UNSTRING	LOCK	REMOVAL
CONTENT	END–WRITE	LOW–VALUE	RENAMES
CONTINUE	ENVIRONMENT	LOW–VALUES	REPLACE
CONTROL[2]	EOP		REPLACING
CONTROLS[2]	EQUAL	MERGE	REPORT[2]
CONVERSION[1]	ERROR	MESSAGE[3]	REPORTING[2]
CONVERTING	ESI[3]	MODE	REPORTS[2]
COPY	EVALUATE	MOVE	RESERVE
CORR	EXCEPTION	MULTIPLE	RESET[2]
CORRESPONDING	EXIT	MULTIPLY	RETURN
COUNT	EXTEND		REWIND
CURRENCY	EXTERNAL	NATIVE	REWRITE
		NEGATIVE	RF
DATA	FALSE	NEXT	RH[2]
DATE	FD	NO	RIGHT
DATE–COMPILED	FILE	NOT	ROUNDED
DATE–WRITTEN	FILE–CONTROL	NUMBER[2]	RUN
DAY	FILLER	NUMERIC	
DAY–OF–WEEK	FINAL[2]	NUMERIC–EDITED	SAME
DE[2]	FIRST		SD
DEBUG–CONTENTS[1]	FOOTING	OBJECT–COMPUTER	SEARCH
DEBUG–ITEM[1]	FOR	OCCURS	SECTION
DEBUG–LENGTH[1]	FROM	OF	SECURITY

Table 1.1

Table 1.1 continued

SEGMENT³	START		VALUE
SEGMENT–LIMIT	STATUS	THAN	VALUES
SELECT	STOP	THEN	VARYING
SEND³	STRING	THROUGH	
SENTENCE	SUB–QUEUE–1³	THRU	WHEN
SEPARATE	SUB–QUEUE–2³	TIME	WITH
SEQUENCE	SUB–QUEUE–3³	TIMES	WORKING–STORAGE
SEQUENTIAL	SUBTRACT	TO	WRITE
SET	SUM²	TOP	
SIGN	SUPPRESS²	TRAILING	ZERO
SIZE	SYMBOLIC	TRUE	ZEROES
SORT	SYNC	TYPE²	ZEROS
SORT–MERGE	SYNCHRONIZED		
SOURCE¹,²		UNIT	+
SOURCE–COMPUTER	TABLE³	UNSTRING	–
SPACE	TALLYING	UNTIL	*
SPACES	TAPE	UP	/
SPECIAL–NAMES	TERMINAL³	UPON	**
STANDARD	TERMINATE²	USAGE	>
STANDARD–1	TEST	USE	<
STANDARD–2	TEXT³	USING	=

1.3.2 Sentences

A COBOL sentence consists of one or more statements and is terminated by a full-stop (period) and a space. When a sentence contains several statements they may be separated by a comma (,) or semi-colon (;). Separators are allowed simply for readability, their presence or absence has no effect on the compiled program. A separator **must** be followed by a space.

1.3.3 Statements

The PROCEDURE DIVISION is composed of a series of statements, each of which calls for some kind of action to be taken. Statements may be *imperative* e.g. ADD SALARY TO ACCOUNT or *conditional* e.g. IF TAX > 500 PERFORM CODE–X. Both types of statement may contain:

> **reserved words**
> **variables**
> **literals**
> **symbols**
> **paragraph names.**

1.3.4 Reserved Words

These have predefined meanings according to their use in a program. Reserved words must be correctly used in context and spelt correctly. Table 1.1. gives a list of COBOL reserved words.

Reserved words fall into two categories, *key* words and *optional* words. Key words are obligatory. Optional words are used to improve the readability of a program, however, if used must be used correctly. For example in the COBOL sentence:

> READ DATAFILE RECORD AT END MOVE 1 TO E–O–F.

READ, END, MOVE and TO are reserved key words, RECORD and AT are reserved optional words. The sentence could be shortened to:

> READ DATAFILE END MOVE 1 TO E–O–F.

and it would be syntactically correct, although its readability leaves something to be desired!

1.3.5 Variables

Variable names are used to identify items of data. In reality they are references to areas of the computer's memory. The programmer has the responsibility of inventing these names. Variable names should therefore convey the meaning and nature of the data and be documented in the form of a glossary. Remember the author of a program is not always the person who has to maintain the program, and there is nothing more frustrating when trying to maintain a program than to have to guess the meaning and nature of variable names that are not your own creation.

The rules of composition for variable names are similar to those for paragraph names. However, the first character must be alphabetic (A through to Z) and the variable name is not terminated by a full-stop (period) unless the variable name is the last word of a sentence.

An example of legal variable names would be:

```
TAX–IN–HAND
P35
POINT–OF–SALE
GROSS–SALARY
```

and illegal variable names would be:

```
COUNT          (reserved word)
8XKT           (begins with a non-alphabetic character)
BANK–NO–       (hyphens must be embedded)
!  COST        (! and embedded space illegal)
PRICE£         (£ illegal)
```

Variable names are also called identifiers or data names in this book.

1.3.6 Literals

Literals give an actual value that is used in the program. They fall into two categories – numeric literals (numeric constants) and non-numeric literals (character strings).

Numeric literals contain up to 18 characters taken from the digits 0 through to 9, and the characters plus (+), minus (−) and the decimal point (.), which is the same character as the full-stop (period). The sign (+ or −) is optional, if it is used it must precede the digits.

Examples of numeric literals are:

```
3     +17.8     −132     0.00394     −526.2     +0.1509
```

Non-numeric literals are character strings containing up to 160 characters taken from either the ASCII or EBCDIC character sets. The character set used will be dependent upon the make of computer being used. For example PR1ME use ASCII , IBM use EBCDIC.

The character string must be delimited by either identical apostrophes or quotation marks, according to the COBOL compiler being used.

Examples of non-numeric literals are:

```
'EMPLOYEE  DETAILS'         '123456'
"TAX  POINT"                "DO'S  &  DON'TS"
'DIVISION'                  'STOCK–ITEM'
```

6

A special case can be made for a third type of literal. This is the *figurative constant* which strictly speaking falls under the category of reserved words.

The figurative constants that are commonly used within this book are:

ZERO   represents numeric 0.

SPACE or SPACES   represents one or more space characters.

HIGH–VALUE or HIGH–VALUES represents one or more of the character that has the highest ordinal position in either the ASCII or EBCDIC codes.

There are other figurative constants but they will not be considered here.

1.4 THE COBOL CHARACTER SET

This must not be confused with either the ASCII or EBCDIC character sets. The COBOL character set describes those characters that are used to write COBOL computer programs and is a subset of the ASCII or EBCDIC character sets.

The COBOL character set consists of:

numeric characters 0 through to 9,
alphabetic characters A through to Z, and a ' ' (space) character,
special characters $+ - */ = < > \$, ; . " ( ) :$

1.5 THE COBOL PROGRAM SHEET

The programmer, regardless of experience, **should refrain from composing programs at the computer terminal.** The purpose of the COBOL program sheet is for writing or coding a COBOL program **having first carefully designed and tested the algorithm.** Figure 1.2 shows the layout of a COBOL program sheet.

Columns 1 through to 6, and 73 through to 80 are part of a hangover from the use of punched cards as an input medium. Their purpose is of no importance here.

The three important areas of the COBOL program sheet are as follows.

Column 7 – this is known as the indicator area. If a hyphen (–) is present in this column it indicates that the current line, containing the hyphen, is to be used as a continuation from the previous line. In the context of this book the hyphen in column 7 will only be used to continue a non-numeric literal from one line to another. This will be explained later in the text.

If an asterisk (*) is used in column 7 then the remainder of the line can be used for writing comments into the program.

Columns 8 through to 11 represent zone A or area A. In the context of this chapter Division and section headings and paragraph names **must** begin in zone A, and be terminated by a full-stop (period).

There are other entries in a COBOL program that must begin in zone A but these will be dealt with in later chapters.

Columns 12 through to 72 represent zone B or area B. Again in the context of this chapter all sentences in the PROCEDURE   DIVISION must be confined to this zone.

7

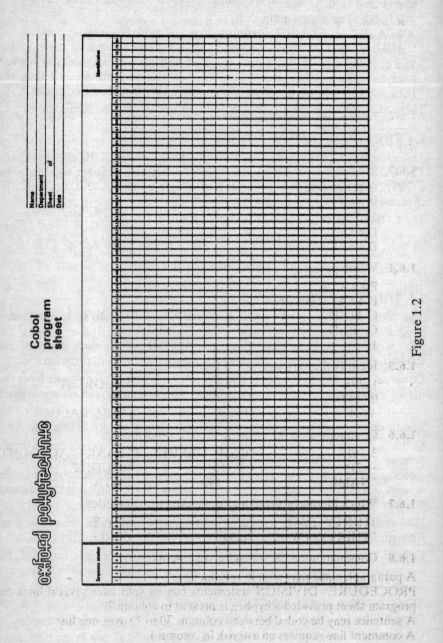

Figure 1.2

1.6 QUESTIONS *(answers begin on page 327)*

1.6.1 Comment upon the following statements.

A COBOL program must have all four Divisions present.

The order in which the Divisions are written is not important.

A sentence may contain one statement.

Variable names and paragraph names can be the same.

The characters , and ; can be used in a sentence.

Each paragraph may contain one sentence.

Paragraph names are not necessary in a PROCEDURE DIVISION.

1.6.2 If the COBOL character set is a subset of the ASCII character set then comment upon which characters are common to both sets.

+ ! ? * / < [↑ a A

1.6.3 Which variable names are illegal and why?

GROSS–SALARY	*PARA 1
WAGE/3	COUNT
23	247.34
DATA	A3
DATA–VALUE	TAX ALLOWANCE

1.6.4 Which paragraph names are illegal and why?

PARA 1	*BEGIN
DATA DIVISION	START
C–ITER	MAX VAL OUT
C END	"A–SEQ"
1	A–END

1.6.5 Identify the various types of literals listed.

123.96	"ABCD"	"ADDRESS"
0.01478	ZERO	−36
+6.4	SPACE	HIGH–VALUE

1.6.6 Comment upon the errors in the following literals.

3,649	HIGH VALUES	"BANK" ACCOUNT'
−.215	467. 63	NOUGHT
"NAME	+0. 147	DATA

1.6.7 Which literals or variables can be used in arithmetic?

THIRTY–TWO	1234	SPACE
"THIRTY–TWO"	"1234"	ZERO

1.6.8 Comment upon the following statements.

A paragraph name may start in column 9.

PROCEDURE DIVISION statements can be split over several lines on a program sheet provided a hyphen is present in column 7.

A sentence may be coded between columns 30 to 70 over one line.

A comment line requires an asterisk in column 1.

Columns 1 through to 6 and 73 through to 80 must never be used when coding a COBOL program.

9

2 Procedure Division Verbs

2.1 INTRODUCTION

The purpose of this chapter is to introduce the reader to those PROCEDURE DIVISION verbs that form the basis of coding simple algorithms. Although an earlier distinction was made between imperative and conditional statements, a more formal classification of the verbs that form these statements will now be developed. The reader who has had some experience of programming in other languages will appreciate that the procedural verbs of any language can be broadly classified into the areas of data movement, arithmetic, input and output, conditional and unconditional branching, and procedural control. These areas will now be considered with reference to the COBOL language.

2.1.1 COBOL Standards

At the time of writing, a new Standard for COBOL is being proposed. The COBOL statements described throughout this book will be based on the Draft Proposed Revised X3.23 American National Standard Programming Language COBOL that was published in September 1981.

In order to illustrate the compatibility of the new Standard with the 1974 Standard the majority of the programs in this book have been compiled using a COBOL compiler based on the 1974 Standard of the language. Where new features in the Draft Proposal are not compatible with the 1974 Standard both methods of coding are illustrated showing how the new COBOL statements enhance structured programming. The coding based on the Draft Proposal is given in Appendix II.

To help the reader assimilate the material of this chapter as quickly as possible the author has purposely reduced the format of many of the COBOL statements to their simplest forms. For the reader who would like a more detailed description of the format and syntax of these statements Appendix III contains extracts from the Draft Proposed Standard relating to PROCEDURE DIVISION statements.

2.1.2 Notation

In defining COBOL statements the following notation will be used.

All reserved words are printed in uppercase letters. Key reserved words are printed in bold type, optional reserved words are printed in normal type.

The use of square brackets [] indicates that items within the square brackets can be omitted.

The use of braces {} indicates that a choice must be made between the various contents of the braces. If the braces contain a single entry no choice is implied.

The use of ellipsis .... represents the position at which the user elects repetition of a portion of the format. The portion of the format that may be repeated is determined as follows.

Given .... in a format, scanning right to left, determine the] or } delimiter immediately to the left of the .... ; continue scanning right to left and determine the logically matching [or { delimiter; the .... applies to the portion of the format between the determined pair of delimiters.

2.2 DATA MOVEMENT

2.2.1 Move

The MOVE statement transfers data from one area of main storage to another.

Format

> **MOVE** $\left\{ \begin{matrix} \text{identifier–1} \\ \text{literal–1} \end{matrix} \right\}$ **TO**   {identifier–2} ....

note: the term identifier has the same meaning as data name or variable.

Examples

> MOVE 21 to AGE

will move the numeric literal 21 into the memory area given the identifier AGE. The original contents of AGE will be lost or overwritten. This can be illustrated by using a simple before (the execution of the instruction) and after (the execution of the instruction) representation.

	AGE
before	56
after	5̶6̶ 21

The next example shows that it is possible to move the same value to more than one area of memory.

> MOVE 16 TO A, B, C

	A	B	C
before	12	9	−14
after	1̶2̶ 16	9̶ 16	−1̶4̶ 16

note: a comma (,) although not part of the format of the MOVE statement can be used to separate identifiers.

> MOVE "GB" TO CODES

	CODES
before	SA
after	S̶A̶ GB

The MOVE statement is not confined to moving literals, the contents of identifiers can also be moved.

> MOVE A TO B, C

	A	B	C
before	21	13	−9
after	21	1̶3̶ 21	−̶9̶ 21

note: the original contents of A remains unchanged only the contents of B and C are overwritten.

Figurative constants can also be used in a MOVE statement.

> MOVE ZERO TO TOTAL

or

> MOVE ZERO TO TOTAL–A, TOTAL–B, TOTAL–C

Both statements move numeric zero to the respective *destination* identifiers.

2.3 ARITHMETIC

2.3.1 Add

The ADD statement adds together two or more numeric values and stores the resulting sum.

Format

Format 1. **ADD** $\begin{Bmatrix} \text{identifier--1} \\ \text{literal--1} \end{Bmatrix}$ .... **TO** identifier--2

Format 2. **ADD** $\begin{Bmatrix} \text{identifier--1} \\ \text{literal--1} \end{Bmatrix}$ .... **TO** $\begin{Bmatrix} \text{identifier--2} \\ \text{literal--2} \end{Bmatrix}$

      GIVING identifier--3

note: in format 2 the reserved word TO is optional, when TO is omitted this format will conform to the 1974 Standard.

Examples

   ADD A TO B

the contents of A is added to the contents of B and the sum is stored in B.

	A	B
before	17	19
after	17	1̶9̶ 36

   ADD A, B GIVING C

the contents of A is added to the contents of B and the sum is stored in C.

	A	B	C
before	5	9	12
after	5	9	1̶2̶ 14

   ADD 36.1 TO ALPHA

	ALPHA
before	20.7
after	56.8

   ADD J, K, L, M GIVING N

	J	K	L	M	N
before	2	3	4	5	6
after	2	3	4	5	6̶ 14

note: the commas between the operands are optional separators.

2.3.2 Subtract

The SUBTRACT statement subtracts one or more numeric data items from a specified item and stores the difference.

Format

Format 1. **SUBTRACT** $\begin{Bmatrix} \text{identifier--1} \\ \text{literal--1} \end{Bmatrix}$ .... **FROM** identifier--2

Format 2. **SUBTRACT** $\begin{Bmatrix} \text{identifier--1} \\ \text{literal--1} \end{Bmatrix}$ .... **FROM** $\begin{Bmatrix} \text{identifier--2} \\ \text{literal--2} \end{Bmatrix}$

      GIVING identifier--3

Examples

SUBTRACT   A   FROM   B

the contents of A is taken from B and the result is stored in B overwriting the original contents of B.

	A	B
before	16	24
after	16	2̶4̶ 8

SUBTRACT   A   FROM   B   GIVING   C

this is similar to the last example only the result is stored in C thus preventing the original contents of B from being overwritten.

	A	B	C
before	17	32	19
after	17	32	1̶9̶ 15

SUBTRACT   A, B,   C   FROM   D

the contents of A, B and C are added together and the result is subtracted from D.

	A	B	C	D
before	1	2	3	4
after	1	2	3	4̶ −2

SUBTRACT   K,   L,   M   FROM   N   GIVING   X

this is similar to the last example only the result is stored in X.

	K	L	M	N	X
before	5	6	7	8	9
after	5	6	7	8	9̶ −10

2.3.3 Multiply

The MULTIPLY statement computes the product of two numeric data items.

Format

Format 1. **MULTIPLY** $\left\{ \begin{array}{l} \text{identifier–1} \\ \text{literal–1} \end{array} \right\}$ **BY**   identifier–2

Format 2. **MULTIPLY** $\left\{ \begin{array}{l} \text{identifier–1} \\ \text{literal–1} \end{array} \right\}$ **BY** $\left\{ \begin{array}{l} \text{identifier–2} \\ \text{literal–2} \end{array} \right\}$ **GIVING** identifier–3

Examples

MULTIPLY   12   BY   YEARS

the contents of YEARS is multiplied by 12 and the result stored in YEARS.

	YEARS
before	5
after	5̶ 60

MULTIPLY   UNITS   BY   PRICE   GIVING   COST

the contents of UNITS is multiplied by the contents of PRICE and the result stored in COST.

	UNITS	PRICE	COST
before	10	20	30
after	10	20	3̶0̶ 200

13

2.3.4 Divide

The DIVIDE statement divides one numeric data item into another and stores the result.

Format

Format 1. **DIVIDE** $\left\{\begin{array}{l}\text{identifier–1}\\\text{literal–1}\end{array}\right\}$ **INTO**   identifier–2

Format 2. **DIVIDE** $\left\{\begin{array}{l}\text{identifier–1}\\\text{literal–1}\end{array}\right\}$ **INTO** $\left\{\begin{array}{l}\text{identifier–2}\\\text{literal–2}\end{array}\right\}$ **GIVING** identifier–3

Examples

DIVIDE 5 INTO SUM

the contents of SUM is divided by 5 and the result is stored in SUM.

	SUM	
	36.20	
before		
after	36.20	7.24

DIVIDE COUNT INTO TOTAL GIVING MEAN

the contents of TOTAL is divided by COUNT and the result stored in MEAN.

	COUNT	TOTAL	MEAN
before	10	140	23
after	10	140	23 14

2.3.5 Compute

The COMPUTE statement evaluates an arithmetic expression, a numeric literal or an identifier and stores the result.

Format

COMPUTE identifier–1 $\;=\;$ $\left\{\begin{array}{l}\text{identifier–2}\\\text{literal–1}\\\text{arithmetic expression}\end{array}\right\}$

Examples

COMPUTE ALLOWANCE = 2300

the contents of ALLOWANCE is changed to 2300

	ALLOWANCE
before	1200
after	1200 2300

COMPUTE ALLOWANCE = CHILD-BENEFIT

the contents of ALLOWANCE is changed to the contents of CHILD–BENEFIT.

	ALLOWANCE	CHILD–BENEFIT
before	1200	240
after	1200 240	240

COMPUTE GROSS–WAGE = HOURLY–RATE * (1.5 * HOURS–WORKED – 20)

the arithmetic expression is evaluated using the contents of HOURLY–RATE and HOURS–WORKED, the result is stored in GROSS–WAGE.

Notes. Parenthesis may be used in arithmetic expressions to specify the order in which operands are used for arithmetic.

A hierarchy of evaluation for operators exists for non-parenthesised expressions:

highest	unary (single) + or − ;
	** exponentiation (raising a number to a power);
	* multiplication and / division;
lowest	+ addition and − subtraction.

If an expression contains operators of the same hierarchy and is not parenthesised then evaluation is from left to right of the expression.

An operator must always be preceded and followed by a space.

A left parenthesis is preceded by one or more spaces, a right parenthesis is followed by one or more spaces.

2.3.6 Comment

The reader may wonder from looking at Appendix III what the options ROUNDED and ON SIZE ERROR do. The options are of little importance in this chapter, however, they will be explained in full in the context of a later chapter.

2.4 INPUT AND OUTPUT

2.4.1 Accept

The ACCEPT statement causes low volume data to be made available to the specified data item.

Format

ACCEPT   identifier–1

Example

   ACCEPT   ALPHA

When this statement is executed the computer will wait for a value for ALPHA to be input. If we assume that a visual display unit (V.D.U.) is used to input data into the system then a value corresponding to ALPHA, terminated by a return character, must be typed at the keyboard. The computer will then continue with the execution of the rest of the program. In the execution of the ACCEPT statement the system does not display a prompt on the screen of the V.D.U.

2.4.2 Display

The DISPLAY statement causes low volume data to be transferred to an appropriate hardware device.

Format

DISPLAY $\left\{ \begin{array}{l} \text{identifer–1} \\ \text{literal–1} \end{array} \right\}$ ....

Example

   DISPLAY   BETA

If we assume that the hardware device is a V.D.U. then the value of BETA, followed by the return, new line characters, will be displayed on the screen of the V.D.U.

The DISPLAY statement can be used to output many different data items on one line.

DISPLAY "GROSS SALARY" G– SALARY

would display the literal GROSS SALARY followed by the numeric value for G–SALARY on the same line.

2.4.3 Note

The reader is advised to check that the format for ACCEPT and DISPLAY given here will function correctly for their system. It is probable that the reader may have to use the statements

ACCEPT identifier–1 **FROM** mnemonic–name

and **DISPLAY** $\left\{ \begin{array}{l} \text{identifier–1} \\ \text{literal–1} \end{array} \right\}$ .... **UPON** mnemonic–name

The details of these two formats are given in section 6.6.2 and Appendix III. The computer used to run the example programs in this book uses the first format for ACCEPT and DISPLAY given in this chapter.

2.5 CONDITIONAL BRANCHING

2.5.1 If

The IF statement causes a condition to be evaluated. The subsequent action of the object program depends on whether the value of the condition is true or false.

Format

Format 1 from Draft Proposal.

IF condition–1 **THEN** $\left\{ \begin{array}{l} \text{\{statement–1\}} \text{ ....} \\ \textbf{NEXT SENTENCE} \end{array} \right\}$

$\left\{ \begin{array}{l} \textbf{ELSE} \text{ \{statement–2\} ...... [END–IF]} \\ \textbf{ELSE NEXT SENTENCE} \\ \textbf{END–IF} \end{array} \right\}$

Format 2 from the 1974 Standard.

IF condition–1 $\left\{ \begin{array}{l} \text{\{statement–1\}} \text{ ....} \\ \textbf{NEXT SENTENCE} \end{array} \right\}$

$\quad\quad$ **ELSE** $\left\{ \begin{array}{l} \text{\{statement–2 \}} \text{........} \\ \textbf{NEXT SENTENCE} \end{array} \right\}$

Conditions

The condition given in both formats can be defined as:

$\left\{ \begin{array}{l} \text{identifier–1} \\ \text{literal–1} \\ \text{arithmetic expression–1} \end{array} \right\}$ $\begin{array}{l} \text{relational} \\ \text{operator} \end{array}$ $\left\{ \begin{array}{l} \text{identifier–2} \\ \text{literal–2} \\ \text{arithmetic expression–2} \end{array} \right\}$

where the relational operator is defined as:

$\quad\quad\quad\quad$ IS [NOT] >
$\quad\quad\quad\quad$ IS [NOT] <
$\quad\quad\quad\quad$ IS [NOT] =

16

The reserved words **GREATER** THAN, **LESS** THAN and **EQUAL** TO can be used in place of the symbols $>$, $<$, and $=$ respectively.

Two or more conditions can be combined by the logical operators AND and OR.

The format for a combined condition would be:

$$\text{IF} \quad \text{condition} \quad \begin{Bmatrix} \text{AND} \\ \text{OR} \end{Bmatrix} \quad \text{condition} \quad \left[\begin{Bmatrix} \text{AND} \\ \text{OR} \end{Bmatrix} \quad \text{condition} \right] \ldots\ldots$$

Examples

The statement if A is greater than 23 replace A by zero can be coded in several ways.

Draft Proposal	1974 Standard
IF A >23 MOVE ZERO TO A END–IF. next sentence	This results in a similar format to that described under the Draft Proposal. The only significant difference is the omission of END–IF.

IF A IS GREATER THAN 23
  MOVE 0 TO A
END–IF.
next sentence
	IF A >23
	  MOVE ZERO TO A.
	next sentence

In the examples given if the condition is true the statement MOVE ZERO TO A is executed, if the condition is false the computer branches to the next sentence.

The syntax does not limit the statement executed in the true (or false) case to one statement as the next example illustrates.

Draft Proposal	1974 Standard

IF A IS NOT ZERO
  ADD C TO D,
  MOVE X TO Y,
  SUBTRACT 6 FROM D
END–IF.
next sentence
	IF A IS NOT ZERO
	  ADD C TO D,
	  MOVE X TO Y,
	  SUBTRACT 6 FROM D.
	next sentence

The statement if AGE is greater than 18 and height is greater than 68 increase COUNT–PERSON by 1, otherwise, increase COUNT–X by 1 can be coded as:

Draft Proposal	1974 Standard

IF AGE >18 AND HEIGHT >68
  ADD 1 TO COUNT–PERSON
ELSE
  ADD 1 TO COUNT–X
END–IF.
next sentence
	IF AGE >18 AND HEIGHT >68
	  ADD 1 TO COUNT–PERSON
	ELSE
	  ADD 1 TO COUNT–X.
	next sentence

Alternatively, the statement could be coded as *nested* IF's.

Draft Proposal	1974 Standard

IF AGE >18
  IF HEIGHT >68
    ADD 1 TO COUNT–PERSON
  ELSE
    ADD 1 TO COUNT–X
  END–IF
ELSE
  ADD 1 TO COUNT–X
END–IF.
next sentence
	IF AGE >18
	  IF HEIGHT >68
	    ADD 1 TO COUNT–PERSON
	  ELSE
	    ADD 1 TO COUNT–X
	ELSE
	  ADD 1 TO COUNT–X.
	next sentence

When the use of a negated condition provides a minor convenience to the programmer the NEXT SENTENCE option can be usefully employed.

The statement if AGE is less than or equal to 18 **and** HEIGHT is less than or equal to 68 increase REJECT–PERSON by 1 can be coded as:

Draft Proposal	1974 Standard
IF AGE >18 OR HEIGHT >68	IF AGE >18 OR HEIGHT >68
NEXT SENTENCE	NEXT SENTENCE
ELSE	ELSE
ADD 1 TO REJECT–PERSON	ADD 1 TO REJECT–PERSON.
END–IF.	next sentence
next sentence	

Notice since the condition has been negated the logical operator AND has also been changed to OR (inclusive OR).

If the reader looks back over this last section it is noticeable that COBOL statements within the IF statement have been **indented.** This is a good habit that the reader should adopt since it makes the readability of the program easier by highlighting the range of the IF....ELSE..... statements.

END–IF is optional in the Draft Proposal, therefore, if END–IF is omitted the format of the IF...ELSE.... statement becomes the same as that defined by the 1974 Standard.

2.5.2 Evaluate

The EVALUATE statement describes a multi-branch, multi-join structure. It can cause multiple conditions to be evaluated. The subsequent actions of the object program depends on the results of these evaluations.

Format (Draft Proposal only).

EVALUATE identifier-1
{**WHEN** {IDENTIFIER-2 / literal–1} imperative-statement–1} ....
[**WHEN OTHER** imperative-statement–2]
[**END-EVALUATE**]

Example.

A library book code indicates the status of a book as being A – active, D – damaged, E – external or L – on loan. The EVALUATE statement can replace the use of several IF....ELSE....END–IF statements in describing the code for a particular book.

```
EVALUATE STATUS–CODE
    WHEN "A" MOVE "ACTIVE" TO DESCRIPTION
    WHEN "D" MOVE "DAMAGED" TO DESCRIPTION
    WHEN "E" MOVE "EXTERNAL" TO DESCRIPTION
    WHEN OTHER MOVE "LOAN" TO DESCRIPTION
END–EVALUATE
```

The alternative coding using IF....ELSE....END-IF would be:

```
IF STATUS–CODE = "A"
    MOVE "ACTIVE" TO DESCRIPTION
```

```
ELSE
  IF STATUS–CODE = "D"
    MOVE "DAMAGED" TO DESCRIPTION
  ELSE
    IF STATUS–CODE = "E"
      MOVE "EXTERNAL" TO DESCRIPTION
    ELSE
      MOVE "LOAN" TO DESCRIPTION
    END–IF
  END–IF
END–IF
```

2.6 UNCONDITIONAL BRANCHING

2.6.1 Goto

The GO TO statement causes control to be transferred from one part of the PROCEDURE   DIVISION to another.

Format

Format 1.   **GO**   TO procedure–name–1

Format 2.   **GO**   TO {procedure–name–1} ....
              DEPENDING ON identifier–1

Examples

GO TO TAX–END.

will transfer control to the procedure-name TAX–END, which can be either a section name or a paragraph name.

GO TO ALPHA–SEL, ALPHA–OR–2, ALPHA–OR–3
DEPENDING ON MAX–VAL.

will transfer control to procedure-name:

ALPHA–SEL if MAX–VAL = 1,
ALPHA–OR–2 if MAX–VAL = 2,
ALPHA–OR–3 if MAX–VAL = 3.

If MAX–VAL is none of these values then control is transfered to the next statement.

2.6.2 Stop

The STOP statement is used to terminate the execution of the object program.

Format

STOP RUN

2.7 PROCEDURAL CONTROL

2.7.1 Perform

The PERFORM statement is used to transfer control explicitly to one or more procedures and to return control implicitly whenever the execution of the specified procedure is complete.

The PERFORM statement is also used to control the execution of one or more imperative/conditional statements which are within the scope of that PERFORM.

Format

Format 1. Draft Proposal – in–line PERFORM.

PERFORM [UNTIL condition–1] imperative–statement–1 **END–PERFORM**

Format 2. Out–of–line PERFORM – compatible in both Standards.

PERFORM procedure–name–1 $\left\{ \begin{array}{l} \textbf{THROUGH} \\ \textbf{THRU} \end{array} \right\}$ procedure–name–2 [UNTIL condition–1]

Examples using in-line PERFORM

If the UNTIL option is omitted the statements between PERFORM and END–PERFORM are executed once. The computer then continues by executing the statements after the END–PERFORM.

    PERFORM   ⎫
      ACCEPT   NUMB   ⎬ these statements would be
      ADD 1 TO NUMB–COUNT   ⎬ executed once.
    END–PERFORM.   ⎭

With the UNTIL option present the in-line PERFORM behaves in the following manner. If the exit condition is true when the PERFORM statement is entered control is passed to the next statement after END–PERFORM, otherwise, the statements within the scope of that PERFORM ......END–PERFORM are executed until the exit condition becomes true. The test for the exit condition is at the beginning of the loop unless otherwise stated in the format of the PERFORM statement.

    MOVE ZERO TO COUNT, TOTAL.
    PERFORM UNTIL COUNT = 5
      ACCEPT NUMB
      ADD NUMB TO TOTAL
      ADD 1 TO COUNT
    END–PERFORM.
    DIVIDE COUNT INTO TOTAL GIVING AVERAGE.

In this program segment COUNT and TOTAL are both initialised to zero prior to entering the loop. Since the exit condition is not true the statements between PERFORM and END–PERFORM are executed 5 times. At the end of the fifth iteration COUNT = 5, control passes to the beginning of the loop and the exit condition is tested, since it is now true, control passes out of the loop to the next statement after END–PERFORM.

Examples using out–of–line PERFORM

If the UNTIL option is omitted control passes to procedure–name–1 and all the COBOL statements between this and those of procedure–name–2 are executed once. Control then returns to the next executable statement after the PERFORM.

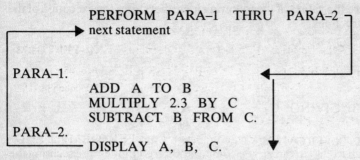

```
                    PERFORM  PARA-1  THRU  PARA-2 ─┐
                    next statement                 │

PARA-1.                                            │
                    ADD  A  TO  B
                    MULTIPLY  2.3  BY  C
                    SUBTRACT  B  FROM  C.
PARA-2.
                    DISPLAY  A,  B,  C.
```

When the UNTIL option is specified the PERFORM mechanism just described is repeated until the exit condition is true. The test for the exit condition will be prior to the execution of the PERFORM. If the condition is false the COBOL statements specified by the two procedure names will be executed repeatedly until the exit condition is true.

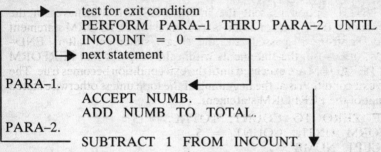

```
                 ┌─ test for exit condition
                 PERFORM  PARA-1  THRU  PARA-2  UNTIL
                 INCOUNT  =  0 ─┐
                 next statement

PARA-1.
                    ACCEPT  NUMB.
                    ADD  NUMB  TO  TOTAL.
PARA-2.
                    SUBTRACT  1  FROM  INCOUNT.
```

If the exit condition is true prior to the execution of the PERFORM statement then PERFORM will **not** be obeyed, but control will revert to the next COBOL statement.

2.7.2 Comment

If the reader makes reference to the PERFORM statements found in Appendix III it is clear that the formats given in this chapter are a simplification of those given in the Draft Proposal. The purpose of the more advanced PERFORM formats will be described in context in a later chapter. The reader now has enough COBOL programming tools to be able to develop PROCEDURE DIVISION code.

2.8 QUESTIONS *(answers begin on page 328)*

2.8.1 Identify the syntax errors in the following arithmetic statements.

```
ADD  A  TO  3.5
SUBTRACT  X  FROM  Y  Z
ADD  A  TO  B  GIVING  C
MULTIPLY  X  TIMES  Y
DIVIDE  X  INTO  5
COMPUTE  =  3.4  *  A  *  B
COMPUTE  a  =  b  +  c
```

2.8.2 What are the values of the following identifiers after the execution of the respective instructions?

MOVE A TO B, C, D	A	B	C	D
	36	98	45	29

ADD A, B, C TO D	A	B	C	D
	10	14	29	36

ADD A, B GIVING C	A	B	C
	24	98	23

SUBTRACT X FROM Y	X	Y
	17	32

SUBTRACT U, V, W FROM X	U	V	W	X
	29	32	84	78

SUBTRACT 3 FROM A GIVING B	A	B
	16	22

MULTIPLY X BY Y GIVING Z	X	Y	Z
	18	3	27

DIVIDE A INTO B	A	B
	6	42

COMPUTE A = A + B	A	B
	3	9

COMPUTE U = V + W * X	U	V	W	X
	17	13	6	4

COMPUTE R = B ** 2 − 4 * A *C	R	A	B	C
	6	2	4	2

2.8.3 Evaluate the following expressions given that A = 6, B = 4, C = 2, D = 16

    A + B / C
    A / (B + C)
    A * B / (C * D)
    (D − B) / 2 / A
    (A − B) * (C + D) ** 2

2.8.4 What are the errors in the following COBOL expressions.

    A.B
    X*−Y
    (64 + B)/−6
    ((A + B) / (C + D) ** 4
    (A − B) (A + B)

2.8.5 Re-write the following COBOL expressions as mathematical expressions.

    X + Y ** 3
    X + 2 / Y + 4
    A * B / (C + 2)
    A / B + C * D / (F * G * H)
    1 / (X + Y) ** 2
    A / B + C / D + E / F

22

2.8.6 Identify the syntax errors in the following statements.

ACCEPT ALPHA, BETA, GAMMA
PRINT "TAX ALLOWANCE", TAX–AL
GO TO PROCEDURE DIVISION DEPENDING UPON
ALPHA.
IF A > 3 ADD B TO C, NEXT SENTENCE.
GOTO PARA1.
PERFORM ADD A TO B, UNTIL B > 1000
END–PERFORM

2.8.7 Trace through the following segments of code (as though you were the computer) and find the final values for A and B.

MOVE 1 TO A, B
PERFORM UNTIL B > 21
  ADD B TO A
  ADD A TO B
END–PERFORM

MOVE 10 TO A
MOVE 15 TO B
PERFORM UNTIL B = 0
  IF A > B
    SUBTRACT B FROM A
  ELSE
    SUBTRACT A FROM B
  END–IF
END–PERFORM.

2.8.8 Write a segment of code to represent:

    ACCEPT X.
PARA1.
      PERFORM UNTIL X < 0
        ACCEPT X
      END–PERFORM
PARA–2.

replacing the PERFORM .... END–PERFORM by IF and GO   TO statements.

2.8.9 Write a segment of code to represent:

PARA.
  IF A >B
    MOVE C TO D
  ELSE
    MOVE E TO D
  END–IF.

replacing IF....ELSE....END–IF by IF and GO   TO statements.

23

2.8.10 Trace through the segment of code and determine the final value for A.

```
MOVE ZERO TO COUNT.
MOVE 2 TO A.
PERFORM P1 UNTIL COUNT = 3
    •
    •
    •
P1.
    COMPUTE X =A ** 2
    ADD 1 TO COUNT
    MOVE X TO A.
```

2.8.11 Replace the following segment of code by the EVALUATE statement.

```
IF MUSIC–CODE = "A"
    MOVE "POPULAR" TO MUSIC–TYPE
ELSE
    IF MUSIC–CODE = "B"
        MOVE "JAZZ" TO MUSIC–TYPE
    ELSE
        MOVE "CLASSICAL" TO MUSIC–TYPE
    END–IF
END–IF
```

3 Procedure Division Coding

3.1 INTRODUCTION

This chapter illustrates how to code the PROCEDURE DIVISION of a COBOL program. It also serves as an introduction to techniques used in the design methodology known as Jackson Structured Programming (JSP) by familiarising the reader with the ideas of a *functions list, conditions list* and *schematic logic*. These ideas will be incorporated into the JSP methodology described later in the book.

3.1.1 Coding Methods

A computer program is a series of instructions that are obeyed by the computer in the order presented. In designing structured computer programs it is necessary to consider that a series of instructions is composed of sequences, selections and repetitions.

The methods used to code sequences, selections and repetitions will vary according to the following circumstances.

The make and model of computer being used and hence COBOL compiler available for that machine. e.g. ICL 2900, PR1ME, IBM 360.

The programming language Standard that was adopted in writing the COBOL compiler.

The manner in which the programmer wishes to implement the program design in the COBOL language.

In order to present a flexible approach to PROCEDURE DIVISION coding three methods are explained in this book.

The method of coding described in Appendix II incorporates the features of selection and repetition described in the Draft Proposed Revised X3.23 American National Standard Programming Language COBOL published in September 1981.

The method of coding described in this chapter is based on the American National Standard Programming Language COBOL X3.23 – 1974. This method will be illustrated throughout the book as computer generated source code that, where necessary, has been compiled and run giving specimen results from the test data available. The reader may be alarmed at the use of GO TO's in this coding, however, **it is important to distinguish the surface appearance of coding from the underlying, well formed, design of a program.**

To quote from M.A. Jackson's book entitled *Principles of Program Design.* "It is vital to distinguish surface appearance from underlying substance. When we write:

```
PXITER.  IF  NOT  CONDITION–1  GO  TO  PXEND.
         ...
         GO  TO  PXITER.
PXEND.
```

25

we are writing an iteration no less well-formed than

    PX: DO WHILE (CONDITION 1);

        ...

        ...

    ENDPX;

We are merely forced, because of shortcomings in the language (which it shares with PL/1 and ALGOL), to code our well-formed iteration in an unusual manner. We are writing by hand the text which we would prefer our compiler to generate automatically. The true objection to GO TO statements is, of course, that they permit unrestrained branching from one part of a program to another. The two GO TO statements in the example do no such thing: they are an utterly standardised implementation of the schematic logic."

Both methods use in–line or flat code for the following reasons.

> The methods produce code that corresponds very closely to the schematic logic.
> The code is efficient in execution.
> The code can be used consistently throughout the JSP methodology – i.e. it will allow inversion and backtracking techniques that will be explained later in the book.

To those readers who would still prefer to write GO TO less code, Chapter 9 illustrates an alternative method that produces GO TO less, hierarchical code from a JSP design. However, beware, this alternative method has shortcomings that will be explained later.

3.2 THE CONSTRUCTS

3.2.1 A Sequence

Consider designing a simple computer program to input via a V.D.U. keyboard the number of hours worked by an employee and his hourly rate of pay. Calculate his gross wage and output to the screen of a V.D.U. the gross wage.

In designing a solution the following instructions to the computer would be necessary.

> Calculate the gross wage.
> Input the hourly rate of pay.
> Input the hours worked.
> Output the gross wage.
> Stop.

These instructions can be numbered to form a **functions list.**

```
1. Calculate the gross wage.
2. Input the hourly rate of pay.
3. Input the hours worked.
4. Output the gross wage.
5. Stop.
```

However, if the computer is presented with the instructions in the numerical order of the functions list it cannot solve the problem since it logically requires the data of rate of pay and hours worked before it can calculate the gross wage.

The instructions must be ordered into a sequence. A notation that is adopted to signify a sequence is:

name–seq
    do (a list of numbers from the functions list showing the **order** in which the instructions are to be obeyed)
name–end

where name, invented by the programmer, is a representative name for the sequence of instructions.

The sequence of instructions for the solution to the stated problem would be represented by the following **schematic logic.**

wages–seq
    do 2,3,1,4,5
wages–end

The name *wages* conveys the nature of the sequence and the list of numbers 2,3,1,4,5 represents the instructions taken from the functions list in the order stated from left to right. This implies that the instruction *input hourly rate of pay* would be obeyed first, followed by *input the hours worked,* etc.

3.2.2 A desk check

A programmer having designed the schematic logic that represents a solution to a problem **must** verify that the design is correct **before** proceeding with the coding. In order to verify that the schematic logic represents a correct solution to a problem it is necessary to follow through the schematic logic using suitable test data. The outcome of a desk check will be the results presented in a tabular format.

When choosing test data the following points should be kept in mind:

I   The type and nature of the data is representative of the situation.

II   Numerical data, where applicable, should be chosen for ease of calculation.

III   Data is meaningful and within defined ranges. This assumes that the procedure being tested will always use valid data. However, this is not always the case since some procedures will be specifically written to trap bad data. In such circumstances the data must be chosen to cover all eventualities.

Data validation is covered as a specific topic later in the book, and it is therefore assumed that all the programs that are designed before that chapter will cater for valid data only, unless otherwise stated.

In the last problem the hourly rate of pay could be chosen as £10 and the hours worked as 40. The desk check on the schematic logic would be written as follows.

Function	Variables		
	hourly rate	hours worked	gross wage
2	10		
3	10	40	
1,4,5	10	40	400

Note: since functions 4 and 5 do not change the values of the variables, they have been written on the same line as function 1 (e.g. 1,4,5).

3.2.3 Coding a Sequence (see also Appendix II)

The schematic logic forms the basis of the PROCEDURE DIVISION, and must now be translated into a suitable format in the COBOL language.

In coding the PROCEDURE DIVISION from the schematic logic wages–seq and wages–end are treated as paragraph names and are used to document the beginning and ending of the sequence of instructions. Because wages–end has no sentence some compilers will flag this as an error, in which case insert the verb EXIT after the paragraph name WAGES–END.

The instructions from the functions list are expanded into COBOL statements and coded in the same order as given in the schematic logic. The numbers from the functions list and the word *do* are **not** included in the COBOL coding.

Note: the Division name and paragraph names **must** begin in zone A (between columns 8 – 11 inclusive) and COBOL statements **must** be coded in zone B (between columns 12 – 72 inclusive).

```
PROCEDURE DIVISION.
WAGES-SEQ.
    ACCEPT HOURLY-RATE.
    ACCEPT HOURS-WORKED.
    MULTIPLY HOURS-WORKED BY HOURLY-RATE
        GIVING GROSS-WAGE.
    DISPLAY GROSS-WAGE.
    STOP RUN.
WAGES-END.
```

3.2.4 A Selection

If the last problem is re-stated to include overtime being paid at 1½ times the hourly rate for work done over 40 hours then the solution must now include a selection based on the number of hours worked.

The condition on which the selection is to be made will be hours worked greater than 40. This and other conditions (if they applied) are documented in a **conditions list.** Each condition is numbered in a similar manner to functions being numbered in a functions list.

1. Hours worked > 40

The previous functions list must now be modified to cater for the solution to the revised problem. The calculation of the gross wage should be sub–divided into:

Calculated gross wage **without** overtime.
Calculate gross wage **with** overtime.

28

These two instructions can be incorporated into the functions list thus:

> 1. Calculate gross wage without overtime.
> 2. Calculate gross wage with overtime.
> 3. Input the hourly rate of pay.
> 4. Input the hours worked.
> 5. Output the gross wage.
> 6. Stop

Notice that in constructing the functions list the order in which the functions appear is **not** important since the correct order is specified in the schematic logic.

The notation used to denote a binary selection is:

> name–sel if (condition number taken from the conditions list)
>> do (a list of numbers from the functions list showing those instructions that are obeyed in the order given if the condition is **true**)
>
> name–or
>> do (a list of numbers from the functions list showing those instructions that are obeyed in the order given if the condition is **false**)
>
> name–end

The selection in the solution to the problem can be represented in the schematic logic as:

> overtime–sel if 1
>> do 2
>
> overtime–or
>> do 1
>
> overtime–end

This selection can now be included within the sequence of instructions to input the hourly rate and hours worked, and output the calculated gross wage.

The selection overtime–sel is indented in the schematic logic since it is regarded as part of the sequence of instructions for wages–seq.

> wages–seq
>> do 3,4
>> overtime–sel if 1
>>> do 2
>>
>> overtime–or
>>> do 1
>>
>> overtime–end
>> do 5,6
>
> wage–end

3.2.5 Desk Check

The schematic logic will be processed twice by hand, on the first occasion with the test data 10 (rate) and 35 (hours), and on the second occasion with the test data 10 (rate) and 45 (hours). Notice that the condition is represented in a separate column.

Function	Condition	Variables		
		hourly rate	hours worked	gross wage
3		10		
4		10	35	
1,5,6	1 False	10	35	350
3		10		
4		10	45	
2,5,6	1 True	10	45	475

3.2.6 Coding a Selection (see also Appendix II)

In representing the part of the schematic logic for a selection in the PROCEDURE DIVISION overtime–sel, overtime–or and overtime–end are represented as paragraph names. The numbers 2 and 1 that follow *do* are coded in COBOL as expanded instructions from the functions list. As before the numbers from the functions list and *do* are **not** included as part of the coding.

The condition if 1 is treated as a COBOL conditional statement using the **negated** condition of the form:

```
IF  NOT condition GO TO ......
    function 2
GO TO   ......
        function 1
```

```
PROCEDURE DIVISION.
WAGES-SEC.
    ACCEPT HOURLY-RATE.
    ACCEPT HOURS-WORKED.
OVERTIME-SEL.
    IF HOURS-WORKED NOT > 40 GO TO OVERTIME-OR.
        COMPUTE GROSS-WAGE
            = HOURLY-RATE * (1.5 * HOURS-WORKED - 20).
    GO TO OVERTIME-END.
OVERTIME-OR.
        MULTIPLY HOURS-WORKED BY HOURLY-RATE GIVING GROSS-WAGE.
OVERTIME-END.
    DISPLAY GROSS-WAGE.
    STOP RUN.
WAGES-END.
```

Comment. The reader may wonder why IF...ELSE.... was not used in the coding of a binary selection. The reason for its exclusion is on the grounds of compatibility of coding method. Since all schematic logic labels are treated as paragraph names, the inclusion of ELSE would imply that one paragraph name would have to revert to being a comment. The method of using IF (negated condition) GO TO .... is also used for multiple branching and repetition.

In calculating the gross wage with overtime the expression has been simplified thus:

GROSS WAGE
$$= (1.5 * HOURLY–RATE) * (HOURS–WORKED - 40) - (HOURLY–RATE * 40)$$
$$= HOURLY–RATE * (1.5 * (HOURS–WORKED - 40) + 40)$$
$$= HOURLY–RATE * (1.5 * HOURS–WORKED - 20)$$

Note: if HOURS–WORKED NOT > 40 is true the computer is directed to the alternative function by using the statement GO TO OVERTIME–OR.

In the problem if it had been required to calculate the overtime pay only then one branch of the selection could be null (empty).

The functions list would be modified to:

> 1. Calculate overtime pay.
> 2. Input the hourly rate of pay.
> 3. Input the hours worked.
> 4. Output the overtime pay.
> 5. Stop.

The schematic logic becomes:

```
Wages–seq
  do 2,3
    Overtime–sel if 1        Note: in catering for the null branch the
      do 1                          Overtime–or is not included.
    Overtime–end
  do 4,5
Wages–end
```

and the COBOL coding is:

```
PROCEDURE DIVISION.
WAGES-SEG.
    ACCEFT HOURLY-RATE.
    ACCEPT HOURS-WORKED.
OVERTIME-SEL.
    IF HCURS-WORKED > 40
      COMPUTE OVERTIME-PAY
            = (HOURS-WORKED - 40) * 1.5 * HOURLY-RATE.
OVERTIME-END.
    DISPLAY OVERTIME-PAY.
    STOP RUN.
WAGES-END.
```

Note: the condition is not negated as with the binary selection.

3.2.7 A Repetition

If the last example is modified to cater for calculating the gross wages for any number of employees then a loop must be introduced in order to repeat the previous set of instructions as many times as is necessary. Assume that all employees are paid at the same hourly rate and the loop will be exited when a negative value for hours worked is input to the computer.

The functions list will remain the same as for the last solution, however, the conditions list must be modified to include the condition for continuing within the loop (hours–worked not less than zero).

> 1. Hours–worked > 40
> 2. Hours–worked not < 0

31

The notation used to denote a loop is:

name–iter while   (condition number for the condition to continue within
——————   the loop, taken from the conditions list)
——————
——————   statements that are to be repeated
——————

name–end

The repetition in the solution to the problem can be represented in schematic logic as:

payroll–iter while 2
——————
——————
——————
payroll–end

The schematic logic for the repetition can now be included in the previous schematic logic representing the input of hourly rate and hours worked, calculation of gross wage taking into account any overtime payments and the output of the gross wage.

```
wages–seq
   do 3,4                      ------------(a)
   payroll–iter while 2
      overtime–sel if 1
         do 2
      overtime–or
         do 1
      overtime–end
         do 5,4               ------------(b)
   payroll–end
   do 6
wages–end
```

Since the repetition is part of wages–seq it is indented in the schematic logic.

The input of the hourly rate is the same for all the employees, it therefore only appears once in the schematic logic, and is represented outside of the loop. See line (a).

To preserve the structure of the loop (testing for an exit condition at the **beginning** of the loop) it is necessary to include the function to input the hours–worked twice. Once outside the loop, line (a) and repeated within the loop, line (b).

3.2.8 Desk Check

The following test data will be used to test the design of the solution represented in the schematic logic. The first number represents the hourly–rate and the last number a *rogue* value to allow the termination of the loop. The numbers between represent the number of hours worked by each employee.

Test data. 10 35 45 40 50 55 30 −1

Function	Condition	Variables		
		hourly rate	hours worked	gross wage
3		10		
4		10	35	
	2 True			
1	1 False	10	35	350
5,4		10	45	
	2 True			
2	1 True	10	45	475
5,4		10	40	
	2 True			
1	1 False	10	40	400
5,4		10	50	
	2 True			
2	1 True	10	50	550
5,4		10	55	
	2 True			
2	1 True	10	55	625
5,4		10	30	
	2 True			
1	1 False	10	30	300
5,4		10	−1	
	2 False			
6				

3.2.9 Coding a Repetition (see also Appendix II)

The schematic logic labels payroll–iter and payroll–end are treated as paragraph names. The condition while 2 is treated as a COBOL conditional statement using the **negated** condition.

```
PROCEDURE DIVISION.
WAGES-SEQ.
    ACCEPT HOURLY-RATE.
    ACCEPT HOURS-WORKED.
PAYROLL-ITER.
    IF HOURS-WORKED < 0 GO TO PAYROLL-END.
OVERTIME-SEL.
    IF HOURS-WORKED NOT > 40 GO TO OVERTIME-OR.
        COMPUTE GROSS-WAGE
            = HOURLY-RATE * (1.5 * HOURS-WORKED -20).
    GO TO OVERTIME-END.
OVERTIME-OR.
    MULTIPLY HOURS-WORKED BY HOURLY-RATE GIVING GROSS-WAGE.
OVERTIME-END.
    DISPLAY GROSS-WAGE.
    ACCEPT HOURS-WORKED.
    GO TO PAYROLL-ITER.
PAYROLL-END.
    STOP RUN.
WAGES-END.
```

Note: in order to construct the loop it is necessary to include GO TO PAYROLL–ITER at the bottom of the loop, before PAYROLL–END. A test for the exit condition from the loop is made immediately after the paragraph name PAYROLL–ITER, i.e. at the beginning of the loop.

3.3 MULTIPLE SELECTION

Problem. The following table shows that the product code of an article indicates the percentage commission a salesman can earn from the value of a sale. Construct a functions list, conditions list, schematic logic and a PROCEDURE DIVISION to input at the keyboard of a V.D.U. the product code (A–D) and the value of the sale, calculate and output to the screen of the V.D.U. the commission on that product.

Product Code	Commission %
A	0.5
B	1.0
C	2.0
D	2.5

3.3.1 The Design

Functions List

1. Input product code.
2. Input value of sale.
3. Output commission.
4. Stop.
5. Calculate commission at 0.5%
6. Calculate commission at 1.0%
7. Calculate commission at 2.0%
8. Calculate commission at 2.5%

Conditions List

1. Product code = A
2. Product code = B
3. Product code = C

The schematic logic for a binary selection can be expanded to include a multiple selection.

```
name–sel if (condition number)
    do (function list number(s))
name–or–2 if (condition number)
    do (function list number(s))
name–or–3 if (condition number)
    do (function list number(s))
    _____
    _____
    _____
    _____
name–end
```

A complete schematic logic for the solution to the problem will incorporate the multiple selection thus:

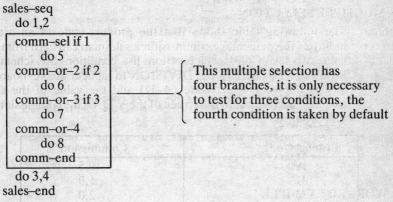

```
sales–seq
    do 1,2
    ┌──────────────────────┐
    │ comm–sel if 1        │
    │     do 5             │
    │ comm–or–2 if 2       │
    │     do 6             │
    │ comm–or–3 if 3       │
    │     do 7             │
    │ comm–or–4            │
    │     do 8             │
    │ comm–end            │
    └──────────────────────┘
    do 3,4
sales–end
```

This multiple selection has four branches, it is only necessary to test for three conditions, the fourth condition is taken by default

3.3.2 Desk Check

The following test data will be used in conjunction with the schematic logic. C 1000; D 2000; A 1500

Function	Condition	Variables		
		product code	sale value	commission
1		C		
2		C	1000	
7	3 True	C	1000	20
3,4				
1		D		
2		D	2000	
8	default	D	2000	50
3,4				
1		A		
2		A	1500	
5	1 True	A	1500	7.5
3,4				

3.3.3 Coding a Multiple Selection (see also Appendix II)

The same convention is used here as was used for the binary selection.

Code all schematic logic labels (i.e. comm–sel, comm–sel–2, etc) as paragraph names in the program.

The conditions given in the schematic logic are coded as COBOL conditional statements using **negated** conditions.

```
PROCEDURE DIVISION.
SALES-SEG.
    ACCEPT PRODUCT-CODE.
    ACCEPT SALE-VALUE.
COMM-SEL.
    IF PRODUCT-CODE NOT = "A" GO TO COMM-OR-2.
        MULTIPLY 0.005 BY SALE-VALUE GIVING COMMISSION,
    GO TC COMM-END.
COMM-OR-2.
    IF PRODUCT-CODE NOT = "B" GO TO COMM-OR-3.
        MULTIPLY 0.01 BY SALE-VALUE GIVING COMMISSION,
    GO TO COMM-END.
COMM-OR-3.
    IF PRODUCT-CODE NOT = "C" GO TO COMM-OR-4.
        MULTIPLY 0.02 BY SALE-VALUE GIVING COMMISSION,
    GO TC COMM-END.
COMM-OR-4.
        MULTIPLY 0.025 BY SALE-VALUE GIVING COMMISSION.
COMM-END.
    DISPLAY COMMISSION, STOP RUN.
SALES-ENC.
```

3.4 WORKED EXAMPLE

In the previous problem if we assume that the salesman sells more than one type of product, amend the functions list, conditions list, schematic logic and PROCEDURE DIVISION to calculate and output to the screen of the V.D.U. his total commission. Terminate the routine when the value of a sale is zero.

3.4.1 The Design

Functions List.

```
1.  Input product code.
2.  Input value of sale.
3.  Output commission on each sale.
4.  Stop.
5.  Calculate commission at 0.5%
6.  Calculate commission at 1.0%
7.  Calculate commission at 2.0%
8.  Calculate commission at 2.5%
9.  Initialise total commission to zero.
10. Output total commission.
11. Increase total commission by commission on current sale.
```

Conditions List.

```
1. Product code = A
2. Product code = B
3. Product code = C
4. Value of sale not = 0
```

Schematic Logic.

```
sales–seq
    do 9,2
    total–sales–iter while 4
        do 1
        comm–sel if 1
            do 5
        comm–or–2 if 2
            do 6
        comm–or–3 if 3
            do 7
        comm–or–4
            do 8
        comm–end
        do 3,11,2
    total–sales–end
    do 10,4
sales–end
```

3.4.2 Desk Check

Test data: 1000 C; 2000 D; 1500 A; 0 (notice the order in which the data is presented is different to that of the last example).

Function	Condition	Variables			
		code	sale	commission	total commission
9					0
2			1000		0
	4 True				
1		C	1000		0
7	3 True	C	1000	20	0
3,11		C	1000	20	20
2		C	2000	20	20
	4 True				
1		D	2000	20	20
8	default	D	2000	50	20
3,11		D	2000	50	70
2		D	1500	50	70
	4 True				
1		A	1500	50	70
5	1 True	A	1500	7.5	70
3,11		A	1500	7.5	77.5
2		A	0	7.5	77.5
	4 False				
10,4					

3.4.3 Coding (see also Appendix II)

```
PROCEDURE DIVISION.
SALES-SEG.
    MOVE ZERO TO TOTAL-COMMISSION.
    ACCEPT SALE-VALUE.
TOTAL-SALES-ITER.
    IF SALE-VALUE = 0 GO TO TOTAL-SALES-END.
        ACCEPT PRODUCT-CODE.
COMM-SEL.
    IF PRODUCT-CODE NOT = "A" GO TO COMM-OR-2.
        MULTIPLY 0.005 BY SALE-VALUE GIVING COMMISSION,
        GO TO COMM-END.
COMM-OR-2.
    IF PRODUCT-CODE NOT = "B" GO TO COMM-OR-3.
        MULTIPLY 0.01 BY SALE-VALUE GIVING COMMISSION,
        GO TO COMM-END.
COMM-OR-3.
    IF PRODUCT-CODE NOT = "C" GO TO COMM-OR-4.
        MULTIPLY 0.02 BY SALE-VALUE GIVING COMMISSION,
        GO TO COMM-END.
COMM-OR-4.
        MULTIPLY 0.025 BY SALE-VALUE GIVING COMMISSION.
COMM-END.
        DISPLAY COMMISSION.
        ADD COMMISSION TO TOTAL-COMMISSION.
        ACCEPT SALE-VALUE.
        GO TO TOTAL-SALES-ITER.
TOTAL-SALES-END.
        DISPLAY TOTAL-COMMISSION.
        STOP RUN.
SALES-END.
```

3.5 QUESTIONS *(answers begin on page 330)*

For questions 1 to 4 inclusive, code a PROCEDURE DIVISION from the information given. For questions 5 to 8 inclusive design functions lists and conditions lists to complete the schematic logic designs that are given with each question. Desk check your designs using suitable test data, and code a PROCEDURE DIVISION for each question.

3.5.1 Write a procedure to input the longest and shortest sides of a rectangular garden plot. Calculate the cost of turfing the plot if turf costs £0.50 m² and the cost of fencing the two long sides and one short side of the plot if fencing cost £2.00 m. Output the cost of the turf and the cost of the fence for the garden plot.

Functions list
1. Input length of long side.
2. Input length of short side.
3. Calculate the cost of turf.
4. Calculate the cost of fencing.
5. Output the cost of turf.
6. Output the cost of fencing.
7. Stop.

Glossary of Identifiers	
L–SIDE	long side of plot
S–SIDE	short side of plot
TURF	cost of turf
FENCE	cost of fencing

Schematic Logic

```
Garden–seq
    do 1,2,3,4,5,6,7
Garden–end
```

3.5.2 Write a procedure to find the arithmetic mean of a list of positive numbers, and output the arithmetic mean. The number of numbers is not known in advance. Terminate the procedure with zero.

Functions list
1. Initialise total to zero.
2. Initialise counter to zero.
3. Increase counter by 1.
4. Input number from list.
5. Increase total by number.
6. Calculate arithmetic mean.
7. Output arithmetic mean.
8. Stop.

Glossary of Identifiers

TOTAL	running total
COUNTER	number of numbers
NUMB	number from a list
MEAN	arithmetic mean

Conditions list.
1. Number not = 0

Schematic Logic

```
Mean–seq
    do 1,2,4
    Calc–iter while 1
        do 5,3,4
    Calc–end
    do 6,7,8
Mean–end
```

3.5.3 Write a procedure to find the largest number from a list of ten positive numbers. Output the largest number.

Functions list
1. Input number.
2. Maxnumber becomes number.
3. Initialise number count to 1.
4. Increase number count by 1.
5. Output maxnumber.
6. Stop.

Glossary of Identifiers

NUMB	number from list
MAXNUMB	largest number from list
COUNTER	number of numbers

Conditions list
1. Number > Maxnumber.
2. Number count not = 10.

Schematic Logic
```
Max–seq
    do 1,3,2
    Comp–iter while 2
        do 1,4
        Largest–sel if 1
            do 2
        Largest–end
    Comp–end
    do 5,6
Max–end
```

3.5.4 Write a procedure to input an amount of money as a whole number of Pounds Sterling and produce a breakdown of the notes required to make up the sum of money using the minimum number of notes. Only £10, £5 and £1 notes are used.

Functions list	Glossary of Identifiers	
1. Input money.	MONEY	amount of money
2. Initialise £10 total to zero.	TOT–10	total number of
3. Initialise £5 total to zero.		£10 notes
4. Increase £10 total by 1.	TOT–5	total number of
5. Increase £5 total by 1.		£5 notes
6. Reduce money by £10.		
7. Reduce money by £5.		
8. Output £10 total.		
9. Output £5 total.		
10. Output money.		
11. Stop.		

Conditions list
1. Money > = 10
2. Money > = 5

Schematic Logic
```
Money–seq
    do 2,3,1
    Ten–iter while 1
        do 6,4
    Ten–end
    Five–sel if 2
        do 7,5
    Five–end
    do 8,9,10,11
Money–end
```

3.5.5 A salesman earns a commission on the value of his sales. The following table shows the scale of the commission.

Value of Sales (£)	Percentage commission on sale value
1 – 999	1
1000 – 9999	5
10000 – 99999	10

Write a procedure to input a figure for the value of his sales (in whole pounds only) and calculate and output his commission. Repeat the procedure for different sales figures. Terminate the procedure when the sales figure is zero.

Schematic Logic	Glossary of Identifiers

Schematic Logic

```
Sales–seq
  do 1
  Salesman–iter while 1
    Comm–sel if 2
      do 5
    Comm–or–2 if 3
      do 4
    Comm–or–3
      do 3
    Comm–end
      do 2,1
  Salesman–end
  do 6
Sales–end
```

Glossary of Identifiers

SALES   value of sale
COMMISSION   % commission

3.5.6 Write a procedure to input the surname, age, weight and height of ten people, and output the name of those persons who fall into **all** the following categories.

Age 18 – 23 years
Weight 80 – 180 Kg
Height 152 – 182 cm

Schematic Logic

```
Details–seq
  do 7
  Person–iter while 1
    do 1,2,3,4,8
    Age–sel if 2
      Weight–sel if 3
        Height–sel if 4
          do 5
        Height–end
      Weight–end
    Age–end
  Person–end
  do 6
Details–end
```

Glossary of Identifiers

SURNAME   name of person
AGE   age in years
WEIGHT   weight in Kg
HEIGHT   height in cm
COUNTER   number of people

41

3.5.7   Consider the following rules for calculating income tax in Utopia.

Personal allowances are £1200 for a single person and £2300 for a married man.

A child allowance is £100 per child.

Taxable income is the amount remaining after deducting the personal allowance and total child allowance from the gross income.

Income tax is calculated from taxable income according to the following table.

Taxable income on	Percentage tax on taxable income
First £1000	no tax
Next £1000	20%
Next £2000	30%
Above £4000	40%

Write a procedure to input the gross salary, tax status (married or single) and number of children, and output the tax paid on that income. Repeat the procedure for different values of gross salary, tax status and number of children. Terminate the procedure with a zero gross salary.

Schematic Logic

```
Inc–seq
   do 1
   Tax–iter while 1
      do 2,3
      Status–sel if 2
         do 5
         Child–sel if 3
            do 6,7
         Child–end
      Status–or
         do 4
      Status–end
      do 8
      Calc–sel if 4
         do 12
      Calc–or–2 if 5
         do 11
      Calc–or–3 if 6
         do 10
      Calc–or–4
         do 9
      Calc–end
      do 13,1
   Tax–end
   do 14
Inc–end
```

Glossary of Identifiers	
G–SALARY	gross salary
TAX–STATUS	married or single
CHILDREN	number of children
ALLOWANCE	personal allowance
CHILD–ALLOWANCE	as stated
TAX–INCOME	taxable income
TAX	income tax

3.5.8 In an examination four pass grades and one fail grade is awarded:

A for marks between 100 and 70 inclusive,
B for marks between   60 and 69 inclusive,
C for marks between   50 and 59 inclusive,
D for marks between   40 and 49 inclusive,
F for marks below 40.

Input an examination mark for a student and output the grade. Repeat the process until the examination mark is 999, then output the total number of students in each of the five grades.

Schematic Logic

		Glossary of Identifiers
Marks–seq	MARK	% examination mark
do 3,1	GRADE	examination grade
Student–iter while 1	TOTAL–A	total number of passes in grade A
Grade–sel if 2	TOTAL–B	total number of passes in grade B
do 4,15	TOTAL–C	total number of passes in grade C
Grade–or–2 if 3	TOTAL–D	total number of passes in grade D
do 5,15	TOTAL–F	total number of passes in grade F

Grade–or–3 if 4
  do 6,15
Grade–or 4 if 5
  do 7,15
Grade–or–5
  do 8,15
Grade–end
  do 2,1
Student–end
do 9,10,11,12,13,14
Marks–end

Note: when deriving the functions list assume one function for initialising the totals for the five grades to zero, otherwise, assume five functions for each of the operations on the totals.

4 The Complete Program

4.1 INTRODUCTION

The end product of this chapter is to present the reader with a complete working COBOL program. The discussion that leads up to this finalé identifies the need for a DATA DIVISION and demonstrates how the format of data values are coded. The chapter by necessity also introduces the reader to the IDENTIFICATION DIVISION. This will be kept to a minimal form since it is largely for documentary purpose and serves of little importance in the design, structure and coding of programs. Finally the problems encountered on compiling and executing complete programs will be discussed towards the end of the chapter.

4.2 THE PICTURE CLAUSE

The PROCEDURE DIVISION for the last worked example of chapter 3 was defined as:

```
PROCEDURE DIVISION.
SALES-SEQ.
    MOVE ZERO TO TOTAL-COMMISSION.
    ACCEPT SALE-VALUE.
TOTAL-SALES-ITER.
    IF SALE-VALUE = 0 GO TO TOTAL-SALES-END.
        ACCEPT PRODUCT-CODE.
COMM-SEL.
        IF PRODUCT-CODE NOT = "A" GO TO COMM-OR-2.
            MULTIPLY 0.005 BY SALE-VALUE GIVING COMMISSION,
        GO TO COMM-END.
COMM-OR-2.
        IF PRODUCT-CODE NOT = "B" GO TO COMM-OR-3.
            MULTIPLY 0.01 BY SALE-VALUE GIVING COMMISSION,
        GO TO COMM-END.
COMM-OR-3.
        IF PRODUCT-CODE NOT = "C" GO TO COMM-OR-4.
            MULTIPLY 0.02 BY SALE-VALUE GIVING COMMISSION,
        GO TO COMM-END.
COMM-OR-4.
            MULTIPLY 0.025 BY SALE-VALUE GIVING COMMISSION.
COMM-END.
        DISPLAY COMMISSION.
        ADD COMMISSION TO TOTAL-COMMISSION.
        ACCEPT SALE-VALUE.
    GO TO TOTAL-SALES-ITER.
TOTAL-SALES-END.
    DISPLAY TOTAL-COMMISSION.
    STOP RUN.
SALES-END.
```

The identifiers in this PROCEDURE DIVISION are:

        TOTAL-COMMISSION
        PRODUCT-CODE
        SALE-VALUE
and   COMMISSION.

The type of data the identifier relates to, and the size of each datum can be summarised in the following table. The term type of data implies either *numeric*, *alphabetic* or *alphanumeric*.

Numeric data consists of the digits 0 through to 9 with or without an operational

44

sign. The decimal point is **not** included as a legal chararcter for a datum that is defined as being numeric.

Alphabetic data consists of the letters of the alphabet A through to Z and a space character.

Alphanumeric data consists of any of the characters of the ASCII or EBCDIC character sets.

Identifier	Data type	Size	Example
TOTAL-COMMISSION	numeric	7 digits inc 2 decimal pl.	25p to £25000
PRODUCE-CODE	alphabetic	1 character	A through to D
SALE-VALUE	numeric	5 digits	£50 to £10000
COMMISSION	numeric	5 digits inc 2 decimal pl.	25p to £250

Note: the size of the SALE-VALUE has been defined by the author of this specific problem; the size of the COMMISSION was calculated by taking 0.5% of £50 for the lowest value and 2.5% of £10000 for the highest value. The size of the TOTAL-COMMISSION was based on a total of 100 sales.

Each identifier must be coded by data type and the **maximum** number of characters that make up the largest data value. This information is coded into a PICTURE clause.

The following characters have specific meanings within a PICTURE clause and represent the position of each character.

     9 – a numeric digit
     A – an alphabetic character
     X – an alphanumeric character
     V – the position only of the decimal point
     S – the datum has an operational sign (+ or −).

The format of the PICTURE clause is:

   $\left\{ \begin{array}{l} \textbf{PICTURE} \\ \textbf{PIC} \end{array} \right\}$ IS character-string

where the character-string is composed from the character subset (9, A, X, V and S). This is purposely described as a subset, since the reader will soon discover that there are many more characters that can be used in a PICTURE character-string.

The following PICTURES (abbreviated to PIC) can be used to define the format of the data represented by the four identifiers.

TOTAL-COMMISSION PIC 99999V99 – consists of up to 7 digits including 2 decimal places.

PRODUCT-CODE PIC A   – consists of 1 alphabetic character.
SALE-VALUE PIC 99999   – consists of up to 5 digits.
COMMISSION PIC 999V99   – consists of up to 5 digits including 2 decimal places.

Where a PICTURE descriptor is repeated a shorter notation may be used.

e.g. PIC 99999 is the same as PIC 9(5) indicating that the item is numeric and contains a maximum of 5 digits.

e.g. PIC AAAAAAAAAA can be coded as A(10), and PIC XXXXXXXX can be coded as PIC X(8).

Every PICTURE clause has a *level number* associated with it. The TOTAL-COMMISSION, PRODUCT-CODE, SALE-VALUE and COMMISSION are **not** by-products of other items of data that have been subdivided and are, therefore, designated the level number 77.

The correct format for describing the four identifiers is:

```
77 TOTAL-COMMISSION   PIC 9(5)V99.
77 PRODUCT-CODE   PIC A.
77 SALE-VALUE   PIC 9(5).
77 COMMISSION   PIC 999V99.
```

4.3 THE DATA DIVISION

In chapter 1 the DATA DIVISION was stated as having three sections (although more are possible). The four identifiers in this problem relate to data that is local to this program (i.e. not stored on tape or disc but stored in the main memory of the computer) and will, therefore, be assigned to the WORKING-STORAGE SECTION of the DATA DIVISION. At this stage the FILE SECTION and LINKAGE SECTION can be omitted and the DATA DIVISION coded as:

```
DATA DIVISION.
WORKING-STORAGE SECTION.
77 TOTAL-COMMISSION PIC 9(5)V99.
77 PRODUCT-CODE PIC A.
77 SALE-VALUE PIC 9(5).
77 COMMISSION PIC 999V99.
```

4.4 THE IDENTIFICATION DIVISION

The format of the IDENTIFICATION DIVISION is given as:

IDENTIFICATION DIVISION.

PROGRAM-ID.   program-name $\left[\text{IS} \ \left\{ \begin{matrix} \textbf{COMMON} \\ \textbf{INITIAL} \end{matrix} \right\} \text{PROGRAM} \right]$.

[**AUTHOR.**   [comment-entry] ...]

[**INSTALLATION.**   [comment-entry] ...]

[**DATE-WRITTEN.**   [comment-entry] ...]

[**DATE-COMPILED.**   [comment-entry] ...]

[**SECURITY.**   [comment-entry] ...]

However, it is only necessary to include the first two statements of this Division in a COBOL program, thus:

```
IDENTIFICATION DIVISION.
PROGRAM-ID. PROG01.
```

is sufficient for our requirements.

The name of the program (PROG01) is invented by the programmer.

4.5 THE PROGRAM

The three Divisions are listed in the order specified in Chapter 1. The ENVIRONMENT DIVISION has been omitted in this solution since the author wants the reader to be able to write complete COBOL programs as quickly as possible with the minimum of coding. The first part of the ENVIRONMENT DIVISION is documentary and the second part relates primarily to external data files (that are not used in this program), therefore, the author feels justified in omitting this Division at this stage.

```
IDENTIFICATION DIVISION.
PROGRAM-ID. PROG01.
DATA DIVISION.
WORKING-STORAGE SECTION.
77 TOTAL-COMMISSION PIC 9(5)V99.
77 PRODUCT-CODE PIC A.
77 SALE-VALUE PIC 9(5).
77 COMMISSION PIC 999V99.
PROCEDURE DIVISION.
SALES-SEG.
    MOVE ZERO TO TOTAL-COMMISSION.
    ACCEPT SALE-VALUE.
TOTAL-SALES-ITER.
    IF SALE-VALUE = 0 GO TO TOTAL-SALES-END.
    ACCEPT PRODUCT-CODE.
COMM-SEL.
    IF PRODUCT-CODE NOT = "A" GO TO COMM-OR-2.
        MULTIPLY 0.005 BY SALE-VALUE GIVING COMMISSION,
    GO TO COMM-END.
COMM-OR-2.
    IF PRODUCT-CODE NOT = "B" GO TO COMM-OR-3.
        MULTIPLY 0.01 BY SALE-VALUE GIVING COMMISSION,
    GO TO COMM-END.
COMM-OR-3.
    IF PRODUCT-CODE NOT = "C" GO TO COMM-OR-4.
        MULTIPLY 0.02 BY SALE-VALUE GIVING COMMISSION,
    GO TO COMM-END.
COMM-OR-4.
        MULTIPLY 0.025 BY SALE-VALUE GIVING COMMISSION.
COMM-END.
    DISPLAY COMMISSION.
    ADD COMMISSION TO TOTAL-COMMISSION.
    ACCEPT SALE-VALUE.
    GO TO TOTAL-SALES-ITER.
TOTAL-SALES-END.
    DISPLAY TOTAL-COMMISSION.
    STOP RUN.
SALES-END.
```

4.6 WORKED EXAMPLE

4.6.1 Problem

A building society requires an interactive computer system for use by its customers who wish to make enquiries about investments. The system is *menu-driven* giving the customer the following choice.

DO YOU WANT INFORMATION ON:
A – THE AMOUNT OF INVESTMENT NEEDED TO GIVE
    AN ANNUAL INCOME OVER A FIXED TERM
B – THE ANNUAL INCOME FROM A FIXED TERM INVESTMENT
C – THE INTEREST PAID AFTER A FIXED TERM ON AN
    INVESTMENT.

The interest rate varies according to the length of the term of the investment.

Term (minimum) Years	Rate Percentage
1	Basic rate
2	Basic rate + 1%
3	Basic rate + 1½%

For example, if the basic rate is assumed to be 10% and the choice is A, the customer enters an annual income (£1000) and term (2 years) to the computer. The calculation 1000 / (0.10 + 0.01) is performed and the investment £9,090.90 is output.

However, if the choice is B, the customer enters the principal invested (£1000) and term of investment (3 years) to the computer. The calculation for simple interest over 1 year is performed 1000 × (0.10 + 0.015) and the annual income £115 is output.

If the choice is C, the customer enters the principal invested (£1000) and term of investment (3 years) to the computer. The calculation for compound interest is performed and the result £385 is output.

At the beginning of a days trading a clerk completes a start-up procedure for the computer system (not part of this program) and then inputs the percentage basic rate of interest. The system runs until 4.30 p.m. each day, and at that time automatically stops. You may assume that the computer updates the time of day after the start up procedure is completed, all input and output will be through a visual display unit, and the COBOL compiler used does not recognise exponentiation (**), therefore, the compound interest formula cannot be used.

4.6.2 Design.

Functions List.
1. Input basic rate of interest.
2. Input principal investment.
3. Input annual income.
4. Input term of investment.
5. Calculate required investment.
6. Calculate annual income.
7. Output required investment.
8. Output calculated interest (income).
9. Store principal investment in temporary area.
10. Increase principal by interest.
11. Decrease term by 1 year.
12. Calculate compound interest.
13. Output menu.
14. Input menu code.
15. Store basic rate.
16. Increase basic rate by 1% and store in rate.
17. Increase basic rate by 1½% and store in rate.
18. Input time.
19. Stop.
20. Calculate simple interest.

Schematic Logic.

```
system-seq
  do 1,18
  enquiry-iter while 1
    init-seq
      do 13,14,4
      rate-sel if 4
        do 17
      rate-or-2 if 5
        do 16
      rate-or-3
        do 15
      rate-end
      code-sel if 2
        do 3,5,7
      code-or
        calc-seq
          do 2
          sim-com-sel if 3
            do 6
          sim-com-or
            com-seq
              do 9
              comp-iter while 6
                do 20,10,11
              comp-end
              do 12
            com-end
          sim-com-end
          do 8
        calc-end
      code-end
      do 18
    init-end
  enquiry-end
  do 19
system-end
```

Conditions List.
1. Time < 16.30.
2. Menu-code = A.
3. Menu-code = B.
4. Term $\geq$ 3.
5. Term = 2.
6. Term not = 0.

4.6.3 Desk Check

The following test data is used to check the design of the program.

100 (10% basic rate of interest per annum)
A; 1; 01000
A; 2; 01000
A; 3; 01000
B; 1; 01000
B; 2; 01000
B; 3; 01000
C; 1; 01000
C; 2; 01000
C; 3; 01000

Note: the time is a function of the system and is not input by the user.

Functions	Conditions	Basic rate	Term	Rate	Code	Income	Investment	Principal	Interest	Temp. store
1,(18)		100								
13,14,4	1 true		1		A					
15	4,5 false			100						
3,5,7	2 true					01000	10000.00			
(18),13,14,4	1 true		2		A					
16	5 true			110						
3,5,7	2 true					01000	09090.90(91)			
(18),13,14,4	1 true		3		A					
17	4 true			115						
3,5,7	2 true					01000	08695.65(22)			
(18),13,14,4	1 true		1		B					
15	4,5 false			100						
2	2 false							01000		
6,8	3 true					00100				
(18),13,14,4	1 true		2		B					
16	5 true			110						
2	2 false							01000		
6,8	3 true					00110				
(18),13,14,4	1 true		3		B					
17	4 true			115						
2	2 false							01000		
6,8	3 true					00115				
(18),13,14,4	1 true		1		C					
15	4,5 false			100						
2	2 false							01000		
9,	3 false									
20,10	6 true		1						00100.00	01000
21,12,8	6 false		0			00100				
(18),13,14,4	1 true	100	2		C					
16	5 true			110						
2	2 false							01000		
9	3 false									
20,10	6 true		2						00110.00	01000
11,20,10			1						00122.10	
11,12,8			0			00232				
(18),13,14,4	1 true		3		C					
17	4 true			115						
2	2 false							01000		
9	3 false									
20,10	6 true		3						00115.00	01000
11,20,10			2						00128.22(5)	
11,20,10			1						00142.94(5)	
11,12,8			0			00385				
(18)	1 false									

Extended glossary.

Identifier	Description	Type	Size
RATE	annual % interest rate	numeric	3 dec.pl.
PRINCIPAL	amount invested (input)	numeric	5 digits
TERM	period of investment	numeric	1 digit
BASIC-RATE	flat rate of annual interest	numeric	3 dec.pl.
MENU-CODE	user's choice from menu	alphabetic	1 character
INVESTMENT	calculated principal (output)	numeric	7 digits inc 2 dec.pl.
INCOME	gain on investment	numeric	5 digits
TIME-OF-DAY	time taken from computer	numeric	8 digits
INTEREST	annual interest	numeric	7 digits inc 2 dec.pl.
TEMP-PRINCIPAL	temporary store	numeric	5 digits

Notes.

Many implementations of COBOL use the reserved word TIME to store an eight digit representation of the current time of day. TIME is composed of the data elements hours, minutes, seconds and hundredths of a second, and is based on elapsed time after midnight on a 24-hour clock basis – thus, 2:41 p.m. would be expressed as 14410000. The minimum value for TIME is 00000000 and the maximum value is 23595999.

The statement ACCEPT TIME-OF-DAY FROM TIME will store the current time, taken momentarily from the computer, in the programmers identifier TIME-OF-DAY.

4.7 PROGRAM IMPLEMENTATION

4.7.1 Storing a Program.

There are two methods of preparing a written program for entry to a computer.

The first method involves typing a line-by-line copy of the program at the keyboard of an on-line data entry terminal and storing the program on magnetic tape or magnetic disc.

The second method (becoming out of date) involves typing a line-by-line copy of the program at the keyboard of an off-line key-punch device and storing the program on either punched paper tape or punched cards. The prepared program must then be read by an on-line input device such as a card reader or paper tape reader so that the program can be transferred to the main memory of the computer.

It is quite probable at this stage, regardless of the method of program entry used, that transcription errors (keying errors) can be introduced into your program. Often double entry preparation techniques are used in order to reduce such errors to the very minimum.

If the first method is used for storing a program then a line-by-line image of the program is stored on a magnetic file, and the contents of that file (your program) is given a name. A future retrieval of the stored program is possible by giving the computer system the command to load the named file.

The commands used to file and load programs are machine specific and will not be considered here. The reader is advised to consult their operations manual (DOS section) for their machine.

4.7.2 Compilation.

Having stored the COBOL program the next stage is to compile it. The commands required to invoke a COBOL compiler and compile the source prorgram are machine specific. The reader is advised to consult the operations manual (JCL section) for their machine.

At the compilation stage a listing of all the syntax errors can be obtained together with a computer generated compiled listing of the source program. To demonstrate this feature the current program has deliberately had syntax errors introduced into it. These errors could have come from two sources – the programmer and the keyboard operator.

The results of the compilation are as follows. Beginners to programming in COBOL can find that the error diagnostics can be very vague and they often become daunted by the number of errors that a COBOL compiler will flag from what appears to be very trivial mistakes. When the compilation of a program reveals that the program contains errors the next stage is to trace through every line of code that has caused an error and annotate the correction on the page of the compiled source listing.

Compiled source program.

```
(0001)        IDENTIFICATION DIVISION.
(0002)        PROGRAM-ID. C462.
(0003)        DATA DIVISION.
(0004)        WORKING STORAGE SECTION.          NO HYPHEN
(0005)        77 RATE PIC V999.
(0006)        77 PRINCIPAL.                     NO PICTURE CLAUSE
(0007)        77 TERM PIC 9.
(0008)        77 BASIC-RATE PIC V999.
(0009)        77 MENU-CODE PIC A.
(0010)        77 INVESTMENT PIC 9(5)V99.
(0011)        77 INCOME PIC 9(5).
(0012)        77 TIME OF DAY PIC 9(8).          NO HYPHENS
(0013)        77 INTEREST PIC 9(5)V99.
(0014)        77 TEMP-PRINCIPAL PIC 9(5).
(0015)        PROCEDURE DIVISION.
(0016)        SYSTEM-SEQ.
(0017)            DISPLAY INPUT BASIC RATE OF INTEREST (3 DEC. PL.)
** SYNTAX ERROR **    PUNCT?                    NO DELIMITERS
(0018)            ACCEPT BASIC-RATE.
(0019)            ACCEPT TIME-OF-DAY FROM TIME.
(0020)        ENQUIRY-ITER.
(0021)            IF TIME-OF-DAY NOT < 16300000 GO TO ENQUIRY-END.

              * display menu

(0022)        INIT-SEQ.
(0023)            DISPLAY "DO YOU WANT INFORMATION ON:"
(0024)            DISPLAY " "
(0025)            DISPLAY "A THE AMOUNT OF INVESTMENT NEEDED TO GIVE"
(0026)            DISPLAY "  AN ANNUAL INCOME OVER A FIXED TERM".
(0027)            DISPLAY " "
(0028)            DISPLAY "B THE ANNUAL INCOME FROM A FIXED TERM INVESTMENT".
(0029)            DISPLAY " "
(0030)            DISPLAY "C THE INTEREST PAID AFTER A FIXED TERM ON AN"
(0031)            DISPLAY "  INVESTMENT".
(0032)            DISPLAY " ".
(0033)            DISPLAY "INPUT CODE A, B OR C"
(0034)            ACCEPT MENU-CODE.
(0035)            DISPLAY " ".
(0036)            DISPLAY "INPUT TERM IN YEARS (1 DIGIT)".
(0037)            ACCEPT TERM.

              * calculate correct rate for term

(0038)        RATE-SEL.
(0039)            IF TEM < 3 GO TO RATE-OR-2.     TERM
(0040)                ADD 1.5, BASIC-RATE GIVING RATE.
(0041)            GO TO RATE-END.
(0042)        RATE-OR-2.
(0043)            IF TERM NOT = 2 GO TO RATE-OR-3.
(0044)                ADD 0.01, BASIC-RATE GIVING RATE.
(0045)            GO TO RATE-END.
(0046)        RATE-OR-3.
(0047)            MOVE BASIC-RATE TO RATE.
(0048)        RATE-END.

              * calculate principal investment
```

(program continued)

```
(0049)             CODE-SEL.
(0050)                  IF MENU-CODE NOT = A GO TO CODE-OR.          NO DELIMITERS
(0051)                  DISPLAY "INPUT ANNUAL INCOME (5 DIGITS)"
(0052)                  ACCEPT INCOME.                         NO PARAGRAPH NAME
(0053)                  DIVIDE RATE INTO INCOME GIVING INVESTMENT.
(0054)                  DISPLAY "PRINCIPAL INVESTMENT REQUIRED " INVESTMENT.
(0055)                  GO TO CODE-END.

                 * calculate interest

(0056)             CALC-SEQ.
(0057)                  DISPLAY "INPUT PRINCIPAL INVESTMENT (5 DIGITS)"
(0058)                  ACCEPT PRINCIPAL.

                 * simple interest per annum

(0059)             SIM-COM-SEL.
(0060)                  IF MENU-CODE NOT = "B" GO TO SIM-COM-OR.
(0061)                  MULTIPLY RATE BY PRINCIPAL GIVING INCOME.
(0062)                  GO TO SIM-COM-END.
(0063)             SIM-COM-OR.
(0064)             COM-SEQ.
(0065)                  MOVE PRINCIPAL TO TEMP-PRINCIPAL.

                 * compound interest over term

(0066)             COMP-ITER.
(0067)                  IF TERM = 0 GO TO COMP-END.          NO PARAGRAPH NAME
(0068)                  MULTIPLY RATE BY PRINCIPAL GIVING INTEREST.
(0069)                  ADD INTEREST TO PRINCIPAL.
(0070)                  SUBTRACT 1 FROM TERM.
(0071)                  SUBTRACT TEMP-PRINCIPAL FROM PRINCIPAL GIVING INCOME.
(0072)             COMM-END.
(0073)             SIM-COM-END.
(0074)                  DISPLAY "INCOME FROM INVESTMENT " INCOME.
(0075)             CODE-END.
(0076)                  ACCEPT TIME-OF-DAY FROM TIME.
(0077)                  GO TO ENQUIRY-ITER.
(0078)             ENQUIRY-END.
(0079)                  STOP              STOP RUN.
(0080)             SYSTEM-END.
```

Listing of errors.

```
0004   SOURCE BYPASSED UNTIL NEXT FD/SECTION. [WORKING    ]
0004   SOURCE BYPASSED UNTIL NEXT FD/SECTION. [STORAGE    ]
0004   SOURCE BYPASSED UNTIL NEXT FD/SECTION. [SECTION    ]
0005   VALUE DELETED DUE TO TYPE CONFLICT.
0006   ITEM ASSUMED TO BE BINARY.
0012   NAME OMITTED; ENTRY BYPASSED. [TIME    ]
0017   STATEMENT DELETED DUE TO ERRONEOUS SYNTAX. [INPUT    ]
0017   UNRECOGNIZABLE ELEMENT IS IGNORED. [BASIC    ]
0017   UNRECOGNIZABLE ELEMENT IS IGNORED. [RATE    ]
0017   UNRECOGNIZABLE ELEMENT IS IGNORED. [(    ]
0017   UNRECOGNIZABLE ELEMENT IS IGNORED. [3    ]
0017   UNRECOGNIZABLE ELEMENT IS IGNORED. [DEC    ]
0017   UNRECOGNIZABLE ELEMENT IS IGNORED. [PL    ]
0017   UNRECOGNIZABLE ELEMENT IS IGNORED. [)    ]
0019   STATEMENT DELETED DUE TO ERRONEOUS SYNTAX. [TIME-OF-DAY    ]
0019   UNRECOGNIZABLE ELEMENT IS IGNORED. [FROM    ]
0019   UNRECOGNIZABLE ELEMENT IS IGNORED. [TIME    ]
0021   UNRECOGNIZABLE ELEMENT IS IGNORED. [TIME-OF-DAY    ]
0021   UNRECOGNIZABLE ELEMENT IS IGNORED. [NOT    ]
0021   UNRECOGNIZABLE ELEMENT IS IGNORED. [<    ]
0021   UNRECOGNIZABLE ELEMENT IS IGNORED. [16300000    ]
0039   UNRECOGNIZABLE ELEMENT IS IGNORED. [TEM    ]
0039   UNRECOGNIZABLE ELEMENT IS IGNORED. [<    ]
0039   UNRECOGNIZABLE ELEMENT IS IGNORED. [3    ]
0050   UNRECOGNIZABLE ELEMENT IS IGNORED. [A    ]
0050   /D/ UNRESOLVED PROCEDURE-NAME; STATEMENT DELETED. [CODE-OR    ]
```

```
0067  /D/ UNRESOLVED PROCEDURE-NAME: STATEMENT DELETED. [COMP-END  ]
0076  STATEMENT DELETED DUE TO ERRONEOUS SYNTAX. [TIME-OF-DAY   ]
0076  UNRECOGNIZABLE ELEMENT IS IGNORED. [FROM   ]
0076  UNRECOGNIZABLE ELEMENT IS IGNORED. [TIME   ]
0080  /W/ PERIOD ASSUMED ABOVE.
0080  INCOMPLETE/TOO LONG STATEMENT DELETED.
 "D" Level errors in program: BINARY file will not be created
0032   Errors   0001 Warnings    COBOL Ver - 19.1  **SYNTAX ONLY**
```

The original source program is then edited using the information from the annotated source listing and then re-compiled. The details relating to editing a source program are machine specific and the reader is again recommended to consult the operations manual (editor section) for their machine.

If having compiled the program for the second time there are still syntax errors, then the process of annotating corrections, editing and compiling must continue until the source program is free from syntax errors and warnings.

4.7.3 Loading and Running. (Program Execution).

The next phase is to load the object program (machine code program generated by the compiler from the COBOL source program) and run or execute the program. Once again the commands to perform these functions are specific to a particular machine, therefore, readers should consult their operations manual (JCL section).

This phase can be prone to the following software errors.

Loading error – the machine code programs necessary for the running of the COBOL program have not been specified or are not available at the time of loading. Consult your operations manual.

Logical errors – the program runs to completion but does not do what you intended it to do. If you have given your program design a careful desk check and coded the design correctly then this type of error can be minimal. In fact the JSP methodology helps to reduce this type of error. In the event of logical errors the programmer should consider the following courses of action.

Check the sizes of the PICTURES, especially decimal fractions, they may not be large enough for the results being generated.

Trace through the source code using the test data that caused the error. This is essentially a desk check on the source code.

Perform another desk check on the design of the program (schematic logic) using the data that caused the error.

If this technique is methodically carried out the error will be detected – this statement is not one of blind faith but years of experience.

Readers must avoid, at all costs, the temptation of sitting at the terminal of a computer editing lines of source code in a haphazard manner in the vague hope that they might fix the errors. Such attempts can only too often result in other errors creeping undetected into the program, and the programmer wastes valuable time, money and computer resources.

The current program still contains errors. If the reader checks the following results with the desk check of the design it is clear to see that a logical error exists.

Part of the results from the test run.

```
INPUT BASIC RATE OF INTEREST (3 DEC. PL.)
100
DO YOU WANT INFORMATION ON:

A THE AMOUNT OF INVESTMENT NEEDED TO GIVE
  AN ANNUAL INCOME OVER A FIXED TERM

B THE ANNUAL INCOME FROM A FIXED TERM INVESTMENT

C THE INTEREST PAID AFTER A FIXED TERM ON AN
  INVESTMENT

INPUT CODE A, B OR C
A

INPUT TERM IN YEARS (1 DIGIT)
1
INPUT ANNUAL INCOME (5 DIGITS)
01000
PRINCIPAL INVESTMENT REQUIRED 1000000

DO YOU WANT INFORMATION ON:

A THE AMOUNT OF INVESTMENT NEEDED TO GIVE
  AN ANNUAL INCOME OVER A FIXED TERM

B THE ANNUAL INCOME FROM A FIXED TERM INVESTMENT

C THE INTEREST PAID AFTER A FIXED TERM ON AN
  INVESTMENT

INPUT CODE A, B OR C
A

INPUT TERM IN YEARS (1 DIGIT)
3
INPUT ANNUAL INCOME (5 DIGITS)                    ERROR
01000
PRINCIPAL INVESTMENT REQUIRED 0166666

DO YOU WANT INFORMATION ON:

A THE AMOUNT OF INVESTMENT NEEDED TO GIVE
  AN ANNUAL INCOME OVER A FIXED TERM

B THE ANNUAL INCOME FROM A FIXED TERM INVESTMENT

C THE INTEREST PAID AFTER A FIXED TERM ON AN
  INVESTMENT

INPUT CODE A, B OR C
B

INPUT TERM IN YEARS (1 DIGIT)
3
INPUT PRINCIPAL INVESTMENT (5 DIGITS)
01000                                            ERROR
INCOME FROM INVESTMENT 00600

DO YOU WANT INFORMATION ON:

A THE AMOUNT OF INVESTMENT NEEDED TO GIVE
  AN ANNUAL INCOME OVER A FIXED TERM

B THE ANNUAL INCOME FROM A FIXED TERM INVESTMENT

C THE INTEREST PAID AFTER A FIXED TERM ON AN
  INVESTMENT
```

(results continued)

55

```
INPUT CODE A, B OR C
C

INPUT TERM IN YEARS (1 DIGIT)
3
INPUT PRINCIPAL INVESTMENT (5 DIGITS)
01000
INCOME FROM INVESTMENT 3096
```
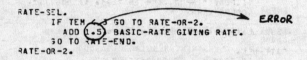
ERROR

When the source program is given a desk check using the test data that caused the error it becomes obvious that the value for the rate of interest is incorrect for a term of three or more years.

```
RATE-SEL.
        IF TEM < 3 GO TO RATE-OR-2.                    ERROR
        ADD 1.5 BASIC-RATE GIVING RATE.
        GO TO RATE-END.
RATE-OR-2.
```

From the compiled source listing it can be seen that in line (0040) the arithmetic statement used to calculate the rate of interest is wrong, the percentage increase should have been 0.015 and not 1.5. The statement should have been coded as:

ADD 0.015, BASIC-RATE GIVING RATE.

The third type of software error that is likely to manifest itself during program execution is the run-time error. This occurs when the program is abandoned by the operating system owing to an unrecoverable error occuring in the program (e.g. file not opened). From the diagnostics given by the system it should be possible to trace the error and correct it.

4.8 THE COMPLETE PROGRAM

4.8.1 The Source Code.

```
(0001)          IDENTIFICATION DIVISION.
(0002)          PROGRAM-ID. C462.
(0003)          DATA DIVISION.
(0004)          WORKING-STORAGE SECTION.
(0005)          77 RATE PIC V999.
(0006)          77 PRINCIPAL PIC 9(5).
(0007)          77 TERM PIC 9.
(0008)          77 BASIC-RATE PIC V999.
(0009)          77 MENU-CODE PIC A.
(0010)          77 INVESTMENT PIC 9(5)V99.
(0011)          77 INCOME PIC 9(5).
(0012)          77 TIME-OF-DAY PIC 9(8).
(0013)          77 INTEREST PIC 9(5)V99.
(0014)          77 TEMP-PRINCIPAL PIC 9(5).
(0015)          PROCEDURE DIVISION.
(0016)          SYSTEM-SEQ.
(0017)              DISPLAY "INPUT BASIC RATE OF INTEREST (3 DEC. PL.)"
(0018)              ACCEPT BASIC-RATE.
(0019)              ACCEPT TIME-OF-DAY FROM TIME.
(0020)          ENQUIRY-ITER.
(0021)              IF TIME-OF-DAY NOT < 16300000 GO TO ENQUIRY-END.
```

(program continued)

```
                    * display menu

(0022)            INIT-SEQ.
(0023)                 DISPLAY "DO YOU WANT INFORMATION ON:"
(0024)                 DISPLAY " "
(0025)                 DISPLAY "A THE AMOUNT OF INVESTMENT NEEDED TO GIVE"
(0026)                 DISPLAY "  AN ANNUAL INCOME OVER A FIXED TERM".
(0027)                 DISPLAY " "
(0028)                 DISPLAY "B THE ANNUAL INCOME FROM A FIXED TERM INVESTMENT".
(0029)                 DISPLAY " "
(0030)                 DISPLAY "C THE INTEREST PAID AFTER A FIXED TERM ON AN"
(0031)                 DISPLAY "  INVESTMENT".
(0032)                 DISPLAY " ".
(0033)                 DISPLAY "INPUT CODE A, B OR C"
(0034)                 ACCEPT MENU-CODE.
(0035)                 DISPLAY " ".
(0036)                 DISPLAY "INPUT TERM IN YEARS (1 DIGIT)".
(0037)                 ACCEPT TERM.

                    * calculate correct rate for term

(0038)            RATE-SEL.
(0039)                 IF TERM < 3 GO TO RATE-OR-2.
(0040)                     ADD 0.015, BASIC-RATE GIVING RATE.
(0041)                 GO TO RATE-END.
(0042)            RATE-OR-2.
(0043)                 IF TERM NOT = 2 GO TO RATE-OR-3.
(0044)                     ADD 0.01, BASIC-RATE GIVING RATE.
(0045)                 GO TO RATE-END.
(0046)            RATE-OR-3.
(0047)                 MOVE BASIC-RATE TO RATE.
(0048)            RATE-END.

                    * calculate principal investment

(0049)            CODE-SEL.
(0050)                 IF MENU-CODE NOT = "A" GO TO CODE-OR.
(0051)                     DISPLAY "INPUT ANNUAL INCOME (5 DIGITS)"
(0052)                     ACCEPT INCOME.
(0053)                     DIVIDE RATE INTO INCOME GIVING INVESTMENT.
(0054)                     DISPLAY "PRINCIPAL INVESTMENT REQUIRED " INVESTMENT.
(0055)                 GO TO CODE-END.

                    * calculate interest

(0056)            CODE-OR.
(0057)            CALC-SEQ.
(0058)                 DISPLAY "INPUT PRINCIPAL INVESTMENT (5 DIGITS)"
(0059)                 ACCEPT PRINCIPAL.

                    * simple interest per annum

(0060)            SIM-COM-SEL.
(0061)                 IF MENU-CODE NOT = "B" GO TO SIM-COM-OR.
(0062)                     MULTIPLY RATE BY PRINCIPAL GIVING INCOME.
(0063)                 GO TO SIM-COM-END.
(0064)            SIM-COM-OR.

                    * compound interest over term

(0065)            COM-SEQ.
(0066)                 MOVE PRINCIPAL TO TEMP-PRINCIPAL.
(0067)            COMP-ITER.
(0068)                 IF TERM = 0 GO TO COMP-END.
(0069)                     MULTIPLY RATE BY PRINCIPAL GIVING INTEREST.
(0070)                     ADD INTEREST TO PRINCIPAL.
(0071)                     SUBTRACT 1 FROM TERM.
(0072)                 GO TO COMP-ITER.
```

(program continued)

```
(0073)          COMP-END.
(0074)                  SUBTRACT TEMP-PRINCIPAL FROM PRINCIPAL GIVING INCOME.
(0075)          COMM-END.
(0076)          SIM-COM-END.
(0077)                  DISPLAY "INCOME FROM INVESTMENT " INCOME.
(0078)          CODE-END.
(0079)                  ACCEPT TIME-OF-DAY FROM TIME.
(0080)                  GO TO ENQUIRY-ITER.
(0081)          ENQUIRY-END.
(0082)              STOP RUN.
(0083)          SYSTEM-END.
```

Note: the line numbers printed down the left-hand side of the COBOL program have been generated by the compiler, they do not form part of the source program and were never included in the original program coding.

4.8.2 The Results.

The results from running the example program are as follows. Notice that the data used in running the program is identical to that used in the desk check, therefore, it is reasonable to assume that the results should also be the same as those calculated in the desk check.

```
INPUT BASIC RATE OF INTEREST (3 DEC. PL.)
100
DO YOU WANT INFORMATION ON:

A THE AMOUNT OF INVESTMENT NEEDED TO GIVE
  AN ANNUAL INCOME OVER A FIXED TERM

B THE ANNUAL INCOME FROM A FIXED TERM INVESTMENT

C THE INTEREST PAID AFTER A FIXED TERM ON AN
  INVESTMENT

INPUT CODE A, B OR C
A

INPUT TERM IN YEARS (1 DIGIT)
1
INPUT ANNUAL INCOME (5 DIGITS)
01000
PRINCIPAL INVESTMENT REQUIRED 1000000
DO YOU WANT INFORMATION ON:

A THE AMOUNT OF INVESTMENT NEEDED TO GIVE
  AN ANNUAL INCOME OVER A FIXED TERM

B THE ANNUAL INCOME FROM A FIXED TERM INVESTMENT

C THE INTEREST PAID AFTER A FIXED TERM ON AN
  INVESTMENT

INPUT CODE A, B OR C
A

INPUT TERM IN YEARS (1 DIGIT)
2
INPUT ANNUAL INCOME (5 DIGITS)
01000
PRINCIPAL INVESTMENT REQUIRED 0909090
DO YOU WANT INFORMATION ON:
```

(results continued)

```
A THE AMOUNT OF INVESTMENT NEEDED TO GIVE
  AN ANNUAL INCOME OVER A FIXED TERM

B THE ANNUAL INCOME FROM A FIXED TERM INVESTMENT

C THE INTEREST PAID AFTER A FIXED TERM ON AN
  INVESTMENT

INPUT CODE A, B OR C
A

INPUT TERM IN YEARS (1 DIGIT)
3
INPUT ANNUAL INCOME (5 DIGITS)
01000
PRINCIPAL INVESTMENT REQUIRED 0869565
DO YOU WANT INFORMATION ON:

A THE AMOUNT OF INVESTMENT NEEDED TO GIVE
  AN ANNUAL INCOME OVER A FIXED TERM

B THE ANNUAL INCOME FROM A FIXED TERM INVESTMENT

C THE INTEREST PAID AFTER A FIXED TERM ON AN
  INVESTMENT

INPUT CODE A, B OR C
B

INPUT TERM IN YEARS (1 DIGIT)
1
INPUT PRINCIPAL INVESTMENT (5 DIGITS)
01000
INCOME FROM INVESTMENT 00100
DO YOU WANT INFORMATION ON:

A THE AMOUNT OF INVESTMENT NEEDED TO GIVE
  AN ANNUAL INCOME OVER A FIXED TERM

B THE ANNUAL INCOME FROM A FIXED TERM INVESTMENT

C THE INTEREST PAID AFTER A FIXED TERM ON AN
  INVESTMENT

INPUT CODE A, B OR C
B

INPUT TERM IN YEARS (1 DIGIT)
2
INPUT PRINCIPAL INVESTMENT (5 DIGITS)
01000
INCOME FROM INVESTMENT 00110
DO YOU WANT INFORMATION ON:

A THE AMOUNT OF INVESTMENT NEEDED TO GIVE
  AN ANNUAL INCOME OVER A FIXED TERM

B THE ANNUAL INCOME FROM A FIXED TERM INVESTMENT

C THE INTEREST PAID AFTER A FIXED TERM ON AN
  INVESTMENT

INPUT CODE A, B OR C
B

INPUT TERM IN YEARS (1 DIGIT)
3
INPUT PRINCIPAL INVESTMENT (5 DIGITS)
01000
INCOME FROM INVESTMENT 00115
```

(results continued)

```
DO YOU WANT INFORMATION ON:

A THE AMOUNT OF INVESTMENT NEEDED TO GIVE
  AN ANNUAL INCOME OVER A FIXED TERM

B THE ANNUAL INCOME FROM A FIXED TERM INVESTMENT

C THE INTEREST PAID AFTER A FIXED TERM ON AN
  INVESTMENT

INPUT CODE A, B OR C
C

INPUT TERM IN YEARS (1 DIGIT)
1
INPUT PRINCIPAL INVESTMENT (5 DIGITS)
01000
INCOME FROM INVESTMENT 00100
DO YOU WANT INFORMATION ON:

A THE AMOUNT OF INVESTMENT NEEDED TO GIVE
  AN ANNUAL INCOME OVER A FIXED TERM

B THE ANNUAL INCOME FROM A FIXED TERM INVESTMENT

C THE INTEREST PAID AFTER A FIXED TERM ON AN
  INVESTMENT

INPUT CODE A, B OR C
C

INPUT TERM IN YEARS (1 DIGIT)
2
INPUT PRINCIPAL INVESTMENT (5 DIGITS)
01000
INCOME FROM INVESTMENT 00232
DO YOU WANT INFORMATION ON:

A THE AMOUNT OF INVESTMENT NEEDED TO GIVE
  AN ANNUAL INCOME OVER A FIXED TERM

B THE ANNUAL INCOME FROM A FIXED TERM INVESTMENT

C THE INTEREST PAID AFTER A FIXED TERM ON AN
  INVESTMENT

INPUT CODE A, B OR C
C

INPUT TERM IN YEARS (1 DIGIT)
3
INPUT PRINCIPAL INVESTMENT (5 DIGITS)
01000
INCOME FROM INVESTMENT 00385
```

4.9 COMMENTS

In this example the test data and resultant size of PICTURE character-strings have been deliberately contrived so as to highlight some potentially error prone situations. When constructing the extended glossary it was assumed that the interest rate would not rise significantly above 10% therefore, the PICTURE character-strings of 9(5)V99 for INVESTMENT and INTEREST and 9(5) for INCOME and PRINCIPAL would be sufficient. However, if the basic rate of interest was increased to 20% and the amount invested was £25,000 over a period of 9 years then the amount at the end of the term would increase to £144,247 using compound interest. When the program is run using this data both PRINCIPAL and INCOME would be insufficient in storage space to represent their respective calculated values. Similarly the investment required to give an annual income of £25,000 with an interest rate of 20% would be £125,000, therefore, INVESTMENT has insufficient storage space to represent this value.

On reflection INVESTMENT, INCOME and PRINCIPAL should have been given PICTURE character-strings of at least 9(6)V99.

When the programmer has allocated PICTURE character-strings that are of adequate size for the storage of data, yet wishes to flag an abnormal event when the data becomes too large to fit into the storage allocated the

ON SIZE ERROR imperative statement

option should be used.

In this example if the PICTURE character-strings were extended to the values specified and an abnormal value for RATE was introduced, say, 50% and the initial value of PRINCIPAL was £50,000 then the amount invested would increase to £1,922,168 over 9 years using compound interest. This figure could not be correctly stored in PRINCIPAL or INCOME using a PICTURE character-string of 9(6)V99.

In order to flag this event line (0070) could be modified to:

ADD INTEREST TO PRINCIPAL ON SIZE ERROR GO TO ERROR-MESSAGE.

The value of PRINCIPAL is **not** increased to the error value and the computer branches to the paragraph ERROR-MESSAGE.

The reader should remember to ensure that PICTURE character-strings are large enough to represent all the data, and that the range of test data is sufficient to detect any discrepancies in the PICTURE clauses as well as the logic of the computer program.

If the reader looks back at the desk check the amount of investment required to yield an annual income of £1000 over a period of 2 years was calculated to be 9090.9091. The effect of using a PICTURE of 9(5)V99 was to *truncate* the decimal fraction, and in real terms this meant that the investor would be losing £0.01 on the investment. To obtain a result of 9090.91, which would be in favour of the investor, the ROUNDED option should be used in conjunction with the appropriate arithmetic statement. In this example line (0053) should be modified to:

DIVIDE RATE INTO INCOME GIVING INVESTMENT ROUNDED.

The reader should also note that in the example program the effect of storing a number containing a decimal fraction in an integer field is to truncate the number to an integer. For example ADD INTEREST TO PRINCIPAL would result in:

	INTEREST 9(5)V99	PRINCIPAL 9(5)
before	00128.22	01115
after	00128.22	01243

The reader can be excused for thinking that the output from the example program leaves something to be desired! The author would agree with these sentiments as well. However, the example has been chosen to illustrate several points regarding the format of data input to the computer and the output of information from the computer.

The input of numeric data through a keyboard must conform in format to the PICTURE clause for that item of data. It is for this reason that screen prompts to the user, informing of the size of each datum, have been used. Without any form of prompt the user would not know when to input data at the terminal since the machine does not offer any form of prompt when using the ACCEPT statement. In order for the data to conform to the PICTURE clause extra leading and trailing zeros have to be inserted into the data. For example the RATE is input as 100 and not as .10, and the INCOME as 01000 and not as 1000. The decimal point is not included in the input data.

On the output of information it is clear to see that decimal fractions are not output with a decimal point, leading zeros are not suppressed and currency signs do not appear immediately to the left of the most significant non-zero digit. For example the investment required to yield an income of £1000 per annum over a period of 2 years is output as 0909090 and it is only by inspecting the PICTURE clause for INVESTMENT that it becomes clear that the amount is really £9,090.90.

The next chapter is about the editing of numerical output so the minor problems discussed here can be resolved.

4.10 QUESTIONS *(answers begin on page 335)*

Write complete COBOL programs to the PROCEDURE DIVISIONS coded as answers to the eight questions in section 3.5 of the last chapter.

Use screen prompts where necessary to improve the input and output of data and information.

Implement the programs on a computer that has a COBOL compiler, and run the object programs using the test data that you invented to desk check your designs in chapter 3.

The glossaries for each of the program designs together with the type and size of each item of data are listed below.

4.10.1 (corresponding to 3.5.1)

Identifier	Meaning	Type	Size
L-SIDE	long side of plot	numeric	2 digits
S-SIDE	short side of plot	numeric	2 digits
TURF	cost of turf in £	numeric	6 digits inc 2 dp
FENCE	cost of fencing £	numeric	3 digits

4.10.2 (corresponding to 3.5.2)

Identifier	Meaning	Type	Size
TOTAL	running total	numeric	4 digits
COUNTER	number of numbers	numeric	2 digits
NUMB	number from list	numeric	2 digits
MEAN	arithmetic mean	numeric	2 digits

4.10.3 (corresponding to 3.5.3)

Identifier	Meaning	Type	Size
NUMB	number from list	numeric	2 digits
MAXNUMB	largest number from list	numeric	2 digits
COUNTER	number of numbers	numeric	2 digits

4.10.4 (corresponding to 3.5.4)

Identifier	Meaning	Type	Size
MONEY	amount of money in £	numeric	3 digits
TOT-10	total number of £10	numeric	2 digits
TOT-5	total number of £5	numeric	1 digit

4.10.5 (corresponding to 3.5.5)

Identifier	Meaning	Type	Size
SALES	value of sale	numeric	5 digits
COMMISSION	% commission	numeric	6 digits inc 2 dp

4.10.6 (corresponding to 3.5.6)

Identifier	Meaning	Type	Size
SURNAME	name of person	alphanumeric	15 chars
AGE	age in years	numeric	2 digits
WEIGHT	weight in Kg	numeric	3 digits
HEIGHT	height in cm	numeric	3 digits
COUNTER	number of people	numeric	2 digits

4.10.7 (corresponding to 3.5.7)

Identifier	Meaning	Type	Size
G-SALARY	gross salary	numeric	5 digits
TAX-STATUS	married or single	alphabetic	1 char.
CHILDREN	number of children	numeric	1 digit
ALLOWANCE	personal allowance	numeric	4 digits
CHILD-ALLOWANCE	as stated	numeric	3 digits
TAX-INCOME	taxable income	signed numeric	5 digits
TAX	income tax	numeric	5 digits

4.10.8 (corresponding to 3.5.8)

Identifier	Meaning	Type	Size
MARK	% examination mark	numeric	3 digits
GRADE	A, B, C, D, F	alphabetic	1 char.
TOTAL-A	⎫	numeric	2 digits
TOTAL-B	total number of	numeric	2 digits
TOTAL-C	passes in each	numeric	2 digits
TOTAL-D	category	numeric	2 digits
TOTAL-F	⎭	numeric	2 digits

4.10.9 There are 21 errors in the following COBOL source code. Identify the errors and re-write the program so that it contains no errors.

```
IDENTIFICATION DIVISION
PROGRAM ID. QUEST09.
DATA DIVISION
77 ITEM-DESC PIC X20.
77 ITEM COST PIC 999V99.
77 VAT 999V99.
77 TOTAL PIC 9999V99.
PROCEDURE-DIVISION.
BILL-SEQ
MOVE 0 TO TOTAL
     INPUT ITEM-DESC
     INPUT ITEM-COST
INPUT-ITER.
     IF ITEM-COST = 0 GOTO INPUT-END
        ADD ITEM-COST TO TOTAL
        ACCEPT ITEM-DESC
        ACCEPT ITEM-COST
     GO TO INPUT ITER.
     CALCULATE VAT = 0.15 X TOTAL
     ADD VAT TO TOTAL
     OUTPUT TOTAL
     STOP-RUN.
BILL-END
```

4.10.10 The following program segment is used to input the weights of parcels, calculate the arithmetic mean weight and output this value. The unit of weight is a Kilogramme.

Desk check the code with the following test data and comment upon the suitability of the PICTURE clauses.

Re-write the WORKING-STORAGE SECTION stating the assumptions that you are making about the data.

```
WORKING-STORAGE SECTION.
77 WEIGHT PIC 9V9999.
77 TOT-WEIGHT PIC 9V9999.
77 PARCEL-COUNT PIC 9V9.
77 AVER-WEIGHT PIC 9.
```

```
PROCEDURE DIVISION.
WT-SEQ.
    MOVE ZERO TO TOT-WEIGHT, PARCEL-COUNT.
    ACCEPT WEIGHT.
CALC-SEL.
    IF WEIGHT = 0 GO TO CALC-END.
        ADD 1 TO PARCEL-COUNT.
        ADD WEIGHT TO TOT-WEIGHT.
        ACCEPT WEIGHT.
    GO TO CALC-SEL.
CALC-END.
    COMPUTE AVER-WEIGHT = TOT-WEIGHT / PARCEL-COUNT.
    DISPLAY AVER-WEIGHT.
    STOP RUN.
WT-END.
```

Test data: 1.3 3.5 12.6 2.1 5.9 13.8 2.5 3.9 14.7 5.5 0

5   Picture Editing

5.1 INTRODUCTION

The aim of this chapter is to present the reader with the tools of picture editing so that the DATA DIVISIONS of future programs can be coded to give a much improved printed output compared with the examples of chapter 4.

5.2 THE PURPOSE OF EDITING PICTURES

Picture editing is used in the output of numerical information. If the reader considers the specimen statement in figure 5.1 all the numerical information under the headings *debit, credit, balance* and *final balance* are printed using picture editing. The different forms of picture edit have been highlighted. Looking through the statement it is clear to see that picture editing involves such features as:

suppressing leading zeros, inserting decimal points, floating + or − signs, commas, floating currency signs and extra characters e.g. DB.

The Universal Bank				
Statement of Account: 04973128 1726493				
Date	Description	Debit	Credit	Balance + credit − debit
May 1	Balance			+103.98
May 3	Salary		1,076.42	+1,180.40
May 5	Domestic charge	423.45		+756.95
May 8	Mortgage	932.84		−175.89
May 10	Credit transfer		2,100.00	+1,924.11
May 12	General stores	376.29		+1,547.82
May 13	Universal B.S.	1,900.00		−352.18
May 17	Insurance	50.75		−402.93
May 21	Petrol A/C	103.84		−506.77
May 30	General stores	147.50		−654.27
May 31	Credit transfer		550.00	−104.27
			Final Balance	£104.27DB

Figure 5.1

These edits take place as the result of a data item being transferred from a source area where the picture is **not** edited, to a destination area where the picture is edited using the MOVE statement or the arithmetic statements. Although the destination identifier in an arithmetic statement can be edited, you must **never** perform arithmetic on data items that have been described using edited pictures.

5.3 EDITED PICTURES

In the examples that follow the symbol b represents the space character.

5.3.1 Suppression of leading zeros

The position of each leading digit in a number is represented by Z. If this digit happens to be a zero then a space will be output.

Examples.

Source	Picture	Edited result
003456	999999	003456
003456	ZZ9999	bb3456
000074	ZZ9999	bb0074
000074	ZZZZ99	bbbb74
001001	ZZZZZ9	bb1001
000000	ZZZZZZ	bbbbbb

5.3.2 Insertion of a currency sign.

A single currency sign $ as the leftmost character of a Picture indicates that the character $ (or equivalent) is to be printed in that position.

Examples.

Source	Picture	Edited result
4567	$9999	$4567
006235	$ZZZZ9	$bb6235
000000	$ZZZZZ	bbbbbbb

A floating currency sign can also be used to suppress leading zeros as well as generating a currency sign immediately to the left of the most significant non-zero digit.

Examples.

Source	Picture	Edited result
0004874	$$$$$9	bb$4874
2300004	$$$$$$$	$2300004
0000000	$$$$$$$	bbbbbbbb
0000000	$$$$$$9	bbbbbb$0

Note: the computer used to run the example programs throughout this book has had the $ character on the lineprinter replaced by a £. An alternative method of changing the currency sign without having to change parts of the printer will be discussed later in the book (chapter 6, section 6.6.2).

5.3.3 Insertion of a decimal point

If a decimal point is inserted into a picture then it will be output in the required position of the edited numerical data item. An alignment is performed between the implied decimal point of the source data item (indicated by a V) and the decimal point of the edited item.

Examples.

Source	Picture	Edited result	
376ᵥ56	999.99	376.56	
1ᵥ4598	999.99999	001.45980	leading and trailing zeros have been inserted
000ᵥ045	ZZZ.ZZZ	bbb.045	Z only suppresses leading zeros
1274ᵥ593	99.99	74.59	since alignment is about the implied point and edited point, leading and trailing digits are lost when the destination field is smaller

5.3.4 Insertion of commas, blanks and zeros

These characters can be inserted into the picture and will be printed in the position indicated by the edited picture.

Examples.

Source	Picture	Edited result	
478935	999,999	478,935	
000593	ZZZ,ZZ9	bbbb593	if the digits to the left of the comma(s) are zeros and zero suppression is used the comma(s) are replaced by spaces
4567234	Z,ZZZ,ZZZ	4,567,234	
7245ᵥ56	9,999.99	7,245.56	
00942ᵥ70	ZZ,ZZZ.99	bbb942.70	
589346ᵥ	$ZZZ,ZZZ.ZZ	$589,346.00	trailing zeros have been inserted despite the zero suppression
180348	99BB99BB99	18bb03bb48	the use of B in the picture will print a space in the stated position – useful for printing dates of birth
7839ᵥ	Z,ZZZ.000	7,839.000	zeros can also be inserted in a picture in the same way as spaces
3459	999900000	345900000	

5.3.5 Insertion of a display sign

A single + or − sign inserted into a picture as the first or last character will be printed in the position indicated. If the data item is negative and a + sign is used a − sign will be printed; if the data item is positive and a − sign is used a space will be printed; otherwise the same sign will be printed that appears in the picture.

Examples.

Source	Operational sign	Picture	Edited result
4563	−	−9999	−4563
376	−	999−	376−
27834	−	+99999	−27834
90045	+	−99999	b90045
7398	+	9999+	7398+
18965	−	−9.9999	−1.8965

Zero suppression can be achieved by using either floating + or − signs in the same way that floating currency signs operate.

Examples.

Source	Operational sign	Picture	Edited result
00036	−	−−−−−9	bbb−36
00528	+	+++999	bb+528
00000	+	−−−−−−	bbbbbb

5.3.6 Insertion of special characters

Either CR or DB may appear as the rightmost two characters in a picture. If the source data item is negative then the respective credit or debit symbols will be inserted.

Examples

Source	Operational sign	Picture	Edited result
1456348	−	$$$,$$9.99DB	$14,563.48DB
4784	+	$$$$9CR	$4784bb

In the printing of bank cheques leading spaces are undesirable. An asterisk can be used with the same effect as a Z for zero suppression, only the character * is printed in place of a space.

Examples.

Source	Picture	Edited result
00045673	*****9.99	***456.73
0003489	$***,**9.99	$*****34.89

5.3.7 Blank when Zero.

The clause BLANK WHEN ZERO can be appended to a numeric or numeric edited picture clause if it is preferred to represent the datum as spaces and not zero.

5.4 THE EFFECTS OF DATA MOVEMENT

Editing is performed on numeric data as the result of either a MOVE statement or arithmetic statement being executed, provided the destination for the data item conforms to an edited picture.

When transfering data the following points should be kept in mind.

The data items are aligned by decimal points, with either the generation of zeros to fill the field or the truncation of digits from the number so that the item will fit into the field.

When the data types of the source field and destination field differ then conversion to the type of the receiving field takes place under the following circumstances.

Source	Destination		
	Numeric	Alphabetic	Alphanumeric
Numeric	legal	illegal	legal
Alphabetic	illegal	legal	legal
Alphanumeric	legal*	legal**	legal

*this is a legal move provided the alphanumeric characters are composed of the numeric character set.

**this is a legal move provided the alphanumeric characters are composed of the alphabetic character set.

When the data being transferred is non-numeric then the following rules will apply.

The characters are **left** justified in the receiving (or destination) field.

If the receiving field is larger than the source field it is space filled to the right.

If the source field is larger than the receiving field the string of characters are truncated from the right.

Examples.

Source	Picture of receiving field	Receiving field
6_V7	9999V99	0006_V70
649_V472	999V999	649_V472
$23467_V392467$	999V999	467_V392
78_V	999V999	078_V000
63_V93	X(6)	6393bb
"45628967"	X(6)	456289
1234567890	9(6)V99	567890_V00
"ABC"	X(12)	ABCbbbbbbbbb
"ABCDEFGHIJ"	X(4)	ABCD

When using non-numeric data if the $\left\{ \begin{array}{l} \textbf{JUSTIFIED} \\ \textbf{JUST} \end{array} \right\}$ RIGHT clause is appended to the picture clause then the string of characters is moved to the right of the receiving field if this is larger than the source field. If, however, the receiving field is smaller than the source field then the string of characters is truncated from the left.

Examples.

Source	Picture of receiving field JUSTIFIED RIGHT	Receiving field
"ABCD"	X(10)	bbbbbbABCD
"ABCDEFGHIJ"	X(5)	FGHIJ

5.5 WORKED EXAMPLE

5.5.1 Problem

The gross annual expenditure of a county council can be broken down into the following areas.

Staff 53%
Goods and services 15%
Premises 8%
Capital charges 7%
Education Grants and Contributions 8%
Miscellaneous 9%

Design and implement a program to input at the keyboard of a V.D.U. the gross annual expenditure (e.g. £210,881,916) and output to the screen of the V.D.U. a breakdown of the expenditure according to the following layout.

REPORT ON COUNTY COUNCIL ANNUAL EXPENDITURE 1983/84	
ITEM	AMOUNT
STAFF	£111,767,415.48
GOODS AND SERVICES	£31,632,287.40
PREMISES	£16,870,553.28
CAPITAL CHARGES	£14,761,734.12
EDUCATION GRANTS AND CONTRIB	£16,870,553.28
MISCELLANEOUS	£18,979,372.44
TOTAL	£210,881,916.00

Note: the total is intended as a check against machine truncation errors.

5.5.2 Design

Functions List
1. Input gross annual expenditure.
2. Initialise total expenditure to zero.
3. Increase total expenditure by respective item.
4. Output headings.
5. Calculate staff expenditure.
6. Calculate goods and services expenditure.
7. Calculate premises expenditure.
8. Calculate capital charges expenditure.
9. Calculate educational grants and contributions expenditure.
10. Calculate miscellaneous expenditure.
11. Output edited staff expenditure.
12. Output edited goods and services expenditure.
13. Output edited premises expenditure.
14. Output edited capital charges expenditure.
15. Output edited educational grants and contributions expenditure.
16. Output edited miscellaneous expenditure.
17. Output edited total expenditure.
18. Stop.

Schematic Logic

```
report–seq
  do 1,2,4
  do 5,3,11,6,3,12,7,3,13,8,3,14,9,3,15,10,3,16,17,18
report–end
```

Extended Glossary

Identifier	Meaning	Type	Size	Edited Picture
GROSS-EXP	gross expenditure	numeric	9 digits	–
TOT-EXP	total expenditure	numeric	11 digits inc 2 dp	–
TOT-EXP-OUT	edited total expenditure	alphanumeric	" "	$$$$,$$$,$$9.99
STAFF	staff expenditure	numeric	11 digits inc 2 dp	–
STAFF-OUT	edited staff expenditure	alphanumeric	" "	$$$$,$$$,$$9.99
GOODS	goods and services	numeric	11 digits inc 2 dp	–
GOODS-OUT	edited goods and serv.	alphanumeric	" "	$$$$,$$$,$$9.99
PREM	premises	numeric	10 digits inc 2 dp	–
PREM-OUT	edited premises	alphanumeric	" "	$$$,$$$,$$9.99
CAPITAL	capital charges	numeric	10 digits inc 2 dp	–
CAPITAL-OUT	edited capital charges	alphanumeric	" "	$$$,$$$,$$9.99
EDUC	educational grants, etc.	numeric	10 digits inc 2 dp	–
EDUC-OUT	edited educ grants, etc.	alphanumeric	" "	$$$,$$$,$$9.99
MISC	miscellaneous expend	numeric	10 digits inc 2 dp	–
MISC-OUT	edited misc expend	alphanumeric	" "	$$$,$$$,$$9.99

5.5.3 Coding

```
(0001)          IDENTIFICATION DIVISION.
(0002)          PROGRAM-ID. C553.
(0003)          DATA DIVISION.
(0004)          WORKING-STORAGE SECTION.
(0005)          77 GROSS-EXP PIC 9(9).
(0006)          77 TOT-EXP PIC 9(9)V99.
(0007)          77 TOT-EXP-OUT PIC £££,£££,££9.99.
(0008)          77 STAFF PIC 9(9)V99.
(0009)          77 STAFF-OUT PIC £££,£££,££9.99.
(0010)          77 GOODS PIC 9(9)V99.
(0011)          77 GOODS-OUT PIC £££,£££,££9.99.
(0012)          77 PREM PIC 9(8)V99.
(0013)          77 PREM-OUT PIC £££,£££,££9.99.
(0014)          77 CAPITAL PIC 9(8)V99.
(0015)          77 CAPITAL-OUT PIC £££,£££,££9.99.
(0016)          77 EDUC PIC 9(8)V99.
(0017)          77 EDUC-OUT PIC £££,£££,££9.99.
(0018)          77 MISC PIC 9(8)V99.
(0019)          77 MISC-OUT PIC £££,£££,££9.99.
(0020)          PROCEDURE DIVISION.
(0021)          REPORT-SEQ.
(0022)              DISPLAY "INPUT GROSS ANNUAL EXPENDITURE (9 DIGITS)"
(0023)              ACCEPT GROSS-EXP.
(0024)              MOVE ZERO TO TOT-EXP.
(0025)              DISPLAY "REPORT ON COUNTY COUNCIL ANNUAL EXPENDITURE 1983/84
(0026)              DISPLAY " ".
(0027)              DISPLAY "ITEM                                    AMOUNT"
(0028)              DISPLAY " ".
(0029)              MULTIPLY 0.53 BY GROSS-EXP GIVING STAFF.
```

(program continued)

```
(0030)              ADD STAFF TO TOT-EXP.
(0031)              MOVE STAFF TO STAFF-OUT.
(0032)              DISPLAY "STAFF                        " STAFF-OUT.
(0033)              MULTIPLY 0.15 BY GROSS-EXP GIVING GOODS.
(0034)              ADD GOODS TO TOT-EXP.
(0035)              MOVE GOODS TO GOODS-OUT.
(0036)              DISPLAY "GOODS AND SERVICES            " GOODS-OUT.
(0037)              MULTIPLY 0.09 BY GROSS-EXP GIVING PREM.
(0038)              ADD PREM TO TOT-EXP.
(0039)              MOVE PREM TO PREM-OUT.
(0040)              DISPLAY "PREMISES                      " PREM-OUT.
(0041)              MULTIPLY 0.07 BY GROSS-EXP GIVING CAPITAL.
(0042)              ADD CAPITAL TO TOT-EXP.
(0043)              MOVE CAPITAL TO CAPITAL-OUT.
(0044)              DISPLAY "CAPITAL CHARGES               " CAPITAL-OUT.
(0045)              MULTIPLY 0.09 BY GROSS-EXP GIVING EDUC.
(0046)              ADD EDUC TO TOT-EXP.
(0047)              MOVE EDUC TO EDUC-OUT.
(0048)              DISPLAY "EDUCATION GRANTS AND CONTRIB.  " EDUC-OUT.
(0049)              MULTIPLY 0.09 BY GROSS-EXP GIVING MISC.
(0050)              ADD MISC TO TOT-EXP.
(0051)              MOVE MISC TO MISC-OUT.
(0052)              DISPLAY "MISCELLANEOUS                 " MISC-OUT.
(0053)              DISPLAY " ".
(0054)              MOVE TOT-EXP TO TOT-EXP-OUT.
(0055)              DISPLAY "TOTAL                         " TOT-EXP-OUT.
(0056)              STOP RUN.
(0057)       REPORT-END.
```

5.5.4 Results

```
INPUT GROSS ANNUAL EXPENDITURE (9 DIGITS)
210881916
REPORT ON COUNTY COUNCIL ANNUAL EXPENDITURE 1983/84

ITEM                             AMOUNT

STAFF                            £111,767,415.48
GOODS AND SERVICES               £31,632,287.40
PREMISES                         £16,870,553.28
CAPITAL CHARGES                  £14,761,734.12
EDUCATION GRANTS AND CONTRIB.    £16,870,553.28
MISCELLANEOUS                    £18,979,372.44

TOTAL                            £210,881,916.00
```

73

5.6 QUESTIONS *(answers begin on page 342)*

5.6.1 What are the edited results when the following items of data are moved from the source field to the edited destination or receiving field?

Picture	Source area Data	Op.sign	Receiving area Picture
9(5)	00067		ZZ,ZZ9
9(7)V99	004527745		Z,ZZZ,ZZZ.99
9(3)V99	25489		ZZZ.ZZ
9(5)V99	0045734		$$$$$$.99
9(6)V99	00009589		$***,***.99
S9(4)V99	029456	−	$$,$$$.99CR
S9(3)	835	+	**9DB
S9999	4573	−	9999−
S9999	0528	+	−Z999
S9999	0067	+	ZZZZ+
S9(5)	00023	−	−−−−−9
S9(6)V99	00004578	−	−−−,−−−.99
S9(6)V99	26784590	+	+++,++9.99
9(6)	145623		BBBB9999BB99
9(6)	000345		ZZZ,ZZZ.00

†5.6.2 What are the edited results when the following items of data are moved from the source field to the edited destination or receiving field?

Picture	Source area Data	Op. sign	Receiving area Picture
9(5)	46389		$$$,$$9.99
9(5)	00467		$$$,$$9.99
9(5)	00000		$$$,$$9.99
9(4)V9	12354		$$$,$$9.99
V9(5)	93764		$$$,$$9.99
S9(5)	00423	+	−−−−−−−.99
S9(5)	00004	−	+++++++.99
S9(5)	00543	+	+++++++.99
S9(5)	00003	−	−−−−−−−.99
9(5)	00832		−−−−−−−.99
9(5)	00382		−−−−−−−.99
S9(5)	04127	+	*******.99CR
S999V99	00008	−	ZZZVZZ
S999V99	00067	−	ZZZVZZ
S9(5)	65489	−	*******.99CR
9999V99	001234		9(4).99 BLANK WHEN ZERO
9999V99	000000		****.99 BLANK WHEN ZERO
9999V99	000000		****.99
9999V99	000000		ZZZZ.ZZ BLANK WHEN ZERO
9999V99	004573		****.99 BLANK WHEN ZERO

† **5.6.3** The gross income for a district council can be broken down into the following areas.

> Rents 39%
> Block grant 12%
> Housing subsidies 6%
> Other Government grants 11%
> Ratepayers 10%
> Fees, charges and mortgagors 12%
> Interest and balances 10%.

Design a report on the income for the district council (use the report in 5.5.1 as the basis of your design).

Design and implement a computer program to input at the keyboard of a V.D.U. the gross annual income for the district council and output to the screen of the V.D.U. the details of the report. Design the program so that it will cater for variable percentages in each area of income and not fixed percentages as given in 5.5.3.

† **5.6.4** Return to your solutions to the following past questions in chapter 4, and modify these solutions to take into account picture editing. Questions 4.10.1, and 4.10.8

Compile your modified solutions and re-run the object programs. Compare the output with that from your earlier solutions.

6 Coding Data Files and Reports

6.1 INTRODUCTION

The purpose of this chapter is to demonstrate how to code in the DATA DIVISION the records of a computer file. The chapter also deals with the ENVIRONMENT DIVISION and the necessary entries in this Division when using computer files.

6.2 ELEMENTS OF A COMPUTER FILE

A computer file is a collection of information stored on magnetic tape and magnetic disc (also magnetic drum but this is much less common). Files can also be stored on punched cards and punched paper tape, however, these storage media are fast becoming old methods of storage and will not be considered any further in this book.

The reader has already come across the concept of a file when storing a computer program on magnetic tape or disc. The program file was composed of a line by line collection of COBOL statements stored under a name given to the file.

Data files are similar in concept. Each line of data (or multiple lines) is known as a *logical* record and is subdivided into smaller areas of discrete information known as *fields*. Each field is composed of a series of characters. The number of characters grouped into a field can vary from field to field in a record. The records of a file can be either fixed length or variable length. For example figure 6.1 illustrates the format of a fixed length record used to store the details of a factory employee.

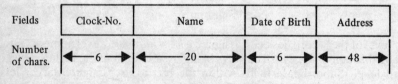

Figure 6.1

Each record in figure 6.1 has a fixed length of 80 characters, however, although such fields as Name and Address have fixed lengths of 20 and 48 characters respectively, their contents will not always fill the size of the fields. Each field that is not completely filled will be padded with space characters (the contents of the field will be left justified unless otherwise stated). The result will be an accumulated waste of space between the records of the file. For this reason the fields of a record can be allowed to vary according to the size of the data contained in them. This in turn will bring about records of varying length throughout the file. The records of such a file are said to be of variable length.

Notice from figure 6.1 that the information contained in the file is related to a specific application, in this example personnel in a factory. Different files are used for different applications, for example, stock records, airline flight reservations, customer details, etc.

One field of a record is normally specified as the *primary* key to that record. For example in figure 6.1 the field clock–number contains a unique value for an employee in a factory and could be used as the key (method of identification) of that record. Thus if one required information relating to an employee whose clock–number was known in advance, the file would be searched comparing the clock–number of each record with the known clock–number. When a match was found between clock–numbers the information for that record could be extracted.

A serial file is one in which the records are positioned one after another yet do **not** form a specific order in relation to the value of a key. Throughout the file, therefore, the keys are **not** arranged into either an ascending or descending order.

By contrast a sequential file contains records whose positions, relative to the other records in the file, are determined by the value of the keys. The keys of the records are **sorted** into either ascending or descending order. Both serial and sequential file organisations will be considered in this chapter.

6.3 CODING RECORDS IN THE DATA DIVISION

Figure 6.2 illustrates the hierarchical division of the record described in figure 6.1.

01	Employee Record								
02	Clock-no.	Name		Date of Birth			Address		
03		Initial	Surname	Day	Month	Year	Street	Town	Postcode

Figure 6.2

Each level of the record has been assigned a *level number*. Level numbers range from 01 through to 49, with 01 always being used to denote the highest level or record level. Subordinate fields within the record are assigned larger level numbers in increments from 01 that the programmer may choose. At the second level in figure 6.2 assigned the level number of 02, the only field that has not been sub–divided further, at a lower level, is that of clock–no. Because clock–no. cannot be subdivided any further it is known as an *elementary item*.

Name, date of birth and address have been sub–divided into fields at a lower level assigned the level number 03. These fields, initial, surname, day, month, year, street, town and postcode, have not been sub–divided any further and are, therefore, known as elementary items.

When any record is represented in the DATA DIVISION **picture clauses are only appended to elementary items.**

When coding the record described in figure 6.2 into COBOL statements the reader should be aware that some of the field descriptors are in fact Reserved Words.

77

The following extended glossary can be used prior to the coding.

Extended glossary

Identifier	Meaning	Type	Size of datum
EMPLOYEE–RECORD	name of record	–	–
CLOCK–NO	clock number	numeric	6 digits
NAME	name of employee	–	–
INIT	initial	alphabetic	1 char.
SURNAME	surname of employee	alphanumeric	19 chars.
DATE–OF–BIRTH	date of birth	–	–
DAY–DATE	day	numeric	2 digits
MONTH	month	numeric	2 digits
YEAR	year	numeric	2 digits
ADDRESS	address of employee	–	–
STREET	street address	alphanumeric	20 chars.
TOWN	town address	alphanumeric	20 chars.
POSTCODE	postcode	alphanumeric	8 chars.

The DATA DIVISION coding of the record illustrated in figure 6.2 is:

```
col  8  |12
     01 EMPLOYEE–RECORD.
        02 CLOCK–NO  PIC  9(6).
        02 NAME.
           03 INIT  PIC  A.
           03 SURNAME  PIC  X(19).
        02 DATE–OF–BIRTH.
           03 DAY–DATE  PIC  99.
           03 MONTH  PIC  99.
           03 YEAR  PIC  99.
        02 ADDRESS.
           03 STREET  PIC  X(20).
           03 TOWN  PIC  X(20).
           03 POSTCODE  PIC  X(8).
```

Note. The 01 level must be coded from zone A, and the subsequent levels should be coded from zone B.

The indented code signifies the hierarchical relationship between the elements of the record.

6.4 CODING REPORTS

6.4.1 Report Layout Forms

The design of a report is made considerably easier if the reader adopts the habit of planning the layout of the report using a report layout document similar to that illustrated in figure 6.3. The document is approximately the same size as one page of lineprinter paper and both the line and column positions are numbered to facilitate designing the report. Such a document is an aid towards the DATA DIVISION coding of the respective records that will eventually form the report.

Figure 6.4 illustrates the typical layout of a credit card statement of account. The design document illustrates each line of the report which represents a record to be coded. Beneath each record is a description of the fields contained in that record. The descriptions show the maximum field widths by using the PICTURE clause character–strings for each field.

6.4.2 Filler

From figure 6.4 many of the fields that have been described using PICTURE clause character–strings do not need an identifier since they will never need to be referenced. When describing such fields in the DATA DIVISION the reserved word FILLER replaces the identifier.

Example.

The DATA DIVISION coding to represent the first record of the report in figure 6.4 is:

```
01 RECORD–1.
   02 FILLER  PIC  X(23).
   02 HEADING–1  PIC  X(20).
```

6.4.3 The Value Clause

The VALUE clause defines the initial values of WORKING–STORAGE SECTION data items. A format for this clause is:

VALUE IS literal–1.

The clause is appended to the PICTURE clause of the data item that is to be initialised.

The descriptive items in the report illustrated in figure 6.4 could be assigned their literal values at the time of coding the format of the records in the DATA DIVISION. Each line of the report is treated as a variable length record and can be described in the WORKING–STORAGE SECTION, thus making use of the VALUE clause.

Example.

```
01 RECORD–1
   02 FILLER PIC X(23) VALUE IS SPACES.
   02 HEADING–1 PIC X(20) VALUE IS "STATEMENT OF ACCOUNT".
```

If HEADING–1 is not to be referenced in the program it can also be replaced by the FILLER.

```
01 RECORD–1
   02 FILLER PIC X(23) VALUE IS SPACES.
   02 FILLER PIC X(20) VALUE IS "STATEMENT OF ACCOUNT".
```

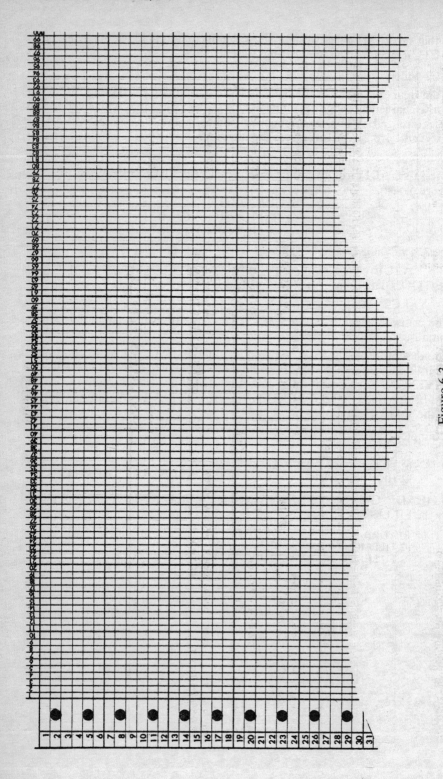

Figure 6.3

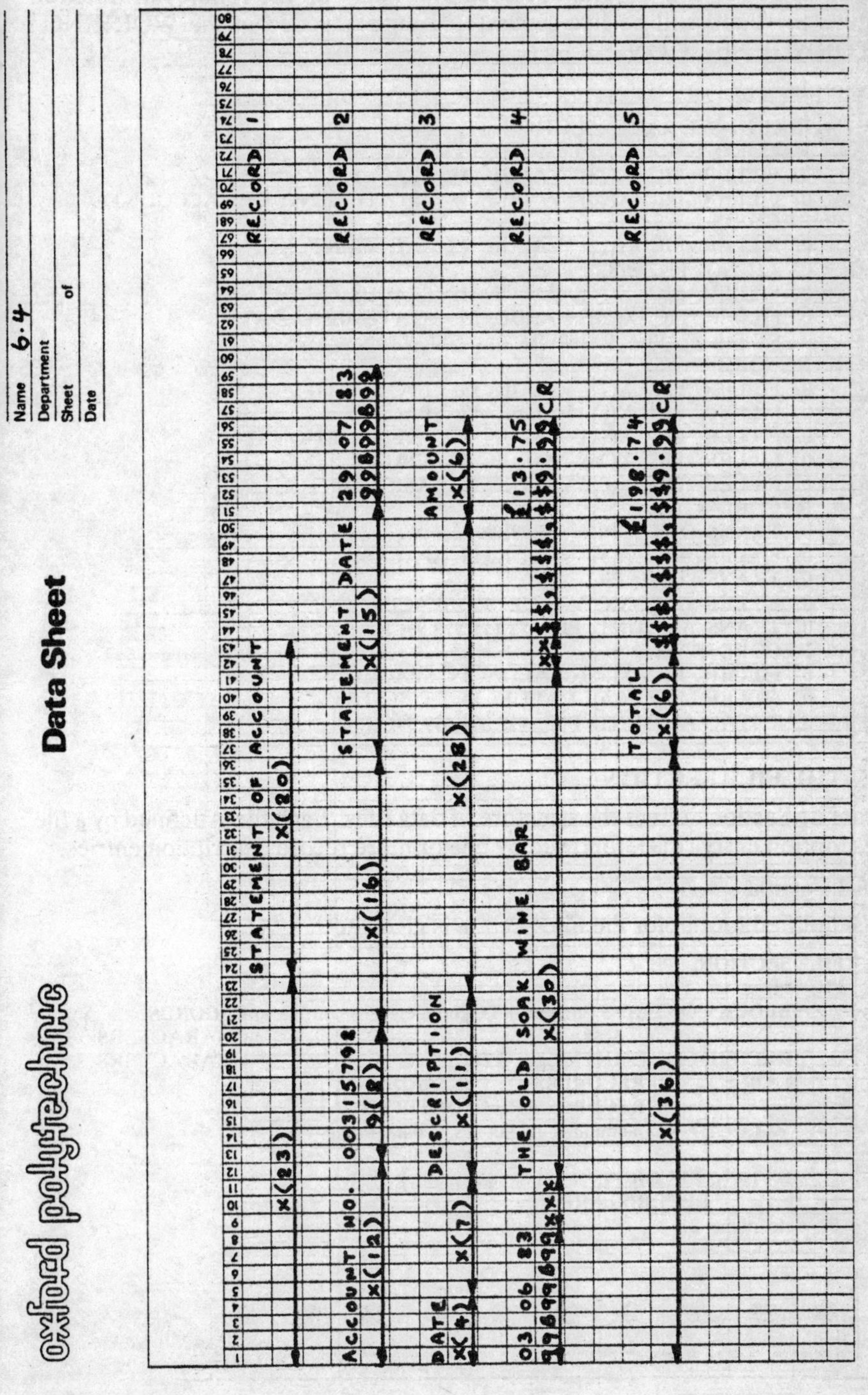

oxford polytechnic

Data Sheet

Name 6.4
Department
Sheet of
Date

RECORD 1
RECORD 2
RECORD 3
RECORD 4
RECORD 5

STATEMENT OF ACCOUNT X(30)
X(23)
STATEMENT DATE X(15)
29 07 83
9980909

ACCOUNT NO. 003157 98 9(8)
ACCOUNT X(12)

DESCRIPTION X(11)
AMOUNT X(6)
X(28)

DATE X(4) X(7)
THE OLD SOAK WINE BAR X(30)
03 06 83 9769 9699 XXX

£ 3.75 £549.29CR
£198.74 £549.29CR
TOTAL X(6)
X(36)

Figure 6.4

81

6.4.4 Coding the Report

Since there are five different records that make up the report illustrated in figure 6.4 there will be five separate 01 entries coded in the WORKING–STORAGE SECTION.

Example.

```
WORKING–STORAGE  SECTION.
01 RECORD–1–WS.
    02 FILLER  PIC  X(23) VALUE  IS  SPACES.
    02 FILLER  PIC  X(20) VALUE  IS  "STATEMENT  OF  ACCOUNT".
01 RECORD–2–WS.
    02 FILLER  PIC  X(12) VALUE  IS  "ACCOUNT  NO.".
    02 AC–NO  PIC  9(8).
    02 FILLER  PIC  X(16) VALUE  IS  SPACES.
    02 FILLER  PIC  X(15) VALUE  IS  "STATEMENT  DATE".
    02 ST–DATE  PIC  99B99B99.
01 RECORD–3–WS.
    02 FILLER  PIC  X(4)  VALUE  IS  "DATE".
    02 FILLER  PIC  X(7)  VALUE  IS  SPACES.
    02 FILLER  PIC  X(11) VALUE  IS  "DESCRIPTION".
    02 FILLER  PIC  X(28) VALUE  IS  SPACES.
    02 FILLER  PIC  X(6)  VALUE  IS  "AMOUNT".
01 RECORD–4–WS.
    02 TRANS–DATE  PIC  99B99B99.
    02 FILLER  PIC  X(3)  VALUE  IS  SPACES.
    02 TRANS–ITEM  PIC  X(30).
    02 FILLER  PIC  XX  VALUE  IS  SPACES.
    02 TRANS–AMOUNT  PIC  $$,$$$,$$9.99CR.
01 RECORD–5–WS.
    02 FILLER  PIC  X(36) VALUE  IS  SPACES.
    02 FILLER  PIC  X(6)  VALUE  IS  "TOTAL".
    02 TOTAL–AMOUNT  PIC  $$$,$$$,$$9.99CR.
```

6.5 THE FILE SECTION

The File Section defines the structure of data files. Each file is defined by a file description entry (FD), followed by one or more record description entries.

6.5.1 Format

A simplified format for the File Section is given here.

```
FILE SECTION.
FD    file–name–1
      [BLOCK CONTAINS [integer–1 TO] integer–2          { RECORDS    } ]
                                                        { CHARACTERS }

      [RECORD CONTAINS integer–3 TO integer–4        CHARACTERS]
      [LABEL      { RECORD IS   } { STANDARD } ]
                  { RECORDS ARE } { OMITTED  }
          [VALUE OF  implementor–name  IS { data–name–1 } ]
                                          { literal–1   }
              [DATA { RECORD IS   } { data–name–2 } .... ]
                    { RECORDS ARE }
      01  date–name–2.
          _____
          _____
          _____
      [01  data–name–3.
          _____
          _____
          _____  ] ....
```

6.5.2 Physical and Logical Records

A *physical* record is defined as one or more *logical* records read into or written from main memory as a unit of information. Records are not usually transferred to and from main memory as single logical records but grouped together and stored in an area of memory known as a *buffer*. When information is transferred to the buffer it is transferred as a *block* of logical records from the storage medium; and when information is transferred from the buffer to the storage medium it is transferred as a block of logical records.

6.5.3 Block Clause

The BLOCK clause specifies the number of logical records contained in a physical record. The clause can be omitted if the size of the block is one logical record. The maximum number of records or characters is specified by integer–2; integer–1 can be regarded as being documentary.

6.5.4 Record Clause

The RECORD clause specifies the number of characters in a record : integer–3 TO integer–4 would signify the minimum and maximum number of characters in variable length records. Since the number of characters is specified in the description of each field of a record this entry in the File Description is not essential.

6.5.5 Label Clause

In order to identify different magnetic files each file will have a unique machine readable label. Labels contain such information as the *external* name of the file, the volume number, the date the file was written and perhaps the date after which the data will be no longer valid (purge date). The clause LABEL RECORDS ARE STANDARD should be used with all magnetic files, and the clause LABEL RECORDS ARE OMITTED should be used in conjunction with all non-magnetic files, for example, terminals, card readers and punches.

6.5.6 Value Of Clause

The VALUE OF clause is used to specify the *external* name of the file which is normally found as one field in the label record. The clause serves the purpose of linking the external name of the file (part of the label) with the *internal* name of the file (file–name–1) invented by the programmer.

6.5.7 Data Record Clause

The DATA RECORD clause specifies the name(s) of the record(s) described at the 01 level. Since these names appear at the 01 level the clause can be regarded as being documentary only.

6.5.8 File Description used in the text

Since all the files used in the worked examples of this book are stored on magnetic disc, the format for every FD entry that is present will be simplified to:

```
FD file–name–1
     LABEL RECORDS ARE STANDARD
     VALUE OF FILE–ID IS literal–1.
```

6.6 THE ENVIRONMENT DIVISION

This Division describes the physical environment in which the COBOL program will be executed.

6.6.1 Format

A simplied format for this Division follows.

```
ENVIRONMENT  DIVISION.
[CONFIGURATION  SECTION.
[SOURCE–COMPUTER.  computer–name.]
[OBJECT–COMPUTER.  computer–name.]
[SPECIAL–NAMES.  paragraph.]]
[INPUT–OUTPUT  SECTION.
 FILE–CONTROL.
    {SELECT  file–name–1  ASSIGN  TO  device–name
    [ORGANIZATION  IS  SEQUENTIAL]
    [ACCESS  MODE  IS  SEQUENTIAL]
    [FILE  STATUS  IS  data–name–1.]}.....]
```

6.6.2 The Configuration Section

The programmer may document the name of the computer used to compile and execute the COBOL program under the paragraph names of SOURCE–COMPUTER and OBJECT–COMPUTER respectively.

Example.

```
ENVIRONMENT  DIVISION.
CONFIGURATION  SECTION.
SOURCE–COMPUTER.  PR1ME  750.
OBJECT–COMPUTER.  PR1ME  750.
```

The SPECIAL–NAMES paragraph can contain the following entries.

```
[SPECIAL–NAMES.
    [implementor–name  IS  mnemonic–name.]
    [CURRENCY  SIGN  IS  literal.]
    [DECIMAL–POINT  IS  COMMA.]]
```

In chapter 2, section 2.4.3 the ACCEPT and DISPLAY verbs were written in an alternative format as:

ACCEPT identifier–1 **FROM** mnemonic–name
and
DISPLAY $\left\{ \begin{array}{l} \text{identifier–1} \\ \text{literal–1} \end{array} \right\}$ ...... **UPON** mnemonic–name

where mnemonic name is invented by the programmer and specified as part of the SPECIAL–NAMES paragraph. The implementor–name is a specific name assigned to a hardware device.

Example.
```
ENVIRONMENT  DIVISION.
CONFIGURATION  SECTION.
SPECIAL–NAMES.
    CONSOLE  IS  TTY.
    PRINTER  IS  PRT.
    _____
    _____
    _____


PROCEDURE  DIVISION.
    _____

    ACCEPT  ALPHA  FROM  TTY.
    _____
    _____
    DISPLAY  BETA  UPON  PRT.
    _____
```

The value of ALPHA will be entered through the keyboard of the console (terminal) and the value of BETA will be output to the printer.

The implementor–name CONSOLE and PRINTER used in this example are machine specific, therefore, the reader is advised to refer to the manufacturers COBOL manual for their computer.

The second entry in the SPECIAL–NAMES paragraph, CURRENCY SIGN IS literal, will allow the programmer to use a single character currency sign for the country the application program is written for.

Example.
```
ENVIRONMENT  DIVISION.
CONFIGURATION  SECTION.
SPECIAL–NAMES.
    CURRENCY  SIGN  IS  "£".
    _____

DATA  DIVISION.
    _____

    02 TOTAL–COMMISSION  PIC  £££,££9.99.
```

The third entry in the SPECIAL–NAMES pargraph is the sentence DECIMAL–POINT IS COMMA. This will allow the programmer to inter–change the functions of the comma and decimal–point (period). This conforms to the European representation of decimal values. The functions of the comma and decimal–point (period) are exchanged in the character–string of the PICTURE clause and in numeric literals.

Example.

345,987.45 output using a PICTURE of ZZZ,ZZ9.99 can be changed to 345.897,45 using a PICTURE of ZZZ.ZZ9,99.

85

6.6.3 The Input–Output Section

This section is used when there are external data files to be accessed in a program. It allows the specification of peripheral devices and the information required to transmit and handle data between the devices and the program.

The SELECT clause enables a file to be assigned to a hardware device. The file–name must be described under the FD for that file in the DATA DIVISION. The name of the device is machine specific, therefore, the reader is advised to refer to the COBOL manual for their computer.

Example.

```
SELECT  EMPLOYEE–FILE  ASSIGN  TO  PFMS.
SELECT  REPORT–FILE  ASSIGN  TO  PRINTER.
SELECT  WAGES–FILE  ASSIGN  TO  MT9.
```

In this example PFMS implies disc storage, PRINTER implies a lineprinter and MT9 a nine–track magnetic tape unit. These names are created by the implementor of the COBOL compiler for a particular make of computer.

The clauses for ORGANIZATION and for ACCESS describe respectively the type of file that is being processed and the manner in which records in the file are to be referenced. This entry, for serial and sequential files, serves no purpose other than being documentary. The relevance of these two entries with respect to other file organisations will be described in context in a later chapter.

The File–Status clause describes an identifier in the WORKING–STORAGE SECTION that has specific values moved to it after the execution of file–processing verbs. The value of the identifier is a code to such information as:

successful completion,
end of file,
permanent I/O error,

and can be useful in detecting run–time errors. The file–status codes and their meanings are defined by the implementor of the COBOL compiler for a particular manufacturers computer.

6.6.4 Simplified Environment Division

In order to reduce the amount of coding so that readers can write complete COBOL programs as quickly as possible the following Environment Division will be used throughout the book when using either serial or sequential files.

```
ENVIRONMENT  DIVISION.
INPUT–OUTPUT  SECTION.
FILE–CONTROL.
    SELECT  file–name  ASSIGN  TO  PFMS.
    SELECT ............
```

6.7 WORKED EXAMPLES

6.7.1 Problem

Two files stored on magnetic disc are to be used in a program. The first file has an external file–name of FILE01 and an internal file–name of MEMBERS–FILE. The organisation of the file is serial, with fixed length records containing the following details about members of a squash club.

86

Name		30 alphanumeric characters
Sex		1 alphabetic character
League	Division	1 digit (numeric)
	Box	1 letter (alphabetic)
Telephone number		15 alphanumeric characters.

The second file has an external file–name of FILE02 and an internal file–name of CLUB–NOTICE. The organisation of this file is also serial with fixed length records. The records contain details taken from the first file and the format of a record is:

Paper control	1 alphanumeric character
Line image	119 alphanumeric characters.

Code COBOL Environment and Data Divisions that fully describe these files.

6.7.2 Solution

```
ENVIRONMENT  DIVISION.
INPUT–OUTPUT  SECTION.
FILE–CONTROL.
    SELECT  MEMBERS–FILE  ASSIGN  TO  PFMS.
    SELECT  CLUB–NOTICE  ASSIGN  TO  PFMS.

DATA  DIVISION.
FILE  SECTION.
FD  MEMBERS–FILE
    LABEL  RECORDS  ARE  STANDARD
    VALUE  OF  FILE–ID  IS  "FILE01".
01  RECORD–1.
    02  NAME  PIC  X(30).
    02  SEX  PIC  A.
    02  LEAGUE.
        03  DIV  PIC  9.
        03  BOX  PIC  A.
    02  TELE–NO  PIC  X(15).
FD  CLUB–NOTICE
    LABEL  RECORDS  ARE  STANDARD
    VALUE  OF  FILE–ID  IS  "FILE02".
01  RECORD–2.
    02  P–CONTROL  PIC  X.
    02  LINE–IMAGE  PIC  X(119).
```

6.7.3 Problem

A design for a report on the members of a squash club is illustrated in figure 6.5. Code a WORKING–STORAGE SECTION entry to represent the four different records that make up the report.

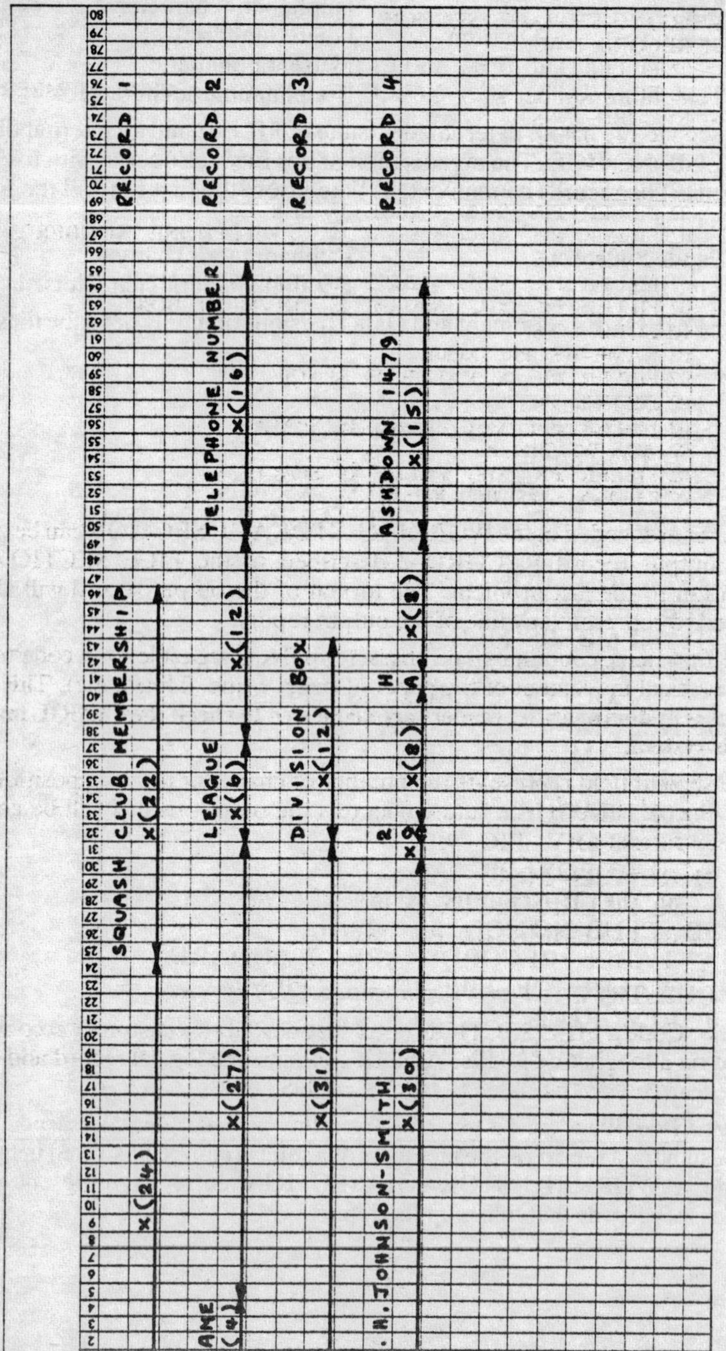
SQUASH CLUB MEMBERSHIP
RECORD 1
X(24)
X(22)
NAME
LEAGUE
TELEPHONE NUMBER
RECORD 2
X(4)
X(27)
X(6)
X(12)
X(16)
DIVISION BOX
RECORD 3
X(31)
X(12)
W. H. JOHNSON-SMITH
2
H
ASHDOWN 1479
RECORD 4
X(30)
X9
X(8)
A
X(8)
X(15)

Figure 6.5

6.7.4 Solution

```
WORKING–STORAGE SECTION.
01 RECORD–1–WS.
   02 FILLER PIC X(24) VALUE IS SPACES.
   02 FILLER PIC X(22) VALUE IS " SQUASH CLUB MEMBERSHIP".
01 RECORD–2–WS.
   02 FILLER PIC X(4) VALUE IS "NAME".
   02 FILLER PIC X(27) VALUE IS SPACES.
   02 FILLER PIC X(6) VALUE IS "LEAGUE".
   02 FILLER PIC X(12) VALUE IS SPACES.
   02 FILLER PIC X(16) VALUE IS " TELEPHONE NUMBER".
01 RECORD–3–WS.
   02 FILLER PIC X(31) VALUE IS SPACES.
   02 FILLER PIC X(12) VALUE IS "DIVISION BOX".
01 RECORD–4–WS.
   02 NAME–WS PIC X(30).
   02 FILLER PIC X VALUE IS SPACE.
   02 DIV–WS PIC 9.
   02 FILLER PIC X(8) VALUE IS SPACES.
   02 BOX–WS PIC A.
   02 FILLER PIC X(8) VALUE IS SPACES.
   02 TELE–NO–WS PIC X(15).
```

The records coded in the WORKING–STORAGE SECTION can be moved to the output record RECORD–2 described in the FILE SECTION of the solution to the last problem. The format of the output record will always be coded to represent any line of the output report.

The first field, containing one character only, is set aside for a code to control the vertical movement of the paper (1 page, 1 line, 2 lines, etc). **This requirement is system specific, readers are requested to check the COBOL manual for their system.**

The second field represents the number of character printing positions across one line of the page. In future chapters the output record will be coded in a similar format to:

```
01 REPORT–LINE.
   02 FILLER PIC X.
   02 LINE–IMAGE PIC X(119).
```

6.8 QUESTIONS *(answers begin on page 342)*

† **6.8.1** Code a FILE SECTION entry that describes a customer account record held on a magnetic disc file. A block contains one logical record and standard labels are used. The name of the file is CUSTOM.

The format of a record is given by the following extended glossary.

Indentifier	Meaning	Type	Size of datum
CUSTOM–REC	name of record	–	–
ACC–NOS	account number	numeric	8 digits
NAME	name of customer	–	–
SURNAME	surname of customer	alphanumeric	19 chars.
FORENAME	first name	alphabetic	12 chars.
ADDRESS	address of customer	–	–
STREET	street address	alphanumeric	20 chars.
TOWN	town address	alphanumeric	20 chars.
POSTCODE	postcode	alphanumeric	8 chars.
CRED–LIMIT	credit limit	numeric	3 digits
BALANCE	credit balance	numeric	5 digits inc 2 dec. pl.

6.8.2 Code a FILE SECTION entry that describes a stock record held on a magnetic tape file. There are 64 records to a block, standard labels are used and the name of the file is STOCK.

The format of a record is given by the following extended glossary.

Identifier	Meaning	Type	Size of datum
STOCK–REC	name of record	–	–
STOCK–NOS	stock number	numeric	8 digits
DESC	description of stock	alphanumeric	20 chars.
QUANT	quantity in stock	numeric	3 digits
RE–ORD	re–order level	numeric	3 digits
COST	price of stock item	numeric	4 digits inc 2 dec.p/.
LOCATION	location of stock	–	–
FAC–CODE	factory area code	alphabetic	1 char.
BIN–CODE	bin number	numeric	2 digits.

†6.8.3 Code a FILE SECTION entry that describes a payroll record held on a magnetic tape file. There are 128 records to a block, standard labels are used and the name of the file is PAYROLL.

The format of a record is given by the following extended glossary.

Identifier	Meaning	Type	Size of datum
PAY–REC	name of record	–	–
EMP–NOS	employee number	numeric	8 digits
EMP–NAME	name of employee	alphanumeric	20 chars.
NAT–INS–NO	National Insurance number	alphanumeric	9 chars.
TAX–CODE	income tax code	alphanumeric	3 chars.
GROSS	gross pay	numeric	6 digits inc 2 dec.pl.
TAX	income tax	numeric	6 digits inc 2 dec.pl.
SUPERAN	superannuation	numeric	5 digits inc 2 dec.pl.
NAT–INS	National Insurance	numeric	5 digits inc 2 dec.pl.
PAYMENT	details of credit transfer	–	–
BANK	bank code	numeric	6 digits
ACC–NOS	bank account number	numeric	10 digits
ACC–NAME	bank account name	alphanumeric	20 chars.

6.8.4 Code a WORKING–STORAGE SECTION entry that describes each of the four records illustrated. The identifiers used to store the county, town, model of car and total sales should be coded as COUNTY–WS, TOWN–WS, MODEL–WS and SALE–WS respectively.

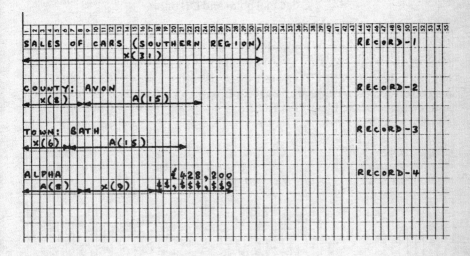

† **6.8.5** Code a WORKING–STORAGE SECTION entry that describes each of the four records illustrated. The identifiers used to store the type of cassette, stock–number and quantity should be coded as MUSIC–WS, STOCK–NUMBER–WS and QUANTITY–WS respectively.

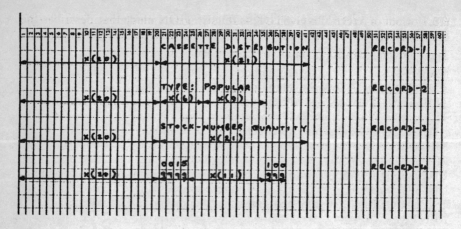

6.8.6 Code a WORKING–STORAGE SECTION entry that describes the following report.

The following identifiers should be used in the coding.

ACCOUNT–NO–WS   15 digits in two groups of 8 digits and 7 digits.
DATE–WS   5 characters
DESCRIPTION–WS   11 characters
DEBIT–WS   9 characters including comma and decimal point
CREDIT–WS   9 characters including comma and decimal point
BALANCE–WS   9 characters including comma and decimal point
FINAL–BALANCE–WS   12 characters including currency–sign, comma, decimal point and DB or bb.

```
THE UNIVERSAL BANK

STATEMENT OF ACCOUNT:  04971328 1726493

DATE  DESCRIPTION      DEBIT      CREDIT        BALANCE

MAY 1  BALANCE                                  103.98
MAY 3  SALARY                    1,076.42     1,180.40
MAY 5  DOMESTIC       423.45                     756.95
                                                    .
                                                    .
                                                    .

                       FINAL BALANCE           £104.27 DB
```

†**6.8.7** Code a WORKING–STORAGE SECTION entry that describes the following report.

The following identifiers should be used in the coding.

NAME–WS	25 characters
ADDRESS–ROAD–WS	20 characters
ADDRESS–TOWN–WS	20 characters
TELE–NO–WS	20 characters
ADDRESS–PC–WS	8 characters
PREV–READ–WS	6 digits with zero suppression
PRES–READ–WS	6 digits with zero suppression
UNIT–PRICE–WS	5 characters inc currency–sign and decimal point
UNITS–USED–WS	6 digits with zero suppression
CALL–COST–WS	9 characters inc decimal point
RENTAL–WS	7 characters inc decimal point
SUB–TOTAL–WS	10 characters inc decimal point
VAT–PERCENT–WS	2 digits
VAT–WS	9 characters inc decimal point
TOTAL–WS	11 characters inc currency–sign and decimal point

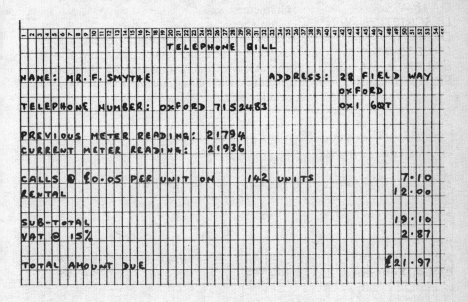

6.8.8 A COBOL program is compiled on a PR1ME 750 computer and executed on a PR1ME 550 computer.

Throughout the PROCEDURE DIVISION the computer CONSOLE is referred to as a TTY and the system PRINTER is referred to as PRT.

The currency symbol used in the printed reports is F for French Francs and since the reports are used by a French bank the printing of a decimal point must be changed to a comma.

The computer uses four data files in conjunction with four different hardware devices.

Filename	Device	System Code	File Organisation
ALPHA	CARD READER	CRO	serial
BETA	LINE PRINTER	LPO	serial
DELTA	MAGNETIC TAPE	MT1	sequential
EPSILON	MAGNETIC DISC	MD1	sequential

Code a complete ENVIRONMENT DIVISION to express these facts.

7 Introduction to File Processing

7.1 INTRODUCTION

7.1.1 Contents of Chapter

The purpose of this chapter is to introduce the reader to the fundamental concepts of file processing. The chapter is divided into three parts.

The first part gives a selection of Procedure Division verbs that are used in file processing.

The second part looks at the creation of a serial file and the production of a report.

The final part investigates the use of the SORT verb to change the organisation of a file from serial to sequential.

7.1.2 An Overview

The only method described up to now for inputting data to a computer program was through the verb ACCEPT. However, as was pointed out earlier this verb is only meant for low volume data input through, say, a keyboard device. Such a verb, although useful for writing interactive computer programs, does have the following disadvantages.

Does not permit the processing of large volumes of data.

The advantage of using a high-speed computer to process work becomes redundant since the speed of the computer system becomes dependent upon the typing speed of the user at the terminal.

Data that is input via a keyboard to the main memory of a computer is **not** permanently stored. Switch the power off from the computer and the data stored in a volatile main memory will be destroyed. Switch the power on again and the user must re-load and run the program again before entering all the data!

The method of outputting information from a computer program was through the DISPLAY verb. Although this verb can be used to output information to say a screen or printer it cannot be used to create files of information on a magnetic medium such as tape or disc.

The storage of data on a magnetic medium has the following advantages.

Peripheral devices such as magnetic tape and magnetic disc units can transfer data from the medium on which it is stored to the main memory of a computer at a very fast speed (hundreds of thousand of characters per second). Thus the speed of data input and output becomes more realistic in terms of the power of the computer.

Data can be permanently stored on both magnetic tape and magnetic disc. Switch the power off and the data remains on the magnetic medium.

Magnetic tapes and disc packs are portable, so not only can data be moved from one computer to another but libraries of data can also be kept.

Data stored on magnetic tape or disc can be duplicated for security.

7.2 FILE PROCESSING VERBS

In this section the trend of describing the formats of COBOL statements in a simplified form continues.

7.2.1 Open

Before a file can be used it must be opened. There are many functions associated with this verb which may include:

ensuring that the device (disc or tape unit) is ready for use;
checking labels on an existing file;
creating labels on a new file;
filling the input buffer with a physical record for a file that is about to be read.

A format for the OPEN statement is:

OPEN $\left\{ \begin{array}{l} \textbf{INPUT} \quad \{\text{file–name}\} \ ... \\ \textbf{OUTPUT} \ \{\text{file–name–3}\} \ ... \end{array} \right\}$ .....

A file is opened in the INPUT mode for reading and in the OUTPUT mode for writing.

Example.

OPEN   INPUT   MEMBERS–FILE,
          OUTPUT   CLUB–NOTICE.

7.2.2 Close

When all processing activities are completed on a file it must be closed.

The activity of closing a file serves the following purposes.

The contents of a buffer, which may be partially full, is written to the file if the mode is set to OUTPUT. An *end of file* record is then appended to the file.

A file must first be closed before it can be re-opened for a different mode of processing. For example, a file that is opened for OUTPUT could be closed and re-opened in the INPUT mode ready for reading.

A format for the CLOSE statement is:

CLOSE {file–name–1} .....

Example.

CLOSE   MEMBERS–FILE,   CLUB–NOTICE.

7.2.3 Read

The READ statement makes available the next logical record from a file. Figure 7.1 illustrates the transfer of a logical record from a buffer area when reading records that are stored on magnetic tape. The execution of subsequent READ statements will cause successive records to be accessed in sequence from the buffer. When all the logical records from the buffer have been accessed, the buffer will be refilled with a physical record.

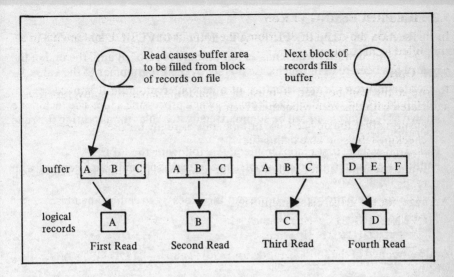

Figure 7.1. An illustration of records being read from a magnetic tape file three logical records are assumed to fill the buffer area.

A format for reading a record from a serial or sequential file stored on either magnetic tape or disc is:

READ file–name–1 RECORD [**INTO** identifier–1]
[AT **END** imperative–statement–1]

Example.

If the MEMBERS–FILE described in the worked example of section 6.7.2 was read using the statement READ MEMBERS–FILE then the values for name, sex, league and telephone number would be moved into the respective fields NAME, SEX, DIV, BOX and TELE–NO described under RECORD–1.

When the INTO option is used the values of the fields are moved into a data area in the WORKING–STORAGE SECTION described by identifier–1.

The repeated execution of a READ file statement will eventually cause the *end of file* record to be accessed. This record marks the end of the file and when it is read implies that all the records in the file have been read.

If the AT END option is omitted then unless a count is kept on the number of records in the file, which is impractical since the number of records is not usually known in advance, the computer will attempt to read beyond the last record and this will flag a run-time error. The AT END option should normally be present so that the end of the file can be detected in the program and the computer directed to execute further instructions. However, it would be a desirable feature to be able to test for the end of the file anywhere in the program, and not simply through a READ ... AT END statement. The imperative statement associated with the AT END option, therefore, takes the form of setting a flag (E–O–F) to show that the end of the file has been reached.

Example.

READ MEMBERS–FILE AT END MOVE 1 TO E–O–F.

E–O–F is an identifier which has an initial value of zero (0) until the end of file record has been read in which case it is set by the programmer to the value 1.

In order to preserve the structure of a computer program it is necessary to introduce at least two READ statements when processing a file. The technique known as *reading ahead* can be summarised by two rules for allocating the read operation.

Rule 1. Read the first record immediately following the OPEN.

Rule 2. Read again at the end of each program component which processes an input record.

A skeletal schematic logic to represent the process of reading ahead is:

```
do 1,2
    _____
    _____

A–iter while 1
    _____
    _____
    _____
    _____

do 2
A–end
```

where the functions are:

1. Open file for Input.
2. Read file.

and the condition is:

1. Not end of file (i.e. E–O–F = 0)

7.2.4 Write

The WRITE statement releases a logical record to an output file. It can also be used for the vertical positioning of lines within a logical page. The format of a logical record would be specified in a program and the fields used to represent that format would be assigned values before writing a record. Figure 7.2 illustrates that the use of successive WRITE statements to magnetic tape will cause the output buffer to be filled, having one logical record placed after the next. When the buffer is full the computer system will store the contents of the buffer as a block of records on the magnetic tape file. The buffer is then empty and ready to receive more logical records.

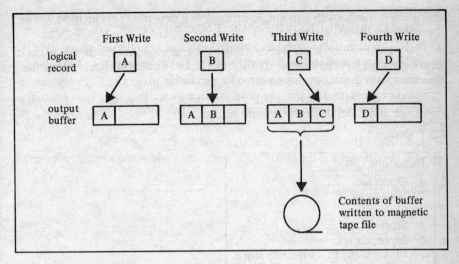

Figure 7.2 Illustration of records being written to a magnetic tape file.

A format for writing a record to a serial or sequential file stored on either magnetic tape or disc is:

WRITE record–name–1   [**FROM** identifier–1]
$$\left[\begin{Bmatrix} \textbf{BEFORE} \\ \textbf{AFTER} \end{Bmatrix} \text{ADVANCING} \begin{Bmatrix} \text{identifier–2} \\ \text{integer–1} \\ \textbf{PAGE} \end{Bmatrix} \begin{bmatrix} \text{LINE} \\ \text{LINES} \end{bmatrix} \right]$$

Examples.

    WRITE RECORD–1.
    WRITE RECORD–2 AFTER ADVANCING 2 LINES.

The first example illustrates the correct format for creating a file that can be re-opened in the INPUT mode for reading.

The second example illustrates the correct format for creating a report file. Such a file contains paper control characters (codes to advance the paper in the lineprinter a specific number of lines or to advance to the top of the page) and should never be re-opened in the INPUT mode for reading.

If the FROM option is used the contents of identifier–1 in the WORKING–STORAGE SECTION is moved to record–name–1 prior to the WRITE operation.

Notice from the formats of the READ and WRITE statements that **files are read** and **records are written**.

7.3 CREATING A SERIAL FILE

There are three methods of creating a serial file. The first is by invoking the system editor and typing each record as a line by line entry at the keyboard of a terminal. This method is machine specific, therefore, the reader is advised to consult the operations manual (editor section) for their make of computer.

The second method involves reading an existing file and writing the information, perhaps in a modified format, to a new file. This method will be covered later in the chapter.

Finally the third method involves writing a program to input the details of each record through, say the keyboard of a V.D.U., and writing each record to a file. This last method will now be explored in greater depth.

To create the MEMBERS–FILE described in section 6.6 the following algorithm and COBOL coding would be used.

7.3.1 Design

```
Functions List.
1. Open file.
2. Write record.
3. Close file.
4. Stop.
5. Input name.
6. Move name to temporary store.
7. Input sex.
8. Input league.
9. Input telephone number.
```

```
Condition List.
1. Name = "XXX"
```

n.b. the process of writing to the file ceases when XXX is typed in response to the prompt for name.

Schematic Logic.

```
File–seq
    do 1,5,6
    Input–iter while not 1
        do 7,8,9,2,5,6
    Input–end
    do 3,4
File–end
```

7.3.2 Coding.

```
(0001)         IDENTIFICATION DIVISION.
(0002)         PROGRAM-ID. C732.
(0003)         ENVIRONMENT DIVISION.
(0004)         INPUT-OUTPUT SECTION.
(0005)         FILE-CONTROL.
(0006)             SELECT MEMBERS-FILE ASSIGN TO PFMS.
(0007)         DATA DIVISION.
(0008)         FILE SECTION.
(0009)         FD MEMBERS-FILE
(0010)             LABEL RECORDS ARE STANDARD
(0011)             VALUE OF FILE-ID IS "FILE01".
(0012)         01 RECORD-1.
(0013)             02 FILLER PIC X(48).
```

(program continued)

```
(0014)          WORKING-STORAGE SECTION.
(0015)          01 RECORD-1-WS.
(0016)             02 NAME PIC X(30).
(0017)             02 SEX PIC A.
(0018)             02 LEAGUE.
(0019)                03 DIV PIC 9.
(0020)                03 BOX PIC A.
(0021)             02 TELE-NO PIC X(15).
(0022)          77 END-STORE PIC XXX.
(0023)          PROCEDURE DIVISION.
(0024)          FILE-SEQ.
(0025)             OPEN OUTPUT MEMBERS-FILE.
(0026)             DISPLAY "INPUT NAME (MAX 30 CHARS) TYPE XXX TO STOP"
(0027)             ACCEPT NAME.
(0028)             MOVE NAME TO END-STORE.

              * input fields of record

(0029)          INPUT-ITER.
(0030)             IF END-STORE = "XXX" GO TO INPUT-END.
(0031)                DISPLAY "INPUT SEX (M OR F)"
(0032)                ACCEPT SEX.
(0033)                DISPLAY "INPUT LEAGUE 1 DIGIT 1 LETTER"
(0034)                ACCEPT LEAGUE.
(0035)                DISPLAY "INPUT TELEPHONE NUMBER (MAX 15 CHARS)"
(0036)                ACCEPT TELE-NO.
(0037)                WRITE RECORD-1 FROM RECORD-1-WS.
(0038)                DISPLAY "INPUT NAME (MAX 30 CHARS) TYPE XXX TO STOP"
(0039)                ACCEPT NAME.
(0040)                MOVE NAME TO END-STORE.
(0041)                GO TO INPUT-ITER.
(0042)          INPUT-END.
(0043)             CLOSE MEMBERS-FILE.
(0044)             STOP RUN.
(0045)          FILE-END.
```

7.3.3 Comments

The format of a record in the MEMBERS–FILE has been coded in the WORKING–STORAGE SECTION. This illustrates the record is to be created in the program using local data (data that is not already part of a file). When a record is complete and is to be written to the file the contents of the record is transferred from the WORKING–STORAGE SECTION to the FILE SECTION. Notice that the specific names of the fields are not required for the output file in the FILE SECTION and therefore, the description of a record has been replaced by the reserved word FILLER. The total number of characters that form one record must be inserted into the PICTURE clause after the word FILLER. This figure is calculated by adding together the number of characters in each field of RECORD–1–WS.

The function of END–STORE is to truncate the name to the left three characters only, thus, enabling a test to be made on the first three characters of the name and not the 30 characters (including spaces) that have been allocated for the storage of name.

Example.

W.H.JOHNSON–SMITHbbbbbbbbbbbbbb is truncated to W.H and
XXXbbbbbbbbbbbbbbbbbbbbbbbbbbbbb is truncated to XXX to enable the condition END–STORE = "XXX" to eventually become true.

The value XXX should not be confused with the PICTURE character–string XXX. The reader will notice that the level numbers 01,02,03 and 77 appear in the WORKING–STORAGE SECTION. This practice is **not** popular amongst many programmers despite it providing a very positive distinction between the fields of a record and a discrete item of data. The current trend is to re–code the 77 level entry as:

01 END–STORE PIC XXX.
or
01 PARAMETER.
  02 END–STORE PIC XXX.

The author will fall into line with such current practices and will not use a level 77 entry again in future programs. It has not done the reader any harm in knowing about its function since level 77 is to be retained in the Draft Proposed Revision to the COBOL Standard.

In line (0037) of the coding the FROM option has been used in writing RECORD–1, this essentially replaces the statements:

MOVE RECORD–1–WS TO RECORD–1,
WRITE RECORD–1.

7.3.4 Extracts from a program test run.

```
INPUT NAME (MAX 30 CHARS) TYPE XXX TO STOP
LONG C
INPUT SEX (M OR F)
M
INPUT LEAGUE 1 DIGIT 1 LETTER
1A
INPUT TELEPHONE NUMBER (MAX 15 CHARS)
CUMNOR 863
INPUT NAME (MAX 30 CHARS) TYPE XXX TO STOP
MCDOUGALL G
INPUT SEX (M OR F)
F
INPUT LEAGUE 1 DIGIT 1 LETTER
3B
INPUT TELEPHONE NUMBER (MAX 15 CHARS)
ABINGDON 81773
INPUT NAME (MAX 30 CHARS) TYPE XXX TO STOP
DIMITRIOU B
INPUT SEX (M OR F)
M
INPUT LEAGUE 1 DIGIT 1 LETTER
3C
INPUT TELEPHONE NUMBER (MAX 15 CHARS)
OXFORD 235
INPUT NAME (MAX 30 CHARS) TYPE XXX TO STOP
ELWIN J
INPUT SEX (M OR F)
F
INPUT LEAGUE 1 DIGIT 1 LETTER
1A
INPUT TELEPHONE NUMBER (MAX 15 CHARS)
PORTWAY 14732
INPUT NAME (MAX 30 CHARS) TYPE XXX TO STOP
PEPPER D
INPUT SEX (M OR F)
M
INPUT LEAGUE 1 DIGIT 1 LETTER
2A
INPUT TELEPHONE NUMBER (MAX 15 CHARS)
LONGWORTH 6498
INPUT NAME (MAX 30 CHARS) TYPE XXX TO STOP
GUNASEKARA A
INPUT SEX (M OR F)
M
INPUT LEAGUE 1 DIGIT 1 LETTER
1A
INPUT TELEPHONE NUMBER (MAX 15 CHARS)
HARWELL 2124
```

7.3.5 Listing of the Created File.

```
STEVENSON G.R            M3ALECHLADE 194
O'FLINN P                M4BCHOLSEY 5259
LOWE J.C                 F1CBICESTER 4268
STOTT P.A                M1AJALLINGFORD 837
BARRETT G.C              F1BSTANDLAKE 87936
ALLEN D.J                M2BICKFORD 947361
OSTLE D.M                M2CCLANFIELD 4932
TILBURY C                M3CDIDCOT 9873
FOX M                    M1CFREELAND 93412
JONES N.L                F4AWITNEY 192
COLLINS P                F3BTHAME 94287
GILLOT D                 F1CHARWELL 6829
LONG C                   M1ACUMNOR 863
MCDOUGALL G              F3BABINGDON 81773
DIMITRIOU B              M3COXFORD 235
ELWIN J                  F1APORTWAY 14732
PEPPER D                 M2ALONGWORTH 6498
GUNASEKARA A             M1AHARWELL 2124
RODRIGUEZ-BACHILLER A    F2BFRITWELL 916
THOMAS K                 F1CDIDCOT 48973
WARD S                   M3CDIDCOT 27918
ANDERSON T               M3CWITNEY 817963
HILL L                   M3CUFFINGTON 36792
WALTON B                 M1BTACKLEY 1134
WINTER M                 M2ABURFORD 223
KEABLE R                 F2ACHOLSEY 1414
GODDARD P                M1ACROWMARSH 81793
MAY N                    F1CDIDCOT 98149
EDWARDS E                M2CWOODSTOCK 931
PRISCOTT M               F2CWITNEY 419523
ALLEN P                  M3BWANTAGE 9696
JACKSON J                M3BTHAME 8137
WINSLET M.J              M3BLECHLADE 2130
CLAYTON A                M4CICKFORD 326
BLACK A                  M4CFILKINS 159
EAST W                   F4ACHILDREY 4267
LYLE S                   M1BGT MILTON 71436
SANDERS M.A              M4CWOODSTOCK 1136
DANIELS J                M3COXFORD 713
ROBBINS H                M2CWITNEY 219597
HARRISON C               F1AABINGDON 2123
BROWN M.L                M4BWANTAGE 416
```

7.4 REPORT GENERATION

There are two methods for producing printed reports from a COBOL program. The first method uses an optional feature of the COBOL language known as *Report Writer*. However, in the implementation of a COBOL compiler the Report Writer module is regarded as not part of the *high* subset of the language. For this reason it is not a common feature of a COBOL compiler and will not be considered here.

The second method uses the techniques already discussed. To illustrate this method the MEMBERS–FILE and CLUB–NOTICE files described in section 6.7 will be used. The members file was already created in the last section.

7.4.1 Problem

Read the MEMBERS–FILE and create a report file called CLUB–NOTICE containing all the records of MEMBERS–FILE. The layout of the CLUB–NOTICE report file is illustrated in figure 6.5.

7.4.2 Design

Functions List.
1. Open files.
2. Close files.
3. Read file.
4. Write record.
5. Stop.
6. Move record–1–ws for output.
7. Move record–2–ws for output.
8. Move record–3–ws for output.
9. Move spaces for output.
10. Format name.
11. Format league.
12. Format telephone number.

Conditions List.
1. Not end of file.

Schematic Logic.

```
File–seq
    do 1,3,6,4,7,4,8,4,9,4
    Input–iter while 1
        do 10,11,12,4,3
    Input–end
    do 2,5
File–end
```

7.4.3 Coding.

```
(0001)          IDENTIFICATION DIVISION.
(0002)          PROGRAM-ID. C743.
(0003)          ENVIRONMENT DIVISION.
(0004)          INPUT-OUTPUT SECTION.
(0005)          FILE-CONTROL.
(0006)              SELECT MEMBERS-FILE ASSIGN TO PFMS.
(0007)              SELECT CLUB-NOTICE ASSIGN TO PFMS.
(0008)          DATA DIVISION.
(0009)          FILE SECTION.
(0010)          FD MEMBERS-FILE
(0011)              LABEL RECORDS ARE STANDARD
(0012)              VALUE OF FILE-ID IS "FILE01".
(0013)          01 RECORD-1.
(0014)              02 NAME PIC X(30).
(0015)              02 SEX PIC A.
(0016)              02 LEAGUE.
(0017)                  03 DIV PIC 9.
(0018)                  03 BOX PIC A.
(0019)              02 TELE-NO PIC X(15).
(0020)          FD CLUB-NOTICE
(0021)              LABEL RECORDS ARE STANDARD
(0022)              VALUE OF FILE-ID IS "FILE02".
(0023)          01 REPORT-OUT.
(0024)              02 FILLER PIC X.
(0025)              02 LINE-IMAGE PIC X(119).
(0026)          WORKING-STORAGE SECTION.
(0027)          01 RECORD-1-WS.
(0028)              02 FILLER PIC X(24) VALUE IS SPACES.
(0029)              02 FILLER PIC X(22) VALUE IS "SQUASH CLUB MEMBERSHIP".
```

(program continued)

```
(0030)        01 RECORD-2-WS.
(0031)           02 FILLER PIC X(4) VALUE IS "NAME".
(0032)           02 FILLER PIC X(27) VALUE IS SPACES.
(0033)           02 FILLER PIC X(6) VALUE IS "LEAGUE".
(0034)           02 FILLER PIC X(12) VALUE IS SPACES.
(0035)           02 FILLER PIC X(16) VALUE IS "TELEPHONE NUMBER".
(0036)        01 RECORD-3-WS.
(0037)           02 FILLER PIC X(31) VALUE IS SPACES.
(0038)           02 FILLER PIC X(12) VALUE IS "DIVISION BOX".
(0039)        01 RECORD-4-WS.
(0040)           02 NAME-WS PIC X(30).
(0041)           02 FILLER PIC X VALUE IS SPACE.
(0042)           02 DIV-WS PIC 9.
(0043)           02 FILLER PIC X(8) VALUE IS SPACES.
(0044)           02 BOX-WS PIC A.
(0045)           02 FILLER PIC X(8) VALUE IS SPACES.
(0046)           02 TELE-NO-WS PIC X(15).
(0047)        01 PARAMETER.
(0048)           02 E-O-F PIC 9 VALUE IS ZERO.
(0049)        PROCEDURE DIVISION.
(0050)        FILE-SEQ.
(0051)           OPEN INPUT MEMBERS-FILE
(0052)                OUTPUT CLUB-NOTICE.
(0053)           READ MEMBERS-FILE.

              * print headings

(0054)           MOVE RECORD-1-WS TO LINE-IMAGE.
(0055)           WRITE REPORT-OUT AFTER ADVANCING PAGE.
(0056)           MOVE RECORD-2-WS TO LINE-IMAGE
(0057)           WRITE REPORT-OUT AFTER ADVANCING 2 LINES.
(0058)           MOVE RECORD-3-WS TO LINE-IMAGE.
(0059)           WRITE REPORT-OUT AFTER ADVANCING 1 LINE.
(0060)           MOVE SPACES TO LINE-IMAGE.
(0061)           WRITE REPORT-OUT AFTER ADVANCING 1 LINE.

              * print body of report

(0062)        INPUT-ITER.
(0063)           IF E-O-F NOT = 0 GO TO INPUT-END.
(0064)              MOVE NAME TO NAME-WS.
(0065)              MOVE DIV TO DIV-WS.
(0066)              MOVE BOX TO BOX-WS.
(0067)              MOVE TELE-NO TO TELE-NO-WS.
(0068)              MOVE RECORD-4-WS TO LINE-IMAGE.
(0069)              WRITE REPORT-OUT AFTER ADVANCING 1 LINE.
(0070)              READ MEMBERS-FILE AT END MOVE 1 TO E-O-F.
(0071)           GO TO INPUT-ITER.
(0072)        INPUT-END.
(0073)           CLOSE MEMBERS-FILE
(0074)                 CLUB-NOTICE.
(0075)           STOP RUN.
(0076)        FILE-END.
```

7.4.4 Comments

The reader will notice from the program listing that two different READ statements have been used. The initial READ statement does not contain the AT END option, whereas the READ statement embedded within the loop does contain the option. Having created the MEMBERS–FILE in the last example the author has assumed that there is at least one record in the file, therefore, the *end–of–file* record will not be read by the initial READ statement.

In catering for the empty file situation the initial READ statement would contain the AT END option. A statement such as:

READ MEMBERS–FILE AT END DISPLAY
"** MEMBERS–FILE EMPTY **",
GO TO INPUT–END.

would be written to inform the operator of the error, close the files and stop the execution of the program.

The GO TO statement violates the manner in which GO TO's have been used in selections and repetitions. Here it is not the controlled use of a GO TO but a haphazard branch to another part of the program code. The use of GO TO's in this manner will be discussed towards the end of the book under the heading of *backtracking*.

In printing the various report headings it has been necessary to use both a MOVE statement and a WRITE statement. The FROM option associated with the WRITE statement has not been used here since it would have the effect of moving, say, RECORD–1–WS to REPORT–OUT and storing the first character of the line in the area reserved for the paper control character. Thus all of the output would be shifted left by one character position.

The output of a blank line is possible by moving spaces to the output record and then writing this record.

Since this program is meant to produce a report the reader may be puzzled by the SELECT clause in line (0007). Here the report is assigned to the disc. system, implying that it will be stored on a disc as a serial data file. The reason for doing this is because the system used to run the example programs is a time-sharing system and no one user is allowed to have total control over the printer through commands in a user's program. In a batch entry system line (0007) would be coded as:

SELECT CLUB–NOTICE ASSIGN TO PRINTER.

The user can obtain a printed copy of the report that is stored on disc by *spooling* a copy of a file to the printer.

7.4.5 Results

SQUASH CLUB MEMBERSHIP

NAME	LEAGUE DIVISION BOX		TELEPHONE NUMBER
STEVENSON G.R	3	A	LECHLADE 194
O'FLINN P	4	B	CHOLSEY 5259
LOWE J.C	1	C	BICESTER 4268
STOTT P.A	1	A	WALLINGFORD 837
BARRETT G.C	1	B	STANDLAKE 87936
ALLEN D.J	2	B	ICKFORD 947361
OSTLE D.M	2	C	CLANFIELD 4932
TILBURY C	3	C	DIDCOT 9873
FOX M	1	C	FREELAND 93412
JONES N.L	4	A	WITNEY 192
COLLINS P	3	B	THAME 94287
GILLOT D	1	C	HARWELL 6829
LONG C	1	A	CUMNOR 863
MCDOUGALL G	3	B	ABINGDON 81773
DIMITRIOU B	3	C	OXFORD 235
ELWIN J	1	A	PORTWAY 14732
PEPPER D	2	A	LONGWORTH 6498
GUNASEKARA A	1	A	HARWELL 2124
RODRIGUEZ-BACHILLER A	2	B	FRITWELL 916
THOMAS K	1	C	DIDCOT 48973
WARD S	3	C	DIDCOT 27918
ANDERSON T	3	C	WITNEY 817963
HILL L	3	C	UFFINGTON 36782
WALTON B	1	B	TACKLEY 1134
WINTER M	2	A	BURFORD 223
KEABLE R	2	A	CHOLSEY 1414

```
GODDARD P            1      A     CROWMARSH 81793
MAY N                1      C     DIDCOT 98149
EDWARDS E            2      C     WOODSTOCK 931
PRISCOTT M           2      C     WITNEY 419523
ALLEN P              3      B     WANTAGE 9696
JACKSON J            3      B     THAME 8137
WINSLET M.J          3      B     LECHLADE 2130
CLAYTON A            4      C     ICKFORD 326
BLACK A              4      C     FILKINS 159
EAST W               4      A     CHILDREY 4267
LYLE S               1      B     GT MILTON 71436
SANDERS M.A          4      C     WOODSTOCK 1136
DANIELS J            3      C     OXFORD 713
ROBBINS H            2      C     WITNEY 219597
HARRISON C           1      A     ABINGDON 2123
BROWN M.L            4      B     WANTAGE 416
```

7.5 SERIAL FILES TO SEQUENTIAL FILES

The information given in the report of section 7.4.5 was not very well presented. This was due to the data on the serial MEMBERS–FILE not being sorted into any pre-determined order. It would be possible to use the same program, with minor modifications, to produce two club reports. The first report would contain a list of members split into two groups – male and female, and have the members names listed alphabetically within each group. The second report would contain a list of members split into their respective league divisions and boxes. Within each box the members names would be listed alphabetically.

To produce the first report the original serial MEMBERS–FILE would need to be sorted on sex as the primary key, and name as the secondary key.

The second report requires that the original serial file is sorted again, this time on division as the primary key, box as the secondary key and name as the tertiary key.

The operation of sorting a serial file on defined keys must by definition result in the file being converted to a sequential file.

7.5.1 The Sort Verb

The function of the SORT statement is to create a sort file by transferring records from another file, sorts the records in the sort file on a set of specified keys, and in the final phase of the sort operation makes available each record of the sort file, in sorted order, to an output file.

A simplified format for the SORT statement is:

SORT file–name–1 $\left\{ \text{ON} \left\{ \begin{array}{l} \textbf{ASCENDING} \\ \textbf{DESCENDING} \end{array} \right\} \text{KEY } \{\text{data–name–1}\} \ldots \right\} \ldots$
USING file–name–2
GIVING file–name–3.

The file to be sorted is file–name–2, the sorted file is file–name–3. Both files are described in the FILE SECTION in the normal manner. The SORT statement uses a work–file file–name–1 that must be described under a SD entry in the FILE SECTION. The SD entry does not contain any of the options available in a FD entry. The format of file–name–1, file–name–2 and file–name–3 must be identical. The keys used in sorting the file must be described under the SD entry of file–name–1. Before the SORT statement can be used file–name–1, file–name–2 and file–name–3 must be closed. The SORT statement will perform all the necessary opening and closing of these files during its execution.

107

The following skeletal COBOL code illustrates how the program of section 7.4.3 can be modified so that the original serial MEMBERS–FILE can be sorted and suitable reports printed.

```
IDENTIFICATION  DIVISION.

ENVIRONMENT  DIVISION.


    SELECT  MEMBERS–FILE–SD  ASSIGN  TO  PFMS.
    SELECT  MEMBERS–FILE–UNSORTED  ASSIGN  TO  PFMS.
    SELECT  MEMBERS–FILE  ASSIGN  TO  PFMS.

DATA  DIVISION.
FILE  SECTION.
SD  MEMBERS–FILE–SD.
01 RECORD–SD.
    02 NAME–SD  PIC  X(30).
    02 SEX–SD  PIC  A.
    02 LEAGUE–SD.
        03 DIV–SD  PIC 9.
        03 BOX–SD  PIC  A.
    02 FILLER  PIC  X(15).
FD  MEMBERS–FILE–UNSORTED
    LABEL  RECORDS  ARE  STANDARD
    VALUE  OF  FILE–ID  IS  "FILE01".
01 RECORD–1.
    02 FILLER  PIC  X(48).
FD  MEMBERS–FILE
    LABEL  RECORDS  ARE  STANDARD
    VALUE  OF  FILE–ID  IS  "FILE03".
01 RECORD–3.
    02 NAME  PIC  X(30).
    02 SEX  PIC  A.
    02 LEAGUE.
        03 DIV  PIC  9.
        03 BOX  PIC  A.
    02 TELE–NO  PIC  X(15).


WORKING–STORAGE  SECTION.



PROCEDURE  DIVISION.
SORT–PROCEDURE.
        SORT  MEMBERS–FILE–SD
            ON  DESCENDING  KEY  SEX–SD
            ON  ASCENDING  KEY  NAME–SD
        USING  MEMBERS–FILE–UNSORTED
        GIVING  MEMBERS–FILE.
```

FILE SEQ.

——————
——————
——————

FILE–END.

To produce the second report described only the paragraph SORT–PROCEDURE need to be changed, and the program re-compiled and executed.

The modification would be:

```
SORT  MEMBERS–FILE–SD
    ON  ASCENDING  KEY DIV-SD, BOX-SD, NAME-SD
USING  MEMBERS–FILE–UNSORTED
GIVING  MEMBERS–FILE.
```

7.5.2 Comment

The original serial MEMBERS–FILE had the external filename FILE01. By changing the internal filename to MEMBERS–FILE–UNSORTED it was possible to sort this file and store the sorted file as a new file with the filename MEMBERS–FILE having an external filename of FILE03. Thus any further reference to MEMBERS–FILE in the PROCEDURE DIVISION then referred to the sorted version of the file and no further modification to the filenames in the PROCEDURE DIVISION was necessary.

7.5.3 Coding.

The skeletal COBOL code described in section 7.5.1 has been incorporated into the program of section 7.4.3 so that the report will contain records that are sorted on sex as the primary key, and members name as secondary key.

```
(0001)       IDENTIFICATION DIVISION.
(0002)       PROGRAM-ID. C753.
(0003)       ENVIRONMENT DIVISION.
(0004)       INPUT-OUTPUT SECTION.
(0005)       FILE-CONTROL.
(0006)           SELECT MEMBERS-FILE-SD ASSIGN TO PFMS.
(0007)           SELECT MEMBERS-FILE-UNSORTED ASSIGN TO PFMS.
(0008)           SELECT MEMBERS-FILE ASSIGN TO PFMS.
(0009)           SELECT CLUB-NOTICE ASSIGN TO PFMS.
(0010)       DATA DIVISION.
(0011)       FILE SECTION.
(0012)       SD MEMBERS-FILE-SD.
(0013)       01 RECORD-SD.
(0014)           02 NAME-SD PIC X(30).
(0015)           02 SEX-SD PIC A.
(0016)           02 LEAGUE-SD.
(0017)               03 DIV-SD PIC 9.
(0018)               03 BOX-SD PIC A.
(0019)           02 FILLER PIC X(15).
(0020)       FD MEMBERS-FILE-UNSORTED
(0021)           LABEL RECORDS ARE STANDARD
(0022)           VALUE OF FILE-ID IS "FILE01".
(0023)       01 RECORD-1.
(0024)           02 FILLER PIC X(48).
```

(program continued)

```
(0025)          FD MEMBERS-FILE
(0026)              LABEL RECORDS ARE STANDARD
(0027)              VALUE OF FILE-ID IS "FILE03".
(0028)          01 RECORD-3.
(0029)              02 NAME PIC X(30).
(0030)              02 SEX PIC A.
(0031)              02 LEAGUE.
(0032)                03 DIV PIC 9.
(0033)                03 BOX PIC A.
(0034)              02 TELE-NO PIC X(15).
(0035)          FD CLUB-NOTICE
(0036)              LABEL RECORDS ARE STANDARD
(0037)              VALUE OF FILE-ID IS "FILE02".
(0038)          01 REPORT-OUT.
(0039)              02 FILLER PIC X.
(0040)              02 LINE-IMAGE PIC X(119).
(0041)          WORKING-STORAGE SECTION.
(0042)          01 RECORD-1-WS.
(0043)              02 FILLER PIC X(24) VALUE IS SPACES.
(0044)              02 FILLER PIC X(22) VALUE IS "SQUASH CLUB MEMBERSHIP".
(0045)          01 RECORD-2-WS.
(0046)              02 FILLER PIC X(4) VALUE IS "NAME".
(0047)              02 FILLER PIC X(27) VALUE IS SPACES.
(0048)              02 FILLER PIC X(6) VALUE IS "LEAGUE".
(0049)              02 FILLER PIC X(12) VALUE IS SPACES.
(0050)              02 FILLER PIC X(16) VALUE IS "TELEPHONE NUMBER".
(0051)          01 RECORD-3-WS.
(0052)              02 FILLER PIC X(31) VALUE IS SPACES.
(0053)              02 FILLER PIC X(12) VALUE IS "DIVISION BOX".
(0054)          01 RECORD-4-WS.
(0055)              02 NAME-WS PIC X(30).
(0056)              02 FILLER PIC X VALUE IS SPACE.
(0057)              02 DIV-WS PIC 9.
(0058)              02 FILLER PIC X(8) VALUE IS SPACES.
(0059)              02 BOX-WS PIC A.
(0060)              02 FILLER PIC X(8) VALUE IS SPACES.
(0061)              02 TELE-NO-WS PIC X(15).
(0062)          01 PARAMETER.
(0063)              02 E-O-F PIC 9 VALUE IS ZERO.
(0064)          PROCEDURE DIVISION.
(0065)          SORT-PROCEDURE.
(0066)              SORT MEMBERS-FILE-SD
(0067)                  ON DESCENDING KEY SEX-SD
(0068)                  ON ASCENDING KEY NAME-SD
(0069)              USING MEMBERS-FILE-UNSORTED
(0070)              GIVING MEMBERS-FILE.
(0071)          FILE-SEQ.
(0072)              OPEN INPUT MEMBERS-FILE
(0073)                   OUTPUT CLUB-NOTICE.
(0074)              READ MEMBERS-FILE.

              * print headings

(0075)              MOVE RECORD-1-WS TO LINE-IMAGE.
(0076)              WRITE REPORT-OUT AFTER ADVANCING PAGE.
(0077)              MOVE RECORD-2-WS TO LINE-IMAGE
(0078)              WRITE REPORT-OUT AFTER ADVANCING 2 LINES.
(0079)              MOVE RECORD-3-WS TO LINE-IMAGE.
(0080)              WRITE REPORT-OUT AFTER ADVANCING 1 LINE.
(0081)              MOVE SPACES TO LINE-IMAGE.
(0082)              WRITE REPORT-OUT AFTER ADVANCING 1 LINE.

              * print body of file

(0083)          INPUT-ITER.
(0084)              IF E-O-F NOT = 0 GO TO INPUT-END.
(0085)              MOVE NAME TO NAME-WS.
(0086)              MOVE DIV TO DIV-WS.
(0087)              MOVE BOX TO BOX-WS.
(0088)              MOVE TELE-NO TO TELE-NO-WS.
```

(program continued)

110

```
(0089)              MOVE RECORD-4-WS TO LINE-IMAGE.
(0090)              WRITE REPORT-OUT AFTER ADVANCING 1 LINE.
(0091)              READ MEMBERS-FILE AT END MOVE 1 TO E-O-F.
(0092)          GO TO INPUT-ITER.
(0093)      INPUT-END.
(0094)          CLOSE MEMBERS-FILE
(0095)               CLUB-NOTICE.
(0096)          STOP RUN.
(0097)      FILE-END.
```

7.5.4 Results

Report with file sorted on sex and name. The alphabetical listing of names
appears twice, once for males from ALLEN D.J. through to WINTER M, and
once for females for BARRETT G.C. through to THOMAS K.

SQUASH CLUB MEMBERSHIP

NAME	LEAGUE DIVISION BOX		TELEPHONE NUMBER
ALLEN D.J	2	B	ICKFORD 947361
ALLEN P	3	B	WANTAGE 9696
ANDERSON T	3	C	WITNEY 817963
BLACK A	4	C	FILKINS 159
BROWN N.L	4	B	WANTAGE 416
CLAYTON A	4	C	ICKFORD 326
DANIELS J	3	C	OXFORD 713
DIMITRIOU B	3	C	OXFORD 235
EDWARDS E	2	C	WOODSTOCK 931
FOX M	1	C	FREELAND 93412
GODDARD P	1	A	CROWMARSH 81793
GUNASEKARA A	1	A	HARWELL 2124
HILL L	3	C	UFFINGTON 36782
JACKSON J	3	B	THAME 8137
LONG C	1	A	CUMNOR 863
LYLE S	1	B	GT MILTON 71436
O'FLINN P	4	B	CHOLSEY 3259
OSTLE D.M	2	C	CLANFIELD 4932
PEPPER D	2	A	LONGWORTH 6498
ROBBINS H	2	C	WITNEY 219597
SANDERS M.A	4	C	WOODSTOCK 1136
STEVENSON G.R	3	A	LECHLADE 194
STOTT P.A	1	A	WALLINGFORD 837
TILBURY C	3	C	DIDCOT 9873
WALTON B	1	B	TACKLEY 1134
WARD S	3	C	DIDCOT 27918
WINSLET M.J	3	B	LECHLADE 2130
WINTER M	2	A	BURFORD 223
BARRETT G.C	1	B	STANDLAKE 87936
COLLINS P	3	B	THAME 94287
EAST W	4	A	CHILDREY 4267
ELWIN J	1	A	PORTWAY 14732
GILLOT D	1	C	HARWELL 6829
HARRISON C	1	A	ABINGDON 2123
JONES N.L	4	A	WITNEY 192
KEABLE R	2	A	CHOLSEY 1414
LOWE J.C	1	C	BICESTER 4268
MAY N	1	C	DIDCOT 98149
MCDOUGALL G	3	B	ABINGDON 81773
PRISCOTT M	2	C	WITNEY 419523
RODRIGUEZ-BACHILLER A	2	B	FRITWELL 916
THOMAS K	1	C	DIDCOT 48973

Report with file sorted on division, box and name.

SQUASH CLUB MEMBERSHIP

NAME	LEAGUE DIVISION	BOX	TELEPHONE NUMBER
ELWIN J	1	A	PORTWAY 14732
GODDARD P	1	A	CROWMARSH 81793
GUNASEKARA A	1	A	HARWELL 2124
HARRISON C	1	A	ABINGDON 2123
LONG C	1	A	CUMNOR 853
STOTT P.A	1	A	WALLINGFORD 837
BARRETT G.C	1	B	STANDLAKE 87936
LYLE S	1	B	GT MILTON 71436
WALTON B	1	B	TACKLEY 1134
FOX M	1	C	FREELAND 93412
GILLOT D	1	C	HARWELL 6829
LOWE J.C	1	C	BICESTER 4269
MAY N	1	C	DIDCOT 98149
THOMAS K	1	C	DIDCOT 48973
KEABLE R	2	A	CHOLSEY 1414
PEPPER D	2	A	LONGWORTH 6498
WINTER M	2	A	BURFORD 223
ALLEN D.J	2	B	ICKFORD 947361
RODRIGUEZ-BACHILLER A	2	B	FRITWELL 916
EDWARDS E	2	C	WOODSTOCK 931
OSTLE D.M	2	C	CLANFIELD 4932
PRISCOTT M	2	C	WITNEY 419523
ROBBINS M	2	C	WITNEY 219597
STEVENSON G.R	3	A	LECHLADE 194
ALLEN P	3	B	WANTAGE 9696
COLLINS P	3	B	THAME 94287
JACKSON J	3	B	THAME 8137
MCDOUGALL G	3	B	ABINGDON 81773
WINSLET M.J	3	B	LECHLADE 2130
ANDERSON T	3	C	WITNEY 817963
DANIELS J	3	C	OXFORD 713
DIMITRIOU B	3	C	OXFORD 235
HILL L	3	C	UFFINGTON 36782
TILBURY C	3	C	DIDCOT 9873
WARD S	3	C	DIDCOT 27918
EAST W	4	A	CHILDREY 4267
JONES N.L	4	A	WITNEY 192
BROWN M.L	4	B	WANTAGE 416
O'FLINN P	4	B	CHOLSEY 3259
BLACK A	4	C	FILKINS 159
CLAYTON A	4	C	ICKFORD 326
SANDERS M.A	4	C	WOODSTOCK 1136

7.6 QUESTIONS *(answers begin on page 343)*

7.6.1 Comment on the following segment of code.

```
PROCEDURE  DIVISION.
P1.
    OPEN  INPUT  FILE-X.
    OPEN  OUTPUT  FILE-Y.
P2.
    READ  FILE-Y  AT  END  GO  TO  P3.
    MOVE  FILE-Y  TO  FILE-X.
    WRITE  FILE-X.
    GO  TO  P2.
P3.
```

7.6.2 If RECORD–1 is used to define the format of a record in FILE–X comment on the following segment of code.

```
PROCEDURE  DIVISION.
P1.
   OPEN  OUTPUT  FILE–X.
P2.
   ACCEPT  RECORD–1.
   IF  RECORD–1  =  "END"  GO  TO  P3.
   WRITE  RECORD–1  AFTER  ADVANCING  2  LINES.
   GO  TO  P2.
P3.
   OPEN  INPUT  FILE–X.
   READ  RECORD–1.
```

7.6.3 If the first three fields of a record for a factory employee are:

```
FULL–NAME  PIC  X(20)
SEX  PIC  A
DATE–OF–BIRTH  PIC  9(6)  presented as  DDMMYY
```

comment on the following SORT statements.

```
SORT  EMPLOYEE–FILE  ON  ASCENDING  KEY
FULL–NAME,  SEX
USING  DATA–FILE–1,  GIVING  DATA–FILE–2.

SORT  EMPLOYEE–FILE  ON  ASCENDING  KEY
DATE–OF–BIRTH
USING  DATA–FILE–1,  GIVING  DATA–FILE–3.
```

†**7.6.4** Create a serial file that contains the details of items of stock in a brewery. Records are of fixed length and contain the following details.

```
STOCK–NUMBER  PIC  X(5)
DESCRIPTION  PIC  X(20)
STOCK–QUANTITY  PIC  999
UNIT–PRICE  PIC  99V99
```

Assume that the records are **not** in STOCK–NUMBER order when they are input into the computer system. Limit the number of test data records to twenty in this question.

Write a complete COBOL program to input and store the test data. Use a program design structure similar to that described in section 7.3.1 as a basis to the PROCEDURE DIVISION coding.

†**7.6.5** Write a complete COBOL program to sort the file created in question 7.6.4 on STOCK–NUMBER as an ascending primary key. The name of the sorted file is STOCK–SORTED.

In the second part of the program read the STOCK–SORTED file and output the following report to a file called REPORT–OUT. Use a program design structure similar to that described in section 7.4.2 as a basis to coding the PROCEDURE DIVISION.

STOCK NO	DESCRIPTION	QUANTITY	PRICE
91189	BEST BITTER BRLS	200	3,158·20
92258	MASTER BREW MILD	40	120·50
9238X	STOCK ALE	125	1,320·80
		TOTAL VALUE	£4,599·50

(Title: STOCK REPORT)

7.6.6 A serial file is to be created containing the details of telephone subscribers. Records are of fixed length and contain the following details.

```
FULL–NAME
   SURNAME  PIC  X(19)
   INITIALS
      INIT–1  PIC  A
      INIT–2  PIC  A
   TITLE  PIC  A(4)
ADDRESS
   ROAD  PIC  X(20)
   TOWN  PIC  X(20)
   POSTCODE  PIC  X(8)
TELE–NUMBER  PIC  X(20)
PREV–READ  PIC  9(6)
PRES–READ  PIC  9(6)
```

Invent a minimum of twenty test data records containing the fields described.

Write a complete COBOL program to input and store the test data. Use a program design structure similar to that described in section 7.3.1 as a basis to the PROCEDURE DIVISION coding.

7.6.7 Write a complete COBOL program to sort the file created in question 7.6.6 and output a report on the contents of the sorted file. The file should be sorted on TOWN as a primary key and SURNAME as a secondary key. Both keys are sorted in ascending order. Use a program design structure similar to that described in section 7.4.2 as a basis to coding the PROCEDURE DIVISION.

The layout of the report is as follows. Units used is the difference between PRES–READ and PREV–READ.

NAME	TELEPHONE NUMBER	UNITS USED
MR F.G. BLOGGS	ABINGDON 41937	2,719
MISS J. BROWN	ABINGDON 21483	645
MRS P.S. ALLEN	BLADON 413	384

(Title: SUBSCRIBERS)

†**7.6.8** A serial file is to be created containing the details of invoice payments against customer orders. Records are of fixed length and contain the following details.

```
CUST–AC  PIC  X(6)
INV–NOS  PIC  X(6)
DATE–OF–INVOICE
   DAY–DATE  PIC  99
   MONTH–DATE  PIC  99
   YEAR–DATE  PIC  99
AMOUNT–RECEIVED  PIC  9(6)V99
AMOUNT–OF–INVOICE  PIC  9(6)V99
```

Invent a minimum of twenty test data records containing the fields described. Assume that there is only one invoice payment per customer. Write a complete COBOL program to input and store the test data. Use a program design structure similar to that described in section 7.3.1 as a basis to the PROCEDURE DIVISION coding.

†**7.6.9** Write a complete COBOL program to sort the file created in question 7.6.8 on DATE–OF–INVOICE using YEAR–DATE as primary key, MONTH–DATE as secondary key and DAY–DATE as tertiary key. The three keys are sorted in ascending order. The name of the sorted file is ACCOUNT–DATE.

Within the same program sort the original data file again using CUST–AC as the primary key taken in ascending order. The name of the sorted file is ACCOUNT–CUST.

In the second part of the program output two reports taken from the files ACCOUNT–DATE and ACCOUNT–CUST respectively. The format of the two reports is identical to the format of a record on the original file created in question 7.6.8.

The purpose of these two reports is for a visual verification that the original data file has been sorted correctly.

†**7.6.10** Write a complete COBOL program to read the file ACCOUNT–DATE created in question 7.6.9 and output a report using the following format.

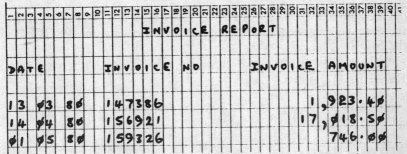

Within the same program read the file ACCOUNT–CUST and output a debtors report on those customers that still owe money on orders for goods. The format of the debtors report is as follows.

CUSTOMER AC	DATE OF INVOICE	INVOICE NO	BALANCE OWING
	DEBTORS LIST		
319874	19 07 81	351176	140.00
492113	11 12 80	129712	59.99
500618	21 03 81	219799	459.99

8 Program Structures from Data Structures

8.1 INTRODUCTION

The essence of the JSP methodology is to derive the structure of a program from the data structures used in the program. In chapter 3 it was stated that in designing structured computer programs it was necessary to consider that a series of instructions was composed from sequences, selections and repetitions. These three constructs will now be considered from the point of view of the data to be processed.

8.2 THE CONSTRUCTS

8.2.1 A Sequence

The schematic logic for a sequence could be written as:

    A–seq
      B
      C
      D
    A–end

where B, C and D are labels of components that can be **associated with functions in the functions list.** Since B, C and D in this example do not form other constructs (ie. other sequences, selections or repetitions) they are regarded as **elementary** components.

The schematic logic can be represented diagramatically.

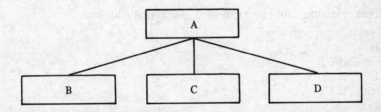

This illustrates that the sequence consists of three parts B, C and D. Each part occurs once in the **order** shown (from left to right), each time the sequence (A) itself occurs. A sequence is not denoted by any special symbol.

8.2.2 Example.

The staff of a college could be composed from administrative, academic and maintenance staff. This could be represented as a sequence in a **structure diagram.**

The structure diagram illustrates that the staff are represented in a set order, from left to right, as stated in the example.

8.2.3 A Selection

The schematic logic for a binary selection could be written as:

```
A–sel if 1
   B
A–or
   C
A–end
```

where B and C are elementary components, and 1 represents a condition from a conditions list. This schematic logic can be represented diagramatically.

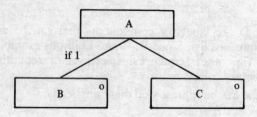

A multiple selection could be expressed in schematic logic as:

```
A–sel if 1
   B
A–or–2 if 2
   C
A–or–3 if 3
   D
A–or–4
   E
A–end
```

where B, C, D and E are elementary components and 1, 2 and 3 are conditions from a conditions list, and represented diagramatically as:

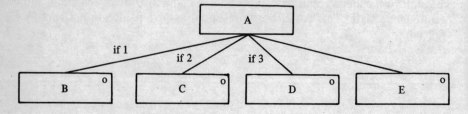

118

These examples illustrate that a selection has two or more parts (B and C for the binary selection and B, C, D, and E for the multiple selection) of which one, **and only one,** occurs once, each time the selection (A) is invoked.

The condition associated with each branch of the selection is annotated in the structure diagram. There is no need to annotate the nth selection (ie. second choice in the binary selection and fourth choice in the multiple selection) since this is taken by default. Each component in a selection is denoted by the character 'o'.

8.2.4 Example.

Staff at a college could be either part-time if they worked for less than 15 hours per week, otherwise they are regarded as full-time. This selection based on the number of hours worked in a week can be represented in a structure diagram.

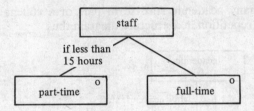

8.2.5 Example.

The last example can be modified to illustrate a multiple selection by stating that workers are classified as casual if they work less than or equal to 5 hours per week, part-time workers work less than 15 hours but greater than 5 hours per week, and full-time workers work at least 15 hours per week.

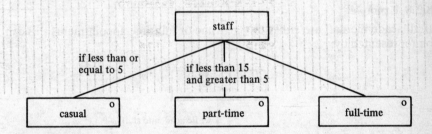

8.2.6 A Repetition

The schematic logic for a repetition could be written as:

    A–iter while 1
      B
    A–end

where B is an elementary component and 1 represents a condition from the conditions list. The schematic logic can be represented diagramatically.

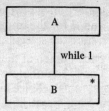

A repetition has only **one part** which occurs zero or more times, each time the repetition occurs. The condition under which the component (B) is repeated (iterated) is annotated in the diagram. The repeated component is denoted by the character '*'.

8.2.7 Example.

The fact that many academic staff form part of a college staff could be represented as a repetition in a structure diagram thus.

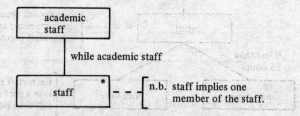

The constructs are used together to represent the structure of the data. The previous examples of staff in a college can be expanded to illustrate this point.

8.2.8 Example.

If all academic staff are either on part-time or full-time appointments this can be represented by:

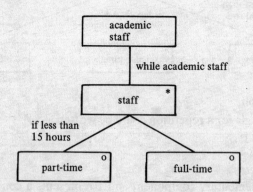

If the academic staff are divided into faculties, and each faculty consists of several departments then the structure diagram can be modified to:

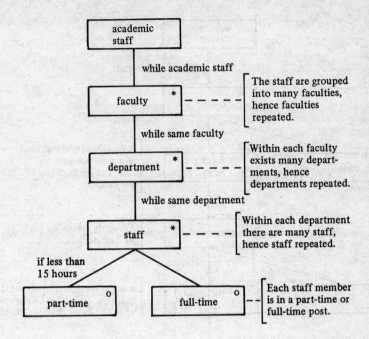

If we further consider that each faculty has a dean, and each department a head, then these staff can be incorporated into the structure diagram.

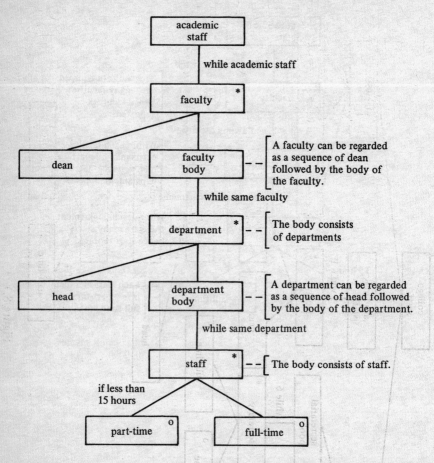

The example can be extended further if we consider the following points. The administrative staff consist of a principal, bursar and secretarial pool. Secretaries are employed on either a part-time or full-time basis. The maintenance staff consist of a caretaker, gardener, cook and ancillary staff. Ancillary staff are employed on either a casual, part-time or full-time basis.

Unless otherwise stated the staff can be regarded as being employed on a full-time basis. The structure of the college staff can be represented in the structure diagram in fig. 8.1.

Notice that the conditions have been collected together under a conditions list, and the conditions have been incorporated in a numbered format on the structure diagram.

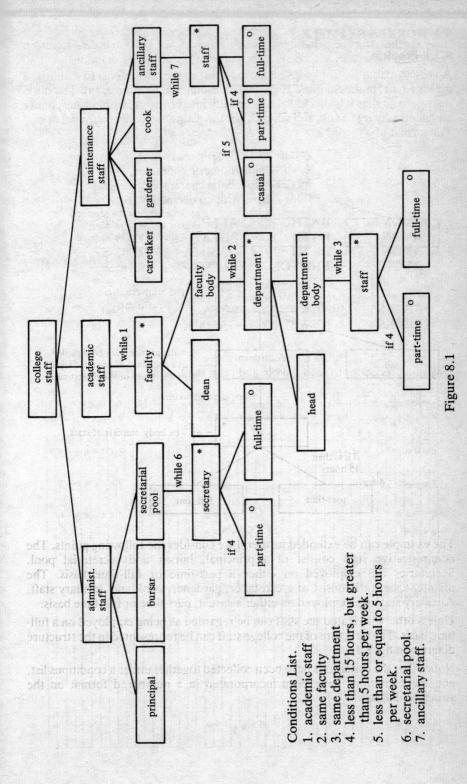

Figure 8.1

Conditions List.
1. academic staff
2. same faculty
3. same department
4. less than 15 hours, but greater than 5 hours per week.
5. less than or equal to 5 hours per week.
6. secretarial pool.
7. ancillary staff.

8.3 WORKED EXAMPLE

8.3.1 Problem

A vehicle manufacturer keeps on file the value of the sales of cars to authorised motor agents in the South of England (excluding the London area). The file is organised so that it is divided alphabetically into counties, within each county alphabetically by towns, and within each town alphabetically by model of car. The format of a record is:

> county 15 alphabetic characters,
> town 15 alphanumeric characters,
> model 8 alphabetic characters,
> sales 7 digits with no decimal places.

e.g.

AVON	BATH	ALPHA	0036100
AVON	BATH	BETA	0147900
AVON	BATH	GAMMA	0294875
AVON	BRISTOL	ALPHA	1376580
.			
.			
BERKS	NEWBURY	BETA	2100500
BERKS	NEWBURY	GAMMA	1701600
.			
.			

Design a procedure to read the file and print the following report.

```
SALES OF CARS (SOUTHERN REGION)              RECORD-1

COUNTY: AVON                                  RECORD-2

TOWN: BATH                                    RECORD-3

ALPHA                    £36,100              RECORD-4
BETA                    £147,900

TOWN: BRISTOL

ALPHA                 £1,376,580




COUNTY: BERKS

TOWN: NEWBURY

ALPHA                   526,750
```

8.3.2 Data Structures

The first stage is to draw structure diagrams for the file which is to be read, and the report that is to be printed.

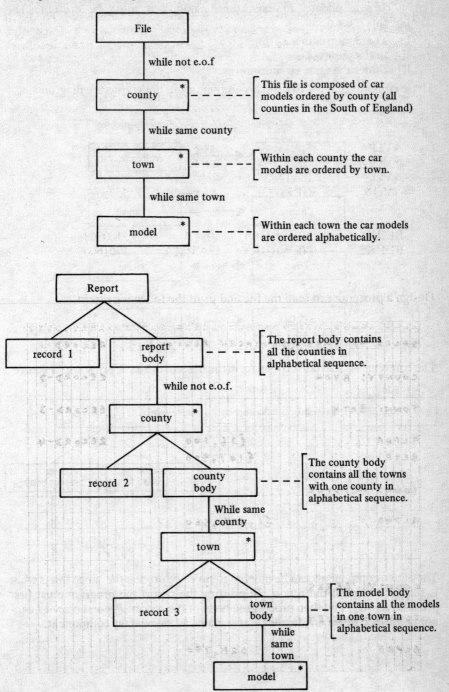

125

The second stage is to identify those components on the structure diagram of the input file that correspond to components on the structure diagram of the report.

For a correspondence to exist **three** conditions must be present. The components must occur:

I   **The same number of times.**
II   **In the same order.**
III **Under the same circumstances.**

These conditions apply to several components in both structure diagrams.

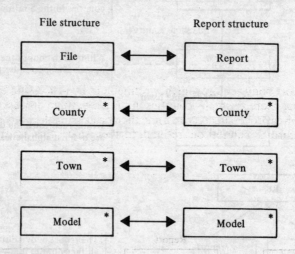

The components that correspond form the basis of the **basic program structure**

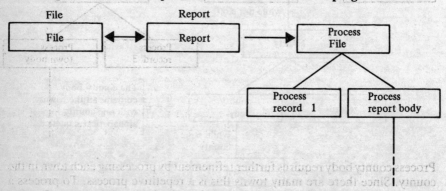

These two components can be merged to produce *process file*, since this is what is required to print the report. In printing the report the program must first *process record 1*, and then process the body of the report. *Process record 1* cannot be refined down any further and remains an **elementary** component.

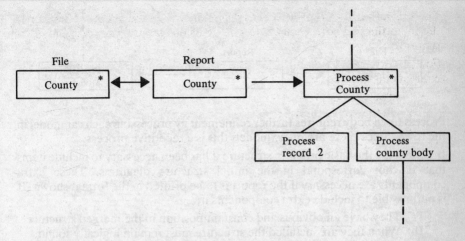

Process report body requires further refinement by processing each county in the file. Since there are many counties this is a repetitive process. To process a county requires processing record 2 and then processing the body of the county. Process record 2 cannot be refined further since this is an elementary component.

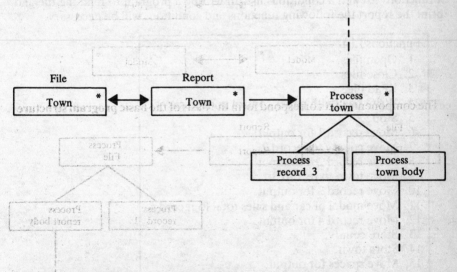

Process county body requires further refinement by processing each town in the county. Since there are many towns this is a repetitive process. To process a town requires processing record 3, and then the body of the town. Process record 3 cannot be refined further since it is an elementary component.

127

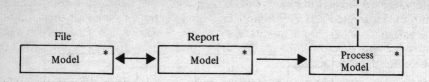

Process town body requires further refinement by processing each car model in the town. Since there are many models this is a repetitive process.

In producing the basic program structure it has been necessary to include items that do not correspond in the initial structure diagrams. These extra components are necessary if the report is to be printed in the format shown. It is permissible to include extra components if:

I   They have an obvious and constant position in the merged structure.
II   When they are included the structure must remain logically sound.

These two criteria are observed by including process record 1, process record 2 and process record 3.

8.3.3 The Functions and Conditions Lists

The third stage is identical to that described in chapter 3 for the production of a functions list and a conditions list. In writing a program to read the file and print the report the following functions and conditions will be necessary.

Functions List.
1. Open files.
2. Close files.
3. Read file.
4. Write line (with paper control as necessary).
5. Stop.
6. Move record 1 for output.
7. Move county to record 2.
8. Move record 2 for output.
9. Move town to record 3.
10. Move record 3 for output.
11. Move model of car and sales total to record 4.
12. Move record 4 for output.
13. Store county.
14. Store town.
15. Move spaces for output.

Conditions List.
1. Not end of file.
2. Same county and (1).
3. Same town and (2).

8.3.4 Detailed Program Structure.

The fourth stage is to distribute the functions to the **elementary** components of the basic program structure, and conditions to the repetitions and selections (if they exist) of the basic program structure.

However, in the distribution it will be necessary to introduce new components into the structure. The new components are to cater for functions that cannot be assigned to existing elementary components. It may also be necessary to introduce further components for selection and iteration, but this will be considered in later examples.

Remember, whenever extra components are introduced into a program structure:

I   They must have an obvious and constant position in the program structure.

II   When they are included the structure must remain logically sound.

For example a component does not exist for the functions of opening files and reading the first record in the file (initialisation) or closing the files and stopping program execution (final procedures).

For the purpose of this example the additional components will be shown in broken lines as

In the following structure diagram the word process has been abbreviated to *P*.

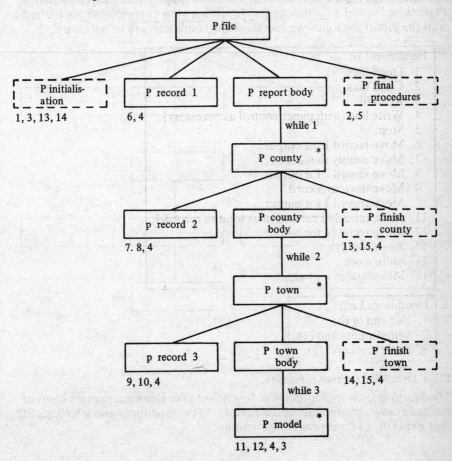

129

8.3.5 The Schematic Logic

The fifth stage in designing the computer program is to represent the detailed program structure that has been developed in the last section into a schematic logic.

Each component in the detailed program structure is allocated a letter from the alphabet. The order in which the components are labelled indicates the order in which the detailed program structure is to be traversed, and ultimately the order in which the COBOL code will be executed. The other reason for labelling the detailed program structure with letters is to serve the purpose of abbreviating the name of the component when writing the schematic logic.

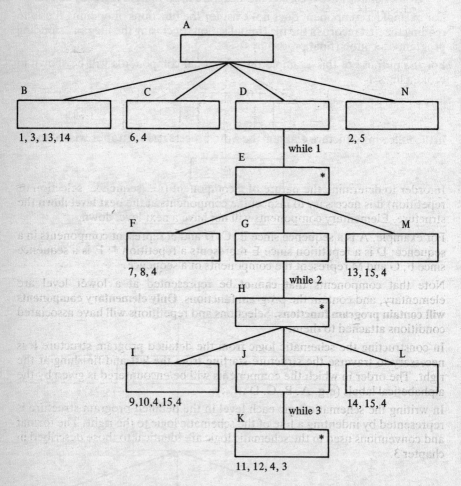

The detailed program structure has been built up in levels. For example:

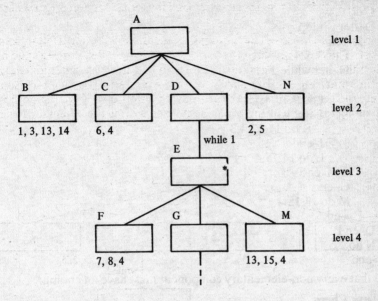

In order to determine the nature of a component (i.e. sequence, selection or repetition) it is necessary to inspect the components at the **next level down** the structure. Elementary components will **not** have a next level down.

For example, A is a sequence since B, C, D and N represent components in a sequence; D is a repetition since E represents a repetition *; E is a sequence since F, G and M represent the components of a sequence.

Note that components that **cannot** be represented at a lower level are elementary, and contain the program functions. **Only elementary components will contain program functions.** Selections and repetitions will have associated conditions attached to them.

In constructing the schematic logic from the detailed program structure it is necessary to traverse the structure starting from the left and finishing at the right. The order in which the components will be encountered is given by the alphabetical labels (e.g. A, B, C, D ......).

In writing the schematic logic each level in the detailed program structure is represented by indenting a line of the schematic logic to the right. The format and conventions used in the schematic logic are identical to those described in chapter 3.

```
A–seq
  B do 1,3,13,14
  C do 6,4
  D–iter while 1
    E–seq
      F do 7,8,4
      G–iter while 2
        H–seq
          I do 9,10,4,15,4
          J–iter while 3
            K do 11,12,4,3
          J–end
          L do 14,15,4
        H–end
      G–end
      M do 13,15,4
    E–end
  D–end
  N do 2,5
A–end
```

Notice that every non-elementary component must have an ending.

8.3.6 Desk Check

In inventing suitable test data for this solution choose data to test the conditions 1,2 and 3.

Test data:			
Avon	Bath	Alpha	458700
Avon	Bath	Beta	679500
Avon	Bristol	Alpha	1105984
Berks	Newbury	Alpha	137280

Each line of the test data is meant to represent one record in the file, thus in this example the file contains 4 records. Although this is a small number of records it is enough to test the logic behind the solution to the problem.

A table containing the functions, conditions and variables is drawn up as illustrated in chapter 3. Whenever function (4)– write line, is executed it is a good idea to write on a separate sheet of paper the output for that instruction. This will help to verify that the output is similar to that required in the original design of the report. In this example the output has been printed at the side of the desk check table to enable the reader to trace the action of the functions. Remember, each time a read file function (3) is executed it reads the **next record in the file**.

Functions	Conditions	Variables: County	Variables: Town	Output	
1,3,13,14		Avon	Bath		
6,4	1 true	Avon	Bath	SALES OF CARS	
				(SOUTHERN REGION)	
7,8,4	2 true	Avon	Bath	COUNTY: AVON	
9,10,4	3 true	Avon	Bath	TOWN: BATH	
11,12,4,3	3 true	Avon	Bath	ALPHA	428200
11,12,4,3	3 false	Avon	Bath	BETA	679500
14,15,4	2 true	Avon	Bristol		
9,10,4	3 true	Avon	Bristol	TOWN: BRISTOL	
11,12,4,3	3 false	Avon	Bristol	ALPHA	1105984
14,15,4	2 false	Avon	Newbury		
13,15,4	1 true	Berks	Newbury		
7,8,4	2 true	Berks	Newbury	COUNTY: BERKS	
9,10,4	3 true	Berks	Newbury	TOWN: NEWBURY	
11,12,4,3	3 false	Berks	Newbury	ALPHA	137280
14,15,4	2 false	Berks	–		
13,15,4	1 false	–			
2,5					

Desk Check Table with specimen output.

Note: if this output is compared with the original design it is obvious that the numbers require editing. Since this is a function of the DATA DIVISION it will not be considered here.

8.4 WORKED EXAMPLE

8.4.1 Problem

A distributor for a chain of music shops receives music cassettes from the manufacturers and distributes the cassettes to individual record shops. Each distribution of a batch of cassettes is entered as a record on a computer file. The format of each record being:

Music code, 1 character. (A – popular, B – jazz, C – classical).
Stock number, 4 digits.
Quantity, 4 digits.

At the end of each month the records in the file are sorted on music code (in ascending order) as primary key, and stock number (in ascending order) as secondary key.

e.g. A00150100
A00240055
A00240100
.
.
B01470200
B02150150
B02150025
.
.
C01280300
C01290550
.
.

Design a computer program to read the file and print the following report. The report contains the total monthly distribution for every different stock number that is stored on file. It is evident from the example that the same stock number can appear many times in the file, yet must only appear once in the report, therefore it will be necessary to keep a running total of the distribution for the same stock number.

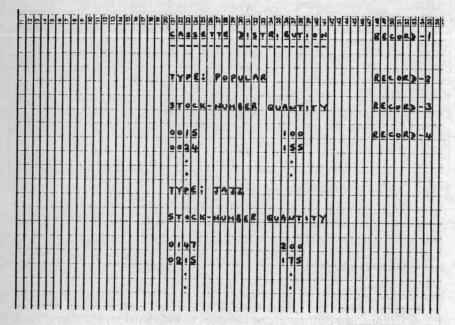

8.4.2 Data Structures

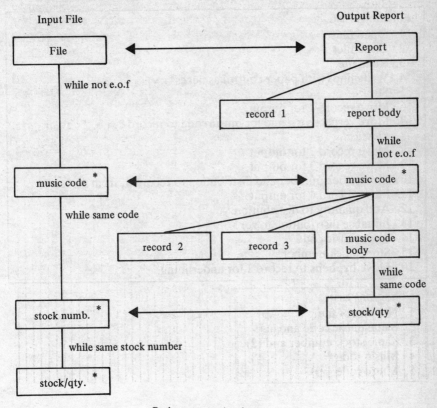

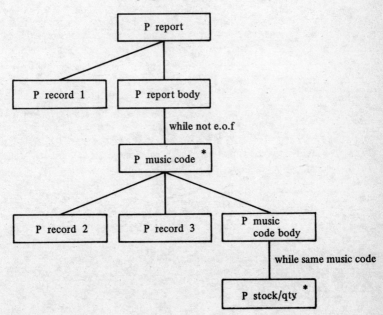

Basic program structure

8.4.3 Functions and Conditions Lists

Functions List.
1. Open files.
2. Close files.
3. Read file.
4. Write line (with paper control as necessary).
5. Stop.
6. Move record 1 for output.
7. Move respective name for music code to record 2. i.e. *Popular, jazz, classical.*
8. Move record 2 for output.
9. Move record 3 for output.
10. Move stock number and distribution to record 4, from store.
11. Move record 4 for output.
12. Add quantity to distribution.
13. Initialise distribution to zero.
14. Store music code.
15. Store stock number.
16. Move hyphens to record 1 for underlining.

Conditions List.
1. Not end of file.
2. Same music code and (1).
3. Same stock number and (2).
4. Music code = A.
5. Music code = B.

Note: The basic program structure has been expanded by including the components B, G, H, I, J, M, O, P and Q. If the functions are to be distributed over this structure then these extra components are necessary in order to process the file and produce a report in the format given. They have an obvious and constant position in the structure and the structure remains logically sound.

8.4.4 Detailed Program Structure

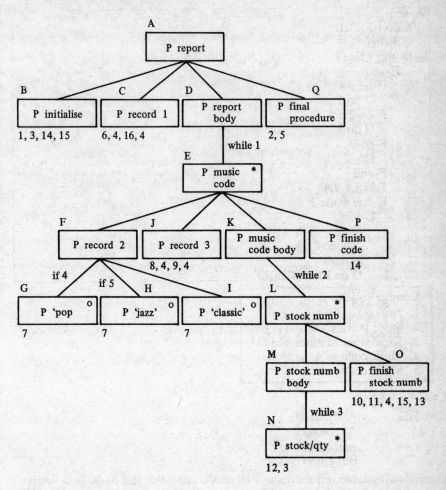

Note: The basic program structure has been expanded by including the components B, G, H, I, L, M. O, P and Q. If the functions are to be distributed over this structure then these extra components are necessary in order to process the file and produce a report in the format given. They have an obvious and constant position in the structure and the structure remains logically sound.

8.4.5 Schematic Logic

```
A–seq
   B do 1,3,14,15
   C do 6,4,16,4
   D–iter while 1
      E–seq
         F–sel if 4
            G do 7
         F–or–2 if 5
            H do 7
         F–or–3
            I do 7
         F–end
         J do 8,4,9,4
         K–iter while 2
            L–seq
               M–iter while 3
                  N do 12,3
               M–end
               O do 10,11,4,15,13
            L–end
         K–end
         P do 14
      E–end
   D–end
   Q do 2,5
A–end
```

8.4.6 Desk Check

Test data: A00150100
                    A00240055
                    A00240100
                    B01470200

The following table represents a desk check using this test data. In a similar manner to the last example specimen output has been provided so that the reader can follow the actions of the functions.

Functions	Conditions	stock number	music code	distribution		
1,3,14,15		0015	A	0		
6,4,16,4	1 true	0015	A	0	CASSETTE DISTRIBUTION	
7	4 true	0015	A	0	TYPE: POPULAR	
8,4,9,4	2 true	0015	A	0	STOCK NUMBER	QUANTITY
12,3	3 true	0015	A	100	0015	100
10,11,4,15,13	3 false	0024	A	0	0024	155
	2 true	0024	A	0		
12,3	3 true	0024	A	55	TYPE: JAZZ	
12,3	3 true	0024	A	155	STOCK NUMBER	QUANTITY
10,11,4,15,13	3 false	0147	A	0	0147	200
14	2 false	0147	B	0		
7	5 true	0147	B	0		
8,4,9,4	2 true	0147	B	0		
12,3	3 true	0147	B	1200		
10,11,4,15,13	3 false	–	B	0		
14	2 false	–		0		
2,5	1 false			0		

Desk check table with specimen output

8.5 QUESTIONS *(answers begin on page 347)*

8.5.1 A passenger train consists of a front-engine, first class carriages, a restaurant car, second class carriages, a mail van and a second engine. Draw a data structure diagram that represents the passenger train. Modify your diagram to show that the mail van may not always be part of the train, and that carriages that are second class will either have compartments or be an open carriage.

8.5.2 Draw a data structure diagram to represent a meal in a restaurant. The restaurant menu consists of:

Starter.	Soup of the day, or fruit juice, or melon.
Main course.	Beef and Yorkshire Pudding, or Lamb. Both meats are served with fresh vegetables.
Dessert.	Fresh fruit, or cheese and biscuits. Coffee (as many cups as you require!).

8.5.3. A computer file contains records with the name, sex and year of birth of all the employees in a factory. The file is sorted on sex as the primary key in ascending order, and year of birth as the secondary key in descending order. It is required to print a report on the contents of the file using the following format. Draw data structure diagrams that describe the file and the report.

```
AGE DISTRIBUTION OF STAFF                          ---- record 1
SEX: FEMALE                                        ---- record 2
YEAR OF BIRTH          NAME                         ---- record 3
1952                   HEMMINGS, P.W.              ---- record 4
1950                   BRADSHAW, S.
   .                        .

SEX: MALE
YEAR OF BIRTH          NAME
1954                   JONES, T.A.
1953                   SMITH, P.W.
1949                   ACKROYD, F.
   .                        .
```

8.5.4 A small building society keeps on file details of all its customers holding ordinary share accounts. A record contains the fields:

Branch code.
Account number.
Number of £1 shares.

The file is sorted on branch code as primary key (in ascending order), and account number as secondary key (in ascending order). It is required to print a report on the contents of the file using the following format. Draw data structure diagrams that described the file and the report.

```
THE HAPPY HOMES BUILDING SOCIETY.                          ---- record 1
DETAILS OF ORDINARY SHARE ACCOUNT CUSTOMERS.               ---- record 2
BRANCH CODE: BRAD2                                         ---- record 3
ACCOUNT NUMBER           £1 SHARES                         ---- record 4
112345                   1,000                             ---- record 5
121456                     550
   .                         .

              TOTAL    £235,643                            ---- record 6
BRANCH CODE: HAL17
ACCOUNT NUMBER           £1 SHARES
101456                   2,578
101577                   1,234
   .                         .
```

8.5.5 Identify the correspondences between the two data structures in question 8.5.3, and derive a basic program structure. Write a functions list and conditions list and derive a detailed program structure.

8.5.6 Repeat question 8.5.5 using the data structures derived in question (8.5.4).

8.5.7 Translate the following detailed program structures into schematic logic.

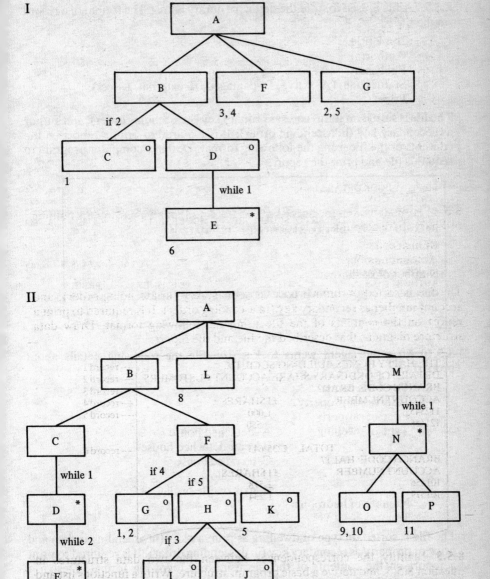

8.5.8 Translate the detailed program structure obtained in question 8.5.5 into a schematic logic. Repeat this question using the detailed program structure obtained in question 8.5.6.

† **8.5.9**   A file is used to store the details of library books. The format of a record on the file is:

> Book title.
> Author(s).
> Publisher.
> Status code. (A–active, D–damaged, E–external, L–lost).
> Price.

The file is sorted on status code as primary key (in ascending order), and author as secondary key (in ascending order). It is required to print a report on the contents of the file using the following format. Design a computer program to read this file and print the report.

LIBRARY BOOK DETAILS				record 1
STATUS: ACTIVE				record 2
AUTHOR	TITLE	PUBLISHER	PRICE	record 3
BELLINGER, C	THE ART OF SCULPTURE	MOORE-HILL	£18.75	record 4
BRAGG, L	DIFFRACTION PHYSICS	HALL	£15.50	
.				
.				
		TOTAL	£764.75	record 5
STATUS: DAMAGED				
AUTHOR	TITLE	PUBLISHER	PRICE	
COLLINS, J	THE VAMPIRE CATCHERS	MINSTER-BELL	£3.75	
.				
.				

† **8.5.10** An estate agent wants to keep on file the following details about properties.

> Vendor's name.
> Address of property.
> Price of property.
> Type of dwelling.
>
> > A–detached house
> > B–semi-detached house
> > C–terraced house
> > D–bungalow
> > E–maisonette or flat
>
> Number of bedrooms.
> Tenure.

The file is sorted on type of dwelling as primary key (in ascending order) and price of property as secondary key (in descending order). It is required to print a report on the contents of the file using the following format. Design a computer program to read this file and print the report.

HOLMES & HOLMES – ESTATE AGENTS EST. 1948					record 1
PROPERTY TYPE: DETACHED					record 2
VENDOR	ADDRESS	PRICE	BEDS	TENURE	record 3
SMITH, C	2 LIBERAL WALK	£45,675	4	F	record 4
BOWYER, F	69 CHURCH VIEW	£44,350	4	F	
SUMNER, S	3 HOPE STREET	£43,000	4	F	
.					
.					
TOTAL NUMBER OF PROPERTIES: 23					record 5
PROPERTY TYPE: SEMI-DETACHED					
VENDOR	ADDRESS	PRICE	BEDS	TENURE	
JONES, M	145 RIVER VIEW	£36,750	4	F	
EVANS, M	27 RIDGE BANK	£35,500	3	F	
.					

143

9 Worked Examples of Complete COBOL Programs

9.1 INTRODUCTION

In this chapter the two designs for the solutions to the last two examples of chapter 8 are coded in COBOL and implemented on a computer. This chapter can be regarded by the reader as a milestone in the book, since it utilises all the concepts and techniques discussed so far.

The problems and designs are re-stated for the readers convenience.

9.2 PROBLEM

A vehicle manufacturer keeps on file the value of the sales of cars to authorised motor agents in the South of England (excluding the London area). The file is organised so that it is divided alphabetically into counties, within each county alphabetically by towns, and within each town alphabetically by model of car. The format of a record is:

county 15 alphabetic characters,
town 15 alphanumeric characters,
model 8 alphabetic characters,
sales 7 digits with no decimal places.

Write a computer program to read the file and print the following report.

```
SALES OF CARS (SOUTHERN REGION)              RECORD-1

COUNTY: AVON                                 RECORD-2

TOWN: BATH                                   RECORD-3

ALPHA                    £36,100             RECORD-4
BETA                    £147,900

TOWN: BRISTOL

ALPHA                  £1,376,580


COUNTY: BERKS

TOWN: NEWBURY

ALPHA                    526,750
```

9.2.1 Program Design

The functions list, conditions list and schematic logic derived in (8.3.3) and (8.3.5) are re-stated.

```
Functions List.
  1.  Open files.
  2.  Close files.
  3.  Read file.
  4.  Write line (with paper control as necessary).
  5.  Stop.
  6.  Move record 1 for output.
  7.  Move county to record 2.
  8.  Move record 2 for output.
  9.  Move town to record 3.
 10.  Move record 3 for output.
 11.  Move model of car and sales total to record 4.
 12.  Move record 4 for output.
 13.  Store county.
 14.  Store town.
 15.  Move spaces for output.
```

```
Conditions List.
  1.  Not end of file.
  2.  Same county and (1).
  3.  Same town and (2).
```

Schematic Logic.

```
A–seq
  B do 1,3,13,14
  C do 6,4
  D iter while 1
    E seq
    F do 7,8,4
      G–iter while 2
        H–seq
          I do 9,10,4,15,4
          J–iter while 3
            K do 11,12,4,3
          J–end
          L do 14,15,4
        H–end
      G–end
      M do 13,15,4
    E–end
  D–end
  N do 2,5
A–end
```

9.2.2 COBOL Source Code (see also Appendix II)

```
(0001)          IDENTIFICATION DIVISION.
(0002)          PROGRAM-ID. C922.
(0003)          ENVIRONMENT DIVISION.
(0004)          INPUT-OUTPUT SECTION.
(0005)          FILE-CONTROL.
(0006)              SELECT SALES-DATA ASSIGN TO PFMS.
(0007)              SELECT SALES-REPORT ASSIGN TO PFMS.
(0008)          DATA DIVISION.
(0009)          FILE SECTION.
(0010)          FD SALES-DATA
(0011)              LABEL RECORDS ARE STANDARD
(0012)              VALUE OF FILE-ID 'SALES'.
(0013)          01 RECORD-LAYOUT.
(0014)              02 COUNTY PIC A(15).
(0015)              02 TOWN PIC X(15).
(0016)              02 MODEL PIC A(8).
(0017)              02 SALE PIC 9(7).
(0018)          FD SALES-REPORT
(0019)              LABEL RECORDS ARE STANDARD
(0020)              VALUE OF FILE-ID 'OUTPUT'.
(0021)          01 REPORT-OUT.
(0022)              02 FILLER PIC X.
(0023)              02 LINE-IMAGE PIC X(119).
(0024)          WORKING-STORAGE SECTION.
(0025)          01 RECORD-1-WS.
(0026)              02 FILLER PIC X(31) VALUE 'SALES OF CARS (SOUTHERN REGION)'.
(0027)          01 RECORD-2-WS.
(0028)              02 FILLER PIC X(8) VALUE 'COUNTY: '.
(0029)              02 COUNTY-WS PIC A(15).
(0030)          01 RECORD-3-WS.
(0031)              02 FILLER PIC X(6) VALUE 'TOWN: '.
(0032)              02 TOWN-WS PIC A(15).
(0033)          01 RECORD-4-WS.
(0034)              02 MODEL-WS PIC A(8).
(0035)              02 FILLER PIC X(9) VALUE SPACES.
(0036)              02 SALE-WS PIC ££,£££,££9.
(0037)          01 PARAMETERS.
(0038)              02 E-O-F PIC 9 VALUE IS ZERO.
(0039)              02 COUNTY-STORE PIC A(15).
(0040)              02 TOWN-STORE PIC X(15).
(0041)
(0042)          PROCEDURE DIVISION.
(0043)          A-SEQ.
(0044)          B.  OPEN INPUT SALES-DATA
(0045)                   OUTPUT SALES-REPORT.
(0046)              READ SALES-DATA.
(0047)              MOVE COUNTY TO COUNTY-STORE.
(0048)              MOVE TOWN TO TOWN-STORE.
(0049)          C.  MOVE RECORD-1-WS TO LINE-IMAGE.
(0050)              WRITE REPORT-OUT AFTER ADVANCING PAGE.
(0051)          D-ITER.
(0052)              IF E-O-F NOT = 0 GO TO D-END.
(0053)          E-SEQ.
(0054)          F.  MOVE COUNTY TO COUNTY-WS.
(0055)              MOVE RECORD-2-WS TO LINE-IMAGE.
(0056)              WRITE REPORT-OUT AFTER ADVANCING 2 LINES.
(0057)          G-ITER.
(0058)              IF COUNTY NOT = COUNTY-STORE OR E-O-F NOT = 0 GO TO G-END.
(0059)          H-SEQ.
(0060)          I.  MOVE TOWN TO TOWN-WS.
(0061)              MOVE RECORD-3-WS TO LINE-IMAGE.
(0062)              WRITE REPORT-OUT AFTER ADVANCING 2 LINES.
(0063)              MOVE SPACES TO LINE-IMAGE.
(0064)              WRITE REPORT-OUT AFTER ADVANCING 1 LINE.
(0065)          J-ITER.
(0066)              IF TOWN NOT = TOWN-STORE OR COUNTY NOT = COUNTY-STORE
(0067)              OR E-O-F NOT = 0 GO TO J-END.
(0068)          K.  MOVE MODEL TO MODEL-WS.
(0069)              MOVE SALE TO SALE-WS.
(0070)              MOVE RECORD-4-WS TO LINE-IMAGE.
```

(program continued)

146

```
(0071)                        WRITE REPORT-OUT AFTER ADVANCING 1 LINE.
(0072)                        READ SALES-DATA AT END MOVE 1 TO E-O-F.
(0073)                        GO TO J-ITER.
(0074)          J-END.
(0075)          L.    MOVE TOWN TO TOWN-STORE.
(0076)                MOVE SPACES TO LINE-IMAGE.
(0077)                WRITE REPORT-OUT AFTER ADVANCING 2 LINES.
(0078)          H-END.
(0079)                GO TO G-ITER.
(0080)          G-END.
(0081)          M.    MOVE COUNTY TO COUNTY-STORE.
(0082)                MOVE SPACES TO LINE-IMAGE.
(0083)                WRITE REPORT-OUT AFTER ADVANCING 2 LINES.
(0084)          E-END.
(0085)                GO TO D-ITER.
(0086)          D-END.
(0087)          N.  CLOSE SALES-DATA
(0088)                    SALES-REPORT.
(0089)              STOP RUN.
(0090)          A-END.
```

9.2.3 Example of test data file SALES.

```
        AVON          BATH          ALPHA     0036100
        AVON          BATH          BETA      0147900
        AVON          BATH          GAMMA     0294875
        AVON          BRISTOL       ALPHA     1376580
        AVON          BRISTOL       BETA      0829640
        AVON          BRISTOL       EPSILON   0507300
        AVON          BRISTOL       GAMMA     0428550
        BERKS         NEWBURY       BETA      2100500
        BERKS         NEWBURY       GAMMA     1701600
        BERKS         READING       ALPHA     0335970
        BERKS         READING       BETA      0015730
        BERKS         READING       EPSILON   0008950
```

9.2.4 Report produced from supplied test data.

```
        SALES OF CARS (SOUTHERN REGION)

        COUNTY: AVON

        TOWN: BATH

        ALPHA              £36,100
        BETA              £147,900
        GAMMA             £294,875


        TOWN: BRISTOL

        ALPHA           £1,376,580
        BETA              £829,640
        EPSILON           £507,300
        GAMMA              £42,855




        COUNTY: BERKS

        TOWN: NEWBURY

        BETA            £2,100,500
        GAMMA           £1,701,600


        TOWN: READING

        ALPHA             £335,970
        BETA               £15,730
        EPSILON             £8,950
```

147

9.2.5 Alternative Coding

The in-line or flat code that has been used to implement the design was taken from the schematic logic. If, however, the coding is taken from the detailed program structure then a hierarchical coding can be derived.

Starting at the top of the detailed program structure the code is divided into levels, corresponding to the levels of the structure. The hierarchical structure of the diagram is maintained in the code by PERFORMing **down** to the next level in the structure. Elementary items cannot be performed further, and their

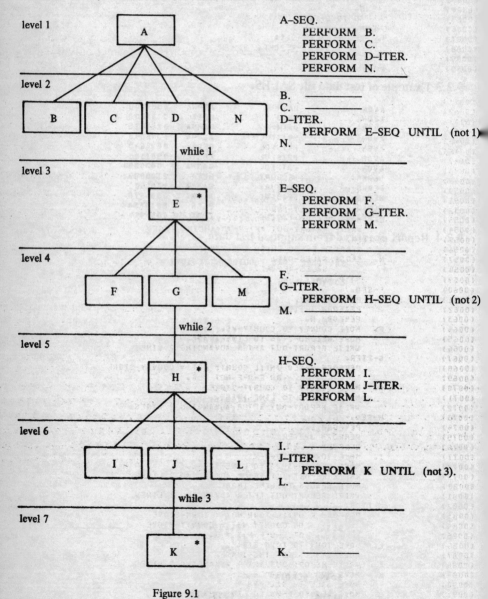

Figure 9.1

148

code is written from the respective elements of the functions list. The description of a construct (A–SEQ; D–ITER; etc) is written into paragraph names in the same manner as flat code. However, endings to the constructs (A–END; D–END; etc) are not used.

To illustrate this technique figure 9.1 shows that the detailed program structure for the last problem has been broken down into its levels and the associated *control* code has been annotated at the side of the structure. Notice that the control of iterations can be represented by the PERFORM paragraph–name UNTIL condition statement in COBOL. The condition is the **negated** condition taken from the conditions list.

The following PROCEDURE DIVISION can replace the previously flat coded PROCEDURE DIVISION and exactly the same results will be obtained when the program is run on a computer. The remaining three Divisions will remain unchanged.

```
(0041)
(0042)              PROCEDURE DIVISION.
(0043)              A-SEQ.
(0044)                  PERFORM B.
(0045)                  PERFORM C.
(0046)                  PERFORM D-ITER.
(0047)                  PERFORM N.
(0048)              B.  OPEN INPUT SALES-DATA
(0049)                       OUTPUT SALES-REPORT.
(0050)                  READ SALES-DATA.
(0051)                  MOVE COUNTY TO COUNTY-STORE.
(0052)                  MOVE TOWN TO TOWN-STORE.
(0053)              C.  MOVE RECORD-1-WS TO LINE-IMAGE.
(0054)                  WRITE REPORT-OUT AFTER ADVANCING PAGE.
(0055)              D-ITER.
(0056)                  PERFORM E-SEQ UNTIL E-O-F NOT = 0.
(0057)              N.  CLOSE SALES-DATA
(0058)                       SALES-REPORT.
(0059)                  STOP RUN.
(0060)              E-SEQ.
(0061)                  PERFORM F.
(0062)                  PERFORM G-ITER.
(0063)                  PERFORM M.
(0064)              F.  MOVE COUNTY TO COUNTY-WS.
(0065)                  MOVE RECORD-2-WS TO LINE-IMAGE.
(0066)                  WRITE REPORT-OUT AFTER ADVANCING 2 LINES.
(0067)              G-ITER.
(0068)                  PERFORM H-SEQ UNTIL COUNTY NOT = COUNTY-STORE
(0069)                               OR E-O-F NOT = 0.
(0070)              M.  MOVE COUNTY TO COUNTY-STORE
(0071)                  MOVE SPACES TO LINE-IMAGE.
(0072)                  WRITE REPORT-OUT AFTER ADVANCING 2 LINES.
(0073)              H-SEQ.
(0074)                  PERFORM I.
(0075)                  PERFORM J-ITER.
(0076)                  PERFORM L.
(0077)              I.  MOVE TOWN TO TOWN-WS.
(0078)                  MOVE RECORD-3-WS TO LINE-IMAGE.
(0079)                  WRITE REPORT-OUT AFTER ADVANCING 2 LINES.
(0080)                  MOVE SPACES TO LINE-IMAGE.
(0081)                  WRITE REPORT-OUT AFTER ADVANCING 1 LINE.
(0082)              J-ITER.
(0083)                  PERFORM K UNTIL TOWN NOT = TOWN-STORE
(0084)                             OR COUNTY NOT = COUNTY-STORE
(0085)                             OR E-O-F NOT = 0.
(0086)              L.  MOVE TOWN TO TOWN-STORE.
(0087)                  MOVE SPACES TO LINE-IMAGE.
(0088)                  WRITE REPORT-OUT AFTER ADVANCING 2 LINES.
(0089)              K.  MOVE MODEL TO MODEL-WS.
(0090)                  MOVE SALE TO SALE-WS.
(0091)                  MOVE RECORD-4-WS TO LINE-IMAGE.
(0092)                  WRITE REPORT-OUT AFTER ADVANCING 1 LINE.
(0093)                  READ SALES-DATA AT END MOVE 1 TO E-O-F.
```

9.3 PROBLEM

A distributor for a chain of music shops receives music cassettes from the manufacturer and distributes the cassettes to individual record shops. Each distribution of a batch of cassettes is entered as a record on a computer file. The format of each record being:

    music code 1 alphabetic character,
    stock number 4 digits,
    quantity 4 digits.

At the end of each month the records in the file are sorted on music code as primary key and stock number as secondary key, both keys being in ascending order.

Write a computer program to read the file and print the following report.

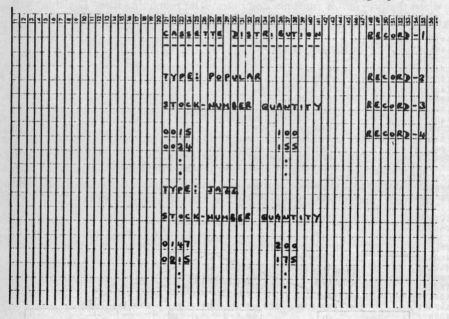

9.3.1 Program Design

The functions list, conditions list and schematic logic derived in (8.4.3) and (8.4.5) are re-stated.

Functions List.
1. Open files.
2. Close files.
3. Read file.
4. Write line (with paper control as necessary).
5. Stop.
6. Move record 1 for output.
7. Move respective name for music code to record 2 i.e. *Popular, jazz, classical.*
8. Move record 2 for output.
9. Move record 3 for output.
10. Move stock number and distribution to record 4, from store.
11. Move record 4 for output.
12. Add quantity to distribution.
13. Initialise distribution to zero.
14. Store music code.
15. Store stock number.
16. Move hyphens to record 1 for underlining.

Conditions List.
1. Not end of file.
2. Same music code and (1).
3. Same stock number and (2).
4. Music code = A.
5. Music code = B.

Schematic Logic.

```
A–seq
  B do 1,3,14,15
  C do 6,4,16,4
  D–iter while 1
    E–seq
      F–sel if 4
        G do 7
      F–or–2 if 5
        H do 7
      F–or–3
        I do 7
      F–end
      J do 8,4,9,4
      K–iter while 2
        L–seq
          M–iter while 3
            N do 12,3
          M–end
          O do 10,11,4,15,13
        L–end
      K–end
      P do 14
    E–end
  D–end
  Q do 2,5
A–end
```

9.3.2 COBOL Source Code (see also Appendix II)

```
(0001)          IDENTIFICATION DIVISION.
(0002)          PROGRAM-ID. C932.
(0003)          ENVIRONMENT DIVISION.
(0004)          INPUT-OUTPUT SECTION.
(0005)          FILE-CONTROL.
(0006)              SELECT MUSIC-DATA ASSIGN TO PFMS.
(0007)              SELECT MUSIC-REPORT ASSIGN TO PFMS.
(0008)          DATA DIVISION.
(0009)          FILE SECTION.
(0010)          FD MUSIC-DATA
(0011)              LABEL RECORDS STANDARD
(0012)              VALUE OF FILE-ID "MUSIC".
(0013)          01 RECORD-FS.
(0014)              02 MUSIC-CODE PIC A.
(0015)              02 STOCK-NUMBER PIC 9(4).
(0016)              02 QUANTITY PIC 9999.
(0017)          FD MUSIC-REPORT
(0018)              LABEL RECORDS STANDARD
(0019)              VALUE OF FILE-ID "OUTPUT".
(0020)          01 REPORT-OUT.
(0021)              02 FILLER PIC X.
(0022)              02 LINE-IMAGE PIC X(119).
(0023)          WORKING-STORAGE SECTION.
(0024)          01 RECORD-1-WS.
(0025)              02 FILLER PIC X(20) VALUE IS SPACES.
(0026)              02 TITLE-1 PIC X(21) VALUE IS "CASSETTE DISTRIBUTION".
```

(program continued)

```
(0027)          01 RECORD-2-WS.
(0028)             02 FILLER PIC X(20) VALUE IS SPACES.
(0029)             02 FILLER PIC X(6) VALUE IS "TYPE: ".
(0030)             02 TITLE-2 PIC A(9).
(0031)          01 RECORD-3-WS.
(0032)             02 FILLER PIC X(20) VALUE IS SPACES.
(0033)             02 FILLER PIC X(21) VALUE IS "STOCK-NUMBER QUANTITY".
(0034)          01 RECORD-4-WS.
(0035)             02 FILLER PIC X(20) VALUE IS SPACES.
(0036)             02 STOCK-NUMBER-WS PIC 9(4).
(0037)             02 FILLER PIC X(10) VALUE IS SPACES.
(0038)             02 QUANTITY-WS PIC ZZZ9.
(0039)          01 PARAMETERS.
(0040)             02 STOCK-NUMBER-STORE PIC 9(4).
(0041)             02 MUSIC-CODE-STORE PIC A.
(0042)             02 E-O-F PIC 9 VALUE IS ZERO.
(0043)             02 TOTAL-QUANTITY PIC 9999 VALUE IS ZERO.
(0044)
(0045)
(0046)          PROCEDURE DIVISION.
(0047)          A-SEQ.
(0048)          B.   OPEN INPUT MUSIC-DATA
(0049)                    OUTPUT MUSIC-REPORT.
(0050)               READ MUSIC-DATA.
(0051)               MOVE MUSIC-CODE TO MUSIC-CODE-STORE.
(0052)               MOVE STOCK-NUMBER TO STOCK-NUMBER-STORE.
(0053)          C.   MOVE RECORD-1-WS TO LINE-IMAGE.
(0054)               WRITE REPORT-OUT AFTER ADVANCING PAGE.
(0055)               MOVE ALL "-" TO TITLE-1.
(0056)               MOVE RECORD-1-WS TO LINE-IMAGE.
(0057)               WRITE REPORT-OUT AFTER ADVANCING 1 LINE.
(0058)          D-ITER.
(0059)               IF E-O-F NOT = 0 GO TO D-END.
(0060)          E-SEQ.
(0061)          F-SEL.
(0062)               IF MUSIC-CODE NOT = "A" GO TO F-OR-2.
(0063)          G.     MOVE "POPULAR" TO TITLE-2, GO TO F-END.
(0064)          F-OR-2.
(0065)               IF MUSIC-CODE NOT = "B" GO TO F-OR-3.
(0066)          H.     MOVE "JAZZ" TO TITLE-2, GO TO F-END.
(0067)          F-OR-3.
(0068)          I.     MOVE "CLASSICAL" TO TITLE-2.
(0069)          F-END.
(0070)          J.   MOVE RECORD-2-WS TO LINE-IMAGE.
(0071)               WRITE REPORT-OUT AFTER ADVANCING 2 LINES.
(0072)               MOVE RECORD-3-WS TO LINE-IMAGE.
(0073)               WRITE REPORT-OUT AFTER ADVANCING 2 LINES.
(0074)          K-ITER.
(0075)               IF MUSIC-CODE NOT = MUSIC-CODE-STORE OR E-O-F NOT = 0
(0076)               GO TO K-END.
(0077)          L-SEQ.
(0078)          M-ITER.
(0079)               IF STOCK-NUMBER NOT = STOCK-NUMBER-STORE OR
(0080)               MUSIC-CODE NOT = MUSIC-CODE-STORE OR E-O-F NOT = 0
(0081)               GO TO M-END.
(0082)          N.     ADD QUANTITY TO TOTAL-QUANTITY.
(0083)                 READ MUSIC-DATA AT END MOVE 1 TO E-O-F.
(0084)               GO TO M-ITER.
(0085)          M-END.
(0086)          O.     MOVE STOCK-NUMBER-STORE TO STOCK-NUMBER-WS.
(0087)                 MOVE TOTAL-QUANTITY TO QUANTITY-WS.
(0088)                 MOVE RECORD-4-WS TO LINE-IMAGE.
(0089)               WRITE REPORT-OUT AFTER ADVANCING 1 LINE.
(0090)               MOVE STOCK-NUMBER TO STOCK-NUMBER-STORE
(0091)               MOVE ZERO TO TOTAL-QUANTITY.
(0092)          L-END.
(0093)               GO TO K-ITER.
(0094)          K-END.
(0095)          P.   MOVE MUSIC-CODE TO MUSIC-CODE-STORE.
(0096)          E-END.
(0097)               GO TO D-ITER.
(0098)          D-END.
(0099)          Q.   CLOSE MUSIC-DATA
(0100)                    MUSIC-REPORT.
(0101)               STOP RUN.
(0102)          A-END.
```

153

9.3.3 Points to Note

The title CASSETTE DISTRIBUTION is underlined by moving 21 hyphens to the TITLE–1 field, then printing this new record. The original contents of this field defined by a VALUE clause has been overwritten. Because TITLE–1 has a PICTURE of X(21), 21 hyphens are moved into this field by coding:

    MOVE   ALL   '–'   TO   TITLE–1

in line (0055).

The reserved word ZERO and the digit 0 are interchangeable in the program coding.

9.3.4 Example of test data file MUSIC.

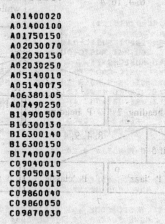

```
A01400020
A01400100
A01750150
A02030070
A02030150
A02030250
A05140010
A05140075
A06380105
A07490250
B14900500
B16300130
B16300140
B16300150
B17400070
C09040010
C09050015
C09060010
C09860040
C09860050
C09870030
```

9.3.5 Report produced from supplied test data.

```
CASSETTE DISTRIBUTION
---------------------

TYPE: POPULAR

STOCK-NUMBER QUANTITY
0140            120
0175            150
0203            470
0514             85
0639            105
0749            250

TYPE: JAZZ

STOCK-NUMBER QUANTITY
1490            500
1630            420
1740             70

TYPE: CLASSICAL

STOCK-NUMBER QUANTITY
0904             10
0905             15
0905             10
0985             90
0987             30
```

9.3.6 Alternative Coding

The detailed program structure for the design of the solution to the last problem was:

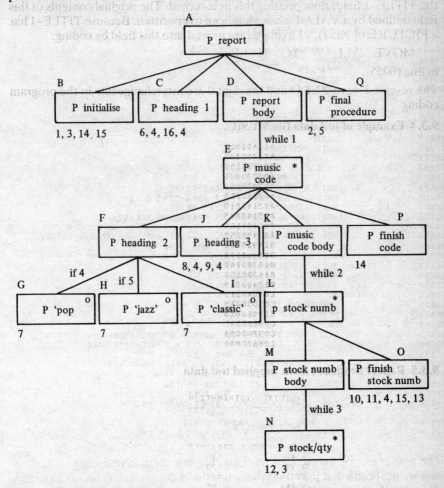

The following hierarchical code illustrates the alternative form of coding the PROCEDURE DIVISION.

```
(0045)
(0046)        PROCEDURE DIVISION.
(0047)        A-SEQ.
(0048)            PERFORM B.
(0049)            PERFORM C.
(0050)            PERFORM D-ITER.
(0051)            PERFORM Q.
(0052)        B.  OPEN INPUT MUSIC-DATA
(0053)                 OUTPUT MUSIC-REPORT.
(0054)            READ MUSIC-DATA.
(0055)            MOVE MUSIC-CODE TO MUSIC-CODE-STORE.
(0056)            MOVE STOCK-NUMBER TO STOCK-NUMBER-STORE.
```

(program continued)

```
(0057)          C.   MOVE RECORD-1-WS TO LINE-IMAGE.
(0058)               WRITE REPORT-OUT AFTER ADVANCING PAGE.
(0059)               MOVE ALL *-* TO TITLE-1.
(0060)               MOVE RECORD-1-WS TO LINE-IMAGE.
(0061)               WRITE REPORT-OUT AFTER ADVANCING 1 LINE.
(0062)          D-ITER.
(0063)               PERFORM E-SEQ UNTIL E-O-F NOT = 0.
(0064)          Q.   CLOSE MUSIC-DATA
(0065)                     MUSIC-REPORT.
(0066)               STOP RUN.
(0067)          E-SEQ.
(0068)               PERFORM F-SEL.
(0069)               PERFORM J.
(0070)               PERFORM K-ITER.
(0071)               PERFORM P.
(0072)          F-SEL.
(0073)               IF MUSIC-CODE = *A*
(0074)                  PERFORM G
(0075)               ELSE
(0076)                  IF MUSIC-CODE = *B*
(0077)                     PERFORM H
(0078)                  ELSE
(0079)                     PERFORM I.
(0080)          J.   MOVE RECORD-2-WS TO LINE-IMAGE.
(0081)               WRITE REPORT-OUT AFTER ADVANCING 2 LINES.
(0082)               MOVE RECORD-3-WS TO LINE-IMAGE.
(0083)               WRITE REPORT-OUT AFTER ADVANCING 2 LINES.
(0084)          K-ITER.
(0085)               PERFORM L-SEQ UNTIL MUSIC-CODE NOT = MUSIC-CODE-STORE
(0086)                             OR E-O-F NOT = 0.
(0087)          P.   MOVE MUSIC-CODE TO MUSIC-CODE-STORE.
(0088)          G.   MOVE *POPULAR* TO TITLE-2.
(0089)          H.   MOVE *JAZZ* TO TITLE-2.
(0090)          I.   MOVE *CLASSICAL* TO TITLE-2.
(0091)          L-SEQ.
(0092)               PERFORM M-ITER.
(0093)               PERFORM O.
(0094)          M-ITER.
(0095)               PERFORM N UNTIL STOCK-NUMBER NOT = STOCK-NUMBER-STORE
(0096)                          OR MUSIC-CODE NOT = MUSIC-CODE-STORE
(0097)                          OR E-O-F NOT = 0.
(0098)          O.   MOVE STOCK-NUMBER-STORE TO STOCK-NUMBER-WS.
(0099)               MOVE TOTAL-QUANTITY TO QUANTITY-WS.
(0100)               MOVE RECORD-4-WS TO LINE-IMAGE.
(0101)               WRITE REPORT-OUT AFTER ADVANCING 1 LINE.
(0102)               MOVE STOCK-NUMBER TO STOCK-NUMBER-STORE.
(0103)               MOVE ZERO TO TOTAL-QUANTITY.
(0104)          N.   ADD QUANTITY TO TOTAL-QUANTITY.
(0105)               READ MUSIC-DATA AT END MOVE 1 TO E-O-F.
```

The reader can be excused for thinking that this method of coding is ideal! A hierarchical code that fully describes a top-down design and no GO TO's within the code. However, although it has these advantages and also offers a small liability to error in coding, and the rules of coding are simple to follow there are disadvantages. These are:

I   The code will run slower because of the need to invoke lower levels of code.

II   The code is broken up into very small logical sections.

III   Because of the hierarchical nature of the code techniques of inversion and backtracking (to be described later in the book) may cause problems.

9.4 QUESTIONS *(answers begin on page 353)*

Write complete COBOL programs for the designs developed to the following questions from chapter 8. Create test data files organised in the manner described in chapter 8, and with records having the respective formats described below. Implement your files and programs on your computer and run the programs to produce the required reports. Invent your own spacing for each report.

9.4.1 A computer file contains records with the name, sex and year of birth of all the employees in a factory. The file is sorted on sex as the primary key in ascending order, and year of birth as the secondary key in descending order. It is required to print a report on the contents of the file using the following format.

```
AGE DISTRIBUTION OF STAFF            – – – – record 1
SEX: FEMALE                          – – – – record 2
YEAR OF BIRTH    NAME                – – – – record 3
1952             HEMMINGS, P.W       – – – – record 4
1950             BRADSHAW, S.
   .
SEX: MALE
YEAR OF BIRTH    NAME
1954             JONES, T.A.
1953             SMITH, P.W.
1949             ACKROYD, F.
   .
```

The format of a record on the file is:

> name 20 alphanumeric characters
> sex 1 character (M or F)
> year of birth 2 digits.

9.4.2 A small building society keeps on file details of all its customers holding ordinary share accounts. A record contains the fields:

> Branch code. 5 alphanumeric characters.
> Account number. 6 numeric characters.
> Number of £1 shares. 5 digits with no decimal places.

The file is sorted on branch code as primary key (in ascending order), and account number as secondary key (in ascending order). It is required to print a report on the contents of the file using the following format.

```
THE HAPPY HOMES BUILDING SOCIETY.              – – – – record 1
DETAILS OF ORDINARY SHARE ACCOUNT CUSTOMERS.   – – – – record 2
BRANCH CODE: BRAD2                             – – – – record 3
ACCOUNT NUMBER        £1 SHARES                – – – – record 4
112345                1,000                    – – – – record 5
121456                  550
        .
           TOTAL  £235,643                      – – – – record 6
BRANCH CODE: HAL17
ACCOUNT NUMBER        £1 SHARES
101456                2,578
101577                1,234
        .
```

† **9.4.3** A file is used to store the details of library books. The format of a record on the file is:

Book title.	30 alphanumeric characters.
Author(s).	20 alphanumeric characters.
Publisher.	15 alphanumeric characters.
Status code.	(A–active, D–damaged, E–external, L–lost).
	1 character.
Price.	4 digits with 2 decimal places.

The file is sorted on status code as primary key (in ascending order), and author as secondary key (in ascending order). It is required to print a report on the contents of the file using the following format.

```
LIBRARY BOOK DETAILS                                              record 1
STATUS: ACTIVE                                                    record 2
AUTHOR          TITLE                   PUBLISHER    PRICE        record 3
BELLINGER, C    THE ART OF SCULPTURE    MOORE-HILL   £18.75       record 4
BRAGG, L        DIFFRACTION PHYSICS     HALL         £15.50
   .
   .

                                        TOTAL   £764.75           record 5

STATUS: DAMAGED
AUTHOR          TITLE                   PUBLISHER    PRICE
COLLINS, J      THE VAMPIRE CATCHERS    MINSTER-BELL £3.75
   .
```

† **9.4.4** An estate agent wants to keep on file the following details about properties.

Vendor's name. 20 alphanumeric characters.
Address of property. 40 alphanumeric characters.
Price of property. 6 digits with no decimal places.
Type of dwelling.　　A–detached house
　　　　　　　　　　B–semi-detached house
　　　　　　　　　　C–terraced house
　　　　　　　　　　D–bungalow
　　　　　　　　　　E–maisonette or flat, 1 character.
Number of bedrooms. 2 digits.
Tenure. F–freehold, L–leasehold, 1 character.

The file is sorted on type of dwelling as primary key (in ascending order) and price of property as secondary key (in descending order). It is required to print a report on the contents of the file using the following format.

```
HOLMES & HOLMES – ESTATE AGENTS EST. 1948        record 1
PROPERTY TYPE: DETACHED                          record 2
VENDOR       ADDRESS          PRICE    BEDS   TENURE   record 3
SMITH, C     2 LIBERAL WALK   £45,675  4      F        record 4
BOWYER, F    69 CHURCH VIEW   £44,350  4      F
SUMNER, S    3 HOPE STREET    £43,000  4      F



TOTAL NUMBER OF PROPERTIES: 23                   record 5

PROPERTY TYPE: SEMI-DETACHED
VENDOR       ADDRESS          PRICE    BEDS   TENURE
JONES, M     145 RIVER VIEW   £36,750  4      F
EVANS, M     27 RIDGE BANK    £35,500  3      F
```

10 File Maintenance

10.1 INTRODUCTION

In the first part of this chapter the JSP methodology is used to define two basic algorithms for file maintenance – merging and updating. The latter part of the chapter explains the errors that can arise when updating files and defines a general algorithm for file updating. Throughout the chapter worked examples are used to develop and implement the algorithms.

10.2 MERGING

Two sequential files, file A and file B, contain records of the names, departments and telephone extension numbers for staff based on two sites of a college. A third file, file C, is to be produced that combines the details of the staff from both sites. The format of a record for the three files is:

    Name (key field) 20 alphanumeric characters,
    Department Code 4 alphabetic characters,
    Extension Number 3 digits.

The following specimen records illustrate the sequential contents of file A and file B, ordered alphabetically on the name field as the key, and also illustrates how the files are combined or *merged* to produce file C.

File A			
	APPLETON J.N	CPS	446
	BAINBRIDGE R	EDUC	210
	BEAUMONT J.E	CATR	415
	BUTLER N.J	COMP	422
	DAINDRIDGE J	LIB	552
	DUNFORD C	ARCI	512

File B			
	AXFORD B	LPE	397
	AYERS C.A	COMP	305
	BARRETT D.A	CONS	579
	ELLIOTT M.J	GPS	447

File C			
	APPLETON J.N	CPS	446
	AXFORD B	LPE	397
	AYERS C.A	COMP	305
	BAINBRIDGE R	EDUC	210
	BARRETT D.A	CONS	579
	BEAUMONT J.E	CATR	415
	BUTLER N.J	COMP	422
	DAINDRIDGE J	LIB	552
	DUNFORD C	ARCI	512
	ELLIOT M.J	GPS	447

File C is shown to be an amalgam of all the records of file A and file B combined together such that the names of the members of staff are kept in strict alphabetical sequence.

10.3 DESIGN OF MERGING ALGORITHM

10.3.1 Data Structures.

The following data structures can be drawn for the three files. For correspondences to exist between the components of the files the components involved must occur:

 the same number of times,
 in the same order, and
 under the same circumstances.

The only correspondence exists at the first level, since there is only one file in each case. Correspondences do not exist at lower levels since the number of records in each file is not the same, and the records are not in the same order.

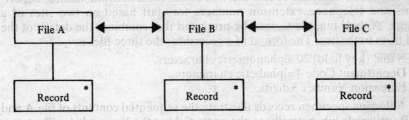

File C is an amalgum of the contents of both input files, file A and file B. Since both files are processed together to produce file C the data structure diagram can be modified to:

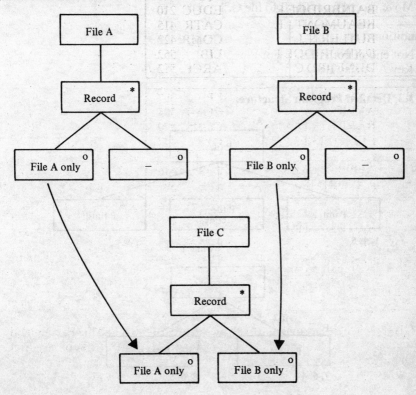

161

The basic program structure becomes:

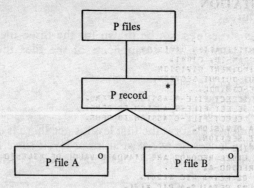

10.3.2 Functions and Conditions Lists.

Functions List
1. Open files.
2. Close files.
3. Stop.
4. Read file A.
5. Read file B.
6. Write record to file C.
7. Move record from file A to file C.
8. Move record from file B to file C.

Conditions List.
1. Not end of both files.
2. Key A < Key B

10.3.3 Detailed Program Structure.

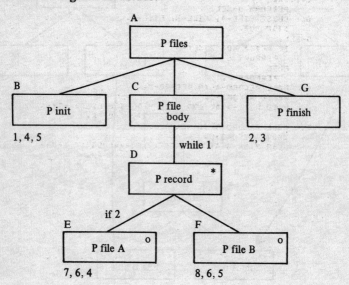

162

10.4 IMPLEMENTATION

10.4.1 Coding.

```
(0001)          IDENTIFICATION DIVISION.
(0002)          PROGRAM-ID. C1041.
(0003)          ENVIRONMENT DIVISION.
(0004)          INPUT-OUTPUT SECTION.
(0005)          FILE-CONTROL.
(0006)              SELECT FILE-A ASSIGN TO PFMS.
(0007)              SELECT FILE-B ASSIGN TO PFMS.
(0008)              SELECT FILE-C ASSIGN TO PFMS.
(0009)          DATA DIVISION.
(0010)          FILE SECTION.
(0011)          FD FILE-A
(0012)              LABEL RECORDS ARE STANDARD VALUE OF FILE-ID IS "FILEA".
(0013)          01 RECORD-A.
(0014)              02 KEY-A PIC X(20).
(0015)              02 DETAILS-A PIC X(7).
(0016)          FD FILE-B
(0017)              LABEL RECORDS ARE STANDARD VALUE OF FILE-ID IS "FILEB".
(0018)          01 RECORD-B.
(0019)              02 KEY-B PIC X(20).
(0020)              02 DETAILS-B PIC X(7).
(0021)          FD FILE-C
(0022)              LABEL RECORDS ARE STANDARD VALUE OF FILE-ID IS "FILEC".
(0023)          01 RECORD-C.
(0024)              02 FILLER PIC X(27).
(0025)          WORKING-STORAGE SECTION.
(0026)          01 FLAGS.
(0027)              02 E-O-FA PIC 9 VALUE IS ZERO.
(0028)              02 E-O-FB PIC 9 VALUE IS ZERO.
(0029)
(0030)
(0031)
(0032)          PROCEDURE DIVISION.
(0033)          A-SEQ.
(0034)              PERFORM B.
(0035)              PERFORM C-ITER UNTIL E-O-FA NOT = 0 AND E-O-FB NOT = 0.
(0036)              PERFORM G.
(0037)          B.  OPEN INPUT FILE-A, FILE-B
(0038)                   OUTPUT FILE-C.
(0039)              READ FILE-A.
(0040)              READ FILE-B.
(0041)          C-ITER.
(0042)              PERFORM D-SEL.
(0043)          G.  CLOSE FILE-A, FILE-B, FILE-C.
(0044)              STOP RUN.
(0045)          D-SEL.
(0046)              IF KEY-A NOT > KEY-B
(0047)                 PERFORM E
(0048)              ELSE
(0049)                 PERFORM F.
(0050)          E.  MOVE RECORD-A TO RECORD-C.
(0051)              WRITE RECORD-C.
(0052)              READ FILE-A AT END MOVE HIGH-VALUES TO KEY-A
(0053)                                  MOVE 1 TO E-O-FA.
(0054)          F.  MOVE RECORD-B TO RECORD-C
(0055)              WRITE RECORD-C.
(0056)              READ FILE-B AT END MOVE HIGH-VALUES TO KEY-B
(0057)                                  MOVE 1 TO E-O-FB.
```

10.4.2 Results.

The program only merges the two files, it does not print the contents of each file. These results were obtained after the program had been executed by listing the contents of the three files.

```
              FILFA
APPLETON J.N          CPS 446
BAINBRIDGE R          EDUC210
BEAUMONT J.E          CATR415
BUTLER N.J            COMP422
DAINDRIDGE J          LIB 552
DUNFORD C             ARCI512
              FILEB
AXFORD B              LPE 397
AYERS C.A             COMP305
BARRETT D.A           CONS579
ELLIOTT M.J           GPS 447
              FILEC
APPLETON J.N          CPS 446
AXFORD B              LPE 397
AYERS C.A             COMP305
BAINBRIDGE R          EDUC210
BARRETT D.A           CONS579
BEAUMONT J.E          CATR415
BUTLER N.J            COMP422
DAINDRIDGE J          LIB 552
DUNFORD C             ARCI512
ELLIOT M.J            GPS 447
```

10.5 THE TERMINOLOGY OF FILE UPDATING

Information that is contained in data files is not always static, it can be subject to changes. Such changes to the information will come about through the insertion, amendment and deletion of records. The process of changing the information held on data files is known as updating.

The most common types of files used in an updating situation are the *master* file and the *transaction* file.

Master files are files of a fairly permanent nature. For example a stock file, a personnel file, a customer file. A feature to note is the regular updating of these files to show a current position. For example when orders are processed the amount of stock should be decreased in the stock file. It is seen, therefore, that master records will contain both data of a static nature, for example, a stock number, description of stock and a minimum re-order level, and data which by its nature will change each time a transaction occurs, for example the depletion of a stock level.

A transaction file is made up from the various transactions created from source documents, e.g. sales invoices. In a stock control application the file will contain a list of stock items that have been sold. This file will be used to update the master file. As soon as it has been used for this purpose it is no longer required. It will, therefore, have a very short life because it will be replaced by another transaction file containing the next list of stock items that have been sold.

In the last problem file C can be regarded as a master file, created from merging the two files A and B together. This master file will eventually require updating. New staff may enter the college (insertions), staff may change either their department, telephone extension number or both (amendments), and staff may leave the college (deletions).

The transaction file could have the following specimen records.

```
File T.    AXFORD B
           BAILEY S.K            SOC    832
           BESWICK K.P           MEDI   654
           BUTLER N.J            MATH   342
           DUNFORD C
           ELLIOT M.J            COMP   422
           HARRIS P.T            CATR   416
```

From this file new members of staff to be inserted into the master file are BAILEY S.K, BESWICK K.P and HARRIS P.T. Those members of staff who already exist on the master file yet require to have their records amended because they have changed departments are BUTLER N.J and ELLIOT M.J. The records of AXFORD B and DUNFORD C are to be deleted since they have left the college.

To distinguish between those records that are to be deleted and those that are to be amended, records that contain only the key field (name) will be deleted in this example.

If the transaction file, file T, is processed against the master file, file C from the previous example, then the following updated master file, file U, will be the outcome.

```
File U.    APPLETON J.N          CPS    446
           AYERS C.A             COMP   305
           BAILEY S.K            SOC    832
           BAINBRIDGE R          EDUC   210
           BARRETT D.A           CONS   579
           BEAUMONT J.E          CATR   415
           BESWICK K.P           MEDI   654
           BUTLER N.J            MATH   342
           DAINDRIDGE J          LIB    552
           ELLIOT M.J            COMP   422
           HARRIS P.T            CATR   416
```

10.6 DESIGN OF A SIMPLE UPDATE ALGORITHM

10.6.1 Data Structures.

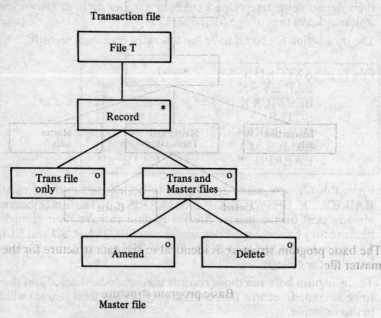

Transaction file

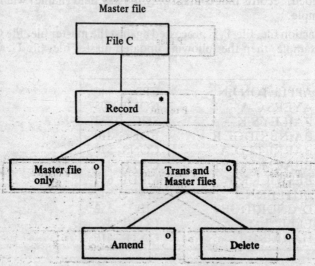

Master file

Updated Master file

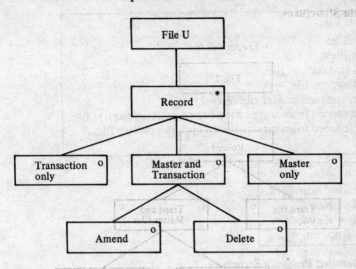

The basic program structure is identical to the data structure for the updated master file.

Basic program structure

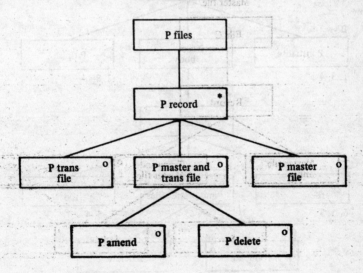

10.6.2 Functions and Conditions Lists.

Functions List.

1. Open files.
2. Close files.
3. Read transaction file.
4. Read master file.
5. Write updated master file record.
6. Move record from transaction file to updated master file.
7. Move record from master file to updated master file.
8. Stop.

Condition List.

1. Not end of both files.
2. Key T < Key C
3. Key T = Key C
4. Field T not empty

10.6.3 Detailed Program Structure.

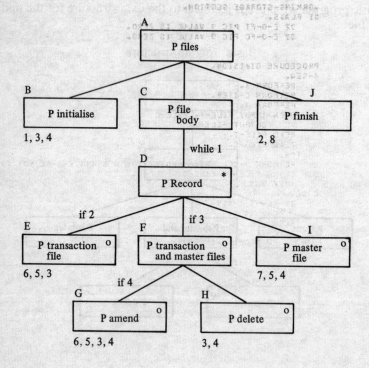

10.7 IMPLEMENTATION

10.7.1 Coding.

```
(0001)          IDENTIFICATION DIVISION.
(0002)          PROGRAM-ID. C1071.
(0003)          ENVIRONMENT DIVISION.
(0004)          INPUT-OUTPUT SECTION.
(0005)          FILE-CONTROL.
(0006)              SELECT FILE-T ASSIGN TO PFMS.
(0007)              SELECT FILE-C ASSIGN TO PFMS.
(0008)              SELECT FILE-U ASSIGN TO PFMS.
(0009)          DATA DIVISION.
(0010)          FILE SECTION.
(0011)          FD FILE-T
(0012)              LABEL RECORDS ARE STANDARD VALUE OF FILE-ID IS "FILET".
(0013)          01 RECORD-T.
(0014)              02 KEY-T PIC X(20).
(0015)              02 DETAILS-T PIC X(7).
(0016)          FD FILE-C
(0017)              LABEL RECORDS ARE STANDARD VALUE OF FILE-ID IS "FILEC".
(0018)          01 RECORD-C.
(0019)              02 KEY-C PIC X(20).
(0020)              02 DETAILS-C PIC X(7).
(0021)          FD FILE-U
(0022)              LABEL RECORDS ARE STANDARD VALUE OF FILE-ID IS "FILEU".
(0023)          01 RECORD-U.
(0024)              02 KEY-U PIC X(20).
(0025)              02 DETAILS-U PIC X(7).
(0026)          WORKING-STORAGE SECTION.
(0027)          01 FLAGS.
(0028)              02 E-O-FT PIC 9 VALUE IS ZERO.
(0029)              02 E-O-FC PIC 9 VALUE IS ZERO.
(0030)
(0031)
(0032)          PROCEDURE DIVISION.
(0033)          A-SEQ.
(0034)              PERFORM B.
(0035)              PERFORM C-ITER.
(0036)              PERFORM J.
(0037)          B.  OPEN INPUT FILE-T, FILE-C
(0038)                   OUTPUT FILE-U.
(0039)              READ FILE-T.
(0040)              READ FILE-C.
(0041)          C-ITER.
(0042)              PERFORM D-SEL UNTIL E-O-FT NOT = 0 AND E-O-FC NOT =0.
(0043)          J.  CLOSE FILE-T, FILE-C, FILE-U.
(0044)              STOP RUN.
(0045)          D-SEL.
(0046)              IF KEY-T < KEY-C
(0047)                PERFORM E
(0048)              ELSE
(0049)                IF KEY-T = KEY-C
(0050)                   PERFORM F-SEL
(0051)                ELSE
(0052)                   PERFORM I.
(0053)          E.  MOVE RECORD-T TO RECORD-U.
(0054)              WRITE RECORD-U.
(0055)              READ FILE-T AT END MOVE HIGH-VALUES TO KEY-T
(0056)                                  MOVE 1 TO E-O-FT.
(0057)          F-SEL.
(0058)              IF DETAILS-T NOT = SPACES
(0059)                PERFORM G
(0060)              ELSE
(0061)                PERFORM H.
(0062)          I.  MOVE RECORD-C TO RECORD-U.
(0063)              WRITE RECORD-U.
(0064)              READ FILE-C AT END MOVE HIGH-VALUES TO KEY-C
(0065)                                  MOVE 1 TO E-O-FC.
```

(program continued)

```
(0066)          G.   MOVE RECORD-T TO RECORD-U.
(0067)               WRITE RECORD-U.
(0068)               READ FILE-T AT END MOVE HIGH-VALUES TO KEY-T
(0069)                                  MOVE 1 TO E-O-FT.
(0070)               READ FILE-C AT END MOVE HIGH-VALUES TO KEY-C
(0071)                                  MOVE 1 TO E-O-FC.
(0072)          H.   READ FILE-T AT END MOVE HIGH-VALUES TO KEY-T
(0073)                                  MOVE 1 TO E-O-FT.
(0074)               READ FILE-C AT END MOVE HIGH-VALUES TO KEY-C
(0075)                                  MOVE 1 TO E-O-FC.
(0076)
(0077)
```

10.7.2 Results.

```
                    FILET
        AXFORD B
        BAILEY S.K          SOC 832
        BESWICK K.P         MEDI654
        BUTLER N.J          MATH342
        DUNFORD C
        ELLIOT M.J          COMP422
        HARRIS P.T          CATR416
                    FILEC
        APPLETON J.N        CPS 446
        AXFORD B            LFE 397
        AYERS C.A           COMP305
        BAINBRIDGE R        EDUC210
        BARRETT D.A         CONS579
        BEAUMONT J.E        CATR415
        BUTLER N.J          COMP422
        DAINDRIDGE J        LIB 552
        DUNFORD C           ARCI512
        ELLIOT M.J          GPS 447
                    FILEU
        APPLETON J.N        CPS 446
        AYERS C.A           COMP305
        BAILEY S.K          SOC 832
        BAINBRIDGE R        EDUC210
        BARRETT D.A         CONS579
        BEAUMONT J.E        CATR415
        BESWICK K.P         MEDI654
        BUTLER N.J          MATH342
        DAINDRIDGE J        LIB 552
        ELLIOT M.J          COMP422
        HARRIS P.T          CATR416
```

10.7.3 Optimisation.

If the reader examines the functions in the detailed program structure then it would appear that functions 3 and 4 are repeated in the components B, G and H. When the design is coded the same code for functions 3 and 4 will appear three times in the program (in practice the same code only appears twice at G and H since the initial READ statements at B do not cater for the end of file). There is a great temptation amongst programmers to reduce the amount of repeated code in any program. However, be warned, such pruning of repeated code can lead to a program that was once structured becoming unstructured. The outcome of such an action would result in a program that is more difficult to maintain and more prone to logical errors.

The technique of making a program smaller by reducing the code is one of the techniques under the heading of *optimisation*. The other technique of optimisation is the *tuning* of a program to make it run faster. The reader who contemplates optimising program code should consider M.A Jackson's rules for optimisation in the *Principles of Program Design*. They are:

> Rule 1: Don't do it.
> Rule 2: Don't do it yet.

The first rule implies that a positive quantified justification for optimisation is necessary before commencing the technique. For example, to spend time trying to make a program run faster is no justification if the computer is idle for a large percentage of its time and output is not required within a time-critical period.

The second rule implies that the original program design should be created without any form of optimisation even though optimisation is planned at a later stage. In the last worked example from the detailed program structure it is clear that functions 3 and 4 are suitable for optimisation since they are repeated three times.

The original design can be optimised by removing functions 3 and 4 and replacing them by a *high-level* function which represents a call to a common segment of code known as a *subroutine*. If the name of this subroutine is SR-A then it can be represented as a separate component (not connected) to the detailed program structure. All references to function 3 and 4 in the main structure are replaced by SR-A.

e.g

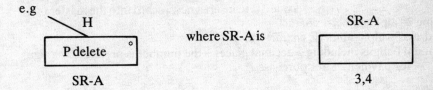

The following skeletal code illustrates how the call to the subroutine is implemented using the PERFORM statement.

```
       PROCEDURE DIVISION.
       A-SEQ.
              _____
              _____
              _____
       B.
              _____
              _____
       PERFORM SR-A.
              _____
              _____
       G.
              _____
       PERFORM SR-A.
       H.
       PERFORM SR-A.
       SR-A.
              READ FILE-T AT END MOVE HIGH-VALUES TO KEY-T
                         MOVE 1 TO E-O-FT.
              READ FILE-C AT END MOVE HIGH-VALUES TO KEY-C
                         MOVE 1 TO E-O-FC.
```

Note: this version of the program caters for the possibility of empty files.

10.8 DESIGN OF AN UPDATE ALGORITHM WITH VALIDATION

10.8.1 Problem.

A transaction file from a customer accounts system contains records with the following format.

Account number (key) 4 digits.

Transaction code 1 digit –   code 1 is to amend a record on the master file,
                             code 2 is to delete a record on the master file,
                             code 3 is to insert a new record into the master file.

Name 20 alphanumeric characters.

Address 30 alphanumeric characters.

Amount 6 digits including 2 decimal places – the number is prefixed by a sign
       – for payment + for purchase.

A sample of records on the file would appear as:

12461	26 AVON CR. BATH	+013000
12533J DAVIES	4 QUEEN MARY WALK SWINDON	+050050
12542		
.		
.		
.		
15103P SMITH	4 WATFORD RD LUTON	+000000
15101		+010050
15101	3 JUNCTION RD AYLESBURY	−010050
15102		
.		

Notice from the transaction code that records can be inserted, amended or deleted from the master file, and that the transaction file may contain multiple records having an identical key. In an extreme case it is possible for a record to be inserted into the master file (new account customer), amendments made to this record in the master file (payments, purchases, change of name, change of address) and the record then deleted from the master file (customer account closed). From the sample records it can be seen that when a record is to be amended the key and the fields to be changed are included, however, when a record is to be deleted only the key is specified in the transaction record (the remaining fields are left blank). New records to be inserted contain the key and information about the customer that is available at the time.

The format of the master file is similar to that of the transaction file, the only exception is that the transaction code is missing. A sample of records on the file would appear as:

1245S JOSEPH	14 HARCOURT CR BATH	+014000
1246P HAMILTON	2 PUMP ST BATH	+013000
1254M MASKINS	18 OXFORD RD WATFORD	+000000
1277P TRENT	1 VICARAGE CR OXFORD	+100000
.		

The insertion, amendment and deletion of records on the master file can appear on the transaction file in any combination, however, some of the combinations are illegal. For example, a record cannot be amended or deleted if it has not first been inserted on to the master file, and a record cannot be inserted more than once on the master file. These situations arise when the record to be amended or deleted does not exist on the master file, or the record to be inserted already exists on the master file.

Such errors in the records of the transaction file cannot be detected before the transaction file is processed against the master file and it is for this reason that the procedure to update the master file should contain a record validation routine.

10.8.2 Data Structures.

The records on both the transaction and master files are in key sequence. In considering the data structures for both files it is necessary to consider the procedures associated with records that have a key match between the two files and those that do not have a key match between the two files.

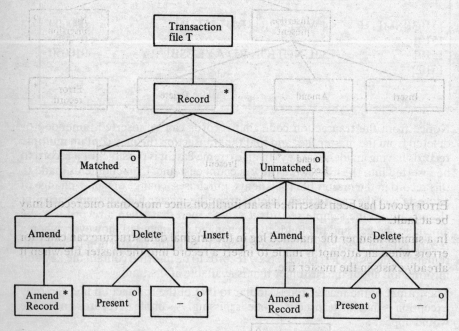

Note: in the unmatched case a record must be inserted before it can be amended or deleted – hence the **sequence** (insert, amend and delete).

In both the matched and unmatched case since the amended record can be repeated zero or more times, and the deletion is either present or absent the combinations of insertion, amendment and deletion are all possible in this data structure.

The unmatched leg of this structure could be modified to cater for error conditions. If the record is **not** matched with a record in the master file the update **must** be an insertion otherwise an error exists in the transaction record key.

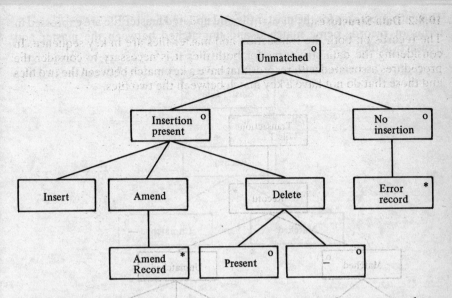

Error record has been described as an iteration since more than one record may be at fault.

In a similar manner the matched leg in the original data structure can cater for errors when an attempt is made to insert a record into the master file when it already exists in the master file.

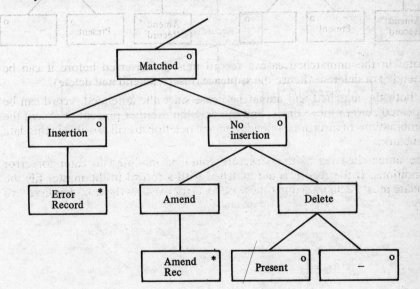

The data structures for the master file and updated master file are expressed in terms of records being matched and unmatched between the master and transaction files.

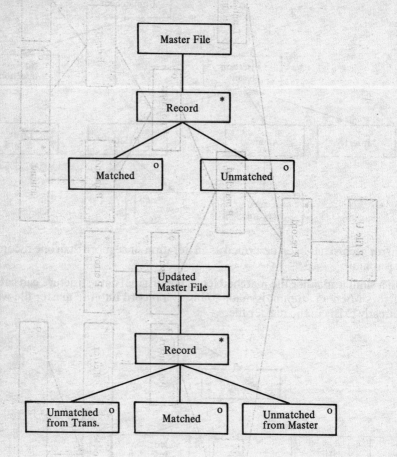

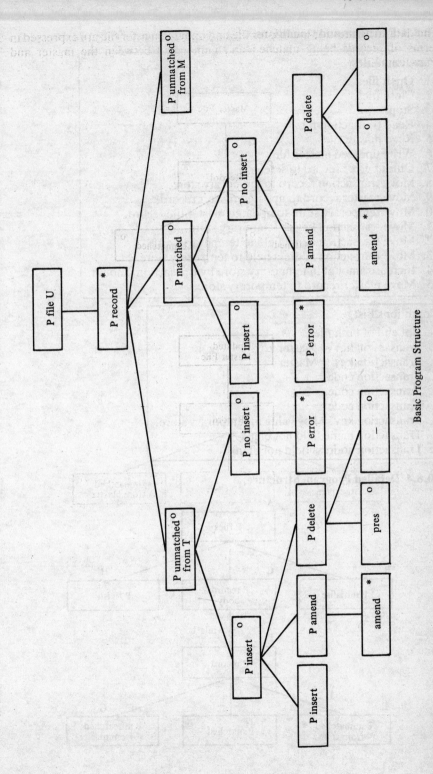

Basic Program Structure

10.8.3 Functions and Conditions.

Functions List.

1. Open files.
2. Close files.
3. Stop.
4. Read transaction file.
5. Read master file.
6. Write updated master file.
7. Output error record to screen.
8. Move transaction record to temporary store.
9. Move master record to updated master record.
10. Move temporary store to updated master file record.
11. Move transaction key to temporary store.
12. Move transaction name field to temporary store.
13. Move transaction address field to temporary store.
14. Increase amount in temporary store by transaction amount.
15. Move master record to temporary store.

Conditions List.

1. Not end of both files.
2. Transaction key < Master key.
3. Transaction key = Master key.
4. Transaction code = 1.
5. Transaction code = 2.
6. Transaction code = 3.
7. Transaction key = key value in temporary store.
8. Transaction name field not blank.
9. Transaction address field not blank.

10.8.4 Detailed Program Structure.

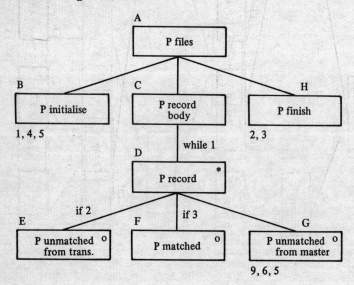

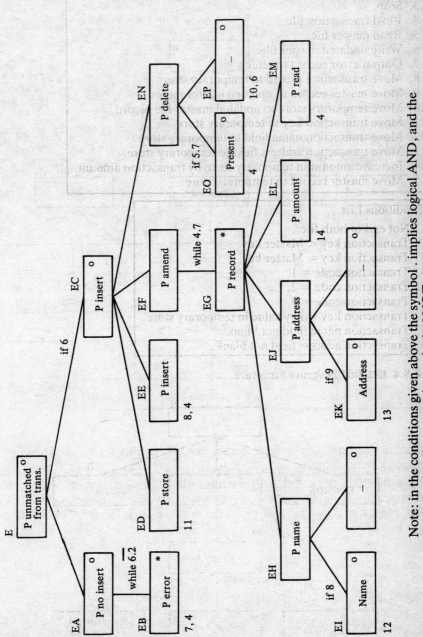

Note: in the conditions given above the symbol . implies logical AND, and the symbol − implies a negation or logical NOT.

When a program structure is too large to fit on to one page it is possible for individual components of that structure to be described on successive pages.

The letter that corresponds to this symbol in the structure diagram will be used to prefix each letter in the expanded structure diagram that has been derived from this one component.

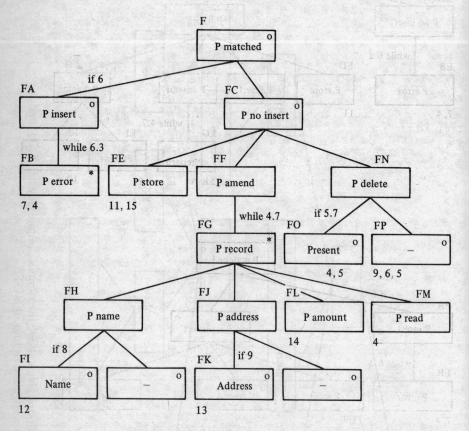

Note: in the conditions given above the symbol . implies logical AND.

From an examination of the detailed program structure all the components of EG and FG are the same and, therefore, will be treated as a subroutine. The structures for E and for F have been re-drawn replacing the components for EG and FG by a single subroutine component which refers to the high-level function SR-A.

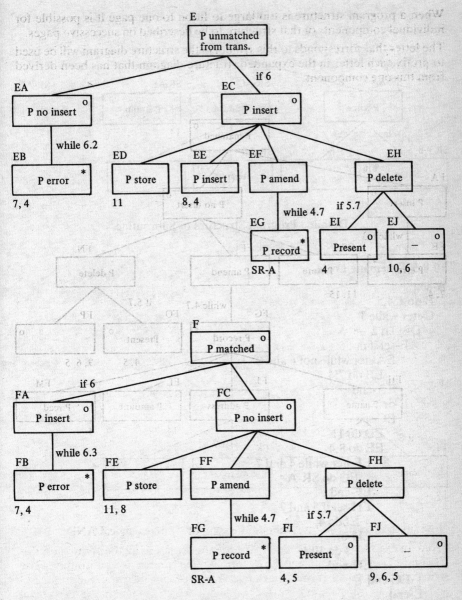

Note: beware of inadvertently using COBOL reserved words as component names – in this structure diagram FD has not been used since it would have ultimately been coded into a paragraph name.

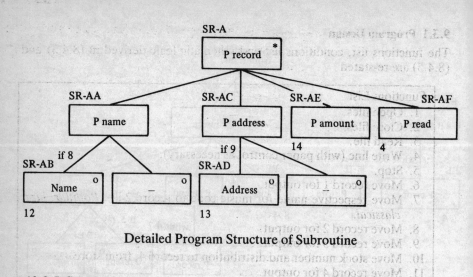

SR-A

P record *

SR-AA   SR-AC   SR-AE   SR-AF

P name   P address   P amount   P read

if 8   if 9   14   4

SR-AB   SR-AD

Name °   — °   Address °   — °

12   13

Detailed Program Structure of Subroutine

10.8.5 Schematic Logic.

```
A-seq
  B do 1,4,5
  C-iter while 1
    D-sel if 2
      E-sel if not 6
        EA-iter while not 6 and 2
          EB do 7,4
        EA-end
      E-or
        EC-seq
          ED do 11
          EE do 8,4
            EF-iter while 4 and 7
              EG do SR-A
            EF-end
            EH-sel if 5 and 7
              EI do 4
            EH-or
              EJ do 10,6
            EH-end
        EC-end
      E-end
    D-or-2 if 3
      F-sel if 6
        FA-iter while 6 and 3
          FB do 7,4
        FA-end
      F-or
        FC-seq
          FE do 11,15
          FF-iter while 4 and 7
```

```
            FG do SR-A
         FF-end
         FH-sel if 5 and 7
            FI do 4,5
         FH-or
            FJ do 9,6,5
         FH-end
      FC-end
    F-end
    D-or-3
       G do 9,6,5
    D-end
  C-end
  H do 2,3
A-end


SR-A-seq
  SR-AA-sel if 8
     SR-AB do 12
  SR-AA-end
  SR-AC-sel if 9
     SR-AD do 13
  SR-AC-end
  SR-AE do 14
  SR-AF do 4
SR-A-end
```

10.9 IMPLEMENTATION

10.9.1 Coding (see also Appendix II)

```
(0001)          IDENTIFICATION DIVISION.
(0002)          PROGRAM-ID. C1031.
(0003)          ENVIRONMENT DIVISION.
(0004)          INPUT-OUTPUT SECTION.
(0005)          FILE-CONTROL.
(0006)              SELECT FILE-A ASSIGN TO PFMS.
(0007)              SELECT FILE-B ASSIGN TO PFMS.
(0008)              SELECT FILE-C ASSIGN TO PFMS.
(0009)          DATA DIVISION.
(0010)          FILE SECTION.
(0011)          FD FILE-A
(0012)              LABEL RECORDS ARE STANDARD VALUE OF FILE-ID IS "FLT".
(0013)          01 RECORD-A.
(0014)              02 KEYA PIC X(4).
(0015)              02 TCODE PIC 9.
(0016)              02 NAME-A PIC X(20).
(0017)              02 ADDRESS-A PIC X(30).
(0018)              02 AMOUNT-A PIC S9(4)V99 SIGN IS LEADING SEPARATE CHARACTER.
(0019)          FD FILE-B
(0020)              LABEL RECORDS ARE STANDARD VALUE OF FILE-ID IS "FLM".
(0021)          01 RECORD-B.
(0022)              02 KEYB PIC X(4).
(0023)              02 NAME-B PIC X(20).
(0024)              02 ADDRESS-B PIC X(30).
(0025)              02 AMOUNT-B PIC S9(4)V99 SIGN IS LEADING SEPARATE CHARACTER.
(0026)          FD FILE-C
(0027)              LABEL RECORDS ARE STANDARD VALUE OF FILE-ID IS "FLU".
```

(program continued)

183

```
( 0028 )          01 RECORD-C.
( 0029 )             02 FILLER PIC X(61).
( 0030 )          WORKING-STORAGE SECTION.
( 0031 )          01 RECORD-X.
( 0032 )             02 KEYX PIC X(4).
( 0033 )             02 NAME-X PIC X(20).
( 0034 )             02 ADDRESS-X PIC X(30).
( 0035 )             02 AMOUNT-X PIC S9(4)V99 SIGN IS LEADING SEPARATE CHARACTER.
( 0036 )          01 PARAMETERS.
( 0037 )             02 E-O-FA PIC 9 VALUE IS ZERO.
( 0038 )             02 E-O-FB PIC 9 VALUE IS ZERO.
( 0039 )             02 STOREY PIC 9(4).
( 0040 )
( 0041 )
( 0042 )
( 0043 )          PROCEDURE DIVISION.
( 0044 )          A-SEQ.
( 0045 )          B.
( 0046 )             OPEN INPUT FILE-A, FILE-B, OUTPUT FILE-C.
( 0047 )             READ FILE-A.
( 0048 )             READ FILE-B.
( 0049 )          C-ITER.
( 0050 )             IF E-O-FA = 1 AND E-O-FB = 1 GO TO C-END.
( 0051 )          D-SEL.
( 0052 )                IF KEYA NOT < KEYB GO TO D-OR-2.

          * unmatched from transaction file

( 0053 )          F-SEL.
( 0054 )                IF TCODE = 3 GO TO E-OR.
( 0055 )          FA-ITER.
( 0056 )                IF TCODE = 3 OR KEYA NOT < KEYB GO TO EA-END.

          * error - record does not exist on master file

( 0057 )          FB.
( 0058 )                DISPLAY "ERROR-ATTEMPT TO AMEND/DELETE NON-EXISTENT"
( 0059 )                   " RECORD" RECORD-A.
( 0060 )                READ FILE-A AT END MOVE 1 TO E-O-FA, MOVE HIGH-VALUES
( 0061 )                   TO KEYA.
( 0062 )                GO TO EA-ITER.
( 0063 )          EA-END.
( 0064 )                GO TO E-END.
( 0065 )          E-OR.
( 0066 )          EC-SEQ.
( 0067 )          ED.

          * insert record

( 0068 )                MOVE KEYA TO STOREY.
( 0069 )          EE.
( 0070 )                MOVE KEYA TO KEYX.
( 0071 )                MOVE NAME-A TO NAME-X.
( 0072 )                MOVE ADDRESS-A TO ADDRESS-X.
( 0073 )                MOVE AMOUNT-A TO AMOUNT-X.
( 0074 )                READ FILE-A AT END MOVE 1 TO E-O-FA, MOVE HIGH-VALUES
( 0075 )                   TO KEYA.
( 0076 )          EF-ITER.
( 0077 )                IF TCODE NOT = 1 OR KEYA NOT = STOREY GO TO EF-END.
( 0078 )          EG.

          * amend record

( 0079 )                PERFORM SR-A-SEQ THRU SR-A-END.
( 0080 )                GO TO EF-ITER.
( 0081 )          EF-END.
( 0082 )          EH-SEL.
( 0083 )                IF TCODE NOT = 2 OR KEYA NOT = STOREY GO TO EH-OR.
( 0084 )          EI.
```

(program continued)

* delete record

```
(0085)                      READ FILE-A AT END MOVE 1 TO E-O-FA, MOVE HIGH-VALUES
(0086)                          TO KEYA.
(0087)                      GO TO EH-END.
(0088)         EH-OR.
(0089)         FJ.
(0090)                      MOVE RECORD-X TO RECORD-C.
(0091)                      WRITE RECORD-C.
(0092)         EH-END.
(0093)         EC-END.
(0094)         F-END.
(0095)             GO TO D-END.
(0096)         D-OR-2.
(0097)                 IF KEYA NOT = KEYB GO TO D-OR-3.
```

* matched on both transaction and master

```
(0098)         F-SEL.
(0099)                 IF TCODE NOT = 3 GO TO F-OR.
(0100)         FA-ITER.
(0101)                 IF TCODE NOT = 3 OR KEYA NOT = KEYB GO TO FA-END.
```

* error - record exists on master

```
(0102)         FB.
(0103)                 DISPLAY "ERROR-ATTEMPT TO INSERT A RECORD THAT"
(0104)                     " EXISTS" RECORD-A.
(0105)                 READ FILE-A AT END MOVE 1 TO E-O-FA,
(0106)                 MOVE HIGH-VALUES TO KEYA.
(0107)                 GO TO FA-ITER.
(0108)         FA-END.
(0109)                 GO TO F-END.
(0110)         F-OR.
(0111)         FC-SEQ.
```

* amend record

```
(0112)         FE.
(0113)                 MOVE KEYA TO STOREY, KEYX.
(0114)                 MOVE NAME-B TO NAME-X.
(0115)                 MOVE ADDRESS-B TO ADDRESS-X.
(0116)                 MOVE AMOUNT-B TO AMOUNT-X.
(0117)         FF-ITER.
(0118)                 IF TCODE NOT = 1 OR KEYA NOT = STOREY GO TO FF-END.
(0119)         FG.
(0120)                 PERFORM SR-A-SEQ THRU SR-A-END.
(0121)                 GO TO FF-ITER.
(0122)         FF-END.
(0123)         FH-SEL.
(0124)                 IF TCODE NOT = 2 OR KEYA NOT = STOREY GO TO FH-OR.
```

* delete record

```
(0125)         FI.
(0126)                 READ FILE-A AT END MOVE 1 TO E-O-FA,
(0127)                 MOVE HIGH-VALUES TO KEYA.
(0128)                 READ FILE-B AT END MOVE 1 TO E-O-FB,
(0129)                 MOVE HIGH-VALUES TO KEYB.
(0130)                 GO TO FH-END.
(0131)         FH-OR.
(0132)         FJ.
(0133)                 MOVE RECORD-X TO RECORD-C.
(0134)                 WRITE RECORD-C.
(0135)                 READ FILE-B AT END MOVE 1 TO E-O-FB,
(0136)                 MOVE HIGH-VALUES TO KEYB.
(0137)         FH-END.
(0138)         FC-END.
(0139)         F-END.
(0140)             GO TO D-END.
(0141)         D-OR-3.
```

(program continued)

```
                         * unmatched from master file

(0142)                   G.
(0143)                           MOVE RECORD-B TO RECORD-C.
(0144)                           WRITE RECORD-C.
(0145)                           READ FILE-B AT END MOVE 1 TO E-O-FB,
(0146)                           MOVE HIGH-VALUES TO KEYB.
(0147)                   D-END.
(0148)                       GO TO C-ITER.
(0149)                   C-END.
(0150)                   H.
(0151)                       CLOSE FILE-A, FILE-B, FILE-C.
(0152)                       STOP RUN.
(0153)                   A-END.
(0154)

                         * subroutine to amend fields of master file record

(0155)                   SR-A-SEQ.
(0156)                   SR-AA-SEL.
(0157)                       IF NAME-A = ALL SPACES GO TO SR-AA-END.
(0158)                   SR-AB.
(0159)                       MOVE NAME-A TO NAME-X.
(0160)                   SR-AA-END.
(0161)                   SR-AC-SEL.
(0162)                       IF ADDRESS-A = ALL SPACES GO TO SR-AC-END.
(0163)                   SR-AD.
(0164)                       MOVE ADDRESS-A TO ADDRESS-X.
(0165)                   SR-AC-END.
(0166)                   SR-AE.
(0167)                       ADD AMOUNT-A TO AMOUNT-X.
(0168)                   SR-AF.
(0169)                       READ FILE-A AT END MOVE 1 TO E-O-FA,
(0170)                       MOVE HIGH-VALUES TO KEYA.
(0171)                   SR-A-END.
```

10.9.2 Results.

```
ERROR-ATTEMPT TO INSERT A RECORD THAT EXISTS13873L S VAUGHAN
                      8 HILLTOP VIEW OXFORD          +100050
ERROR-ATTEMPT TO AMEND/DELETE NON-EXISTENT RECORD13942


            FLT
   12461                   26 AVON CR. BATH            +013000
   12533J DAVIES           4 QUEEN MARY WALK SWINDON   +050050
   12542
   12871                                               +031475
   12871                                               -017850
   12871                                               -005000
   13461                   16 HOOK ST WALLINGFORD      +005070
   13493P T JONES          49 BROOK ST ABINGDON        +010000
   13491                                               -035000
   13571P V EVANS                                      +035070
   13873L S VAUGHAN        8 HILLTOP VIEW OXFORD       +100050
   13942
   14821                                               -007575
   15031                                               +010070
   15103P SMITH            4 WATFORD RD LUTON          +000000
   15101                                               +010050
   15101                   3 JUNCTION RD AYLESBURY     -010050
   15102
   16321                                               +175436
   16321                                               +219321
   16321                   14 HAYMARKET OXFORD         -330000
   16433S SPENCER          184 PALACE RD WITNEY        +005000
```

```
          FLM
1245S JOSEPH          14 HARCOURT CR BATH           +014000
1246P HAMILTON         2 PUMP ST BATH               +013000
1254M MASKINS         18 OXFORD       RD WATFORD     +000000
1277P TRENT            1 VICARAGE CR OXFORD          +103000
1278M VICARS          28 BOW WALK STRATFORD          +001000
1287P BILLINGS        18 KNOLL ST WATFORD            +010050
1300T JONES           29 PARK RD WITNEY              +001075
1346M TYRER            2 COTTAGE ST DIDCOT           +015870
1357P V EVANS          2 CHURCH RD DIDCOT            +000000
1387L S VAUGHAN        8 HILLTOP VIEW OXFORD         +000000
1482A ANDREWS         29 HIGH RD WATFORD             +030050
1503M GAYNOR           2 LUX LANE DIDCOT             +000000
1612V LORD            77 RIVER ST ABINGDON           +015720
1632N MELLOR          64 HOE ST WATFORD              +000000
          FLU
1245S JOSEPH          14 HARCOURT CR BATH           +014000
1246P HAMILTON        26 AVON CR. BATH              +026000
1253J DAVIES           4 QUEEN MARY WALK SWINDON     +050050
1277P TRENT            1 VICARAGE CR OXFORD          +100000
1278M VICARS          28 BOW WALK STRATFORD          +001000
1287P BILLINGS        18 KNOLL ST WATFORD            +018675
1300T JONES           29 PARK RD WITNEY              +001075
1346M TYRER           16 HOOK ST WALLINGFORD         +020940
1349P T JONES         49 BROOK ST ABINGDON           +005000
1357P V EVANS          2 CHURCH RD DIDCOT            +035070
1387L S VAUGHAN        8 HILLTOP VIEW OXFORD         +000000
1482A ANDREWS         29 HIGH RD WATFORD             +022475
1503M GAYNOR           2 LUX LANE DIDCOT             +010070
1612V LORD            77 RIVER ST ABINGDON           +015720
1632N MELLOR          14 HAYMARKET OXFORD            +094757
1643S SPENCER        184 PALACE RD WITNEY            +005000
```

10.9.3 Comments.

In lines (0018), (0025) and (0035) the clause SIGN IS LEADING SEPARATE CHARACTER has been used to indicate the presence of an operational sign. The general format of the SIGN clause is:

[SIGN IS] $\begin{Bmatrix} \text{LEADING} \\ \text{TRAILING} \end{Bmatrix}$ [SEPARATE CHARACTER]

and is used to specify the position and the mode of representation of the operational sign when it is necessary to describe these properties explicitly.

10.10 QUESTIONS

† **10.10.1** Three files contain lists of English words and their meanings in alphabetical sequence. Each word (key) and its meaning occupies one fixed length record. Design and write a program to merge the three files into one file and output the contents of the new file as a dictionary. Assume the format of a record is:

word (key) 10 characters.
meaning 70 characters.

† **10.10.2** In a simplified weekly wage system, factory employees are allocated one fixed length record per employee on a wages master file. The format of a record on this file is:

Employee number – 10 charactres.
Hourly rate of pay – 4 digits inc 2 dec.pl.
Fixed allowances against pay – 5 digits inc 2 dec.pl.
Total gross income to date – 7 digits inc 2 dec.pl.
Total tax paid to date – 7 digits inc 2 dec.pl.
Total pension contributions to date – 6 digits inc 2 dec.pl.
Total National Insurance contributions to date – 6 digits inc 2 dec.pl.

187

For every employee the pension contribution is 6% of the gross income, the National Insurance is £10.50 and income tax is levied at 30% of taxable income.

Taxable income is calculated as the difference between gross income and pension contributions and fixed allowances.

A transaction file contains fixed length records with the format:

Employee number – 10 characters
Hours worked in week (including overtime) – 3 digits.

Design and write a program to process the transaction file against the employee master file and produce both an updated master file and pay-slips for each employee on the transaction file.

Assume that both files are sequential and ordered on employee number. The number of employees on the transaction file is less than those on the master file and only amendments to the master file are required (no deletions or insertions).

The format of a pay-slip is:

```
Employee number: X342567SMI
Gross wage: £307.69
                    Pension:   £18.46
                    NatIns:    £10.50
                    Tax:       £77.77
Nett wage: £200.96
```

† **10.10.3** A small college keeps on file a description of the use of all its rooms. The format of a record on the master room file is:-

room number (key)   2 digits
description of use   20 alphanumeric characters.

The records on the master room file are stored in ascending key order.

Over the period of a year the use each room is put to may change. The records on the master room file will, therefore, have to be updated. Such changes that exist will be:-

change of use of room (amendment to the description)
room demolished (deletion)
new room built (insertion)

These changes are described in a transaction file the format of which is:-

room number (key)   2 digits
transaction code   1 digit $\begin{bmatrix} 1 \text{ amend} \\ 2 \text{ delete} \\ 3 \text{ insert} \end{bmatrix}$
description of use   20 alphanumeric characters
(this field is absent when a record on the master file is to be deleted).

The records on the transaction file are stored in ascending key order, and each record has a unique key.

Devise a JSP detailed program structure for a procedure to update the master file from the transaction file. Incorporate into your design error conditions that might exist between the keys on the two files.

Implement the program design using hierarchical COBOL code.

Invent your own test data files and execute your compiled program.

11 Tables

11.1 INTRODUCTION

The only data structures that have been encountered so far in the text are serial and sequential files. The storage of these data files is independent of the main memory of the computer and consequently access to the data is a serial process; information cannot be accessed directly since each record of the file has to be read in order to locate the required record.

A table is a data structure that enables data to be stored in the main memory of the computer. By specifying a unique location within the structure it is possible to access the data in a direct manner without having to perform a serial search through the data structure.

The advantages of using a table to store data are as follows.

Each item of data does not have a unique variable name.
The homogeneous nature of data can be classified under one name;
for example the heights of a population sample.
Direct access to an item of data becomes possible.
Program coding is reduced.

Within this chapter the methods of defining tables, and storing and accessing data within tables is explained. The latter part of the chapter investigates the methods available in COBOL for searching tables.

11.2 THE CONCEPT OF A TABLE

The main memory of a computer is divided into many storage areas each of which has a unique memory address. The size of a computer memory is dependent upon the model of computer and varies in size between tens of thousands to millions of storage areas. Each storage area is known as either a byte or a word. Generally a word is a multiple number of bytes.

The following diagram serves to illustrate the **linear** nature of a computer memory. Each small rectangle represents a byte of computer memory and has a unique memory address in order for the storage location to be accessed.

A table uses part of the main memory to store data, however, the programmer need not be aware of which part of the memory is being used. The table is accessed by specifying a unique location, however, the mapping of this location into a memory address is a function of the computer system and is seldom of any concern to the programmer.

11.2.1 A one-dimensional table.

A one-dimensional table can be represented diagramatically as a linear set of storage areas. Each storage area, despite having a unique memory address, is given a unique location number or **subscript** to enable the programmer to make reference to the location.

A subscript must be a positive integer, the lowest value is normally 1, and represents the first storage area in the table. The following diagram illustrates a one-dimensional table containing five storage areas.

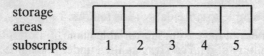

A JSP diagram can also be used to represent this data structure.

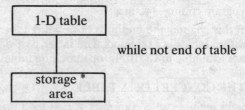

11.2.2 A two-dimensional table.

A two-dimensional table should be thought of as a number of one-dimensional tables with each one-dimensional table being given a subscript value.

Diagramatically the two-dimensional table appears as:

```
table 1        ┌───┬───┬───┬───┬───┐
               └───┴───┴───┴───┴───┘
subscripts       1   2   3   4   5

table 2        ┌───┬───┬───┬───┬───┐
               └───┴───┴───┴───┴───┘
subscripts       1   2   3   4   5

table 3        ┌───┬───┬───┬───┬───┐
               └───┴───┴───┴───┴───┘
subscripts       1   2   3   4   5
```

This type of structure can be thought of as a matrix, in which the one-dimensional tables form *rows,* and the respective storage areas between the different one-dimensional tables form *columns*.

Access to a particular location in a two-dimensional table is first by *row* subscript and then by *column* subscript.

A JSP diagram to represent this structure would be:

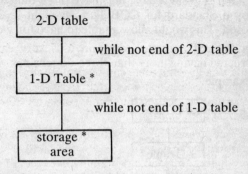

11.2.3 A three-dimensional table.

A three-dimensional table should be thought of as a number of two-dimensional tables, with each two-dimensional table given a subscript value.

Diagramatically the three-dimensional table appears as:

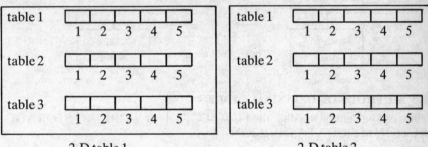

Access to a specific location in the three-dimensional table is by two-dimensional table subscript, and within the appropriate two-dimensional table by row and column subscripts respectively.

A JSP diagram to represent this structure would be:

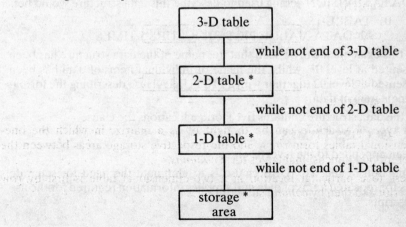

The ANS 1974 Standard for COBOL specified three levels of addressing a table, that is to say a table may have three-dimensions. However, in the draft proposed Standard for COBOL forty-eight levels of addressing have been proposed. This would allow a table to have forty-eight dimensions!

Using the JSP structure diagram it is very easy to imagine tables being constructed having more than three-dimensions.

For example.

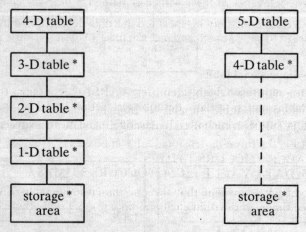

11.3 METHODS OF DEFINING TABLES

Tables can be defined in either the FILE SECTION or WORKING-STORAGE SECTION of the DATA DIVISION.

11.3.1 A one-dimensional table.

A one-dimensional table given the identifier of TABLE-1 is to be defined so that it contains five storage locations, and within each storage location it is required to store an item of data having the identifier DATA-VALUE, is numeric and contains a maximum of three digits.

The DATA DIVISION coding used to describe this data structure would be:

```
01  TABLE-1.
    02  DATA-VALUE PIC 9(3) OCCURS 5 TIMES.
```

From this example it can be seen that the name of the data structure has been represented at level 01, whilst the name of individual items of data has been represented at level 02 together with a PICTURE clause describing the format of a single item of data.

Since the data structure contains five storage locations the clause

```
        OCCURS 5 TIMES
```

has been appended to the level 02 entry.

The function of the OCCURS clause is to eliminate the need for separate entries for repeated items of data and supplies information required for the use of subscripts.

A general format for the OCCURS clause is:

> **OCCURS** integer-1 TIMES
> $\left[\begin{Bmatrix} \textbf{ASCENDING} \\ \textbf{DESCENDING} \end{Bmatrix}\right.$ KEY IS {data-name-1} .....].....
> [**INDEXED** BY {index-name-1} ......]

Clearly the format used to describe the one-dimensional array does not contain the options. The relevance of these will be explained later in the chapter.

The OCCURS clause must not be specified in a data description entry that has a level-number of 01,66,77 or 88; and mut not have a VALUE clause associated with it.

11.3.2 A two-dimensional table.

A two-dimensional table with identifier TABLE-2 contains three one-dimensional tables similar to those described in section 11.3.1.

The DATA DIVISION coding used to describe this data structure would be:

```
01 TABLE-2.
   02 TABLE-1 OCCURS 3 TIMES.
      03 DATA-VALUE PIC 9(3) OCCURS 5 TIMES.
```

From this coding it is evident that the one-dimensional table TABLE-1 is repeated three times, and within each one-dimensional table there exists five storage areas.

11.3.3 A three-dimensional table.

The three-dimensional table illustrated in section 11.2.3, given the identifier TABLE-3, and containing the two-dimensional tables described in section 11.3.2 can be described by the following DATA DIVISION coding.

```
01 TABLE-3.
   02 TABLE-2 OCCURS 2 TIMES.
      03 TABLE-1 OCCURS 3 TIMES.
         04 DATA-VALUE PIC 9(3) OCCURS 5 TIMES.
```

11.3.4 Subscripts.

At the same time as defining the table it is also important to define the subscripts that are to be used in accessing the storage locations of the table.

Subscripts are normally defined in the WORKING-STORAGE SECTION and are represented as unsigned integers. There should exist the same number of defined subscripts as there are dimensions in the table. In the last example, section 11.3.3, a three-dimensional table was defined, therefore, three subscripts should also be defined. The size of each subscript in this example is less than ten, therefore, a typical WORKING-STORAGE entry would be:

```
01 SUBSCRIPTS.
   02 SUB-1 PIC 9.
   02 SUB-2 PIC 9.
   02 SUB-3 PIC 9.
```

11.3.5 Variable length tables.

An alternative format of the OCCURS clause exists. This can be used when the number of entries in a table is known to vary and the programmer does not wish to invoke the overhead of using memory space to store an empty part of a table.

For example, the contents of a table could vary between 100 and 500 entries depending upon the use the table is put to in a program. If the table is used to store names of components that contain ten alphanumeric characters, and the varying size of the table is given at different points in the program by the identifier SIZE-OF-TABLE, then the following declaration of the table would be necessary.

```
01 TABLE-1.
    02 COMPONENT PIC X(10) OCCURS 100 TO 500 TIMES
       DEPENDING ON SIZE-OF-TABLE.
```

11.4 INITIALISATION OF TABLES

There are two methods of initialising a table with data. The first involves assigning the data to the table within the DATA DIVISION of the program, whilst the second method requires the storing of the data in the table when the program is being executed. The latter method would involve reading the data from a file, or in the case of a small table, typing the data at the keyboard of, say, a visual display unit.

11.4.1 Method 1 – worked example.

A one-dimensional table called TABLE-1 is to contain five three digit numbers as illustrated.

TABLE-1

038	049	100	079	084

The required WORKING-STORAGE coding is:

```
01 DATA-STRING PIC X(15) VALUE IS "038049100079084".
01 TABLE-1 REDEFINES DATA-STRING.
    02 DATA-VALUE PIC 9(3) OCCURS 5 TIMES.
```

An area of memory contains the alphanumeric string DATA-STRING.

DATA-STRING   038049100079084

However, this data can be viewed by the programmer in a different way by using a REDEFINES clause.

The area DATA-STRING can be regarded as consisting of five, three digit numbers, with the new name of TABLE-1.

TABLE-1   038 | 049 | 100 | 079 | 084

The original alphanumeric string has not been destroyed, the REDEFINES clause allows the programmer to view an area of memory using a different classification of data.

Each of the five numbers has the same identifier of DATA-VALUE, therefore, the only way in which individual items can be distinguished is by the subscript of the location in which they are stored. For example:

DATA-VALUE (1)   contains 038
DATA-VALUE (2)   contains 049
DATA-VALUE (3)   contains 100
DATA-VALUE (4)   contains 079
DATA-VALUE (5)   contains 084

The method of accessing data stored in a table is by specifying the name of the identifier for the data followed by the subscript in parenthesis for the storage area to be referenced.

The function of the REDEFINES clause is to allow the same computer storage area to be described by different data description entries.

The general format for this clause is:

level number $\begin{bmatrix} \text{data-name-1} \\ \text{FILLER} \end{bmatrix}$ **REDEFINES** data-name-2

Note: level-number, data-name-1 and FILLER are shown in the above format to improve clarity. Level-number, data-name-1 and FILLER are not part of the REDEFINES clause.

The REDEFINES clause, when specified, must immediately follow the subject of the entry. The level-numbers of data–name–2 and the subject of the entry must be identical, but must not be level 66 or 88. This clause must not be used in level 01 entries in the File Section. The data description entry for data–name–2 cannot contain an OCCURS clause. The entries giving the new description of the character positions must not contain any VALUE clauses, except in condition-name entries.

A two-dimensional table called POPULAR-CARS contains six ten-character non-numeric literals as illustrated.

FORD	B.L.	VAUXHALL
RENAULT	VOLKSWAGEN	FIAT

To initialise this table with these values in the WORKING-STORAGE SECTION would require the following coding.

```
01 CAR-MANUFAC.
   02 FILLER PIC X(10) VALUE IS "FORD".
   02 FILLER PIC X(10) VALUE IS "B.L.".
   02 FILLER PIC X(10) VALUE IS "VAUXHALL".
   02 FILLER PIC X(10) VALUE IS "RENAULT".
   02 FILLER PIC X(10) VALUE IS "VOLKSWAGEN".
   02 FILLER PIC X(10) VALUE IS "FIAT".
01 POPULAR-CARS REDEFINES CAR-MANUFAC.
   02 BRITISH-FOREIGN OCCURS 2 TIMES.
      03 MANUFAC PIC X(10) OCCURS 3 TIMES.
```

An alternative coding for CAR-MANUFAC is:

```
01 CAR-MANUFAC PIC X(60) VALUE IS "FORDbbbbbbB.L.bbbbbbVAUXHALLbb
   "RENAULTbbbVOLKSWAGENFIATbbbbbb".
```

An area of memory contains the alphanumeric string CAR-MANUFAC.

```
FORDbbbbbbB.L.bbbbbbVAUXHALLbbRENAULTbbbVOLKSWAGENFIATbbbbbb
```

The data string is split up into two components using the statement

```
02 BRITISH-FOREIGN OCCURS 2 TIMES.
```

1	FORDbbbbbb B.L.bbbbbb VAUXHALLbb
2	RENAULTbbbVOLKSWAGENFIATbbbbbb

Each of the one-dimensional tables that have been formed is split up into three components using the statement

03 MANUFAC PIC X(10) OCCURS 3 TIMES.

1	FORDbbbbbb	B.L.bbbbbb	VAUXHALLbb
2	RENAULTbbb	VOLKSWAGEN	FIATbbbbbb
	1	2	3

Access to any component within the two-dimensional table will be through two subscripts. The first will define the one-dimensional table (row) and the second the component within the appropriate one-dimensional table (column).

MANUFAC (1 2) = B.L.   MANUFAC (2 1) = RENAULT
MANUFAC (2 3) = FIAT etc.

11.4.2 Method 2 – worked example.

The second method of storing data in a table requires the data to be either input at the keyboard of a V.D.U. or read from a computer file. This method requires the subscript(s) of the table to be assigned values so that the data can be stored in the correct storage location.

Using the JSP methodology an alternative method to that given in section 11.4.1 for the initialisation of TABLE-1 would be as follows.

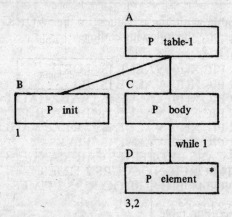

Functions List.
1. Set subscript to 1.
2. Increase subscript by 1.
3. Input data.

Conditions List.
1. Subscript not > 5.

The DATA and PROCEDURE DIVISION coding for initialising TABLE-1 is:

```
DATA DIVISION.
WORKING-STORAGE SECTION.
01  TABLE-1.
    02  NUM-VALUE PIC 999 OCCURS 5 TIMES.
01  SUB-1 PIC 9.

PROCEDURE DIVISION.
A-SEQ.
B.  MOVE 1 TO SUB-1.
C-ITER.
    IF SUB-1 > 5 GO TO C-END.
D.  ACCEPT NUM-VALUE (SUB-1).
    ADD 1 TO SUB-1.
    GO TO C-ITER.
C-END.
```

Alternatively the procedure could be rewritten to read data from a file.

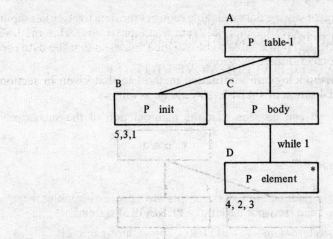

Functions List.
1. Set subscript to 1.
2. Increase subscript by 1.
3. Read file.
4. Transfer record to table.
5. Open file.

Conditions List.
1. Not end of file.

```
DATA DIVISION.
FILE SECTION.
FD DATAFILE
   LABEL RECORDS ARE STANDARD VALUE OF FILE-ID IS
   "TABLE".
01 RECORD-1.
   02 DATA-IN PIC 999.
WORKING-STORAGE SECTION.
01 TABLE-1.
   02 NUM-VALUE PIC 999 OCCURS 5 TIMES.
01 PARAMETERS.
   02 SUB-1 PIC 9.
   02 E-O-F PIC 9 VALUE IS ZERO.

PROCEDURE DIVISION.
A-SEQ.
B. OPEN INPUT DATAFILE.
   READ DATAFILE.
   MOVE 1 TO SUB-1.
C-ITER.
   IF E-O-F NOT = 0 GO TO C-END.
   MOVE RECORD-1 TO NUM-VALUE (SUB-1).
   ADD 1 TO SUB-1.
   READ DATAFILE AT END MOVE 1 TO E-O-F.
   GO TO C-ITER.
C-END.
```

In the first example it can be seen that the manipulation of the subscript comprises:

> initialisation,
> incrementing, and
> testing.

In order to simplify the manipulation of subscripts when processing tables these three functions have been incorporated into a PERFORM statement.

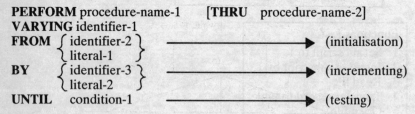

PERFORM procedure-name-1   **[THRU**   procedure-name-2]
VARYING identifier-1
FROM { identifier-2 / literal-1 } ⟶ (initialisation)
BY { identifier-3 / literal-2 } ⟶ (incrementing)
UNTIL   condition-1 ⟶ (testing)

Thus the procedure to initialise the table by typing values at the keyboard during run-time can be re-written as:

```
    PROCEDURE DIVISION.
    A-ITER.
        PERFORM B VARYING SUB-1
                FROM 1
                BY 1
                UNTIL SUB-1 > 5

        ────
        ────
        ────

    B.
        ACCEPT NUM-VALUE (SUB-1).
```

To initialise the two-dimensional table illustrated in the second example of section 11.4.1 by typing values at the keyboard of a V.D.U. during run-time, the following JSP program design would be necessary.

Functions List.	Conditions List.
1. Set row subscript to 1.	1. Row subscript not > 2.
2. Set column subscript to 1.	2. Column subscript not > 3.
3. Increase row subscript by 1.	
4. Increase column subscript by 1.	
5. Input data.	

Detailed program structure.

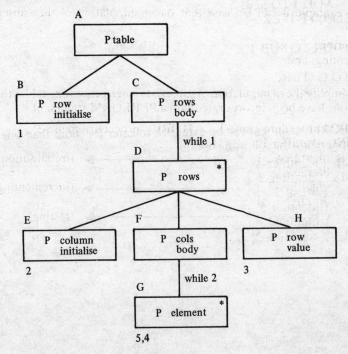

199

Schematic logic.

```
A-seq
  B do 1
  C-iter while 1
    D-seq
      E do 2
      F-iter while 2
        G do 5,4
      F-end
      H do 3
    D-cnd
  C-end
A-end
```

Coding.

```
PROCEDURE DIVISION.
A-SEQ.
B.    MOVE 1 TO SUB-1.
C-ITER.
      IF SUB-1 > 2 GO TO C-END.
D-SEQ.
E.        MOVE 1 TO SUB-2.
F-ITER.
          IF SUB-2 > 3 GO TO F-END.
G.            ACCEPT MANUFAC (SUB-1, SUB-2).
              ADD 1 TO SUB-2.
              GO TO F-ITER.
F-END.
H.        ADD 1 TO SUB-1.
D-END
      GO TO C-ITER.
C-END.
A-END.
```

The PERFORM statement can be extended to cater for more than one subscript by appending the following option.

```
[AFTER    identifier-4
 FROM  {  identifer-5  }
       {  literal-3    }
 BY    {  identifier-6 }
       {  literal-4    }
 UNTIL    condition-2]  .....
```

The coding used to initialise the two-dimensional table can now be simplified to:

```
PROCEDURE DIVISION.
A-ITER.
    PERFORM B VARYING SUB-1
                FROM 1
                BY 1
                UNTIL SUB-1 > 2
                AFTER SUB-2
                FROM 1
                BY 1
                UNTIL SUB-2 > 3.

    ___
    ___
    ___

B.
        ACCEPT MANUFAC (SUB-1, SUB-2).
```

where the second subscript SUB-2 varies faster than the first subscript SUB-1.

By using the PERFORM statement the initialisation of a table and access to elements within a table has been reduced to an iteration of the elements within the table.

The initialisation of the one and two-dimensional tables previously described can be illustrated as:

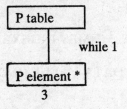

function 3: input data
condition 1: subscript not > 5.

and

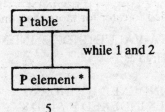

function 5: input data
condition 1: row subscript
    not > 2
condition 2: column subscript
    not > 3

respectively, when it is the intention of the programmer to code these structures using a PERFORM statement. In comparing these structure diagrams with earlier diagrams it is clear that the functions of initialising and incrementing the subscripts do not appear in these diagrams as individual functions but have become part of the PERFORM statement.

If this method of coding is used then the programmer should resort to hierarchical coding from the detailed program structure. Any attempt to introduce in-line coding would result in the schematic logic no longer mapping accurately into the coding.

When in-line coding is to be preferred the programmer should either use the methods of table access described prior to the introduction of the PERFORM statement in this chapter, or treat table access as a subroutine.

11.5 INDICES

An **index** serves the same purpose as a subscript, however, there are advantages of using indices compared with subscripts. These advantages are as follows.

The name of the index is defined within the declaration of the table.

A PICTURE clause is not required when defining an index since an index is stored within a fixed number of bytes in the memory of the computer.

The use of indices will allow the SEARCH and SEARCH ALL verbs to be used to find an item of data within an array when the position of the item is not known in advance.

11.5.1 Defining an index.

An index is defined by using an option of the OCCURS clause. One format of the OCCURS clause that is used to describe the index is:

    OCCURS integer-1 TIMES   **INDEXED** BY index-name-1

The examples of table declarations given in section 11.3 can be re-stated to include indices and **not** separate subscripts.

The one-dimensional table would be declared as:

```
01 TABLE-1.
   02 DATA-VALUE PIC 9(3) OCCURS 5 TIMES INDEXED BY
      INDX-1.
```

Access to the data in this table would be through DATA-VALUE (INDX-1).

The two-dimensional table would be declared as:

```
01 TABLE-2.
   02 TABLE-1 OCCURS 3 TIMES INDEXED BY INDX-2.
      03 DATA-VALUE PIC 9(3) OCCURS 5 TIMES INDEXED BY
         INDX-1.
```

Access to this table would be through DATA-VALUE (INDX-2, INDX-1).

The three-dimensional table would be declared as:

```
01 TABLE-3.
   02 TABLE-2 OCCURS 2 TIMES INDEXED BY INDX-3.
      03 TABLE-1 OCCURS 3 TIMES INDEXED BY INDX-2.
         04 DATA-VALUE PIC 9(3) OCCURS 5 TIMES INDEXED
            BY INDX-1.
```

Access to this table would be through DATA-VALUE (INDX-3, INDX-2, INDX-1).

11.5.2 Index modification.

A minor limitation in the use of indices is that arithmetic can only be performed on an index by using the PERFORM, SEARCH, SEARCH ALL and SET statements.

If the reader refers to the format of the PERFORM verb given in Appendix III, the inclusion of index names in format 4 shows how the statement can be used to manipulate indices.

The SET verb replaces the MOVE, ADD and SUBTRACT verbs that were used to initialise and modify subscripts.

The SET statement has two formats:

$$\textbf{SET}\ \begin{Bmatrix} \text{index-name-1} \\ \text{identifier-1} \end{Bmatrix}\ \dots\dots\ \textbf{TO}\ \begin{Bmatrix} \text{index-name-2} \\ \text{identifier-2} \\ \text{integer-1} \end{Bmatrix}$$

which is equivalent to the MOVE statement in respect of initialising either an index name or an identifier, and

$$\textbf{SET}\ \{\text{index-name-3}\}\ \dots\dots\ \begin{Bmatrix} \textbf{UP BY} \\ \textbf{DOWN BY} \end{Bmatrix} \begin{Bmatrix} \text{identifier-3} \\ \text{integer-2} \end{Bmatrix}$$

which is equivalent to the ADD and SUBTRACT statements in respect of modifying a subscript.

Examples.

The index INDX-1 can be intialised to the value 1 by using:

    SET INDX-1 TO 1

or initialised to the value of INDX-2 by using:

    SET INDX-1 TO INDX-2

or initialised to the value of the identifier COUNTER by using:

    SET INDX-1 TO COUNTER.

The index INDX-1 can be increased by the value 1 by using:

    SET INDX-1 UP BY 1

or be increased by the value of STEP-VALUE (assuming STEP-VALUE is > 0) by using:

    SET INDX-1 UP BY STEP-VALUE.

In a similar manner INDX-1 may be decreased by using:

    SET INDX-1 DOWN BY 1

or   SET INDX-1 DOWN BY STEP-VALUE.

11.5.3 Relative indexing.

An index can be increased or decreased by a fixed amount by appending a positive or negative integer to the index name (the same technique also applies to subscripts).

The format of relative addressing is:

$$\text{identifier-1}\ (\ \begin{Bmatrix} \text{index-name-1} \\ \text{identifier-2} \end{Bmatrix} \{\pm\}\ \text{integer-1}\ [\ ,\begin{Bmatrix} \text{index-name-2} \\ \text{identifier-3} \end{Bmatrix} \{\pm\}\ \text{integer-2} \dots])$$

Examples.

    SET INDX-1 TO 5.

    ADD TABLE-1 (INDX-1 + 3) TO TOTAL-VALUE

    IF TABLE-1 (INDX-1) > TABLE-1 (INDX-1 + 1) PERFORM KJ.

11.6 THE SEARCH VERBS

In processing a table it is often necessary to search a table until a particular item of data can be found. The COBOL language provides a facility for searching tables.

The SEARCH statement provides a method of performing a serial search through a table when the keys to the items within the table are **not** sorted. Whereas the SEARCH ALL statement perform a binary search through a table provided the keys to items within the table are sorted into either ascending or descending order.

The general formats for the SEARCH and SEARCH ALL verbs can be found in Appendix III.

11.6.1 Example.

A one-dimensional table contains the costs for the replacement of major components of a bicycle.

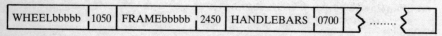

| WHEELbbbbb | 1050 | FRAMEbbbbb | 2450 | HANDLEBARS | 0700 |

If the table contains ten pairs of data and each entry in the table can be located by the index POS-TABLE then the table can be declared by:

```
01 BICYCLE-COMPONENTS.
   02 PARTS OCCURS 10 TIMES INDEXED BY POS-TABLE.
      03 COMPONENT PIC X(10).
      03 COST PIC 99V99.
```

When a description of the bicycle component, DESC-COMP, is input to the computer system the table can be searched using COMPONENT as a key, and when a match is found the cost of the component can be output.

To search the BICYCLE-COMPONENTS table the following statements would be necessary.

```
SET POS-TABLE TO 1.
SEARCH PARTS VARYING POS-TABLE
    AT END DISPLAY "COMPONENT NOT FOUND"
WHEN DESC-COMP = COMPONENT (POS-TABLE)
    MOVE COST (POS-TABLE) TO COST-ED,
    DISPLAY "COST OF COMPONENT" COST-ED.
```

Notice that it is the responsibility of the programmer to initialise the index to the first storage location in the table.

If a key match is not made then the end of the table will have been reached and the programmer should provide a notification of this.

When a key match is made the programmer must state through imperative-statement-2 (ref. Appendix III) what action is to be taken.

The system automatically increases the value of the index by 1 so that each location in turn can be examined and tested for condition-1 (ref. Appendix III) being true.

11.6.2 Example.

A one-dimensional table contains the first four characters of a postal code as a key, and the name of the postal district as the remainder of the entry. There are 984 entries in this table, and the keys are sorted into ascending order.

A selection of typical entries could be:

If each entry in the table can be located by the index P-INDEX then the table can be declared by the following statement.

```
01  POSTAL-CODE-TABLE.
    02  DISTRICTS OCCURS 984 TIMES INDEXED BY P-INDEX
        ASCENDING KEY IS POSTAL-CODE.
        03  POSTAL-CODE PIC X(4).
        03  POSTAL-DISTRICT PIC X(15).
```

From the general format of the OCCURS clause given in section 11.3.1, the option to give the name of the key and the manner in which the keys are sorted must be specified when defining a table that is to be given a binary search.

When the first four characters of the postal code P-CODE are input to the computer the table is given a binary search using the POSTAL-CODE as key, and when a match is found between P-CODE and POSTAL-CODE the name of the POSTAL-DISTRICT can be output.

For information on the binary search the reader is recommended to study the chapter on *Sorting and Searching Techniques* in another book in this series *BASIC Programming* by B.J. Holmes.

To search the POSTAL-CODE-TABLE the following statement would be used.

```
SEARCH ALL DISTRICTS
    AT END DISPLAY "POST CODE NOT LISTED"
WHEN P-CODE = POSTAL-CODE (P-INDEX)
    DISPLAY "NAME OF DISTRICT"
    POSTAL-DISTRICT (P-INDEX)
```

11.7 QUESTIONS *(answers begin on page 356)*

11.7.1 Use the descriptions of the OCCURS and REDEFINES clauses to identify the errors in the following lines of code.

```
01  ITEM PIC X(10) OCCURS 50 TIMES.
```

```
01  TABLE-1.
    02  DATA-VALUE PIC 99 OCCURS 6 TIMES VALUE IS 30.
```

```
01  TABLE-X.
    02  DATA-X PIC X(20) OCCURS 6 TIMES.
        03  DATA-Y PIC X(20) OCCURS 10 TIMES.
```

```
77  DATA-VALUE PIC X(20) OCCURS 5 TIMES.
```

FILE SECTION.
01 RECORD-1.
    ‾‾‾‾‾
    ‾‾‾‾‾

01 RECORD-2 REDEFINES RECORD-1.
    ‾‾‾‾‾
    ‾‾‾‾‾

WORKING-STORAGE SECTION.
01 ALPHA.
    ‾‾‾‾‾
    ‾‾‾‾‾
    ‾‾‾‾‾

    02 BETA REDEFINES ALPHA.
        ‾‾‾‾‾
        ‾‾‾‾‾
        ‾‾‾‾‾

01 RECORD-1-WS.
    02 ALPHA PIC X(6).
    02 BETA PIC X(6).
01 RECORD-2-WS.
    02 DELTA REDEFINES ALPHA.
        03 GAMMA PIC X OCCURS 12 TIMES

11.7.2 Code WORKING-STORAGE SECTION entries to define the following tables.

A one-dimensional table containing 50 entries, each entry represents a three digit integer ALPHA.

A two-dimensional table containing 10 rows and 3 columns, each entry represents a real number BETA with 7 digits including 2 decimal places.

A two-dimensional table contains 10 rows and 50 columns, each entry represents a 20 character string GAMMA followed by a 3 digit code DELTA.

A three-dimensional table represents 5 two-dimensional tables, each two-dimensional table represents 10 one-dimensional tables, each one-dimensional table has 8 entries and each entry represents a 3 digit integer EPSILON.

11.7.3 A selection of towns in three counties in the South of England have the following populations.

County	Town	Population
Cornwall	Penzance	19,360
	Truro	15,690
	Newquay	13,890
Dorset	Poole	118,922
	Dorchester	13,880
	Shaftesbury	4,180
Hampshire	Southampton	204,406
	Basingstoke	60,910
	Winchester	31,620

Write segments of code to initialise the following tables.

A one-dimensional table containing the names of the counties.

A two-dimensional table containing the names of the towns, where each row represents a different county in the order given in the first table.

A second two-dimensional table containing the population of each town, where each row represents a different county and each column a different town in the order given in the first two-dimensional table.

11.7.4 Using the tables defined in the last question (11.7.3) write a procedure to input the name of the county and the name of the town and perform a serial search of the one-dimensional table to match the county and obtain a row subscript, then perform a serial search of the first two-dimensional table to match the town and obtain a column subscript. Using the row and column subscript access the second two-dimensional table and display the value for the population.

Write a second procedure to input the name of a county and output the total population for the towns listed in the county. Re-express this figure as a percentage of the population in all the towns defined in the table.

11.7.5 For each of the tables defined in question 11.7.2 write separate procedures that will initialise the four tables with either spaces or zeros depending on their contents being defined as alphanumeric or numeric.

Hint: use the PERFORM statement.

11.7.6 The surnames of friends and their telephone numbers are stored in a one-dimensional table.

JONES	0296-41573	COLLINS	128-273	SMYTHE	01-111-9147

The following code is used to define the table and search the table for a telephone number given a particular name. The coding, however, contains 12 deliberate errors. Identify these errors then re-write the code correctly.

```
WORKING-STORAGE SECTION.
01 TELE-TABLE.
   02 RECORD OCCURS 50 TIMES INDEXED BY I.
   ASCENDING-KEY IS NAME (I).
      03 NAME PIC X(12).
         04 TELE-NUMBER PIC 9(12).
77 I PIC 99.
   ____
   ____

PROCEDURE DIVISION.
   ____

   MOVE 1 TO I.
   ACCEPT INPUT-NAME (I).
   SEARCH ALL TELE-TABLE CHANGING NAME
   WHEN INPUT-NAME (I) = NAME (I)
   DISPLAY TELE-NUMBER (I).
   ____
   ____
```

†**11.7.7** A sequential file is used to store information relating to different items of clothing that are distributed by a garment manufacturer. The format of records on the file is:

> Code number of garment (key) – 5 digits.
> Brief description of article – 20 characters.
> Discount quantity.
> > Ten percent – 3 digits.
> > Twenty percent – 3 digits.
> > Thirty percent – 4 digits.
> Unit price – 5 digits inc 2 dec.pl.

Note the discount quantity implies the minimum quantity of garments that are sold in order to attract the appropriate discount on the unit price of the article.

The contents of the file, which contains 250 records, is also stored in a one-dimensional table and access to the table is through the code number as key.

Define the format of the table as a WORKING-STORAGE entry. Write code for the following procedures.

Initialise the table with the contents of the file.

Input a code number and the quantity of garments to be sold at the keyboard of a computer terminal, search the table and output to the screen of the terminal the description of the garment and percentage discount on the unit price of the garment. Also output the cost of buying that quantity of garments.

†**11.7.8** When travelling on the M3 motorway westwards between junction 1 and junction 6 the towns that are accessible are as follows.

Junction	Road number	Town	Distance (Miles)
1	A308	Sunbury Kingston	 5
	A316	Central London	14
2	M25	The North (M1) Heathrow (M4) Staines (A30) Chertsey (A320)	 10 4 4
3	A322	Guildford Bracknell	11 6
4	A325	Farnborough Farnham	3 8
	A321	Camberley	3
5	A32	Alton Reading	10 14
6	A339	Basingstoke Newbury	2 21

Write a program to store this information in a one-dimensional table having the name of the town as the key to each entry. When the name of a town is input at the keyboard of a terminal the junction number, road number and distance from the junction will be output at the terminal.

Hint: since the names of the towns are not given in alphabetical sequence use the SEARCH verb to locate the appropriate town.

12 Table Processing – Worked Examples

12.1 PROBLEM

A sporting league is divided into four divisions, within each division there are eight teams and each team is named after its home town.

Division 1	Division 2	Division 3	Division 4
Southampton	Portsmouth	Basingstoke	Newbury
Winchester	Reading	Banbury	Witney
Oxford	Bicester	Gloucester	Cheltenham
Thame	Swindon	Cirencester	Salisbury
Poole	Bournemouth	Dorchester	Aylesbury
Bristol	Bath	Exeter	Torquay
St. Albans	Colchester	Chelmsford	Ipswich
Cambridge	Birmingham	Coventry	Leicester

Write a COBOL program to store the names of the teams in a two-dimensional table.

Code a menu driven PROCEDURE DIVISION to interrogate the table and display the following information.

On the input of a division number a list of the teams in that division.

On the input of a division number and team position the name of the team.

On the input of a league position a listing of the name of the teams in that position for the four divisions.

12.1.1 JSP Structure diagrams.

The two-dimensional table used to store the names of the teams can be expressed as:

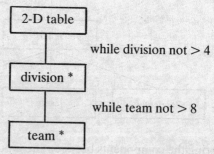

where the rows represent the divisions and the columns the team names.

The information displayed on the screen would appear as:

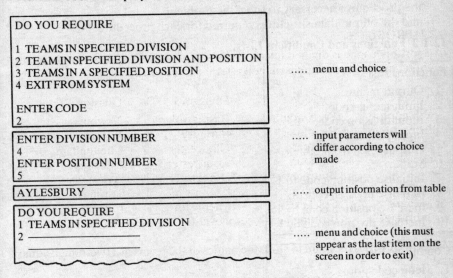

DO YOU REQUIRE

1 TEAMS IN SPECIFIED DIVISION
2 TEAM IN SPECIFIED DIVISION AND POSITION
3 TEAMS IN A SPECIFIED POSITION
4 EXIT FROM SYSTEM

ENTER CODE
2

..... menu and choice

ENTER DIVISION NUMBER
4
ENTER POSITION NUMBER
5

..... input parameters will differ according to choice made

AYLESBURY

..... output information from table

DO YOU REQUIRE
1 TEAMS IN SPECIFIED DIVISION
2 _____

..... menu and choice (this must appear as the last item on the screen in order to exit)

The corresponding structure diagram for this report is:

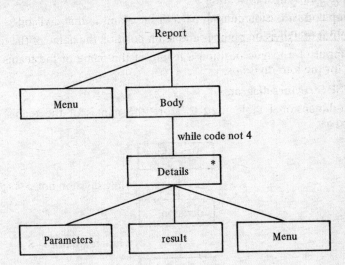

In comparing the components between the input and output data structures it would appear that no correspondence exists between them. Where access to records in a table (or file) is direct there is no requirement for the records in both structures to be in the same order or occur the same number of times. However, when a sequence of records in a table is required they should be treated in the same manner as records from a sequential file, implying that the three criteria for correspondence should be tested.

The author has assumed, therefore, that when access to records in a table (or file) is **direct** the structure diagram for the input table (or file) need not be drawn. The program structure will be based on:

the procedures necessary to solve the problem
and the output data structures required for each procedure.

12.1.2 Functions and Conditions Lists.

Functions List.
1. Output menu.
2. Input menu-code.
3. Input division code.
4. Input position code.
5. Output team from table.
6. Stop.
7. Initialise position code to 1.
8. Initialise division code to 1.
9. Increase position code by 1.
10. Increase division code by 1.

Conditions List.
1. Menu code not = 4.
2. Menu code = 1.
3. Menu code = 2.
4. Division code not > 4.
5. Position code not > 8.

12.1.3 Detailed Program Structure.

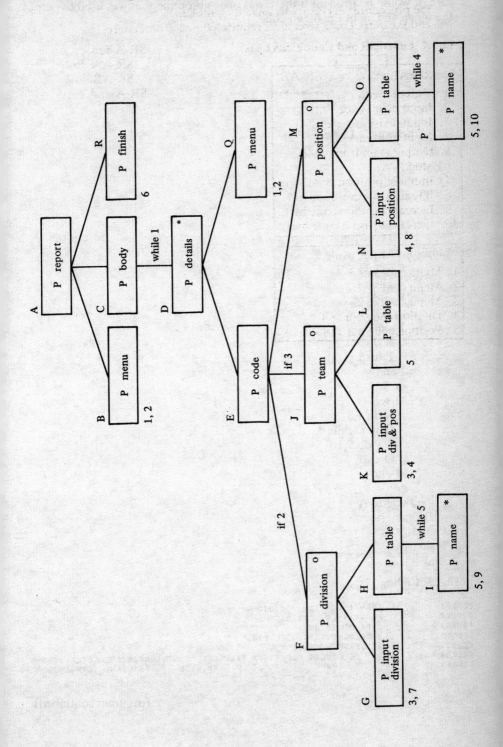

From the detailed program structure components B and Q are the same, therefore, it would be prudent if there was one subroutine that was used to output the menu and input the menu-code.

```
SR-A-seq
  SR-AA do 1
  SR-AB do 2
SR-A-end
```

12.1.4 Schematic Logic.

```
A-seq
  B do SR-A
  C-iter while 1
    D-seq
      E-sel if 2
        F-seq
          G do 3,7
          H-iter while 5
            I do 5,9
          H-end
        F-end
      E-or-2 if 3
        J-seq
          K do 3,4
          L do 5
        J-end
      E-or-3
        M-seq
          N do 4,8
          O-iter while 4
            P do 5,10
          O-end
        M-end
      E-end
      Q do SR-A
    D-end
  C-end
  R do 6
A-end
```

12.1.5 Coding.

```
(0001)          IDENTIFICATION DIVISION.
(0002)          PROGRAM-ID. C1215.
(0003)          DATA DIVISION.
(0004)          WORKING-STORAGE SECTION.
(0005)          01 LEAGUE-DIVISIONS.
(0006)             02 FILLER PIC X(88) VALUE IS "SOUTHAMPTONWINCHESTER OXFORD
(0007)          -    "  THAME       POOLE        BRISTOL     ST.ALBANS  CAMBRIDGE ".
```

(program continued)

```
(0008)              02 FILLER PIC X(88) VALUE IS "PORTSMOUTH READING    BICESTER
(0009)         -    "  SWINDON    BOURNEMOUTHBATH      COLCHESTER BIRMINGHAM ".
(0010)              02 FILLER PIC X(88) VALUE IS "BASINGSTOKEBANBURY    GLOUCESTE
(0011)         -    "R CIRENCESTERDORCHESTER EXETER      CHELMSFORD COVENTRY   ".
(0012)              02 FILLER PIC X(88) VALUE IS "NEWBURY    WITNEY    CHELTENHA
(0013)         -    "M SALISBURY  AYLESBURY  TORQUAY    IPSWICH    LEICESTER ".
(0014)           01 LEAGUE REDEFINES LEAGUE-DIVISIONS.
(0015)              02 DIVISIONS OCCURS 4 TIMES.
(0016)                 03 TEAMS PIC X(11) OCCURS 8 TIMES.
(0017)           01 SUBSCRIPTS.
(0018)              02 DIVISION-CODE PIC 9.
(0019)              02 POSITION-CODE PIC 9.
(0020)           01 MENU-CODE PIC 9.
(0021)
(0022)           PROCEDURE DIVISION.
(0023)           A-SEQ.
(0024)           B.
(0025)               PERFORM SR-A-SEQ THRU SR-A-END.
(0026)           C-ITER.
(0027)               IF MENU-CODE = 4 GO TO C-END.
(0028)           D-SEQ.
(0029)           E-SEL.
(0030)               IF MENU-CODE NOT = 1 GO TO E-OR-2.

      * List teams in specific division

(0031)           F-SEQ.
(0032)           G.
(0033)               DISPLAY "ENTER DIVISION NUMBER"
(0034)               ACCEPT DIVISION-CODE.
(0035)               MOVE 1 TO POSITION-CODE.
(0036)           H-ITER.
(0037)               IF POSITION-CODE > 8 GO TO H-END.
(0038)           I.    DISPLAY TEAMS (DIVISION-CODE, POSITION-CODE)
(0039)               ADD 1 TO POSITION-CODE.
(0040)               GO TO H-ITER.
(0041)           H-END.
(0042)           F-END.
(0043)               GO TO E-END.
(0044)           E-OR-2.
(0045)               IF MENU-CODE NOT = 2 GO TO E-OR-3.

      * List team by division and position

(0046)           J-SEQ.
(0047)           K.
(0048)               DISPLAY "ENTER DIVISION NUMBER"
(0049)               ACCEPT DIVISION-CODE.
(0050)               DISPLAY "ENTER POSITION NUMBER"
(0051)               ACCEPT POSITION-CODE.
(0052)           L.
(0053)               DISPLAY TEAMS (DIVISION-CODE, POSITION-CODE).
(0054)           J-END.
(0055)               GO TO E-END.
(0056)           E-OR-3.

      * List teams in same position

(0057)           M-SEQ.
(0058)           N.
(0059)               DISPLAY "ENTER POSITION NUMBER"
(0060)               ACCEPT POSITION-CODE.
(0061)               MOVE 1 TO DIVISION-CODE.
(0062)           O-ITER.
(0063)               IF DIVISION-CODE > 4 GO TO O-END.
(0064)           P.
(0065)               DISPLAY TEAMS (DIVISION-CODE, POSITION-CODE).
(0066)               ADD 1 TO DIVISION-CODE.
(0067)               GO TO O-ITER.
(0068)           O-END.
```

(program continued)

215

```
(0069)              4-END.
(0070)              E-END.
(0071)              0.
(0072)                   PERFORM SR-A-SEQ THRU SR-A-END.
(0073)              D-END.
(0074)                   GO TO C-ITER.
(0075)              C-END.
(0076)              R.
(0077)                   STOP RUN.
(0078)              A-END.

            * subroutine to print menu

(0079)              SR-A-SEQ.
(0080)              SR-AA.
(0081)                   DISPLAY "DO YOU REQUIRE"
(0082)                   DISPLAY " "
(0083)                   DISPLAY "1 TEAMS IN SPECIFIED DIVISION"
(0084)                   DISPLAY "2 TEAM IN SPECIFIED DIVISION AND POSITION"
(0085)                   DISPLAY "3 TEAMS IN A SPECIFIED POSITION"
(0086)                   DISPLAY "4 EXIT FROM SYSTEM"
(0087)                   DISPLAY " ".
(0088)              SR-AB.
(0089)                   DISPLAY "ENTER CODE".
(0090)                   ACCEPT MENU-CODE.
(0091)              SR-A-END.
```

12.1.6 Extract from results.

```
DO YOU REQUIRE

1 TEAMS IN SPECIFIED DIVISION
2 TEAM IN SPECIFIED DIVISION AND POSITION
3 TEAMS IN A SPECIFIED POSITION
4 EXIT FROM SYSTEM

ENTER CODE
1
ENTER DIVISION NUMBER
1
SOUTHAMPTON
WINCHESTER
OXFORD
THAME
POOLE
BRISTOL
ST.ALBANS
CAMBRIDGE
DO YOU REQUIRE

1 TEAMS IN SPECIFIED DIVISION
2 TEAM IN SPECIFIED DIVISION AND POSITION
3 TEAMS IN A SPECIFIED POSITION
4 EXIT FROM SYSTEM

ENTER CODE
2
ENTER DIVISION NUMBER
1
ENTER POSITION NUMBER
7
ST.ALBANS
DO YOU REQUIRE

1 TEAMS IN SPECIFIED DIVISION
2 TEAM IN SPECIFIED DIVISION AND POSITION
3 TEAMS IN A SPECIFIED POSITION
4 EXIT FROM SYSTEM
```

(results continued)

```
ENTER CODE
3
ENTER POSITION NUMBER
1
SOUTHAMPTON
PORTSMOUTH
BASINGSTOKE
NEWBURY
DO YOU REQUIRE

1 TEAMS IN SPECIFIED DIVISION
2 TEAM IN SPECIFIED DIVISION AND POSITION
3 TEAMS IN A SPECIFIED POSITION
4 EXIT FROM SYSTEM

ENTER CODE
4
```

12.2 PROBLEM

A national union of workers is divided into six regions. Within each region there are five branches. In a national ballot to elect a union president every worker is allowed to vote for one of the four candidates. The votes for the candidates are stored by region and by branch within a three-dimensional table.

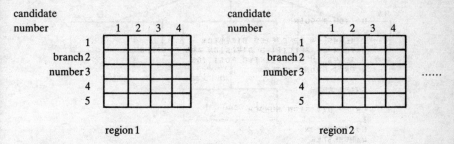

The names of the four candidates are Bloggs, Davies, Jones and Smith and are stored in a separate one dimensional table which is accessed on candidate number as subscript.

Write a COBOL program to execute the following procedures.

Initialise a three-dimensional table from a sequential file that contains the votes for every candidate sorted on region as primary key, branch as secondary key and candidate as tertiary key.

Process and output the following information.

The total number of votes cast for all the candidates.
The total number of votes cast for each candidate in each region.
The percentage number of votes cast for each candidate.
The winner of the election.

Where a result applies to an individual candidate the name of the candidate should be printed and not the candidate number.

217

12.2.1 Procedures.

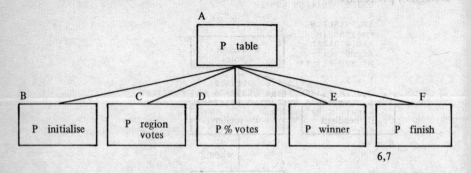

12.2.2 Design of procedure B.

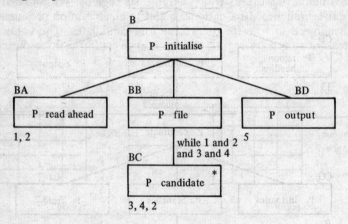

Functions List for B and F.
1. Open file.
2. Read file.
3. Move candidate vote to table.
4. Increase total votes cast by candidate vote.
5. Output total votes cast.
6. Close file
7. Stop.

Conditions List for B.
1. Not end of file.
2. Region not > 6.
3. Branch not > 5.
4. Candidate not > 4.

12.2.3
Design of procedure C.

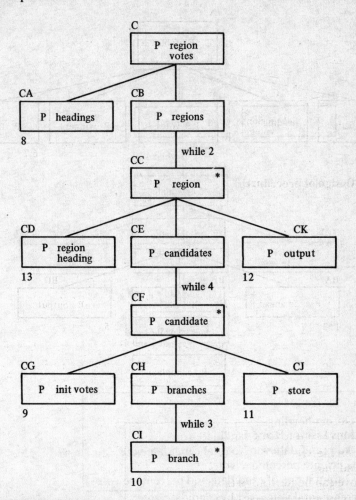

Functions list for C.
  8. Output headings.
  9. Move zero to total regional votes.
  10. Add candidate vote to total regional vote.
  11. Store total regional vote in candidate vote table.
  12. Output candidates regional votes.
  13. Move region to W-S for regional votes output line.

Conditions list for C.
  2. Region not > 6.
  3. Branch not > 5.
  4. Candidate not > 4.

12.2.4

Design of procedure D.

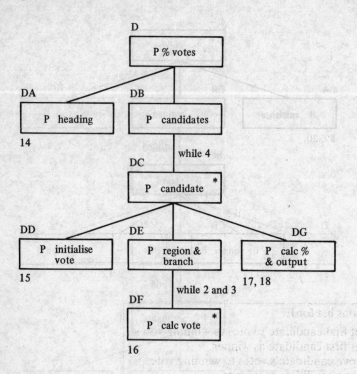

Functions list for D.

14. Output headings.
15. Move zero to total candidate vote.
16. Add candidate vote to total candidate vote.
17. Calculate percentage vote.
18. Output name of candidate and percentage vote.

Conditions list for D.

2. Region not > 6.
3. Branch not > 5.
4. Candidate not > 4.

12.2.5
Design of procedure E.

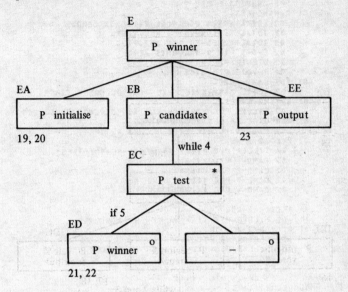

Functions list for E.

19. Set first candidate's votes to winning votes.
20. Set first candidate as winner.
21. Move candidate's votes to winning votes.
22. Move candidate to winner.
23. Output winning candidate.

Conditions list for E.

4. Candidate not > 4.
5. Candidate's votes < Candidate + 1 votes.

12.2.6 Coding.

```
(0001)          IDENTIFICATION DIVISION.
(0002)          PROGRAM-ID. C1153.
(0003)          ENVIRONMENT DIVISION.
(0004)          INPUT-OUTPUT SECTION.
(0005)          FILE-CONTROL.
(0006)              SELECT VOTING-FILE ASSIGN TO PFMS.
(0007)          DATA DIVISION.
(0008)          FILE SECTION.
(0009)          FD VOTING-FILE
(0010)              LABEL RECORDS ARE STANDARD VALUE OF FILE-ID IS "VOTING".
(0011)          01 RECORD-1.
(0012)              02 VOTE PIC 9(4).
(0013)          WORKING-STORAGE SECTION.
(0014)          01 VOTING-TABLE.
(0015)              02 REGIONS OCCURS 6 TIMES.
(0016)                  03 BRANCHES OCCURS 5 TIMES.
(0017)                      04 CANDIDATE-VOTES PIC 9(4) OCCURS 4 TIMES.
```

(program continued)

```
(0018)           01 SUBSCRIPTS.
(0019)              02 REGION PIC 9.
(0020)              02 BRANCH PIC 9.
(0021)              02 CANDIDATE PIC 9.
(0022)           01 PARAMETERS.
(0023)              02 TOTAL-VOTES PIC 9(6) VALUE IS ZERO.
(0024)              02 TOTAL-REGION-VOTES PIC 9(5).
(0025)              02 TOTAL-VOTES-ED PIC ZZZ,ZZ9.
(0026)              02 E-O-F PIC 9 VALUE IS ZERO.
(0027)              02 WINNER PIC 9.
(0028)              02 P-VOTE PIC 9(6)V99.
(0029)           01 TOT-CAND-VOTE.
(0030)              02 TOTAL-CAND-VOTES PIC 9(6) OCCURS 4 TIMES.
(0031)           01 VOTING-NAMES.
(0032)              02 FILLER PIC X(24) VALUE IS "BLOGGSDAVIESJONES SMITH ".
(0033)           01 NAMES REDEFINES VOTING-NAMES.
(0034)              02 CAND-NAME PIC X(6) OCCURS 4 TIMES.
(0035)           01 RECORD-1-WS.
(0036)              02 FILLER PIC X(17) VALUE IS "CANDIDATES".
(0037)              02 CAND-1 PIC X(15).
(0038)              02 CAND-2 PIC X(15).
(0039)              02 CAND-3 PIC X(15).
(0040)              02 CAND-4 PIC X(15).
(0041)
(0042)           01 RECORD-2-WS.
(0043)              02 FILLER PIC X(7) VALUE IS "REGIONS".
(0044)           01 RECORD-3-WS.
(0045)              02 REGION-WS PIC 9.
(0046)              02 FILLER PIC X(14) VALUE IS SPACES.
(0047)              02 VOTES-CAST OCCURS 4 TIMES.
(0048)                 03 VOTE-ED PIC ZZZ,ZZ9.
(0049)                 03 SP-WS PIC X(8).
(0050)           01 RECORD-4-WS.
(0051)              02 FILLER PIC X(23) VALUE IS "CANDIDATE   X TOTAL VOTE".
(0052)           01 RECORD-5-WS.
(0053)              02 CAND-WS PIC X(13).
(0054)              02 VOTE-WS PIC Z9.
(0055)
(0056)           PROCEDURE DIVISION.
(0057)           A-SEQ.
(0058)              PERFORM B-SEQ.
(0059)              PERFORM C-SEQ.
(0060)              PERFORM D-SEQ.
(0061)              PERFORM E-SEQ.
(0062)              PERFORM F.
(0063)           B-SEQ.
(0064)              PERFORM BA.
(0065)              PERFORM BB-ITER.
(0066)              PERFORM BD.
(0067)           BA.
(0068)              OPEN INPUT VOTING-FILE.
(0069)              READ VOTING-FILE.
(0070)           BB-ITER.
(0071)              PERFORM BC VARYING REGION
(0072)                        FROM 1 BY 1 UNTIL E-O-F NOT = 0
(0073)                              AND REGION > 6
(0074)                        AFTER BRANCH FROM 1 BY 1 UNTIL BRANCH > 5
(0075)                        AFTER CANDIDATE FROM 1 BY 1 UNTIL CANDIDATE > 4.
(0076)           BC.
(0077)              MOVE VOTE TO CANDIDATE-VOTES (REGION, BRANCH, CANDIDATE)
(0078)              ADD CANDIDATE-VOTES (REGION, BRANCH, CANDIDATE)
(0079)              TO TOTAL-VOTES.
(0080)              READ VOTING-FILE AT END MOVE 1 TO E-O-F.
(0081)           BD.
(0082)              MOVE TOTAL-VOTES TO TOTAL-VOTES-ED.
(0083)              DISPLAY "TOTAL NUMBER OF VOTES CAST FOR ALL CANDIDATES "
(0084)              TOTAL-VOTES-ED.
(0085)           C-SEQ.
(0086)              PERFORM CA.
(0087)              PERFORM CB-ITER.
```

(program continued)

```
(0088)          CA.
(0089)              MOVE CAND-NAME (1) TO CAND-1.
(0090)              MOVE CAND-NAME (2) TO CAND-2.
(0091)              MOVE CAND-NAME (3) TO CAND-3.
(0092)              MOVE CAND-NAME (4) TO CAND-4.
(0093)              DISPLAY " "
(0094)              DISPLAY RECORD-1-WS.
(0095)              DISPLAY RECORD-2-WS.
(0096)          CB-ITER.
(0097)              PERFORM CC-SEQ VARYING REGION
(0098)                          FROM 1 BY 1 UNTIL REGION > 6.
(0099)          CC-SEQ.
(0100)              PERFORM CD.
(0101)              PERFORM CE-ITER.
(0102)              PERFORM CK.
(0103)          CD.
(0104)              MOVE REGION TO REGION-WS.
(0105)          CE-ITER.
(0106)              PERFORM CF-SEQ VARYING CANDIDATE FROM 1 BY 1
(0107)                          UNTIL CANDIDATE > 4.
(0108)          CK.
(0109)              DISPLAY RECORD-3-WS.
(0110)          CF-SEQ.
(0111)              PERFORM CG.
(0112)              PERFORM CH-ITER.
(0113)              PERFORM CJ.
(0114)          CG.
(0115)              MOVE ZERO TO TOTAL-REGION-VOTES.
(0116)          CH-ITER.
(0117)              PERFORM CI VARYING BRANCH
(0118)                          FROM 1 BY 1 UNTIL BRANCH > 5.
(0119)          CJ.
(0120)              MOVE TOTAL-REGION-VOTES TO VOTE-ED (CANDIDATE).
(0121)              MOVE SPACES TO SP-WS (CANDIDATE).
(0122)          CI.
(0123)              ADD CANDIDATE-VOTES (REGION, BRANCH, CANDIDATE)
(0124)                  TO TOTAL-REGION-VOTES.
(0125)          D-SEQ.
(0126)              PERFORM DA.
(0127)              PERFORM DB-ITER.
(0128)          DA.
(0129)              DISPLAY " ".
(0130)              DISPLAY RECORD-4-WS.
(0131)          DB-ITER.
(0132)              PERFORM DC-SEQ VARYING CANDIDATE
(0133)                          FROM 1 BY 1 UNTIL CANDIDATE > 4.
(0134)          DC-SEQ.
(0135)              PERFORM DD.
(0136)              PERFORM DE-ITER.
(0137)              PERFORM DG.
(0138)          DD.
(0139)              MOVE CAND-NAME (CANDIDATE) TO CAND-WS.
(0140)              MOVE ZERO TO TOTAL-CAND-VOTES (CANDIDATE).
(0141)          DE-ITER.
(0142)              PERFORM DF VARYING REGION
(0143)                          FROM 1 BY 1 UNTIL REGION > 6
(0144)                          AFTER BRANCH
(0145)                          FROM 1 BY 1 UNTIL BRANCH > 5.
(0146)          DF.
(0147)              ADD CANDIDATE-VOTES (REGION, BRANCH, CANDIDATE)
(0148)                  TO TOTAL-CAND-VOTES (CANDIDATE).
(0149)          DG.
(0150)              DIVIDE TOTAL-VOTES INTO TOTAL-CAND-VOTES (CANDIDATE)
(0151)              GIVING P-VOTE ROUNDED.
(0152)              MULTIPLY 100 BY P-VOTE GIVING VOTE-WS.
(0153)              DISPLAY RECORD-5-WS.
(0154)          E-SEQ.
(0155)              PERFORM EA.
(0156)              PERFORM EB-ITER.
(0157)              PERFORM EE.
```

(program continued)

```
(0158)          FA.
(0159)              MOVE TOTAL-CAND-VOTES (1) TO TOTAL-VOTES.
(0160)              MOVE 1 TO WINNER.
(0161)          EB-ITER.
(0162)              PERFORM EC-SEL VARYING CANDIDATE
(0163)                          FROM 2 BY 1 UNTIL CANDIDATE > 4.
(0164)          EC-SEL.
(0165)              IF TOTAL-CAND-VOTES (CANDIDATE) > TOTAL-VOTES
(0166)                 PERFORM ED.
(0167)          ED.
(0168)              MOVE TOTAL-CAND-VOTES (CANDIDATE) TO TOTAL-VOTES.
(0169)              MOVE CANDIDATE TO WINNER.
(0170)          EE.
(0171)              MOVE TOTAL-VOTES TO TOTAL-VOTES-ED.
(0172)              DISPLAY " ".
(0173)              DISPLAY "ELECTED PRESIDENT OF UNION IS MR. "
(0174)              CAND-NAME (WINNER)
(0175)              " WITH " TOTAL-VOTES-ED " VOTES".
(0176)          F.
(0177)              CLOSE VOTING-FILE.
(0178)              STOP RUN.
```

12.2.7 Results.

```
TOTAL NUMBER OF VOTES CAST FOR ALL CANDIDATES 132,521
```

CANDIDATES	BLOGGS	DAVIES	JONES	SMITH
REGIONS				
1	6,055	5,592	5,582	5,141
2	4,704	5,472	3,912	3,251
3	10,822	8,413	13,821	7,331
4	4,202	5,005	3,606	2,875
5	4,717	4,532	5,122	5,393
6	4,282	4,289	4,901	3,501

CANDIDATE	% TOTAL VOTE
BLOGGS	26
DAVIES	25
JONES	28
SMITH	21

```
ELECTED PRESIDENT OF UNION IS MR. JONES WITH 36,944 VOTES
```

12.2.8 Modular Programming.

This last worked example illustrates a technique of refining the design of a program to a series of smaller procedures or *modules,* where each module performs a specific task, for example initialisation, calculation of regional votes, calculation of percentage votes, and determining the winner of the election.

As problems increase in their complexity so the size of the computer programs required to solve these problems will also increase. To apply a JSP design to a complex problem so that a single program structure chart encompassed the whole program would be impractical. A practical approach is to reduce the solution to the problem to a set of procedures and construct a program structure chart for each procedure. Each procedure is PERFORMed from a higher level as indicated by the procedure structure, and each procedure, in turn, is coded using either the hierarchical method or the in-line method of coding.

12.3 PROBLEM

A sequential file contains the names of telephone exchanges in a particular area of Oxfordshire and their respective local dialling codes. The format of a record on the file is:

name of exchange (key)	25 alphanumeric characters
local dialling code	7 alphanumeric characters

and the file is sorted into ascending key sequence.

If the file contains 25 entries write a COBOL program to execute the following procedures.

Initialise a one-dimensional table with the contents of the file.

Interrogate the table on name of exchange as key or local dialling code as key and output either the local dialling code or name or exchange respectively.

This example is used to illustrate the use of SEARCH ALL and SEARCH. Since the names of the exchanges are sorted into ascending order the SEARCH ALL verb will be used to find the corresponding local dialling code for a particular exchange, whereas the SEARCH verb will be used to find the corresponding exchange for a particular dialling code.

12.3.1 Procedures.

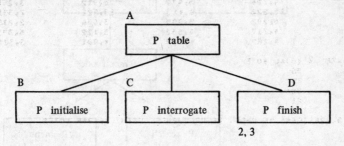

12.3.2 Design of procedure B.

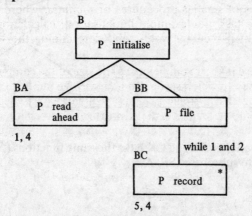

Functions List for B and D.

1. Open file.
2. Close file.
3. Stop.
4. Read file.
5. Move record to table.

Conditions List for B.

1. Not end of file.
2. Index not > 25.

12.3.3 Design of procedure C.

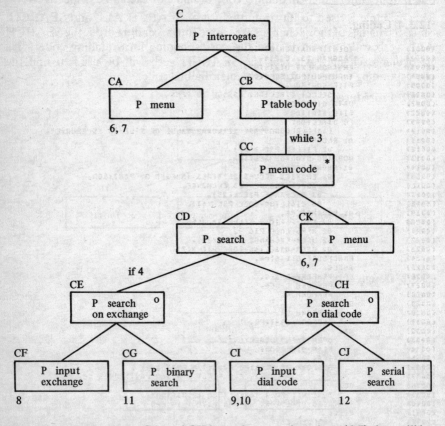

Note. Since components CA and CK have the same functions (6,7) they will be coded as a separate subroutine SR-A.

Functions List for C.

  6. Output menu.
  7. Input menu-code.
  8. Input exchange name.
  9. Input dialling code.
10. Initialise index to 1.
11. Perform binary search and output result.
12. Perform serial search and output result.

Conditions List for C.

3. Menu-code not = 3.
4. Menu-code = 1.

12.3.4 Coding.

```
(0001)          IDENTIFICATION DIVISION.
(0002)          PROGRAM-ID. C1234.
(0003)          ENVIRONMENT DIVISION.
(0004)          INPUT-OUTPUT SECTION.
(0005)          FILE-CONTROL.
(0006)              SELECT DIRECTORY ASSIGN TO PFMS.
(0007)          DATA DIVISION.
(0008)          FILE SECTION.
(0009)          FD DIRECTORY
(0010)              LABEL RECORDS ARE STANDARD VALUE OF FILE-ID IS "PHONE".
(0011)          01 RECORD-1.
(0012)              02 FILLER PIC X(32).
(0013)          WORKING-STORAGE SECTION.
(0014)          01 PHONE-TABLE.
(0015)              02 ENTRIES OCCURS 25 TIMES INDEXED BY POSITION,
(0016)                  ASCENDING KEY IS EXCHANGE.
(0017)                  03 EXCHANGE PIC X(25).
(0018)                  03 DIALLING-CODE PIC X(7).
(0019)          01 PARAMETERS.
(0020)              02 E-O-F PIC 9 VALUE IS ZERO.
(0021)              02 MENU-CODE PIC 9.
(0022)              02 USER-EXCHANGE PIC X(25).
(0023)              02 USER-DIALLING-CODE PIC X(7).
(0024)          PROCEDURE DIVISION.
(0025)          A-SEQ.
(0026)              PERFORM B-SEQ.
(0027)              PERFORM C-SEQ.
(0028)              PERFORM D.
(0029)          B-SEQ.
(0030)              PERFORM BA.
(0031)              PERFORM BB-ITER.
(0032)          BA.
(0033)              OPEN INPUT DIRECTORY.
(0034)              READ DIRECTORY.
(0035)          BB-ITER.
(0036)              PERFORM BC VARYING POSITION FROM 1 BY 1
(0037)                      UNTIL E-O-F NOT = 0 AND POSITION > 25.
(0038)          BC.
(0039)              MOVE RECORD-1 TO ENTRIES (POSITION).
(0040)              READ DIRECTORY AT END MOVE 1 TO E-O-F.
(0041)          C-SEQ.
(0042)              PERFORM CA.
(0043)              PERFORM CB-ITER.
(0044)          CA.
(0045)              PERFORM SR-A-SEQ THRU SR-A-END.
(0046)          CB-ITER.
(0047)              PERFORM CC-SEQ UNTIL MENU-CODE = 3.
(0048)          CC-SEQ.
(0049)              PERFORM CD-SEL.
(0050)              PERFORM CK.
```

(program continued)

```
(0051)            CD-SEL.
(0052)                IF MENU-CODE = 1
(0053)                    PERFORM CE-SEQ
(0054)                ELSE
(0055)                    PERFORM CH-SEQ.
(0056)            CK.
(0057)                PERFORM SR-A-SEQ THRU SR-A-END.
(0058)            CE-SEQ.
(0059)                PERFORM CF.
(0060)                PERFORM CG.
(0061)            CH-SEQ.
(0062)                PERFORM CI.
(0063)                PERFORM CJ.
(0064)            CF.
(0065)                DISPLAY "ENTER EXCHANGE NAME"
(0066)                ACCEPT USER-EXCHANGE.
(0067)            CG.
(0068)                SEARCH ALL ENTRIES
(0069)                    AT END DISPLAY "EXCHANGE NOT LISTED"
(0070)                WHEN USER-EXCHANGE = EXCHANGE (POSITION)
(0071)                    DISPLAY "LOCAL DIALLING CODE IS " DIALLING-CODE (POSITION).
(0072)            CI.
(0073)                DISPLAY "ENTER DIALLING-CODE"
(0074)                ACCEPT USER-DIALLING-CODE.
(0075)                SET POSITION TO 1.
(0076)            CJ.
(0077)                SEARCH ENTRIES VARYING POSITION
(0078)                    AT END DISPLAY "DIALLING CODE NOT LISTED"
(0079)                WHEN USER-DIALLING-CODE = DIALLING-CODE (POSITION)
(0080)                    DISPLAY "NAME OF EXCHANGE IS " EXCHANGE (POSITION).
(0081)            SR-A-SEQ.
(0082)                DISPLAY "DO YOU REQUIRE"
(0083)                DISPLAY " "
(0084)                DISPLAY "1 DIALLING CODE"
(0085)                DISPLAY "2 EXCHANGE NAME"
(0086)                DISPLAY "3 EXIT FROM SYSTEM".
(0087)                DISPLAY " ".
(0088)                ACCEPT MENU-CODE.
(0089)            SR-A-END.
(0090)            D.
(0091)                CLOSE DIRECTORY.
(0092)                STOP RUN.
```

12.3.5 Results.

```
DO YOU REQUIRE

1 DIALLING CODE
2 EXCHANGE NAME
3 EXIT FROM SYSTEM

1
ENTER EXCHANGE NAME
GREAT TEW
LOCAL DIALLING CODE IS 0983
DO YOU REQUIRE

1 DIALLING CODE
2 EXCHANGE NAME
3 EXIT FROM SYSTEM

1
ENTER EXCHANGE NAME
NUNEHAM COURTENAY
LOCAL DIALLING CODE IS 918 38
DO YOU REQUIRE
```

(results continued)

```
1 DIALLING CODE
2 EXCHANGE NAME
3 EXIT FROM SYSTEM

1
ENTER EXCHANGE NAME
TACKLEY
LOCAL DIALLING CODE IS 086 983
DO YOU REQUIRE

1 DIALLING CODE
2 EXCHANGE NAME
3 EXIT FROM SYSTEM

1
ENTER EXCHANGE NAME
BICESTER
LOCAL DIALLING CODE IS 086 92
DO YOU REQUIRE

1 DIALLING CODE
2 EXCHANGE NAME
3 EXIT FROM SYSTEM

2
ENTER DIALLING-CODE
9274
NAME OF EXCHANGE IS BARTON-ON-THE-HEATH
DO YOU REQUIRE

1 DIALLING CODE
2 EXCHANGE NAME
3 EXIT FROM SYSTEM

2
ENTER DIALLING-CODE
86
NAME OF EXCHANGE IS RAMSDEN
DO YOU REQUIRE

1 DIALLING CODE
2 EXCHANGE NAME
3 EXIT FROM SYSTEM

2
ENTER DIALLING-CODE
91
NAME OF EXCHANGE IS OXFORD
DO YOU REQUIRE

1 DIALLING CODE
2 EXCHANGE NAME
3 EXIT FROM SYSTEM

2
ENTER DIALLING-CODE
036 786
NAME OF EXCHANGE IS FILKINS
DO YOU REQUIRE

1 DIALLING CODE
2 EXCHANGE NAME
3 EXIT FROM SYSTEM

3
```

229

With reference to the last example it is quite likely that different local dialling exchanges will have the same dialling code. For example in Oxfordshire the exchanges of Charlbury, Chipping Norton, Hook Norton, Moreton-in-Marsh and Shipton-on-Stour all have the same dialling code of 92 if dialled from the Witney area. Therefore, if the name of an exchange is to be found using a dialling code as key, only the first entry in the table with that dialling code will be accessed despite there being other exchanges with the same dialling code. The program can be modified to search the table and output the names of exchanges that have duplicate dialling codes, as follows.

CJ.

> PERFORM CK VARYING POSITION FROM 1 BY 1
> UNTIL POSITION > 25.

CK.

> IF USER-DIALLING-CODE = DIALLING-CODE (POSITION)
> DISPLAY "NAME OF EXCHANGE IS" EXCHANGE (POSITION).

12.4 QUESTIONS

† **12.4.1** Each team in the sporting league described in the example of 12.1 plays a weekly home or away match with another member of the same division, and is awarded points on the following basis.

	Home	Away
Win	2	3
Draw	1	2
Lose	0	1

A sequential file ordered on primary key division number and secondary key points awarded to date in the season, contains records with the following format.

> Division number – 1 digit.
> Team name – 11 characters.
> Points – 3 digits.

A second sequential file ordered on primary key division number only contains details of current fixtures and the results of those matches played. The format of records on this file is:

> Division number – 1 digit.
> Team name (home) – 11 characters.
> Score (home team) – 2 digits.
> Team name (away) – 11 characters.
> Score (away team) – 2 digits.

Write a COBOL program to execute the following procedures.

Initialise a two-dimensional table with the contents of the first sequential file.

Use the second sequential file to update the table with the latest results thus increasing the points awarded to date for all the teams in the league.

Assume that all the fixtures are played.

† **12.4.2** Five integers are stored in a one-dimensional table, their order is from highest to lowest. However, it is required to sort the contents of the table so

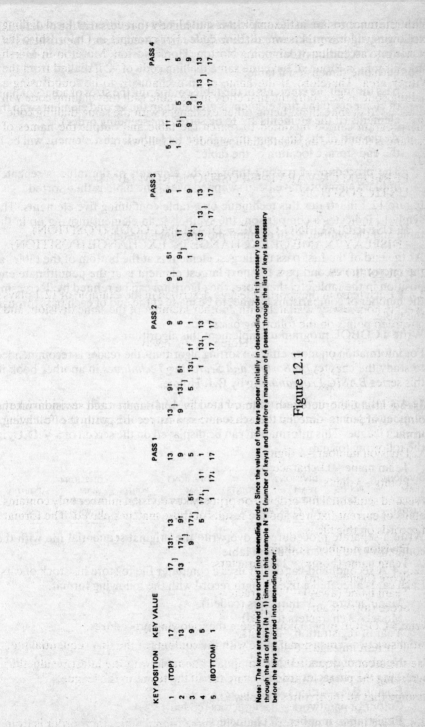

Figure 12.1

Note: The keys are required to be sorted into ascending order. Since the values of the keys appear initially in descending order it is necessary to pass through the list of keys (N − 1) times. In this example N = 5 (number of keys) and therefore a maximum of 4 passes through the list of keys is necessary before the keys are sorted into ascending order.

that the numbers are in the order lowest to highest (a reversal in the order). The following algorithm, known as the *bubble sort* is used to sort the contents of a table into ascending order.

For each one-dimensional table:

pass through the elements of the table comparing the sizes of adjacent pairs of elements, if the first element is greater than the second element swap the elements (if the elements are to be sorted in ascending order).

At the end of the first pass through the table the largest element will be in the end storage location of the table.

The procedure of passing through the elements of the table is repeated until no elements have been swapped over. The table is then sorted.

Figure 12.1 illustrates this technique on a table containing five elements. The symbol] indicates a comparison, the symbol ↑ an element moving up in the table and the symbol ↓ an element moving down the table.

At the end of the first pass the largest element is at the bottom of the table, at the end of the second pass the next largest element is at the penultimate end position in the table etc, therefore, the algorithm can be refined by decreasing the number of comparisons by one, to be made at the end of each pass through the table.

Write a COBOL program to implement this algorithm.

For information on more efficient sorting algorithms the reader is recommended to study the chapter on *Sorting and Searching Techniques* in another book in this series *BASIC Programming* by B.J. Holmes.

† **12.4.3** Using the updated table created in 12.4.1 sort each division on the number of points awarded to each team, and output the position of each team in each league. This information can be displayed on the screen of a V.D.U. in the following format.

DIVISION 1		DIVISION 2		DIVISION 3		DIVISION 4	
TEAM	POINTS	TEAM	POINTS	TEAM	POINTS	TEAM	POINTS
POOLE	58	BATH	67	BANBURY	45	WITNEY	54
OXFORD	56	COLCHESTER	63	EXETER	44	IPSWICH	50

Write a separate procedure to overwrite the original sequential file with the contents of the sorted, updated table.

† **12.4.4** A secondhand-car dealer uses a computer file to store his stock of cars. Each car is allocated a fixed length record with the following format.

Manufacturer – 2 characters (coded).
Model – 3 characters (coded).
Year of registration – 2 digits.
Current mileage – 6 digits.
Number of doors – 1 digit.
Type – 1 character (coded).
Engine size – 4 digits.
Colour of paintwork – 2 characters (coded).
Registration number – 7 characters.
Engine number – 12 characters.
Chassis number – 12 characters.
Sale price – 5 digits.

The organisation of the file is sequential, records being ordered on manufacturer code as primary key, model code as secondary key, and type of car code as tertiary key.

The car dealer requires a comprehensive report on his stock. The report must not contain the codes used for manufacturer, model, type and colour of paintwork, but be replaced by a full description for each of the codes.

The descriptions for each of the codes are stored in four one-dimensional tables, for example.

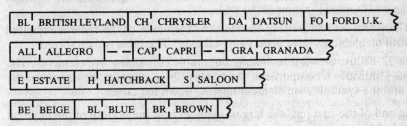

Invent suitable data for the four one-dimensional tables and the sequential file.

Design the layout of a comprehensive report.

Design and write a complete COBOL program to read the sequential file, translate all the coded fields into full descriptions and output the information found in every record to the report.

13 Random Access Files

13.1 INTRODUCTION

The organisation of the files used so far in the text have been either serial or sequential. In order to retrieve a record from a serial file it is necessary to read successive records from the beginning of the file until a key match is found. However, in retrieving a record from a sequential file the records are read in succession from the beginning of the file until either a key match is found or the transaction key is smaller than the master key when the keys on both files are in ascending order.

Both methods of file organisation do not allow for *random* access to records given specific keys. The term random implies processing in no particular order. There are three commonly used methods of organising files for random access – *Indexed Sequential, Relative* and *Direct*. Direct file organisation, also known as *Relative track* organisation, is **not** described in the ANS 1974 Standard or in the Draft Proposal and, therefore, will not be considered further in this chapter.

13.2 DESCRIPTION OF INDEXED SEQUENTIAL FILES

Files organised in this manner are stored on magnetic disc to allow for random access to records as well as sequential access to records on the file. The file organisation uses three areas for data storage:

- an index area,
- a main record storage area,
- and a record overflow area.

The index to the file contains a list of sorted (sequential) record keys. Not every key to a record is stored in the index, but only those necessary to reference a physical record. Associated with each key in the index is an address that corresponds to a position on the surface of the disc where the record belonging to that key is stored. A record may contain a primary key and possibly alternative secondary keys. Therefore, by specifying either the primary key or a secondary key it is possible to access a record directly from the disc.

Records stored in the primary storage area are **not** necessarily in sequential order, however, this is dependent upon the system being used, and does not affect the sequential access to the file since the index is organised in a sequential manner. Records in the main (and overflow) storage areas can be amended, deleted and inserted in the one file without having to create a separate updated master file. However, it is recommended to create a separate serial file that logs all changes to the master file as a matter of security.

Track Index

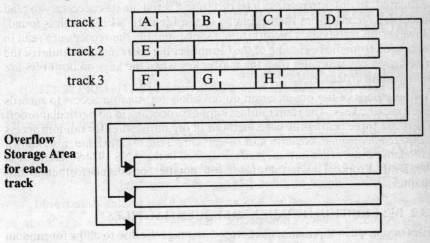

The highest key found on each track of the disc is stored in the track index. If a record has a key of, say, G the index is searched until either a match for G is found or G is less than the the next highest key in the index. In this example the next highest key is H which has a track number of 3. Track 3 is read into a buffer area and the record keys are searched until a match for the key G can be found. The record having key G has then been accessed.

Each track can have an overflow storage area so that when a track is full the overflowed records can be written to the appropriate overflow track. The system must also change the value for the highest key for that track in the index since an insertion of records into a track will result in the original highest key value changing.

When records are deleted from an indexed sequential file gaps appear between records in the file and storage space becomes wasted, yet if records are inserted into the file there will eventually be no more room in the main storage area and records are then stored in an overflow area. After a considerable number of changes to the file the main storage area may contain an unacceptable amount of wasted space and the utilisation of the overflow area becomes too great. This imbalance in the storage of records is of little concern to the COBOL programmer since computer systems provide utility programs to condense indexed sequential files, closing the gaps in the main file and emptying the overflow area.

13.3 COBOL STATEMENTS ASSOCIATED WITH INDEXED SEQUENTIAL FILES

13.3.1 File Control

The general format for FILE CONTROL in the ENVIRONMENT DIVISION is:

SELECT file-name **ASSIGN** TO device-name
ORGANIZATION IS INDEXED
[ACCESS MODE IS $\left\{\begin{array}{l}\textbf{SEQUENTIAL}\\ \textbf{RANDOM}\\ \textbf{DYNAMIC}\end{array}\right\}$]
RECORD KEY IS data-name-1
[**ALTERNATE RECORD** KEY IS data-name-2 [WITH **DUPLICATES**]] .....
[**FILE STATUS** IS data-name-3]

The SELECT clause specifies the name of the indexed sequential file in the COBOL program and assigns the file to a hardware device (e.g. PFMS for the PR1ME disc system).

The ORGANIZATION clause (note the spelling) specifies that the file-name in the SELECT clause contains data organised by indices.

The ACCESS clause specifies how an indexed file is written or retrieved.

If the ACCESS mode is not specified then the default mode is taken to be sequential. The **sequential** mode specifies that records will be written or retrieved sequentially. When a WRITE statement is used the record must be submitted in ascending sequence by RECORD KEY value. A READ statement retrieves a record sequentially.

When the **random** mode is specified a record will be written or retrieved randomly (directly) based on the value stored in the RECORD KEY field **prior** to a READ or WRITE. The random mode precludes a sequential READ or WRITE.

When the **dynamic** mode is specified an indexed file can be written to or retrieved from in either a random or sequential mode.

The RECORD KEY clause specifies the field within each record that is used as the primary index.

This field must be defined in the record description of the file, and must be the first field in the record. The value of the primary index must be unique for each record.

The primary index cannot be subscripted (i.e. defined using an OCCURS clause).

The ALTERNATE RECORD KEY clause specifies secondary keys that may be present in a record. A secondary key cannot be embedded within the primary key. Secondary keys can have values in the file that are not unique, in which case WITH DUPLICATES should be appended to the ALTERNATE RECORD KEY clause.

The FILE STATUS clause specifies a two digit unsigned integer described in the WORKING-STORAGE SECTION that is used to store a code signifying either a successful or an unsuccessful operation on the file. Since this clause is considered as a transitional element (to be phased out) in the Draft Proposal it will not be considered further in this chapter.

236

13.3.2 The OPEN and CLOSE statements.

The general format for the OPEN statement is:

OPEN $\left\{ \begin{array}{l} \text{I-O} \\ \text{INPUT} \\ \text{OUTPUT} \end{array} \right\}$ $\left\{ \text{index-file-name} \right\}$ ..... $\left. \right\}$ ....

A file opened for INPUT can be read, opened for OUTPUT can be written to, and opened for I-O (INPUT and OUTPUT) can be either read or written to.

The general format for the CLOSE statement is:

CLOSE {index-file-name} ......

13.3.3 The READ and START statements.

The READ statement has two formats:

Format 1 – for sequential or dynamic access.

 READ file-name **NEXT RECORD INTO** data-name-1
[AT **END** {imperative-statement} .....]

Format 2 – for sequential, random or dynamic access.

 READ file-name **INTO** data-name-1
[**KEY** IS data-name-2]
[**INVALID** KEY {imperative statement} .....]

When format 1 is used for sequential access the continuous execution of READ will cause successive records in the file to be accessed until the end of the file is reached. Since the primary keys are stored in sequence they ensure that access to the records in the file will be sequential even if the records themselves are not stored sequentially. The NEXT RECORD clause is not required for a file described as having sequential access, therefore, the statement becomes identical to the format the reader has already used. If, however, the dynamic mode of access is specified and sequential access is required then the NEXT RECORD clause must be present when using format 1.

When format 2 is used for either random or dynamic access a record will be retrieved directly based on the value found in data-name-2 of the KEY IS clause. If the key cannot be matched with a key in the file then the imperative statement in the INVALID KEY clause, if present, will be executed. If the INVALID KEY clause is not present and a key match is not possible then the outcome will be a run-time error. The value of data-name-2 can be that of a primary key or a secondary key. Since the primary key is unique the READ statement will access a unique record, however, if a secondary key is used the READ statement will access the first record in the sequence of records with that secondary key. If the dynamic mode has been specified then further access to those records with the same secondary key is possible by using the format 1 READ statement.

The START statement allows an indexed organised file to be positioned for reading at a specified key value. This is permitted for files opened in either the sequential or dynamic modes. The START verb is **not** allowed with random access.

The general format of the START statement is:

START file-name [**KEY** IS $\left[\left\{\begin{array}{l}\textbf{GREATER THAN}\\ \textbf{NOT LESS THAN}\\ \textbf{EQUAL TO}\end{array}\right\}\right]$ data-name]

[**INVALID** KEY {imperative-statement} .....]

START file-name positions the file to the value contained in the primary key.

START file-name KEY IS data-name positions the file to the value contained in either the primary key or secondary key data-name.

When the full format of the START statement contains either of the options GREATER THAN or NOT LESS THAN the file is positioned for the next access to be greater than or less than the value specified in data-name. This option allows the keys to contain partial values.

The START statement only positions the file ready for access it does **not** read the file.

If the INVALID KEY clause is absent and either a key match or key positioning is impossible then a run-time error will be the outcome.

13.3.4 Examples

An indexed sequential file is described in the following manner.

```
ENVIRONMENT DIVISION.
INPUT-OUTPUT SECTION.
FILE-CONTROL.
    SELECT STAFF ASSIGN TO PFMS,
    ORGANIZATION IS INDEXED,
    ACCESS MODE IS DYNAMIC,
    RECORD KEY IS SURNAME,
    ALTERNATE RECORD KEY IS TELE-NO WITH DUPLICATES.
DATA DIVISION.
FILE SECTION.
FD STAFF LABEL RECORDS ARE STANDARD, VALUE OF FILE-ID
    IS "STAFF".
01  RECORD-1.
    02  SURNAME PIC X(20).
    02  TELE-NO PIC XXX.
    02  STATUS-SUBJECT PIC X(20).
```

From the COBOL description of the file it can be seen that the name of the primary key is SURNAME and the name of the secondary key is TELE-NO for which duplicate values are allowed. A typical selection of records from the file could be:

```
BLANCHARD       328HEAD-SCIENCE
COLLINS         397LECTURER-MATHS
EVANS           397LECTURER-COMPUTING
HOUGHTON        397LECTURER-PHYSICS
JEFFRIES        405TECHNICIAN-SCIENCE
    .               .
    .               .
    .               .
```

The following segments of code will produce the described output.

```
PROCEDURE DIVISION.
A-SEQ.
    OPEN STAFF INPUT.
B.
    MOVE "EVANS" TO SURNAME.
    READ STAFF KEY IS SURNAME.
    DISPLAY TELE-NO "        " STATUS-SUBJECT.
```

The value EVANS has been provided as the primary key, retrieval will be direct and the values 397   LECTUTER-COMPUTING will be output.

```
C.
    MOVE "397" TO TELE-NO, TELE-STORE.
    START STAFF KEY IS TELE-NO.
    READ STAFF NEXT RECORD.
D-ITER.
    IF TELE-NO NOT = TELE-STORE GO TO D-END.
        DISPLAY SURNAME.
        READ STAFF NEXT RECORD.
    GO TO D-ITER.
D-END.
```

The value 397 has been provided as a secondary key that also has duplicate values in the file. The START statement positions the file for access to the first record with the secondary key TELE-NO of 397, the file is then READ and the surname of the member of staff with that telephone number is output.

The records in the file with the same secondary key value are accessed in sequence and output. The result would be:

```
        COLLINS
        EVANS
        HOUGHTON
```

```
E.
    MOVE "H" TO SURNAME.
    START STAFF KEY IS NOT LESS THAN SURNAME.
    READ STAFF NEXT RECORD
    AT END MOVE 1 TO E-O-F.
F-ITER.
    IF E-O-F NOT = 0 GO TO F-END.
        DISPLAY SURNAME.
        READ STAFF NEXT RECORD
        AT END MOVE 1 TO E-O-F.
    GO TO F-ITER.
F-END.
    CLOSE STAFF.
    STOP RUN.
A-END.
```

The value H has been provided as a partially complete primary key. The file is positioned such that the first record to be accessed will have a key value that is greater than the value H found in SURNAME. The file is READ at this position and the SURNAME is output. The file is read sequentially until the end of file is encountered. The output using the specimen data is:

   —   HOUGHTON
       JEFFRIES
       .
       .

13.3.5 The WRITE AND REWRITE statements.

The WRITE statement releases a logical record for an output or I-O file. The general format of the statement is:

    WRITE record-name [**FROM** data-name-1]
    [**INVALID** KEY {imperative-statement} .....]

Prior to the WRITE statement being executed a valid, unique value must be stored in the primary record key data-name. If the FROM option is used the unique value in the primary key data-name must be stored in the relative location of data-name-1. If the primary key is not unique the imperative statement in the INVALID KEY clause, if present, will be executed.

The REWRITE statement is used to amend a record in an indexed sequential file. The format of the REWRITE statement is:

    REWRITE record-name [**FROM** data-name-1]
    [**INVALID** KEY {imperative-statement} .....]

The REWRITE statement physically replaces an existing record, and is used to change any or all of the data fields in a record **except** the primary key value. The file must be opened in an I-O mode, and must have been READ successfully prior to the execution of REWRITE.

If the FROM data-name-1 option is used the primary record key must have the same value as the key from the previous READ statement otherwise INVALID KEY conditions will occur, and the imperative-statement in the INVALID KEY clause will be executed, if present, since the value of the primary key has been changed.

13.3.6 The DELETE Statement.

The DELETE statement logically removes a data record from the indexed file together with all the indices.

The format of the DELETE statement is:

    DELETE file-name [**INVALID** KEY {imperative-statement} .....]

When this statement is used in either random or dynamic access modes only a value of the key for the record to be deleted need be placed in the primary record key field prior to the execution of DELETE. If the record does not exist on the file the INVALID KEY clause will be invoked, if present.

In sequential access the record to be deleted must have been successfully read before a delete can be executed. Should the value of the primary key be changed between the operations of READ and DELETE the INVALID KEY clause will be invoked, if present.

Table 13.1 summarises the types of OPEN statements which are permissible with the different access modes and procedural statements.

Access mode	Procedural statement	Open option being used		
		INPUT	OUTPUT	I–O
SEQUENTIAL	READ	yes		yes
	WRITE		yes	
	REWRITE			yes
	START	yes		yes
	DELETE			yes
RANDOM	READ	yes		yes
	WRITE		yes	yes
	REWRITE			yes
	START			
	DELETE			yes
DYNAMIC	READ	yes		yes
	WRITE		yes	yes
	REWRITE			yes
	START	yes		yes
	DELETE			yes

Table 13.1

13.4 WORKED EXAMPLE

13.4.1 Problem

An indexed sequential file contains details about staff in a college. The format of a record on the file is as follows.

Department code – 1 character   B – Business Studies
E – Engineering
G – General Studies
S – Science.
Surname of member of staff – 20 characters.
(note: the department code and surname together form the primary key)
Telephone extension number – 3 digits.
Status of a member of staff – 1 character   H – Head of
Department
L – Lecturer
S – Secretary
T – Technician
(note: the telephone extension number and the status of a member of staff both represent secondary (alternate) keys and can have duplicate entries).
Qualifications of staff member – 10 characters.
Academic subjects member of staff teaches – 20 characters.

Design and write a program to maintain the file catering for the amendment, deletion and insertion of records. Since the maintenance is to take place on a master file we should assume that a copy of this file is made each day and that every change made to a record is stored on a serial log file. In the event of a disc head-crash or the file being accidently erased the file can be re-built using the copy of the master file and the serial log file.

The program is to be menu-driven using the following codes:

    1 – Amend record
    2 – Delete record
    3 – Insert record

and access to a record will be through the primary key only.

13.4.2 Design

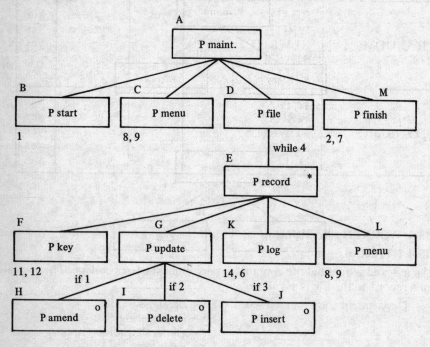

Note. Since the components C and L have the same functions (8,9) they will be coded as a separate subroutine SR-A.

Components F, HD, IE and JE have the same functions (11,12) they will be coded as a separate subroutine SR-B.

Components HF and JA have the same function (10) which will be coded as SR-C.

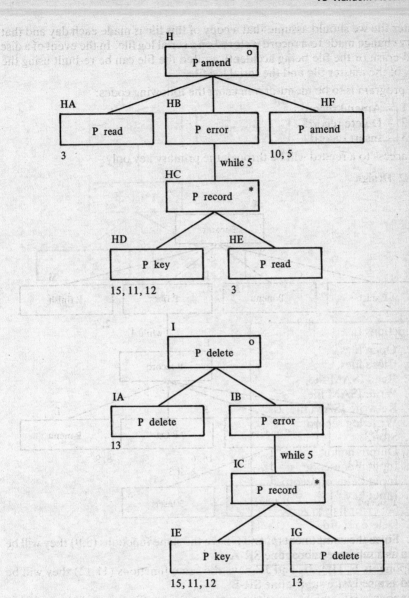

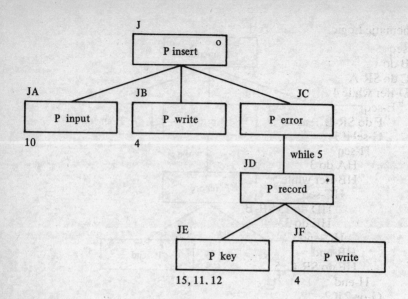

Functions List.
1. Open files.
2. Close files.
3. Read ISAM file.
4. Write ISAM file.
5. Re-write ISAM file.
6. Write log record.
7. Stop.
8. Output menu.
9. Input menu-code.
10. Input fields of record.
11. Input key.
12. Set error flag to zero.
13. Delete record.
14. Format record for output.
15. Output error message.

Conditions List.
1. Menu-code = 1.
2. Menu-code = 2.
3. Menu-code = 3.
4. Menu-code not 4.
5. Error flag = 1.

Schematic Logic.

A-seq
  B do 1
  C do SR-A
  D-iter while 4
    E-seq
      F do SR-B
      G-sel if 1
        H-seq
          HA do 3
          HB-iter while 5
            HC-seq
              HD do 15 SR-B
              HE do 3
            HC-end
          HB-end
          HF do SR-C, 5
        H-end
      G-or-2 if 2
        I-seq
          IA do 13
          IB-iter while 5
            IC-seq
              IE do 15 SR-B
              IG do 13
            IC-end
          IB-end
        I-end
      G-or-3
        J-seq
          JA do SR-C
          JB do 4
          JC-iter while 5
            JD-seq
              JE do 15 SR-B
              JF do 4
            JD-end
          JC-end
        J-end
      G-end
      K do 14,6
      L do SR-A
    E-end
  D-end
  M do 2,7
A-end

13.4.3 Coding.

```
(0001)              IDENTIFICATION DIVISION.
(0002)              PROGRAM-ID. C1343.
(0003)              ENVIRONMENT DIVISION.
(0004)              INPUT-OUTPUT SECTION.
(0005)              FILE-CONTROL.
(0006)                  SELECT STAFF-FILE ASSIGN TO PFMS,
(0007)                  ORGANIZATION IS INDEXED,
(0008)                  ACCESS MODE IS DYNAMIC
(0009)                  RECORD KEY IS DEPT-NAME,
(0010)                  ALTERNATE RECORD KEY IS TELE-NO WITH DUPLICATES,
(0011)                  ALTERNATE RECORD KEY IS STAFF-STATUS WITH DUPLICATES.
(0012)
(0013)                  SELECT LOG-FILE ASSIGN TO PFMS.
(0014)              DATA DIVISION.
(0015)              FILE SECTION.
(0016)              FD STAFF-FILE
(0017)                  LABEL RECORDS ARE STANDARD
(0018)                  VALUE OF FILE-ID IS "STAFF".
(0019)              01 RECORD-1.
(0020)                  02 DEPT-NAME.
(0021)                      03 DEPT-CODE PIC A.
(0022)                      03 STAFF-NAME PIC X(20).
(0023)                  02 TELE-NO PIC 999.
(0024)                  02 STAFF-STATUS PIC A.
(0025)                  02 QUALIFICATIONS PIC X(10).
(0026)                  02 SUBJECTS PIC X(20).
(0027)              FD LOG-FILE
(0028)                  LABEL RECORDS ARE STANDARD VALUE OF FILE-ID IS "LOG".
(0029)              01 RECORD-2.
(0030)                  02 TRANS-CODE PIC 9.
(0031)                  02 STAFF-RECORD PIC X(60).
(0032)              WORKING-STORAGE SECTION.
(0033)              01 PARAMETERS.
(0034)                  02 MENU-CODE PIC 9.
(0035)                  02 ERROR-FLAG PIC 9.
(0036)
(0037)              PROCEDURE DIVISION.
(0038)              A-SEQ.
(0039)              B.
(0040)                  OPEN I-O STAFF-FILE,
(0041)                       OUTPUT LOG-FILE.
(0042)              C.
(0043)                  PERFORM SR-A-SEQ THRU SR-A-END.
(0044)              D-ITER.
(0045)                  IF MENU-CODE = 4 GO TO D-END.
(0046)              E-SEQ.
(0047)              F.
(0048)                  PERFORM SR-B-SEQ THRU SR-B-END.
(0049)              G-SEL.
(0050)                  IF MENU-CODE NOT = 1 GO TO G-OR-2.
(0051)              H-SEQ.

 * amend record

(0052)              HA.
(0053)                  READ STAFF-FILE KEY IS DEPT-NAME
(0054)                  INVALID KEY MOVE 1 TO ERROR-FLAG.
(0055)              HB-ITER.
(0056)                  IF ERROR-FLAG NOT = 1 GO TO HB-END.
(0057)              HC-SEQ.
(0058)              HD.
(0059)                  DISPLAY "ERROR - INVALID KEY"
(0060)                  PERFORM SR-B-SEQ THRU SR-B-END.
(0061)              HE.
(0062)                  READ STAFF-FILE KEY IS DEPT-NAME
(0063)                  INVALID KEY MOVE 1 TO ERROR-FLAG.
(0064)              HC-END. GO TO HB-ITER.
(0065)              HB-END.
```

(program continued)

```
(0066)        HF.
(0067)               PERFORM SR-C-SEQ THRU SR-C-END.
(0068)               REWRITE RECORD-1.
(0069)            GO TO G-END.
(0070)        H-END.
(0071)        G-OR-2.

           * delete record

(0072)        I-SEQ.
(0073)        IA.   IF MENU-CODE NOT = 2 GO TO G-OR-3.
(0074)               DELETE STAFF-FILE
(0075)               INVALID KEY MOVE 1 TO ERROR-FLAG.
(0076)        IB-ITER.
(0077)               IF ERROR-FLAG NOT = 1 GO TO IB-END.
(0078)        IC-SEQ.
(0079)        IE.
(0080)               DISPLAY "ERROR - INVALID KEY"
(0081)               PERFORM SR-B-SEQ THRU SR-B-END.
(0082)        IG.
(0083)               DELETE STAFF-FILE
(0084)               INVALID KEY MOVE 1 TO ERROR-FLAG.
(0085)        IC-END.
(0086)               GO TO IB-ITER.
(0087)        IB-END.
(0088)            GO TO G-END.
(0089)        I-END.
(0090)        G-OR-3.

           * insert record

(0091)        J-SEQ.
(0092)        JA.
(0093)               PERFORM SR-C-SEQ THRU SR-C-END.
(0094)        JB.
(0095)               WRITE RECORD-1
(0096)               INVALID KEY MOVE 1 TO ERROR-FLAG.
(0097)        JC-ITER.
(0098)               IF ERROR-FLAG NOT = 1 GO TO JC-END.
(0099)        JD-SEQ.
(0100)        JE.
(0101)               DISPLAY "ERROR - INVALID KEY"
(0102)               PERFORM SR-B-SEQ THRU SR-B-END.
(0103)        JF.
(0104)               WRITE RECORD-1
(0105)               INVALID KEY MOVE 1 TO ERROR-FLAG.
(0106)        JD-END.
(0107)               GO TO JC-ITER.
(0108)        JC-END.
(0109)        J-END.
(0110)        G-END.
(0111)        K.
(0112)            MOVE MENU-CODE TO TRANS-CODE.
(0113)            MOVE RECORD-1 TO STAFF-RECORD.
(0114)            WRITE RECORD-2.
(0115)        L.
(0116)            PERFORM SR-A-SEQ THRU SR-A-END.
(0117)        E-END.
(0118)            GO TO D-ITER.
(0119)        D-END.
(0120)        M.
(0121)            CLOSE STAFF-FILE
(0122)                  LOG-FILE.
(0123)            STOP RUN.
(0124)        A-END.
```

(program continued)

247

```
                    * menu for type of update
(0125)        SR-A-SEQ.
(0126)            DISPLAY "DO YOU REQUIRE TO:"
(0127)            DISPLAY " "
(0128)            DISPLAY "1  AMEND RECORD"
(0129)            DISPLAY "2  DELETE RECORD"
(0130)            DISPLAY "3  INSERT RECORD"
(0131)            DISPLAY "4  EXIT FROM SYSTEM".
(0132)            DISPLAY "INPUT CODE".
(0133)            ACCEPT MENU-CODE.
(0134)        SR-A-END.

                    * menu for department code etc

(0135)        SR-B-SEQ.
(0136)            DISPLAY "INPUT DEPARTMENT CODE"
(0137)            DISPLAY "B BUSINESS STUDIES"
(0138)            DISPLAY "E ENGINEERING"
(0139)            DISPLAY "G GENERAL STUDIES"
(0140)            DISPLAY "S SCIENCE".
(0141)            ACCEPT DEPT-CODE.
(0142)            DISPLAY " "
(0143)            DISPLAY "INPUT SURNAME"
(0144)            ACCEPT STAFF-NAME.
(0145)            MOVE ZERO TO ERROR-FLAG.
(0146)        SR-B-END.

                    * menu for staff status code etc

(0147)        SR-C-SEQ.
(0148)            DISPLAY "INPUT THE FOLLOWING DETAILS"
(0149)            DISPLAY "TELEPHONE NUMBER"
(0150)            ACCEPT TELE-NO.
(0151)            DISPLAY "STATUS OF STAFF H-HEAD"
(0152)            DISPLAY "            L-LECTURER"
(0153)            DISPLAY "            S-SECRETARY"
(0154)            DISPLAY "            T-TECHNICIAN"
(0155)            ACCEPT STAFF-STATUS.
(0156)            DISPLAY "QUALIFICATIONS"
(0157)            ACCEPT QUALIFICATIONS.
(0158)            DISPLAY "SUBJECT SPECIALISM"
(0159)            ACCEPT SUBJECTS.
(0160)        SR-C-END.
```

13.4.4 Results from trial run.

```
            DO YOU REQUIRE TO:

            1  AMEND RECORD
            2  DELETE RECORD
            3  INSERT RECORD
            4  EXIT FROM SYSTEM
            INPUT CODE
            1
            INPUT DEPARTMENT CODE
            B BUSINESS STUDIES
            E ENGINEERING
            G GENERAL STUDIES
            S SCIENCE
            S

            INPUT SURNAME
            TOMPKINS
            INPUT THE FOLLOWING DETAILS
            TELEPHONE NUMBER
            593
            STATUS OF STAFF H-HEAD
                        L-LECTURER
                        S-SECRETARY
                        T-TECHNICIAN
```

(results continued)

```
S
QUALIFICATIONS
B.A
SUBJECT SPECIALISM

DO YOU REQUIRE TO:

1   AMEND RECORD
2   DELETE RECORD
3   INSERT RECORD
4   EXIT FROM SYSTEM
INPUT CODE
2
INPUT DEPARTMENT CODE
B BUSINESS STUDIES
E ENGINEERING
G GENERAL STUDIES
S SCIENCE
G

INPUT SURNAME
VICKERS
DO YOU REQUIRE TO:

1   AMEND RECORD
2   DELETE RECORD
3   INSERT RECORD
4   EXIT FROM SYSTEM
INPUT CODE
3
INPUT DEPARTMENT CODE
B BUSINESS STUDIES
E ENGINEERING
G GENERAL STUDIES
S SCIENCE
B

INPUT SURNAME
BROWNE
INPUT THE FOLLOWING DETAILS
TELEPHONE NUMBER
224
STATUS OF STAFF H-HEAD
                L-LECTURER
                S-SECRETARY
                T-TECHNICIAN
L
QUALIFICATIONS
M.A
SUBJECT SPECIALISM
PRODUCTION
DO YOU REQUIRE TO:

1   AMEND RECORD
2   DELETE RECORD
3   INSERT RECORD
4   EXIT FROM SYSTEM
INPUT CODE
4
```

Listing of log file.

```
1STOMPKINS        593SB.A
2GVICKERS         593SB.A
3HBROWNE          224LM.A          PRODUCTION
```

13.5 WORKED EXAMPLE

13.5.1 Problem

Design and write a menu-driven program to interrogate the indexed sequential file defined in the last worked example. The menu should allow for interrogation on the following information.

1 – department and staff name
2 – department only
3 – staff name only
4 – telephone extension number
5 – department and staff status

When the appropriate record has been accessed the information should be displayed on the screen of a visual display unit.

13.5.2 Design.

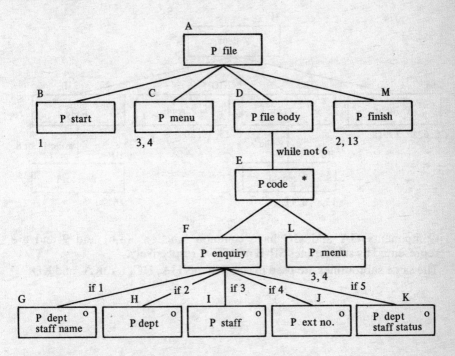

Components C and L have common functions (3,4) and are represented by subroutine SR-A.

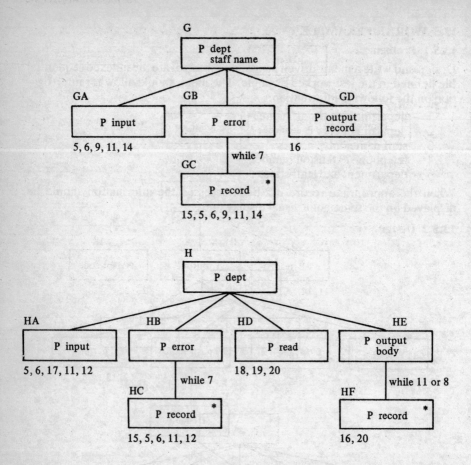

Components GA and GC have common functions (5,6) and 9 and are represented by subroutines SR-B and SR-C respectively.

The same subroutines are used in components HA, HC, IA, KA, and KD.

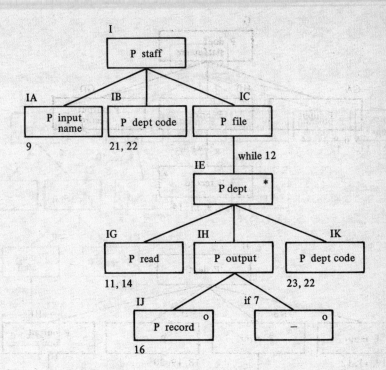

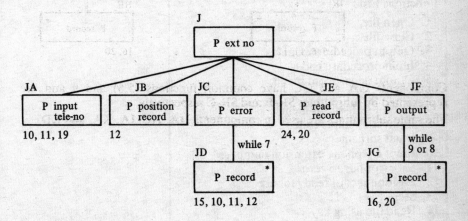

Components JA and JD have function 10 in common, which is represented by subroutine SR-D.

Components GD, HF, IJ, JG, KJ and KL have function 16 in common which is represented by subroutine SR-E.

Functions (7,8) in KE are replaced by subroutine SR-F.

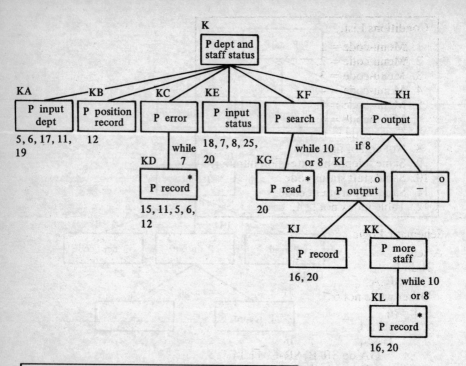

Functions List.

1. Open file.
2. Close file.
3. Output procedure menu.
4. Input procedure code.
5. Output department menu.
6. Input department code.
7. Output staff-status menu.
8. Input staff-status code.
9. Input surname.
10. Input telephone extension number.
11. Set error flag to zero.
12. Position record ready for access.
13. Stop.
14. Read file using key.
15. Output error message.
16. Output contents of record.
17. Fill staff name with spaces.
18. Store department code.
19. Set end of file flag to zero.
20. Read file sequentially.
21. Set table index to 1.
22. Move element in table to department code.
23. Increase table index by 1.
24. Store telephone number.
25. Store status code.

Conditions List.

1. Menu-code = 1.
2. Menu-code = 2.
3. Menu-code = 3.
4. Menu-code = 4.
5. Menu-code = 5.
6. Menu-code = 6.
7. Error code = 1.
8. Not end of file.
9. Same telephone extension number.
10. Same staff status code.
11. Same department code.
12. Table index not > 4.

Schematic Logic.

```
A-seq
  B do 1
  C do SR-A
  D-iter while not 6
    E-seq
      F-sel if 1
        G-seq
          GA do SR-B, SR-C, 11,14
          GB-iter while 7
            GC do 15 SR-B, SR-C, 11,14
          GB-end
          GD do SR-E
        G-end
      F-or-2 if 2
        H-seq
          HA do SR-B, 17,11,12
          HB-iter while 7
            HC do 15 SR-B, 11,12
          HB-end
          HD do 18,19,20
          HE-iter while 11 or 8
            HF do SR-E, 20
          HE-end
        H-end
      F-or-3 if 3
        I-seq
          IA do SR-C
          IB do 21,22
          IC-iter while 12
            IE-seq
              IG do 11,14
              IH-sel if not 7
                IJ do SR-E
              IH-end
```

255

```
                    IK do 23,22
                 IE-end
                 IC-end
              I-end
           F-or-4 if 4
           J-seq
              JA do SR-D, 11,19
              JB do 12
              JC-iter while 7
                 JD do 15 SR-D, 11,12
              JC-end
              JE do 24,20
              JF-iter while 9 or 8
                 JG do SR-E, 20
              JF-end
           J-end
           F-or-5 if 5
           K-seq
              KA do SR-B, 17,11,19
              KB do 12
              KC-iter while 7
                 KD do 15,11 SR-B, 12
              KC-end
              KE do 18 SR-F, 25,20
              KF-iter while 10 or 8
                 KG do 20
              KF-end
              KH-sel if 8
                 KI-seq
                    KJ do SR-E, 20
                    KK-iter while 10 or 8
                       KL do SR-E, 20
                    KK-end
                 KI-end
              KH-end
           K-end
        F-end
        L do SR-A
     E-end
  D-end
  M do 2,13
A-end
```

13.5.3 Coding.

```
(0001)          IDENTIFICATION DIVISION.
(0002)          PROGRAM-ID. C1353.
(0003)          ENVIRONMENT DIVISION.
(0004)          INPUT-OUTPUT SECTION.
(0005)          FILE-CONTROL.
(0006)              SELECT STAFF-FILE ASSIGN TO PFMS,
(0007)              ORGANIZATION IS INDEXED,
(0008)              ACCESS MODE IS DYNAMIC,
(0009)              RECORD KEY IS DEPT-NAME,
(0010)              ALTERNATE RECORD KEY IS TELE-NO WITH DUPLICATES,
(0011)              ALTERNATE RECORD KEY IS STAFF-STATUS WITH DUPLICATES.
(0012)          DATA DIVISION.
(0013)          FILE SECTION.
(0014)          FD STAFF-FILE
(0015)              LABEL RECORDS ARE STANDARD
(0016)              VALUE OF FILE-ID IS "STAFF".
(0017)          01 RECORD-1.
(0018)              02 DEPT-NAME.
(0019)                  03 DEPT-CODE PIC X.
(0020)                  03 STAFF-NAME PIC X(20).
(0021)              02 TELE-NO PIC 999.
(0022)              02 STAFF-STATUS PIC X.
(0023)              02 QUALIFICATIONS PIC X(10).
(0024)              02 SUBJECTS PIC X(20).
(0025)          WORKING-STORAGE SECTION.
(0026)          01 PARAMETERS.
(0027)              02 MENU-CODE PIC 9.
(0028)              02 ERROR-FLAG PIC 9.
(0029)              02 DEPT-STORE PIC A.
(0030)              02 TELE-STORE PIC 999.
(0031)              02 STATUS-STORE PIC A.
(0032)              02 E-O-F PIC 9.
(0033)          01 CODES.
(0034)              02 FILLER PIC A(4) VALUE IS "BEGS".
(0035)          01 CODE-TABLE REDEFINES CODES.
(0036)              02 CODE PIC A OCCURS 4 TIMES INDEXED BY POS.
(0037)          PROCEDURE DIVISION.
(0038)          A-SEQ.
(0039)          B.
(0040)              OPEN INPUT STAFF-FILE.
(0041)          C.
(0042)              PERFORM SR-A-SEQ THRU SR-A-END.
(0043)          D-ITER.
(0044)              IF MENU-CODE = 6 GO TO D-END.
(0045)          E-SEQ.
(0046)          F-SEL.
(0047)                  IF MENU-CODE NOT = 1 GO TO F-OR-2.

         * process file on department code and staff name keys

(0048)          G-SEQ.
(0049)          GA.
(0050)                  PERFORM SR-B-SEQ THRU SR-B-END.
(0051)                  PERFORM SR-C-SEQ THRU SR-C-END.
(0052)                  MOVE ZERO TO ERROR-FLAG.
(0053)                  READ STAFF-FILE KEY IS DEPT-NAME,
(0054)                  INVALID KEY MOVE 1 TO ERROR-FLAG.
(0055)          GB-ITER.
(0056)                  IF ERROR-FLAG NOT = 1 GO TO GB-END.
(0057)          GC.
(0058)                  DISPLAY "ERROR - INVALID KEY".
(0059)                  PERFORM SR-B-SEQ THRU SR-B-END.
(0060)                  PERFORM SR-C-SEQ THRU SR-C-END.
(0061)                  MOVE ZERO TO ERROR-FLAG.
(0062)                  READ STAFF-FILE KEY IS DEPT-NAME,
(0063)                  INVALID KEY MOVE 1 TO ERROR-FLAG.
(0064)                  GO TO GB-ITER.
(0065)          GB-END.
```

(program continued)

```
(0066)          GD.
(0067)               PERFORM SR-E-SEQ THRU SR-E-END.
(0068)               GO TO F-END.
(0069)          G-END.
(0070)          F-OR-2.
(0071)               IF MENU-CODE NOT = 2 GO TO F-OR-3.

           * process file on department code key

(0072)          H-SEQ.
(0073)          HA.
(0074)               PERFORM SR-B-SEQ THRU SR-B-END.
(0075)               MOVE SPACES TO STAFF-NAME.
(0076)               MOVE ZERO TO ERROR-FLAG.
(0077)               START STAFF-FILE KEY IS NOT LESS THAN DEPT-NAME,
(0078)               INVALID KEY MOVE 1 TO ERROR-FLAG.
(0079)          HB-ITER.
(0080)               IF ERROR-FLAG NOT = 1 GO TO HB-END.
(0081)          HC.
(0082)               DISPLAY "ERROR - INVALID KEY"
(0083)               PERFORM SR-B-SEQ THRU SR-B-END
(0084)               MOVE ZERO TO ERROR-FLAG.
(0085)               START STAFF-FILE KEY IS NOT LESS THAN DEPT-NAME,
(0086)               INVALID KEY MOVE 1 TO ERROR-FLAG.
(0087)               GO TO HB-ITER.
(0088)          HB-END.
(0089)          HD.
(0090)               MOVE DEPT-CODE TO DEPT-STORE.
(0091)               MOVE ZERO TO E-O-F.
(0092)               READ STAFF-FILE NEXT RECORD
(0093)               AT END MOVE 1 TO E-O-F.
(0094)          HE-ITER.
(0095)               IF DEPT-CODE NOT = DEPT-STORE
(0096)               OR E-O-F NOT = 0 GO TO HE-END.
(0097)          HF.
(0098)               PERFORM SR-E-SEQ THRU SR-E-END.
(0099)               READ STAFF-FILE NEXT RECORD
(0100)               AT END MOVE 1 TO E-O-F.
(0101)               GO TO HE-ITER.
(0102)          HE-END.
(0103)          H-END.
(0104)               GO TO F-END.
(0105)          F-OR-3.
(0106)               IF MENU-CODE NOT = 3 GO TO F-OR-4.

           * process file on staff name key

(0107)          I-SEQ.
(0108)          IA.
(0109)               PERFORM SR-C-SEQ THRU SR-C-END.
(0110)          IB.
(0111)               SET POS TO 1.
(0112)               MOVE CODE (POS) TO DEPT-CODE.
(0113)          IC-ITER.
(0114)               IF POS > 4 GO TO IC-END.
(0115)          IE-SEQ.
(0116)          IG.
(0117)               MOVE ZERO TO ERROR-FLAG.
(0118)               READ STAFF-FILE KEY IS DEPT-NAME,
(0119)               INVALID KEY MOVE 1 TO ERROR-FLAG.
(0120)          IH-SEL.
(0121)               IF ERROR-FLAG NOT = 0 GO TO IH-END.
(0122)          IJ.
(0123)               PERFORM SR-E-SEQ THRU SR-E-END.
(0124)          IH-END.
(0125)          IK.
(0126)               SET POS UP BY 1.
(0127)               MOVE CODE (POS) TO DEPT-CODE.
(0128)               GO TO IC-ITER.
(0129)          IE-END.
```

(program continued)

```
(0130)          IC-END.
(0131)          I-END.
(0132)               GO TO F-END.
(0133)          F-OR-4.
(0134)               IF MENU-CODE NOT = 4 GO TO F-OR-5.

          * process file on extension number key

(0135)          J-SEQ.
(0136)          JA.
(0137)               PERFORM SR-D-SEQ THRU SR-D-END.
(0138)               MOVE ZERO TO ERROR-FLAG, E-O-F.
(0139)          JB.
(0140)               START STAFF-FILE KEY IS NOT LESS THAN TELE-NO,
(0141)               INVALID KEY MOVE 1 TO ERROR-FLAG.
(0142)          JC-ITER.
(0143)               IF ERROR-FLAG NOT = 1 GO TO JC-END.
(0144)          JD.
(0145)                 DISPLAY "ERROR - INVALID KEY"
(0146)                 PERFORM SR-D-SEQ THRU SR-D-END.
(0147)               MOVE ZERO TO ERROR-FLAG.
(0148)               START STAFF-FILE KEY IS NOT LESS THAN TELE-NO,
(0149)               INVALID KEY MOVE 1 TO ERROR-FLAG.
(0150)               GO TO IC-ITER.
(0151)          JC-END.
(0152)          JE.
(0153)               MOVE TELE-NO TO TELE-STORE.
(0154)               READ STAFF-FILE NEXT RECORD
(0155)               AT END MOVE 1 TO E-O-F.
(0156)          JF-ITER.
(0157)               IF TELE-NO NOT = TELE-STORE
(0158)               OR E-O-F NOT = 0 GO TO JF-END.
(0159)          JG.
(0160)                 PERFORM SR-E-SEQ THRU SR-E-END.
(0161)               READ STAFF-FILE NEXT RECORD
(0162)               AT END MOVE 1 TO E-O-F.
(0163)               GO TO JF-ITER.
(0164)          JF-END.
(0165)          J-END.
(0166)               GO TO F-END.
(0167)          F-OR-5.

          * process file on department code and staff status code keys

(0168)          K-SEQ.
(0169)          KA.
(0170)               PERFORM SR-B-SEQ THRU SR-B-END.
(0171)               MOVE SPACES TO STAFF-NAME.
(0172)               MOVE ZERO TO ERROR-FLAG, E-O-F.
(0173)          KB.
(0174)               START STAFF-FILE KEY IS NOT LESS THAN DEPT-NAME,
(0175)               INVALID KEY MOVE 1 TO ERROR-FLAG.
(0176)          KC-ITER.
(0177)               IF ERROR-FLAG NOT = 1 GO TO KC-END.
(0178)          KD.  DISPLAY "ERROR - INVALID KEY DEPARTMENT CODE".
(0179)               PERFORM SR-B-SEQ THRU SR-B-END.
(0180)               MOVE ZERO TO ERROR-FLAG.
(0181)               START STAFF-FILE KEY IS NOT LESS THAN DEPT-NAME,
(0182)               INVALID KEY MOVE 1 TO ERROR-FLAG.
(0183)               GO TO KC-ITER.
(0184)          KC-END.
(0185)          KE.
(0186)               MOVE DEPT-CODE TO DEPT-STORE.
(0187)               PERFORM SR-F-SEQ THRU SR-F-END.
(0188)               MOVE STAFF-STATUS TO STATUS-STORE.
(0189)               READ STAFF-FILE NEXT RECORD,
(0190)               AT END MOVE 1 TO E-O-F.
```

(program continued)

259

```
(0191)          KF-ITER.
(0192)              IF STAFF-STATUS = STATUS-STORE OR E-O-F NOT = 0
(0193)              GO TO KF-END.
(0194)          KG.   READ STAFF-FILE NEXT RECORD
(0195)              AT END MOVE 1 TO E-O-F.
(0196)              GO TO KF-ITER.
(0197)          KF-END.
(0198)          KH-SEL.
(0199)              IF E-O-F NOT = 0 GO TO KH-END.
(0200)          KI-SEQ.
(0201)          KJ.
(0202)              PERFORM SR-E-SEQ THRU SR-E-END.
(0203)              READ STAFF-FILE NEXT RECORD
(0204)              AT END MOVE 1 TO E-O-F.
(0205)          KK-ITER.
(0206)              IF STAFF-STATUS NOT = STATUS-STORE OR E-O-F NOT = 0
(0207)              GO TO KK-END.
(0208)          KL.
(0209)              PERFORM SR-E-SEQ THRU SR-E-END.
(0210)              READ STAFF-FILE NEXT RECORD
(0211)              AT END MOVE 1 TO E-O-F.
(0212)              GO TO KK-ITER.
(0213)          KK-END.
(0214)          KI-END.
(0215)          KH-END.
(0216)          K-END.
(0217)          F-END.
(0218)          L.
(0219)              PERFORM SR-A-SEQ THRU SR-A-END.
(0220)          E-END.
(0221)              GO TO D-ITER.
(0222)          D-END.
(0223)          M.   CLOSE STAFF-FILE.
(0224)              STOP RUN.
(0225)          A-END.

              * menu for type of access

(0226)          SR-A-SEQ.
(0227)              DISPLAY "DO YOU REQUIRE RECORD ACCESS ON:"
(0228)              DISPLAY " "
(0229)              DISPLAY "1. DEPARTMENT AND STAFF NAME".
(0230)              DISPLAY "2. DEPARTMENT ONLY".
(0231)              DISPLAY "3. STAFF NAME ONLY".
(0232)              DISPLAY "4. TELEPHONE EXTENSION NUMBER".
(0233)              DISPLAY "5. DEPARTMENT AND STAFF STATUS".
(0234)              DISPLAY " "
(0235)              DISPLAY "6. EXIT FROM SYSTEM".
(0236)              DISPLAY " "
(0237)              DISPLAY "INPUT NUMERIC CODE 1-6".
(0238)              ACCEPT MENU-CODE.
(0239)          SR-A-END.

              * menu for department code

(0240)          SR-B-SEQ.
(0241)              DISPLAY "INPUT DEPARTMENT CODE"
(0242)              DISPLAY "B BUSINESS STUDIES"
(0243)              DISPLAY "E ENGINEERING"
(0244)              DISPLAY "G GENERAL STUDIES"
(0245)              DISPLAY "S SCIENCE"
(0246)              ACCEPT DEPT-CODE.
(0247)          SR-B-END.
(0248)          SR-C-SEQ.
(0249)              DISPLAY "INPUT SURNAME"
(0250)              ACCEPT STAFF-NAME.
(0251)          SR-C-END.
(0252)          SR-D-SEQ.
(0253)              DISPLAY "INPUT TELEPHONE EXTENSION NUMBER"
(0254)              ACCEPT TELE-NO.
(0255)          SR-D-END.
```

(program continued)

```
                  * output of information from file

(0256)            SR-E-SEQ.
(0257)                DISPLAY "DEPARTMENT CODE: " DEPT-CODE.
(0258)                DISPLAY "SURNAME:         " STAFF-NAME.
(0259)                DISPLAY "EXTENSION:       " TELE-NO.
(0260)                DISPLAY "STAFF STATUS:    " STAFF-STATUS.
(0261)                DISPLAY "QUALIFICATIONS:  " QUALIFICATIONS.
(0262)                DISPLAY "SUBJECT(S):      " SUBJECTS
(0263)                DISPLAY " ".
(0264)            SR-E-END.

                  * menu for staff status code

(0265)            SR-F-SEQ.
(0266)                DISPLAY "INPUT STAFF STATUS CODE"
(0267)                DISPLAY "H HEAD OF DEPARTMENT"
(0268)                DISPLAY "L LECTURER"
(0269)                DISPLAY "S SECRETARY"
(0270)                DISPLAY "T TECHNICIAN".
(0271)                ACCEPT STAFF-STATUS.
(0272)            SR-F-END.
```

13.5.4 Results from test run.

```
DO YOU REQUIRE RECORD ACCESS ON:

1. DEPARTMENT AND STAFF NAME
2. DEPARTMENT ONLY
3. STAFF NAME ONLY
4. TELEPHONE EXTENSION NUMBER
5. DEPARTMENT AND STAFF STATUS

6. EXIT FROM SYSTEM

INPUT NUMERIC CODE 1-6
1
INPUT DEPARTMENT CODE
B BUSINESS STUDIES
E ENGINEERING
G GENERAL STUDIES
S SCIENCE
B
INPUT SURNAME
JEFFRIES
DEPARTMENT CODE: B
SURNAME:         JEFFRIES
EXTENSION:       213
STAFF STATUS:    H
QUALIFICATIONS:  B.SC
SUBJECT(S):      PRODUCTION

DO YOU REQUIRE RECORD ACCESS ON:

1. DEPARTMENT AND STAFF NAME
2. DEPARTMENT ONLY
3. STAFF NAME ONLY
4. TELEPHONE EXTENSION NUMBER
5. DEPARTMENT AND STAFF STATUS

6. EXIT FROM SYSTEM

INPUT NUMERIC CODE 1-6
2
INPUT DEPARTMENT CODE
B BUSINESS STUDIES
E ENGINEERING
G GENERAL STUDIES
S SCIENCE
S
```

(results continued)

```
                    DEPARTMENT CODE: S
                    SURNAME:          EDWARDS
                    EXTENSION:        234
                    STAFF STATUS:     L
                    QUALIFICATIONS:   B.SC
                    SUBJECT(S):       MATHS

                    DEPARTMENT CODE: S
                    SURNAME:          FAULDS
                    EXTENSION:        364
                    STAFF STATUS:     H
                    QUALIFICATIONS:   M.A
                    SUBJECT(S):       BIOLOGY

                    DEPARTMENT CODE: S
                    SURNAME:          JONES
                    EXTENSION:        591
                    STAFF STATUS:     L
                    QUALIFICATIONS:   B.SC
                    SUBJECT(S):       CHEMISTRY

                    DEPARTMENT CODE: S
                    SURNAME:          SMITH
                    EXTENSION:        591
                    STAFF STATUS:     T
                    QUALIFICATIONS:
                    SUBJECT(S):

                    DEPARTMENT CODE: S
                    SURNAME:          TOMPKINS
                    EXTENSION:        593
                    STAFF STATUS:     S
                    QUALIFICATIONS:   B.A
                    SUBJECT(S):

                    DO YOU REQUIRE RECORD ACCESS ON:

                    1. DEPARTMENT AND STAFF NAME
                    2. DEPARTMENT ONLY
                    3. STAFF NAME ONLY
                    4. TELEPHONE EXTENSION NUMBER
                    5. DEPARTMENT AND STAFF STATUS

                    6. EXIT FROM SYSTEM

                    INPUT NUMERIC CODE 1-6
                    3
                    INPUT SURNAME
                    JONES
                    DEPARTMENT CODE: E
                    SURNAME:          JONES
                    EXTENSION:        318
                    STAFF STATUS:     L
                    QUALIFICATIONS:   B.SC
                    SUBJECT(S):       STRUCTURES

                    DEPARTMENT CODE: S
                    SURNAME:          JONES
                    EXTENSION:        591
                    STAFF STATUS:     L
                    QUALIFICATIONS:   B.SC
                    SUBJECT(S):       CHEMISTRY

                    DO YOU REQUIRE RECORD ACCESS ON:

                    1. DEPARTMENT AND STAFF NAME
                    2. DEPARTMENT ONLY
                    3. STAFF NAME ONLY
                    4. TELEPHONE EXTENSION NUMBER
                    5. DEPARTMENT AND STAFF STATUS

                    6. EXIT FROM SYSTEM
```

(results continued)

```
     INPUT NUMERIC CODE 1-6
     4
     INPUT TELEPHONE EXTENSION NUMBER
     512
     DEPARTMENT CODE: 6
     SURNAME:         SPOONER
     EXTENSION:       512
     STAFF STATUS:    H
     QUALIFICATIONS:  PH.D
     SUBJECT(S):      GEOGRAPHY

     DO YOU REQUIRE RECORD ACCESS ON:

     1. DEPARTMENT AND STAFF NAME
     2. DEPARTMENT ONLY
     3. STAFF NAME ONLY
     4. TELEPHONE EXTENSION NUMBER
     5. DEPARTMENT AND STAFF STATUS

     6. EXIT FROM SYSTEM

     INPUT NUMERIC CODE 1-6
     5
     INPUT DEPARTMENT CODE
     B BUSINESS STUDIES
     E ENGINEERING
     G GENERAL STUDIES
     S SCIENCE
     S
     INPUT STAFF STATUS CODE
     H HEAD OF DEPARTMENT
     L LECTURER
     S SECRETARY
     T TECHNICIAN
     H
     DEPARTMENT CODE: S
     SURNAME:         FAULDS
     EXTENSION:       364
     STAFF STATUS:    H
     QUALIFICATIONS:  M.A
     SUBJECT(S):      BIOLOGY

     DO YOU REQUIRE RECORD ACCESS ON:

     1. DEPARTMENT AND STAFF NAME
     2. DEPARTMENT ONLY
     3. STAFF NAME ONLY
     4. TELEPHONE EXTENSION NUMBER
     5. DEPARTMENT AND STAFF STATUS

     6. EXIT FROM SYSTEM

     INPUT NUMERIC CODE 1-6
     6
```

13.6 DESCRIPTION OF RELATIVE FILES

Files organised in this manner are stored on magnetic disc and will allow either sequential or random access to records. A relative record key is a positive numeric integer that represents the relative position of a logical record with respect to the beginning of a file. For example a record with a key value of 10 represents the record occupying the tenth logical record area in the file, irrespective of whether the relative record areas 1 through to 9 have been filled.

Potentially, Relative files are efficient because records are in sequence, access is fast, and there are no problems with overflow. However, with record deletions or the fact that the keys are numerically spaced far apart, gaps of wasted space can soon occur in such a file organisation.

13.7 COBOL STATEMENTS ASSOCIATED WITH RELATIVE FILES

13.7.1 File Control.

The general format for FILE CONTROL in the ENVIRONMENT DIVISION is very similar to that for Indexed Sequential files.

SELECT file-name ASSIGN TO PFMS
ORGANIZATION IS RELATIVE
[ACCESS MODE IS $\left\{ \begin{array}{l} \text{SEQUENTIAL} \\ \text{RANDOM} \\ \text{DYNAMIC} \end{array} \right\}$]
RELATIVE KEY IS data-name-1
[FILE STATUS IS data-name-2]

The differences should be apparent to the reader. The organisation of the file has been described as RELATIVE, the record key is described as RELATIVE KEY with the description for data-name-1 being given in the WORKING-STORAGE SECTION and **not** as the first field of the record in the FILE SECTION. The Relative file organisation does **not** support secondary keys, since they have no meaning here, therefore, the ALTERNATE RECORD clause is **not** included as part of the format for FILE CONTROL. The value contained within data-name-1 must be a unique positive integer, duplicates are invalid.

13.7.2 Procedure Division Verbs.

The verbs already described for processing Indexed Sequential files are identical to those used for processing Relative files, however, the only exception to this statement is the second format of the READ statement. The KEY IS clause is omitted from the format of the statement, however, a value for the Relative key should be stored in the WORKING-STORAGE entry prior to the READ statement being executed.

13.8 WORKED EXAMPLE

13.8.1 Problem

A relative file is used to store the details of aircraft departures from an airport in the U.K. The format of a record on the file is as follows.

Departure time – 4 digits.
Flight number – 6 characters.
Destination – 30 characters.

The records are organised into departure time order and the relative key is the time of day based on a 24 hour clock.

Design and write a program to maintain the file catering for the amendment, deletion and insertion of records. Since this is a demonstration example a serial log file will not be kept on the changes made to the master file.

The design and structure of this program is very similar to the file maintenance program used for updating the indexed sequential file, therefore, the design phase will be omitted and only the source listing of the program and the test run will be given.

13.8.2 Program.

```
(0001)          IDENTIFICATION DIVISION.
(0002)          PROGRAM-ID. C1382.
(0003)          ENVIRONMENT DIVISION.
(0004)          INPUT-OUTPUT SECTION.
(0005)          FILE-CONTROL.
(0006)              SELECT DEPARTURES ASSIGN TO PFMS,
(0007)              ORGANIZATION IS RELATIVE,
(0008)              ACCESS MODE IS RANDOM,
(0009)              RELATIVE KEY IS CLOCK.
(0010)          DATA DIVISION.
(0011)          FILE SECTION.
(0012)          FD DEPARTURES
(0013)              LABEL RECORDS ARE STANDARD VALUE OF FILE-ID IS "FLIGHT".
(0014)          01 RECORD-1.
(0015)              02 DEPARTURE-TIME PIC 9(4).
(0016)              02 FLIGHT-NO PIC X(6).
(0017)              02 DESTINATION PIC X(30).
(0018)          WORKING-STORAGE SECTION.
(0019)          01 PARAMETERS.
(0020)              02 MENU-CODE PIC 9.
(0021)              02 ERROR-FLAG PIC 9.
(0022)              02 CLOCK PIC 9(4).
(0023)          PROCEDURE DIVISION.
(0024)          A-SEQ.
(0025)          B.
(0026)              OPEN I-O DEPARTURES.
(0027)          C.
(0028)              PERFORM SR-A-SEQ THRU SR-A-END.
(0029)          D-ITER.
(0030)              IF MENU-CODE = 4 GO TO D-END.
(0031)          E-SEQ.
(0032)          F.
(0033)              PERFORM SR-B-SEQ THRU SR-B-END.
(0034)          G-SEL.
(0035)              IF MENU-CODE NOT = 1 GO TO G-OR-2.

                * amend record

(0036)          H-SEQ.
(0037)          HA.
(0038)              READ DEPARTURES
(0039)              INVALID KEY MOVE 1 TO ERROR-FLAG.
(0040)          HB-ITER.
(0041)              IF ERROR-FLAG NOT = 1 GO TO HB-END.
(0042)          HC-SEQ.
(0043)              DISPLAY "ERROR - INVALID KEY".
(0044)          HD.
(0045)              PERFORM SR-B-SEQ THRU SR-B-END.
(0046)          HE.
(0047)              READ DEPARTURES
(0048)              INVALID KEY MOVE 1 TO ERROR-FLAG.
(0049)          HC-END. GO TO HB-ITER.
(0050)          HB-END.
(0051)          HF.
(0052)              PERFORM SR-C-SEQ THRU SR-C-END.
(0053)              REWRITE RECORD-1.
(0054)              GO TO G-END.
(0055)          H-END.
(0056)          G-OR-2.

                * delete record

(0057)          I-SEQ.
(0058)          IA.
(0059)              IF MENU-CODE NOT = 2 GO TO G-OR-3.
(0060)              DELETE DEPARTURES
(0061)              INVALID KEY MOVE 1 TO ERROR-FLAG.
```

(program continued)

265

```
(0062)              IB-ITER.
(0063)                    IF ERROR-FLAG NOT = 1 GO TO IB-END.
(0064)              IC-SEQ.
(0065)              IE.
(0066)                        DISPLAY "ERROR - INVALID KEY"
(0067)                        PERFORM SR-B-SEQ THRU SR-B-END.
(0068)              IFF.
(0069)                        DELETE DEPARTURES
(0070)                        INVALID KEY MOVE 1 TO ERROR-FLAG.
(0071)              IC-END. GO TO IB-ITER.
(0072)              IB-END.
(0073)                    GO TO G-END.
(0074)              I-END.
(0075)              G-OR-3.

              * insert record

(0076)              J-SEQ.
(0077)              JA.
(0078)                    PERFORM SR-C-SEQ THRU SR-C-END.
(0079)              JB.
(0080)                        WRITE RECORD-1
(0081)                        INVALID KEY MOVE 1 TO ERROR-FLAG.
(0082)              JC-ITER.
(0083)                    IF ERROR-FLAG NOT = 1 GO TO JC-END.
(0084)              JD-SEQ.
(0085)              JE.
(0086)                        DISPLAY "ERROR - INVALID KEY"
(0087)                        PERFORM SR-B-SEQ THRU SR-B-END.
(0088)              JF.
(0089)                        WRITE RECORD-1
(0090)                        INVALID KEY MOVE 1 TO ERROR-FLAG.
(0091)                        GO TO JC-ITER.
(0092)              JC-END.
(0093)              J-END.
(0094)              G-END.
(0095)              K.
(0096)                    PERFORM SR-A-SEQ THRU SR-A-END.
(0097)              E-END.
(0098)                 GO TO D-ITER.
(0099)              D-END.
(0100)              L.
(0101)                 CLOSE DEPARTURES.
(0102)                 STOP RUN.
(0103)              A-END.

              * menu for type of update

(0104)              SR-A-SEQ.
(0105)                 DISPLAY "DO YOU REQUIRE TO:"
(0106)                 DISPLAY " "
(0107)                 DISPLAY "1 AMEND RECORD"
(0108)                 DISPLAY "2 DELETE RECORD"
(0109)                 DISPLAY "3 INSERT RECORD"
(0110)                 DISPLAY "4 EXIT FROM SYSTEM".
(0111)                 DISPLAY "INPUT CODE"
(0112)                 ACCEPT MENU-CODE.
(0113)              SR-A-END.
(0114)              SR-B-SEQ.
(0115)                 DISPLAY "INPUT TIME OF DEPARTURE AS A FOUR DIGIT NUMBER"
(0116)                 DISPLAY "EXAMPLE 2.15 P.M. AS 1415"
(0117)                 DISPLAY "           2.15 A.M. AS 0215"
(0118)                 ACCEPT CLOCK.
(0119)                 MOVE CLOCK TO DEPARTURE-TIME.
(0120)                 MOVE ZERO TO ERROR-FLAG.
(0121)              SR-B-END.
(0122)              SR-C-SEQ.
(0123)                 DISPLAY "INPUT FLIGHT NUMBER (MAX 6 CHARACTERS)"
(0124)                 ACCEPT FLIGHT-NO.
(0125)                 DISPLAY "INPUT DESTINATION (MAX 30 CHARACTERS)"
(0126)                 ACCEPT DESTINATION.
(0127)              SR-C-END.
```

13.8.3 Results of test run.

```
DO YOU REQUIRE TO:

1 AMEND RECORD
2 DELETE RECORD
3 INSERT RECORD
4 EXIT FROM SYSTEM
INPUT CODE
1
INPUT TIME OF DEPARTURE AS A FOUR DIGIT NUMBER
EXAMPLE 2.15 P.M. AS 1415
        2.15 A.M. AS 0215
1200
INPUT FLIGHT NUMBER (MAX 6 CHARACTERS)
C2345
INPUT DESTINATION (MAX 30 CHARACTERS)
GLASGOW
DO YOU REQUIRE TO:

1 AMEND RECORD
2 DELETE RECORD
3 INSERT RECORD
4 EXIT FROM SYSTEM
INPUT CODE
2
INPUT TIME OF DEPARTURE AS A FOUR DIGIT NUMBER
EXAMPLE 2.15 P.M. AS 1415
        2.15 A.M. AS 0215
1201
DO YOU REQUIRE TO:

1 AMEND RECORD
2 DELETE RECORD
3 INSERT RECORD
4 EXIT FROM SYSTEM
INPUT CODE
3
INPUT TIME OF DEPARTURE AS A FOUR DIGIT NUMBER
EXAMPLE 2.15 P.M. AS 1415
        2.15 A.M. AS 0215
1415
INPUT FLIGHT NUMBER (MAX 6 CHARACTERS)
PA342
INPUT DESTINATION (MAX 30 CHARACTERS)
NEW YORK
DO YOU REQUIRE TO:

1 AMEND RECORD
2 DELETE RECORD
3 INSERT RECORD
4 EXIT FROM SYSTEM
INPUT CODE
4
```

13.9 WORKED EXAMPLE

13.9.1 Problem.

Design and write a program to access the relative file defined in the last worked example and output a *real-time* display of the next ten flights that are scheduled to depart from the airport. Using the TIME facility available in COBOL change the departure display every minute. Assume that the departure details are for one 24 hour period and that the system will stop at midnight.

The layout for the display is as follows:

DATE: 15/12/83
TIME: 12 01

FLIGHT DEPARTURES

TIME	FLIGHT	DESTINATION
12 01	BA274	GENEVA
12 05	BC0113	ATHENS VIA ROME
12 07	LU0777	MAJORCA
12 15	IB193	NICE
12 20	PA7461	NEW YORK
12 25	PA7469	CHICAGO
12 30	BA275	PARIS
12 35	BC0115	GLASGOW
12 40	BA444	STOCKHOLM
12 45	BC0197	GENEVA

13.9.2 Design.

Data structure diagrams.

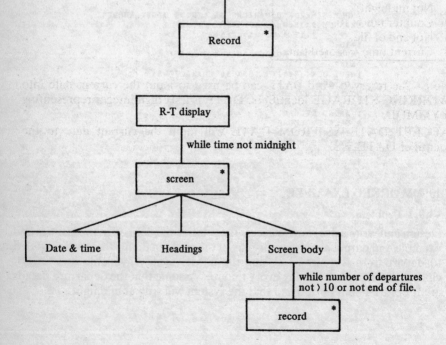

The order in which the records are stored on the relative file and the order in which the records are displayed is the same.

The number of different records that are displayed over a 24 hour period and the number of records stored on the relative file is the same.

Functions List.
1. Open file.
2. Close file.
3. Position record for access.
4. Read file sequentially.
5. Output record.
6. Format record ready for output.
7. Output time.
8. Output date.
9. Output headings.
10. Set end of file flag to zero.
11. Set departure counter to 1.
12. Increase departure counter by 1.
13. Store current time.
14. Input current time.
15. Input current date.
16. Stop.

Conditions List.
1. Not midnight.
2. Counter not > 10.
3. Not end of file.
4. Current time = stored time.

Note. The reserved word **DATE** can be used to input the current date into WORKING-STORAGE identifiers. DATE is a six digit integer representing YYMMDD.

ACCEPT DATE-WS FROM DATE will input the current date to the identifier DATE-WS.

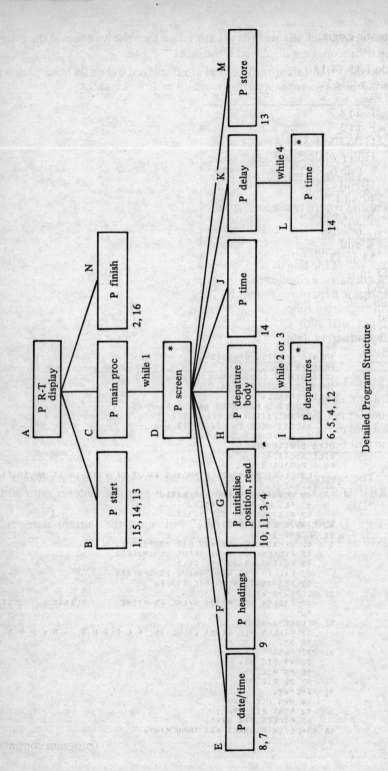

Detailed Program Structure

Schematic Logic.

A-seq
   B do 1,15,14,13
   C-iter while 1
      D-seq
         E do 8,7
         F do 9
         G do 10,11,3,4
         H-iter while 2 or 3
           I do 6,5,4,12
         H-end
         J do 14
         K-iter while 4
           L do 14
         K-end
         M do 13
      D-end
   C-end
   N do 2,16
A-end

13.9.3 Coding.

```
(0001)          IDENTIFICATION DIVISION.
(0002)          PROGRAM-ID. C1393.
(0003)          ENVIRONMENT DIVISION.
(0004)          INPUT-OUTPUT SECTION.
(0005)          FILE-CONTROL.
(0006)              SELECT DEPARTURES ASSIGN TO PFMS,
(0007)              ORGANIZATION IS RELATIVE,
(0008)              ACCESS MODE IS SEQUENTIAL,
(0009)              RELATIVE KEY IS CLOCK.
(0010)          DATA DIVISION.
(0011)          FILE SECTION.
(0012)          FD DEPARTURES
(0013)              LABEL RECORDS ARE STANDARD VALUE OF FILE-ID IS "FLIGHT".
(0014)          01 RECORD-1.
(0015)              02 DEPARTURE-TIME PIC 9(4).
(0016)              02 FLIGHT-NO PIC X(6).
(0017)              02 DESTINATION PIC X(30).
(0018)          WORKING-STORAGE SECTION.
(0019)          01 RECORD-1-WS.
(0020)              02 DEPARTURE-TIME-WS PIC 99B99.
(0021)              02 FILLER PIC X(5) VALUE IS SPACES.
(0022)              02 FLIGHT-NO-WS PIC X(6).
(0023)              02 FILLER PIC X(5) VALUE IS SPACES.
(0024)              02 DESTINATION-WS PIC X(30).
(0025)          01 RECORD-2-WS.
(0026)              02 FILLER PIC X(32) VALUE IS "TIME      FLIGHT      DESTINATIO
(0027)        -     "N".
(0028)          01 RECORD-3-WS.
(0029)              02 FILLER PIC X(34) VALUE IS "F L I G H T    D E P A R T U R
(0030)        -     "E S".
(0031)          01 DATE-WS.
(0032)              02 YY PIC 99.
(0033)              02 MM PIC 99.
(0034)              02 DD PIC 99.
(0035)          01 TIME-WS.
(0036)              02 HRS PIC 99.
(0037)              02 MINS PIC 99.
(0038)              02 FILLER PIC 9(4).
(0039)          66 RT-CLOCK RENAMES HRS THRU MINS.
```

(program continued)

```
(0040)            01 TIME-STORE.
(0041)               02 FILLER PIC 9(4).
(0042)            01 PARAMETERS.
(0043)               02 COUNTER PIC 99.
(0044)               02 E-O-F PIC 9.
(0045)               02 CLOCK PIC 9(4).
(0046)            PROCEDURE DIVISION.
(0047)            A-SEQ.
(0048)            B.
(0049)               OPEN INPUT DEPARTURES.
(0050)               ACCEPT DATE-WS FROM DATE.
(0051)               ACCEPT TIME-WS FROM TIME.
(0052)               MOVE RT-CLOCK TO TIME-STORE, CLOCK.
(0053)            C-ITER.
(0054)               IF TIME-WS = ZERO GO TO C-END.

                  * output headings

(0055)            D-SEQ.
(0056)            E.
(0057)               DISPLAY " ".
(0058)               DISPLAY "DATE: " DD "/" MM "/" YY.
(0059)               DISPLAY "TIME: " HRS " " MINS.
(0060)               DISPLAY " ".

                  * initialise

(0061)            F.
(0062)               DISPLAY RECORD-3-WS.
(0063)               DISPLAY " "
(0064)               DISPLAY RECORD-2-WS.
(0065)               DISPLAY " ".
(0066)            G.  MOVE ZERO TO E-O-F.
(0067)               MOVE 1 TO COUNTER.
(0068)               START DEPARTURES KEY IS NOT LESS THAN CLOCK.
(0069)               READ DEPARTURES AT END MOVE 1 TO E-O-F.

                  * output next ten flights on departure screen

(0070)            H-ITER.
(0071)               IF COUNTER > 10 OR E-O-F NOT = 0 GO TO H-END.
(0072)            I.
(0073)               MOVE DEPARTURE-TIME TO DEPARTURE-TIME-WS.
(0074)               MOVE FLIGHT-NO TO FLIGHT-NO-WS.
(0075)               MOVE DESTINATION TO DESTINATION-WS.
(0076)               DISPLAY RECORD-1-WS.
(0077)               READ DEPARTURES AT END MOVE 1 TO E-O-F.
(0078)               ADD 1 TO COUNTER.
(0079)               GO TO H-ITER.
(0080)            H-END.
(0081)            J.
(0082)               ACCEPT TIME-WS FROM TIME.

                  * delay loop

(0083)            K-ITER.
(0084)               IF RT-CLOCK NOT = TIME-STORE GO TO K-END.
(0085)            L.
(0086)               ACCEPT TIME-WS FROM TIME.
(0087)               GO TO K-ITER.
(0088)            K-END.
(0089)            M.
(0090)               MOVE RT-CLOCK TO TIME-STORE, CLOCK.
(0091)            D-END.
(0092)               GO TO C-ITER.
(0093)            C-END.
(0094)            N.
(0095)               CLOSE DEPARTURES.
(0096)               STOP RUN.
(0097)            A-END.
```

13.9.4 Results of test run.

```
DATE: 15/12/83
TIME: 12 00

F L I G H T    D E P A R T U R E S

TIME        FLIGHT      DESTINATION

12 00       BA271       ROME
12 01       BA274       GENEVA
12 05       BC0113      ATHENS VIA ROME
12 07       LU0777      MAJORCA
12 15       IB193       NICE
12 20       PA7461      NEW YORK
12 25       PA7469      CHICAGO
12 30       BA275       PARIS
12 35       BC0115      GLASGOW
12 40       BA444       STOCKHOLM

DATE: 15/12/83
TIME: 12 01

F L I G H T    D E P A R T U R E S

TIME        FLIGHT      DESTINATION

12 01       BA274       GENEVA
12 05       BC0113      ATHENS VIA ROME
12 07       LU0777      MAJORCA
12 15       IB193       NICE
12 20       PA7461      NEW YORK
12 25       PA7469      CHICAGO
12 30       BA275       PARIS
12 35       BC0115      GLASGOW
12 40       BA444       STOCKHOLM
12 45       BC0197      GENEVA

                    |
                    |
                    |

DATE: 15/12/83
TIME: 12 09

F L I G H T    D E P A R T U R E S

TIME        FLIGHT      DESTINATION

12 15       IB193       NICE
12 20       PA7461      NEW YORK
12 25       PA7469      CHICAGO
12 30       BA275       PARIS
12 35       BC0115      GLASGOW
12 40       BA444       STOCKHOLM
12 45       BC0197      GENEVA
12 50       BC0203      EDINBURGH **CANCELLED**
13 00       B181        GUERNSEY
13 01       M76         MADRID
```

13.9.5 Comment.

The reader should notice that a new level number has been introduced in line (0039) in the program coding. A level 66 entry is used when an existing area of memory is to be referenced by a different name. The RENAMES clause permits alternative, possible overlapping, grouping of elementary items. The format of the RENAMES clause is:

66 data-name-1 **RENAMES** data-name-2 $\left\{ \begin{array}{l} \text{THROUGH} \\ \text{THRU} \end{array} \right\}$ data-name-3

Note: Level number 66 and data-name-1 are shown in the format to improve clarity, they are not part of the RENAMES clause.

In the program coding HRS and MINS were defined as:

02 HRS PIC 99.
02 MINS PIC 99.

This area of memory that contains a total of 4 digits can be given an alternative name RT-CLOCK by using:

66 RT-CLOCK RENAMES HRS THRU MINS.

All references to RT-CLOCK in the program are now references to a 4 digit number composed of HRS and MINS.

13.10 QUESTIONS

† **13.10.1** A Police computer is used to keep records of all registered vehicles. Use an indexed sequential file to create a simplified version of this system. Assume that records in the file are of fixed length with the following format.

Vehicle registration number (primary key) – 7 characters.
Date of registration – 4 digits MMYY.
Manufacturer – 10 characters.
Model – 10 characters. $\Big\}$ alternative key with duplicates.
Colour – 8 characters.
Name of registered owner – 25 characters.
Address where vehicle is kept – 30 characters.
Date of expiry of excise licence – 4 digits MMYY.

Write a file maintenance program to cater for a change in the owner of a vehicle (amendment), vehicles being scrapped (deletion) and new vehicles being registered (insertion).

† **13.10.2** Using the file created in question (13.10.1) write a program to retrieve and output all the information contained in record(s) with access on either a specified primary key, or specified alternative key. The alternative key may have duplicate entries, therefore several records will be output.

Print a report of those vehicle owners who have failed to re-new their vehicle excise licence.

† **13.10.3** A doctor requires a computerised appointments system for use in his surgery. He holds a two hour surgery in the morning (10.00 – 12.00) and a two hour surgery in the evening (17.00 – 19.00) each day from Monday to Friday. Write a program to allow his patients to make and cancel appointments throughout the week. The appointments file is a relative file having a key coded as a 3 digit integer. The coding of this key is as follows:

First digit (0–9) day and session e.g. 0 – Monday A.M. 1 – Monday P.M. 2 – Tuesday A.M. 3 – Tuesday P.M. etc.

Next two digits is the time of the appointment e.g. 01 – first time slot 02 – second time slot 03 – third time slot etc. Assume every appointment is allocated a 10 minute time slot.

An appointment record consists of the name (25 characters) and address (30 characters) of the patient.

† **13.10.4** Using the file created in (13.10.3) write a program to output a list of the vacant appointment slots for each day and a list of the names and addresses of the patients the doctor can expect to see.

14 Data Validation

14.1 INTRODUCTION

This chapter investigates the meaning of good and error data, the types of errors that can occur in data and the way in which such errors can be detected using statements in the COBOL language.

14.2 DEFINITION OF GOOD AND ERROR DATA

In designing a computer program it is vital to cater for both good and error data. There is a clear distinction to be made between valid and invalid data. Valid data is expected data, a program has been designed to process it and the results are predictable. Invalid data is unexpected data, a program has not been designed to process it and, therefore, the results are unpredictable.

Good data is regarded as being correct valid data, whereas error data is incorrect valid data.

A program can be designed to cater for valid data only.

The process of inspecting all valid data that is input to the computer and rejecting data that is unsuitable for use in a program (error data) is known as data validation. A data validation program should ensure that:

> all errors present in input data are detected,
> the type of errors are notified to the user of the system, and
> only good data is passed on for processing.

14.3 CLASSIFICATION OF ERRORS

Data that is input to a computer program could contain one or more of the following errors.

14.3.1 Type error.

The identifier to be assigned a data value has a PICTURE string that does not represent the type of data being input. The types of data are numeric, alphabetic and alphanumeric, and **irrespective of how the data item has been defined the error data will still be stored.**

Example. An identifier defined as, 02 DATUM PIC 999, could be used to represent a numeric field in a record, yet if that field contained a non-numeric item of data the error value would still be stored in DATUM.

An error situation can also exist between integer and real numeric types. For example if a data value is input as a subscript to a table then an error will occur if the data value is a real value. In a one-dimensional table, TABLE-1 (SUB) has no meaning if the value of SUB is 3.75.

14.3.2 Format error.

This is the result of the size or arrangement of the data not conforming to what is expected in the program. Such an error can result from an excessive number of characters in a string or areas within a data format that have not been correctly defined. For example, if DD, MM and YY represent three two-digit integers describing a date as day, month and year respectively, then if the format of a date is described within a program as DDMMYY yet input as MMDDYY (031048) then the date will be translated as the 3rd October 1948 and not the 10th March 1948 as input by the user. Similarly if the date was input as 31048 this would not conform to the six digit number that is expected.

14.3.3 Range error.

Such an error results from the value of the data not being within pre-defined limits. For example the numerical value of a month is recognised as being in the range 1 to 12, any value for a month outside these limits would be in error.

14.3.4 Relationship error.

If one item of data is related to another item of data, then a specific value for one item can dictate the range of values for a second item. For example when validating a date in a year, if the month is March, then the maximum value permissible for the number of days would be 31. This maximum value would change for, say, the month of September. However, the maximum value would not only be different for February but dependent upon whether the year was a Leap Year or not.

14.3.5 Feasibility error.

Certain items of data cannot be given exact limits, therefore, in such cases values that are thought of as being reasonable would be chosen for the range limits when performing a range check on the data. For example in validating the weights of humans a maximum weight of 160 Kg would be reasonable, however, weights above this value are likely to be in error.

14.3.6 Transcription error.

It is a very common practice to use a numeric code as a key to access records in a file e.g. bank account number, stock number. Because it is very easy to make a mistake when entering these numbers to a computer each number normally contains a check digit. This digit provides a means for the computer to check that the number has not had any digits transposed when it has been entered into the computer. The check digit method will ensure a detection of all transcription and transposition errors and 91% of random errors.

The modulus 11 check digit for a code number is calculated in the following way.

Using the code number 9118 as an example: multiply each digit by its associated weight, here we have the weights 5,4,3,2, and calculate the sum of the partial products.

i.e. $(5 \times 9) + (4 \times 1) + (3 \times 1) + (2 \times 8) = 68$.

The sum 68 is then divided by 11 and the remainder 2 is then subtracted from 11, the result 9 is the check digit. The code number, including the check digit as the last digit, is 91189. If the value of the check digit is computed to be 10 this is replaced by the letter X.

To check whether a code number has been entered into the computer correctly a similar calculation is carried out. Each digit is multipled by a weight, the check digit has a weight of 1, and the sum of the partial products is calculated.

i.e. $(5 \times 9) + (4 \times 1) + (3 \times 1) + (2 \times 8) + (1 \times 9) = 77$.

The sum 77 is divided by 11 and the remainder is zero. If the remainder was non-zero then a transcription error would have been made when entering the number.

14.4 FEATURES OF COBOL THAT AID DATA VALIDATION

14.4.1 Class Conditions.

A PICTURE clause is used to define a datum as being numeric, alphabetic or alphanumeric, however, to ensure that the data stored using such a description is of the correct type a class test can be made.

The general format of the class condition is:

identifier-1   IS   [NOT] $\begin{cases} \text{NUMERIC} \\ \text{ALPHABETIC} \end{cases}$

however, an extension of this to include **ALPHABETIC-LOWER** and **ALPHABETIC-UPPER** characters has been made in the Draft Proposal.

e.g. To ensure that the value stored under the description

02 DATUM PIC 999

is numeric, the following PROCEDURE DIVISION test can be made.

IF DATUM NUMERIC GO TO VALID-END.
    DISPLAY "ERROR – DATA TYPE" DATUM
        .
        .
        .

VALID-END.

If the value stored under the description

02 DATUM PIC A(10)

was to be tested for alphabetic type the PROCEDURE DIVISION code would be modified to:

IF DATUM ALPHABETIC GO TO VALID-END.

The class condition NUMERIC must only be used on a data descriptor that is designated as being numeric, and the class condition ALPHABETIC must only be used on a data descriptor that is designated as being alphabetic.

14.4.2 Condition Names.

When the value or range of values of an identifier are known in advance of program execution they can be specified in the DATA DIVISION using a level 88 entry.

The general format of a level 88 entry is:

88 condition-name-1 $\begin{cases} \text{VALUE IS} \\ \text{VALUES ARE} \end{cases}$ $\begin{cases} \text{literal-1} \end{cases}$ $\begin{bmatrix} \begin{cases} \text{THROUGH} \\ \text{THRU} \end{cases} \text{literal-2} \end{bmatrix}$ $\begin{cases} \end{cases}$ ....

A level 88 must follow directly after the description of the datum that has these values.

e.g.   02 DATUM PIC 999.
            88 COND VALUE IS 500.

If the only legal value for DATUM is 500 then the test

IF DATUM = 500 .....

can be replaced by

     IF COND .....

in the PROCEDURE DIVISION.

If a datum has several legal ranges of values then more than one level 88 is permitted for each identifier.

e.g.   02 DATUM PIC 999.
           88 COND-1 VALUES ARE 1 THRU 100.
           88 COND-2 VALUES ARE 201 THRU 300.
           88 COND-3 VALUE IS 500.

The PROCEDURE DIVISION coding to detect legal values of DATUM would normally be:

     IF (DATUM > 0 AND DATUM < 101) OR
         (DATUM > 200 AND DATUM < 301) OR
         DATUM = 500 .....

however, using the condition names specified, the coding can be reduced to:

     IF COND-1 OR COND-2 OR COND-3 .....

e.g. In a menu-driven system if the only legal values for MENU-CODE are A,B,C and D, the DATA DIVISION entry could be coded as:

     02 MENU-CODE PIC A.
         88 LEGAL-CODE VALUES ARE "A", "B", "C", "D".

The PROCEDURE DIVISION code used to test the validity of MENU-CODE would be:

       ACCEPT MENU-CODE.
    REPEAT-ITER.
     IF LEGAL-CODE GO TO REPEAT-END.
       DISPLAY "ERROR – RE-TYPE MENU CODE".
       ACCEPT MENU-CODE.
     GO TO REPEAT-ITER.
    REPEAT-END.

14.4.3 The INSPECT statement.

The INSPECT statement can be used to check every character in an item of data and replace specified characters with other characters, and/or count the number of characters in part of, or throughout the item of data.

A common error that can occur when entering numbers into a computer is to introduce spaces in place of zeros. For example a date might be input as b1b184 instead of 010184. The INSPECT statement can be used to detect the spaces present in the date and replace the spaces by zeros.

The general format for the INSPECT statement is given in Appendix III, however, only a simplified version of format 2 is required for processing the date.

e.g. If date is defined in the WORKING-STORAGE SECTION as:

     02 DATE-WS PIC 9(6).
  then
      INSPECT DATE-WS REPLACING ALL SPACES BY ZEROS

would be a sufficient PROCEDURE DIVISION statement to edit b1b184 to 010184.

279

If the format of an unsigned number is five digits to the left of the decimal point, the decimal point, and two digits to the right of the decimal point, then the format of this number can be checked by using a simplified version of the INSPECT statement given in format 1, in Appendix III.

The test in the PROCEDURE DIVISION to ensure that the decimal point is in the correct place is:

```
ACCEPT DEC-NUMB-WS.
INSPECT DEC-NUMB-WS TALLYING DIGIT-COUNT FOR
CHARACTERS BEFORE INITIAL ".".
REPEAT-ITER.
IF MAX-DIGITS GO TO REPEAT-END.
    DISPLAY "ERROR – RE-TYPE NUMBER"
    ACCEPT DEC-NUMB-WS.
    INSPECT DEC-NUMB-WS TALLYING DIGIT-COUNT FOR
    CHARACTERS BEFORE INITIAL ".".
GO TO REPEAT-ITER.
REPEAT-END.
```

Note it is the responsibility of the programmer to define an identifier that can be used by the INSPECT statement for keeping a tally (or count) of the number of characters before the delimiting character.

The DATA DIVISION entry that describes the identifiers in this would be:

```
02  DEC-NUMB-WS PIC X(8).
02  DIGIT-COUNT PIC 9.
    88 MAX-DIGITS VALUE IS 5.
```

14.5 WORKED EXAMPLE.

14.5.1 Problem.

Design and write a procedure to validate a date between 1980 and 1999. The format of the date is a six digit integer representing DDMMYY.

14.5.2 Design.

```
Functions List.
1.  Input date.
2.  Output error message.
3.  Set error flag to zero.
4.  Set error flag to 1.
5.  Replace spaces by zeros.
6.  Validate date.
```

```
Conditions List.
1.  Error flag not = 0.
2.  Date not numeric.
3.  Month out of range.
4.  Year out of range.
5.  Month February and Leap Year.
6.  Day out of range for month.
7.  Day > 29.
```

280

Detailed program structure.

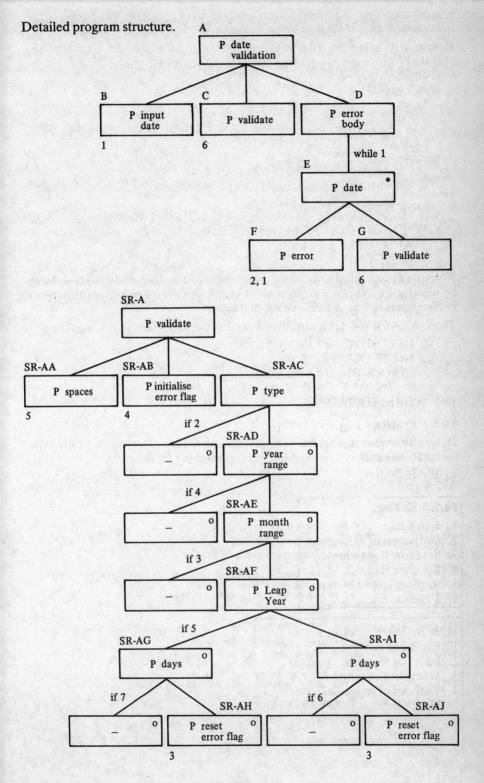

Schematic logic – main program.

```
A-seq
  B do 1
  C do SR-A
  D-iter while 1
    E-seq
      F do 2,1
      G do SR-A
    E-end
  D-end
A-end
```

Schematic logic – function 6 subroutine.

```
SR-A-seq
  SR-AA do 5
  SR-AB do 4
  SR-AC-sel if not 2
    SR-AD-sel if not 4
      SR-AE-sel if not 3
        SR-AF-sel if 5
          SR-AG-sel if not 7
            SR-AH do 3
          SR-AG-end
        SR-AF-or
          SR-AI-sel if not 6
            SR-AJ do 3
          SR-AI-end
        SR-AF-end
      SR-AE-end
    SR-AD-end
  SR-AC-end
SR-A-end
```

14.5.3 Coding.

```
(0001)        IDENTIFICATION DIVISION.
(0002)        PROGRAM-ID. C1453.
(0003)        DATA DIVISION.
(0004)        WORKING-STORAGE SECTION.
(0005)        01 DAY-LIST.
(0006)           02 FILLER PIC X(24) VALUE IS "312831303130313130313031".
(0007)        01 DAY-TABLE REDEFINES DAY-LIST.
(0008)           02 MAX-DAYS PIC 99 OCCURS 12 TIMES.
(0009)        01 DATE-WS.
(0010)           02 DD PIC 99.
(0011)              88 COND-0 VALUE IS 0.
(0012)           02 MM PIC 99.
(0013)              88 COND-1 VALUES  1 THRU 12.
(0014)              88 COND-2 VALUE IS 2.
(0015)           02 YY PIC 99.
(0016)              88 COND-3 VALUES  80 THRU 99.
(0017)              88 COND-4 VALUES  80, 84, 88, 92, 96.
(0018)        01 PARAMETER.
(0019)           02 ERROR-FLAG PIC 9.
```

(program continued)

```
(0020)          PROCEDURE DIVISION.
(0021)          A-SEQ.
(0022)          B.
(0023)              DISPLAY "TYPE DATE IN FORMAT DDMMYY".
(0024)              ACCEPT DATE-WS.
(0025)          C.
(0026)              PERFORM SR-A-SEQ THRU SR-A-END.
(0027)          D-ITER.
(0028)              IF ERROR-FLAG = 0 GO TO D-END.
(0029)          E-SEQ.
(0030)          F.
(0031)              DISPLAY "ERROR - RETYPE DATE".
(0032)              ACCEPT DATE-WS.
(0033)          G.
(0034)              PERFORM SR-A-SEQ THRU SR-A-END.
(0035)          E-END.
(0036)              GO TO D-ITER.
(0037)          D-END.
(0038)          A-END.
(0039)
(0040)          SR-A-SEQ.
(0041)          SR-AA.
(0042)              INSPECT DATE-WS REPLACING ALL SPACES BY ZEROS.
(0043)          SR-AB.
(0044)              MOVE 1 TO ERROR-FLAG.
(0045)          SR-AC-SEL.
(0046)              IF DATE-WS NOT NUMERIC GO TO SR-AC-END.
(0047)          SR-AD-SEL.
(0048)              IF NOT COND-3 GO TO SR-AD-END.
(0049)          SR-AE-SEL.
(0050)              IF NOT COND-1 GO TO SR-AE-END.
(0051)          SR-AF-SEL.
(0052)              IF NOT (COND-2 AND COND-4) GO TO SR-AF-OR.
(0053)          SR-AG-SEL.
(0054)              IF DD > 29 GO TO SR-AG-END.
(0055)          SR-AH.
(0056)              MOVE ZERO TO ERROR-FLAG.
(0057)          SR-AG-END.
(0058)              GO TO SR-AF-END.
(0059)          SR-AF-OR.
(0060)          SR-AI-SEL.
(0061)              IF COND-0 OR DD > MAX-DAYS (MM) GO TO SR-AI-END.
(0062)          SR-AJ.
(0063)              MOVE ZERO TO ERROR-FLAG.
(0064)          SR-AI-END.
(0065)          SR-AF-END.
(0066)          SR-AE-END.
(0067)          SR-AD-END.
(0068)          SR-AC-END.
(0069)          SR-A-END.
```

14.5.4 Results.

```
TYPE DATE IN FORMAT DDMMYY
010184
TYPE DATE IN FORMAT DDMMYY
280283
TYPE DATE IN FORMAT DDMMYY
290283
ERROR - RETYPE DATE
290284
TYPE DATE IN FORMAT DDMMYY
 2 445
ERROR - RETYPE DATE
 2 480
TYPE DATE IN FORMAT DDMMYY
HSJKLLO
ERROR - RETYPE DATE
303080
ERROR - RETYPE DATE

ERROR - RETYPE DATE
131380
ERROR - RETYPE DATE
BBBBBBB
ERROR - RETYPE DATE
```

14.6 WORKED EXAMPLE

14.6.1 Problem.

A serial file is used to store details about stock held in warehouses throughout the U.K. Each record on the file has the following format.

Field 1 stock number – 5 characters including a modulus-11 check digit as the last character.

Field 2 unit cost – 6 characters including a decimal point and two decimal places.

Field 3 location – 6 characters comprising a four letter warehouse code indicating the location of the warehouse in the U.K. (GLAS, LIVE, BIRM, COVE, LOND and SOUT) followed by a two-digit code indicating the storage bay in a particular warehouse.

Design and write a procedure to validate every record on the serial file.

A good record is one in which the three fields contain no errors. An error record is one in which at least one field is in error.

Good records are to be written to an output file ready for processing, therefore, the decimal point will be removed from the unit cost in field 2 before writing each record to this file.

Error records are to be written to an error report file and annotated with the error field numbers.

The format of this report will be as follows.

VALIDATION PROCEDURE ERROR REPORT			
FIELD 1	FIELD 2	FIELD 3	ERROR FIELDS
1543X	1234.5	POOL24	1 2 3
1544X	123.45	POOL24	3
15411	312.67	MANC37	1 3

14.6.2 Design.
Serial file.

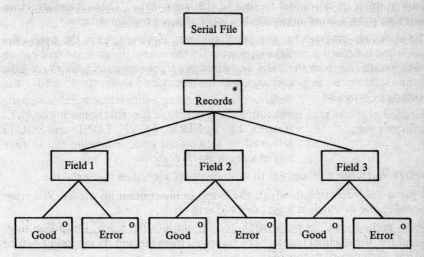

Output file.

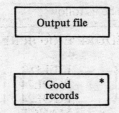

Error file.

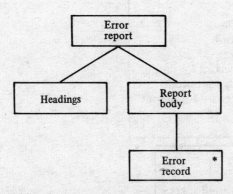

The records described in the serial file do **not** correspond with records in the output file and error file since the records between the files do not occur the same number of times and are not in the same order. These three structure diagrams cannot be amalgamated to form a basic program structure.

The structure diagram for the serial file can, however, form the basis of a validation subroutine, and the structures for the output file and error file can be amalgamated to form the basis of a main program structure. (An alternative design strategy to this approach will be discussed in chapter 15 under the heading of *program inversion*).

Detailed program structures.
Main program.

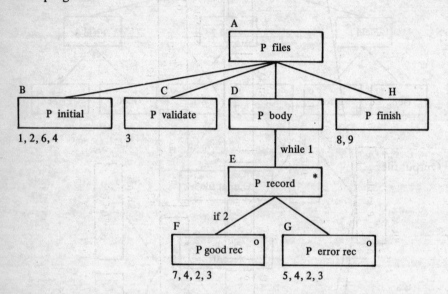

Functions List.
1. Open files.
2. Read serial file.
3. Validate record.
4. Write record.
5. Move error record for output.
6. Move heading for output.
7. Move good record for output.
8. Close files.
9. Stop.

Conditions List.
1. Not end of file.
2. Table elements all spaces.

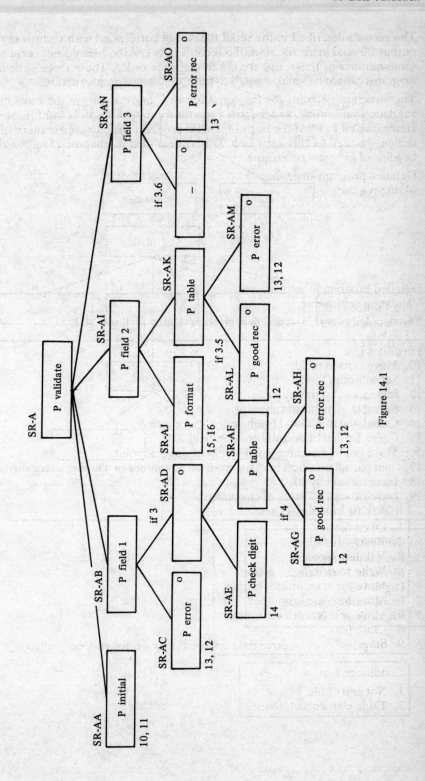

Figure 14.1

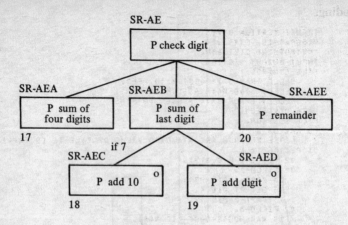

Figure 14.2

Detailed Program Structure.
Validation subroutine.

The detailed program structure is given in figures 14.1 and 14.2.

Functions List.
10. Move zero to table.
11. Set subscript to 1.
12. Increase subscript by 1.
13. Set table element to subscript.
14. Calculated modulus-11 remainder – subroutine.
15. Check format of decimal point in field-2.
16. Move field-2 to numeric field without decimal point.
17. Sum partial products of digits from stock number (excluding check digit).
18. Increase sum by 10.
19. Increase sum by value of check digit.
20. Calculate modulus-11 remainder.

Conditions List.
3. Field is numeric.
4. Modulus-11 remainder = 0.
5. Digits = 3.
6. Legal warehouse code.
7. Check digit = X.

Note: the position of an error field is stored in a one-dimensional table.

14.6.3 Coding.

```
(0001)          IDENTIFICATION DIVISION.
(0002)          PROGRAM-ID. C1463.
(0003)          ENVIRONMENT DIVISION.
(0004)          INPUT-OUTPUT SECTION.
(0005)          FILE-CONTROL.
(0006)              SELECT RAW-DATA ASSIGN TO PFMS.
(0007)              SELECT GOOD-DATA ASSIGN TO PFMS.
(0008)              SELECT ERROR-DATA ASSIGN TO PFMS.
(0009)          DATA DIVISION.
(0010)          FILE SECTION.
(0011)          FD RAW-DATA
(0012)              LABEL RECORDS ARE STANDARD VALUE OF FILE-ID IS "RAW".
(0013)          01 RECORD-1.
(0014)              02 FIELD-1 PIC X(5).
(0015)              02 FIELD-2.
(0016)                 03 PART-1 PIC 999.
(0017)                 03 DEC-PT PIC X.
(0018)                 03 PART-2 PIC 99.
(0019)              02 FIELD-3.
(0020)                 03 WAREHOUSE-CODE PIC A(4).
(0021)                    88 COND-1 VALUES      "GLAS", "LIVE", "BIRM", "COVE", "LON
(0022)         -           "D", "SOUT".
(0023)                 03 BAY PIC 99.
(0024)          01 RECORD-2.
(0025)              02 STOCK-NUMBER.
(0026)                 03 DIGIT-5 PIC 9.
(0027)                 03 DIGIT-4 PIC 9.
(0028)                 03 DIGIT-3 PIC 9.
(0029)                 03 DIGIT-2 PIC 9.
(0030)              02 CHECK-DIGIT PIC 9.
(0031)              02 FILLER PIC X(12).
(0032)          FD GOOD-DATA
(0033)              LABEL RECORDS ARE STANDARD VALUE OF FILE-ID IS "GOOD".
(0034)          01 RECORD-3.
(0035)              02 STOCK-NUM PIC X(5).
(0036)              02 UNIT-COST.
(0037)                 03 INTEGER PIC 999.
(0038)                 03 FRACTION PIC 99.
(0039)              02 LOCATION PIC X(6).
(0040)          FD ERROR-DATA
(0041)              LABEL RECORDS ARE STANDARD VALUE OF FILE-ID IS "ERROR".
(0042)          01 REPORT-OUT.
(0043)              02 FILLER PIC X.
(0044)              02 LINE-IMAGE PIC X(119).
(0045)          WORKING-STORAGE SECTION.
(0046)          01 RECORD-1-WS.
(0047)              02 FILLER PIC X(33) VALUE IS "VALIDATION PROCEDURE ERROR REPO
(0048)         -      "RT".
(0049)          01 RECORD-2-WS.
(0050)              02 FILLER PIC X(45) VALUE IS "FIELD 1    FIELD 2     FIELD 3
(0051)         -      " ERROR FIELDS".
(0052)          01 RECORD-3-WS.
(0053)              02 FIELD-1-WS PIC X(10).
(0054)              02 FIELD-2-WS PIC X(11).
(0055)              02 FIELD-3-WS PIC X(12).
(0056)              02 ERROR-FIELDS.
(0057)                 03 FIELD-NO PIC ZZZ OCCURS 3 TIMES.
(0058)          01 PARAMETERS.
(0059)              02 E-O-F PIC 9 VALUE IS ZERO.
(0060)              02 SUBSCRIPT PIC 9.
(0061)              02 CHECK-SUM PIC 999.
(0062)              02 REM PIC V99.
```

(program continued)

```
(0063)              PROCEDURE DIVISION.
(0064)              A-SEQ.
(0065)              B.
(0066)                  OPEN INPUT RAW-DATA
(0067)                      OUTPUT GOOD-DATA, ERROR-DATA.
(0068)                  READ RAW-DATA.
(0069)                  MOVE RECORD-1-WS TO LINE-IMAGE.
(0070)                  WRITE REPORT-OUT AFTER ADVANCING PAGE.
(0071)                  MOVE RECORD-2-WS TO LINE-IMAGE.
(0072)                  WRITE REPORT-OUT AFTER 2 LINES.
(0073)              C.
(0074)                  PERFORM SR-A-SEQ THRU SR-A-END.
(0075)              D-ITER.
(0076)                  IF E-O-F NOT = 0 GO TO D-END.
(0077)              E-SEL.
(0078)                  IF ERROR-FIELDS NOT = ALL SPACES GO TO E-OR.

        * good record

(0079)              F.
(0080)                      MOVE FIELD-1 TO STOCK-NUM.
(0081)                      MOVE FIELD-3 TO LOCATION.
(0082)                      WRITE RECORD-3.
(0083)                      READ RAW-DATA AT END MOVE 1 TO E-O-F.
(0084)                      PERFORM SR-A-SEQ THRU SR-A-END.
(0085)                      GO TO E-END.
(0086)              E-OR.

        * error record

(0087)              G.
(0088)                      MOVE FIELD-1 TO FIELD-1-WS.
(0089)                      MOVE FIELD-2 TO FIELD-2-WS.
(0090)                      MOVE FIELD-3 TO FIELD-3-WS.
(0091)                      MOVE RECORD-3-WS TO LINE-IMAGE.
(0092)                      WRITE REPORT-OUT AFTER 1 LINE.
(0093)                      READ RAW-DATA AT END MOVE 1 TO E-O-F.
(0094)                      PERFORM SR-A-SEQ THRU SR-A-END.
(0095)              E-END.
(0096)                  GO TO D-ITER.
(0097)              D-END.
(0098)              H.
(0099)                  CLOSE RAW-DATA, GOOD-DATA, ERROR-DATA.
(0100)                  STOP RUN.
(0101)              A-END.
(0102)              SR-A-SEQ.
(0103)              SR-AA.
(0104)                  MOVE ZERO TO FIELD-NO (1), FIELD-NO (2), FIELD-NO (3).
(0105)                  MOVE 1 TO SUBSCRIPT.

        * check field 1

(0106)              SR-AB-SEL.
(0107)                  IF STOCK-NUMBER NOT NUMERIC OR
(0108)                      (CHECK-DIGIT NOT NUMERIC AND CHECK-DIGIT NOT = "X")
(0109)                      GO TO SR-AB-OR.
(0110)              SR-AD-SEQ.
(0111)              SR-AE.
(0112)                  PERFORM SR-AE-SEQ THRU SR-AE-END.
(0113)              SR-AF-SEL.
(0114)                      IF REM NOT = 0 GO TO SR-AF-OR.
(0115)              SR-AG.    ADD 1 TO SUBSCRIPT.
(0116)                      GO TO SR-AF-END.
(0117)              SR-AF-OR.
(0118)              SR-AH.
(0119)                      MOVE SUBSCRIPT TO FIELD-NO (SUBSCRIPT).
(0120)                      ADD 1 TO SUBSCRIPT.
(0121)              SR-AF-END.
(0122)              SR-AD-END.
(0123)                  GO TO SR-AB-END.
```

(program continued)

```
(0124)          SR-AB-OR.
(0125)          SR-AC.
(0126)              MOVE SUBSCRIPT TO FIELD-NO (SUBSCRIPT).
(0127)              ADD 1 TO SUBSCRIPT.
(0128)          SR-AB-END.

                * check field 2

(0129)          SR-AI-SEQ.
(0130)          SR-AJ.
(0131)          SR-AK-SEL.
(0132)              IF PART-1 NOT NUMERIC OR PART-2 NOT NUMERIC
(0133)                OR DEC-PT NOT = "." GO TO SR-AK-OR.
(0134)          SR-AL.
(0135)              MOVE PART-1 TO INTEGER.
(0136)              MOVE PART-2 TO FRACTION.
(0137)              ADD 1 TO SUBSCRIPT.
(0138)              GO TO SR-AK-END.
(0139)          SR-AK-OR.
(0140)          SR-AM.
(0141)              MOVE SUBSCRIPT TO FIELD-NO (SUBSCRIPT).
(0142)              ADD 1 TO SUBSCRIPT.
(0143)          SR-AK-END.
(0144)          SR-AI-END.

                * check field 3

(0145)          SR-AN-SEL.
(0146)              IF COND-1 AND BAY NUMERIC GO TO SR-AN-END.
(0147)              MOVE SUBSCRIPT TO FIELD-NO (SUBSCRIPT).
(0148)          SR-AN-END.
(0149)          SR-A-END.

                * check for transcription error

(0150)          SR-AE-SEQ.
(0151)          SR-AEA.
(0152)              COMPUTE CHECK-SUM = 5 * DIGIT-5 + 4 * DIGIT-4 + 3 * DIGIT-3
(0153)                              + 2 * DIGIT-2.
(0154)          SR-AEB-SEL.
(0155)              IF CHECK-DIGIT NOT = "X" GO TO SR-AEB-OR.
(0156)          SR-AEC.
(0157)              ADD 10 TO CHECK-SUM.
(0158)              GO TO SR-AEB-END.
(0159)          SR-AEB-OR.
(0160)          SR-AED.
(0161)              ADD CHECK-DIGIT TO CHECK-SUM.
(0162)          SR-AEB-END.
(0163)          SR-AEE.
(0164)              DIVIDE 11 INTO CHECK-SUM GIVING REM.
(0165)          SR-AE-END.
```

14.6.4 Results showing the contents of the data files being used.

Raw data.

```
                        RAW
            4345X138.76GLAS06
            91189012.50LIVE84
            912781.27 LOND 3
            91367027.50SOUT32
            91855 12.000UTH96
            80317 57.26BIRM74
            92479094.50BRMI26
            10732£13.76LIV 91
            93467050.23LOND38
            93866075.45LOND48
            94625120.75LIVE27
            95125350.86BIRM
            93271086.00LON 21
            95621045.00COVE4-
            96024213.20GLAS49
            93876176.50GLAS52
            97047 21.7 BIRM53
            97322300.00LIVE75
            97608120.75COVE04
            97705130.40COVE05
            98108076.20LOND22
```

Good data.

```
              GOOD
      9118901250LIVE84
      9136702750SOUT32
      9346705023LOND38
      9386607545LOND48
      9462512075LIVE27
      9602421320GLAS49
      9732230000LIVE75
      9760812075COVE04
      9770513040COVE05
      9810807620LOND22
```

Error data.

```
VALIDATION PROCEDURE ERROR REPORT
```

FIELD 1	FIELD 2	FIELD 3	ERROR FIELDS
4345X	138.76	GLASO6	1
91278	1.27	LOND 3	2 3
91855	12.00	OUTH96	2 3
80317	57.26	BIRM74	1 2
92479	094.50	BRMI26	3
10732	£13.76	LIV 91	1 2 3
95125	350.86	BIRM	3
93271	086.00	LON 21	1 3
95621	045.00	COVE4-	3
93876	176.50	GLAS52	1
97047	21.7	BIRM53	2

14.7 QUESTIONS.

14.7.1 Detect the errors in the following segments of code.

```
01 PARAMETERS.
    02  ALPHA PIC 99.
        88  ALPHA-TEST VALUES "A", "B", "C".
    02  BETA PIC 99V9.
    02  GAMMA PIC X(10).
        88  BETA-TEST PIC 99V9 VALUES 21.6, 38.4, 98.5

01 PARAMETERS.
    02  DELTA PIC 99.
        88  DELTA-TEST VALUES 21 THRU 39.
PROCEDURE DIVISION.
A-SEQ.
        IF DELTA-TEST NOT NUMERIC GO TO .....

H-SEL.
        IF DELTA GO TO H-OR.
```

14.7.2 Detect the syntax error in the following statements.

EXAMINE ALPHA TALLYING ALL LEADING SPACES AFTER INITIAL ".".

INSPECT BETA REPLACING ALL CHARACTERS BEFORE INITIAL "." BY ZERO.

IF GAMMA ALPHANUMERIC PERFORM .....

14.7.3 Write a validation procedure for the time of day input as a four digit number using the 24-hour clock representation, e.g. 1436.

†**14.7.4** Write a validation procedure for the date in a non-leap year input as a five character string e.g. MAR18. The year is not input. Your routine should allow for dates being input as MAR1b or MARb1 to represent the 1st March.

†**14.7.5** Every bona fide user of a computer system has a system-log record in an indexed sequential file. The format of a record on this file is:

> User account number (key) – 6 digits preceded by either PS or TP.
> Password – 10 characters composed from the digits 0-9 and the alphabet; the first character must be alphabetic.
> Time of last log-out – 6 digit integer representing hours, minutes and seconds on a 24 hour clock format.

When a user logs on to the computer system he must type his user account number and password. These two entries are fully validated by the system and if either entry proves to be wrong, or if the time of the last log-out was less than 30 minutes ago, the user will be denied access to the system.

Design and write a complete validation system for the system access procedure.

15 Program Implementation Techniques

15.1 INTRODUCTION

The programming problems encountered so far have resulted in straight-forward solutions. However, life is not that simple, this chapter investigates several areas that can complicate the design of structured programs and illustrates techniques for solving these problems. The chapter is divided into two parts, the first part deals with *structure clashes* between components of data structure diagrams and the second part deals with the problems of *recognition* in the design of programs. This chapter serves as an introduction to these two topics and the reader is advised to refer to M.A. Jackson's book on the *Principles of Program Design* for an in depth treatment of the subject.

15.2 STRUCTURE CLASHES

In attempting to form a basic program structure correspondence must exist between the respective components of the initial data structure diagrams. For a correspondence to exist three conditions must be satisfied. The components must occur:

I   The same number of times.
II   In the same order.
III Under the same circumstances.

If one of these conditions is not satisfied then there is likely to be a structure clash between the components of the initial data structure diagrams. Structure clashes can be categorised into either an *ordering* clash or a *boundary* clash depending upon the problem.

15.2.1 Ordering Clash.

The following problem serves to illustrate an ordering clash between the components of data structure diagrams.

A file contains records of the names and academic details of staff at a college. The file is sorted by department as primary key, staff status as secondary key and staff name as tertiary key. A report is to be printed on the contents of the file, however, the format of the report is such that only the names of the members of staff are to be printed under the headings of the various staff statuses for the entire college. The staff names will **not** be categorised by department.

The data structure diagrams for the staff file and report are as follows.

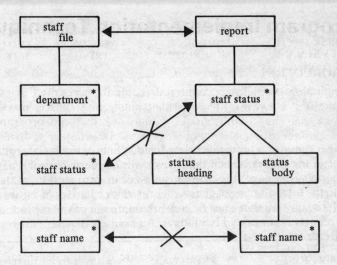

A structure clash exists between two components in these structures. Staff status will appear a different number of times on each structure (once for each department on the staff file and only once in the report). Staff name will also appear in a different order in each structure.

Since the difference between the staff file and the report is the ordering of the records this type of structure clash is known as an ordering clash.

This structure clash is very easily resolved. The staff file (input file) is re-sorted using the staff status as the primary key and the staff name as the secondary key. In effect the re-sorted file becomes an intermediate file, and it is this file that is read in printing the report.

In resolving this structure clash it is necessary in theory to:

> design two programs,
> one program to produce an intermediate file (revised input file),
> one program to produce the output required in the problem.

15.2.2 Boundary Clash.

The following problem serves to illustrate a boundary clash between the components of data structure diagrams.

A hotel manager keeps a register of all his guests on a computer file. The records on the file are of fixed length with the format.

> date of end-of-week: 6 digits
> day number: 1 digit
> guest details: 73 characters.

For each room occupied in the hotel there is a guest record. At the end of each week the records are stored in a batch, each batch is identified by a batch header record that contains the date of the end of the week with the remaining fields blank. An example of part of the file is:

```
311283
3112831MR P JONES          136 WELSH WAY      WATFORD     BRITISH 45
3112831MRS E SMYTHE        24 ANVIL CR        LUTON       BRITISH 23
3112832REV S EVANS         7 CHURCH RD        TRING       BRITISH 13
              .

070184
070184MR S DAVIES          36 BLACK ST        COVENTRY    BRITISH 16
              .
              .
```

The manager requires a report based on the contents of the serial register file. The layout of the report is such that the details of guests for each new week must begin on a new page; the date for the week ending must be at the top of every page; the total number of guests registered for each day of the week must be printed; the day number must be converted into the day name before printing on the report (assume day 1 is Sunday). An example of part of the report is:

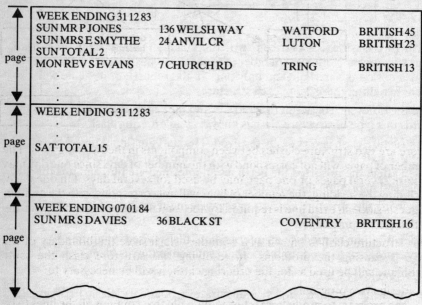

```
WEEK ENDING 31 12 83
SUN MR P JONES        136 WELSH WAY      WATFORD     BRITISH 45
SUN MRS E SMYTHE      24 ANVIL CR        LUTON       BRITISH 23
SUN TOTAL 2
MON REV S EVANS       7 CHURCH RD        TRING       BRITISH 13
```

```
WEEK ENDING 31 12 83


SAT TOTAL 15
```

```
WEEK ENDING 07 01 84
SUN MR S DAVIES       36 BLACK ST        COVENTRY    BRITISH 16
        .
        .
```

The data structure diagrams for the serial file and the report are:

There are two structure clashes between components in the two diagrams. The number of pages will not correspond with the number of days since one day may require several pages or one page may be used for several days. On one page, excluding the heading, the number of lines will not correspond with the number of guests since an extra line is required for the total number of guests registering at the hotel in one day.

This structure clash is known as a boundary clash since the boundary of the page is causing the problems. In resolving this structure clash the same technique will be used as for the ordering clash; it will be necessary to:

    design two programs,
    one program to produce an intermediate file that contains all the lines to be printed (revised input file),
    one program to produce the output required in the problem.

15.3 PROGRAM INVERSION

Program inversion is a technique whereby the intermediate file invented at the program design stage is **not** created at the program implementation stage. The two separate programs developed at the design stage are used, however, one program becomes a *subprogram* of the other, and the *main* program calls the subprogram every time it would have accessed the intermediate file had it still existed.

15.3.1 Modifications to Program Designs.

The two separate programs can be represented diagramatically as:

    Input file ⟶ Program 1 ⟶ Intermediate file

297

Program 1 will read the input file and write to the intermediate file.

Intermediate file ⟶ Program 2 ⟶ Output file

Program 2 will read the intermediate file and write to the output file.

If program 2 is chosen as the main routine all references to reading the intermediate file are replaced by calls to program 1 as a subprogram. The subprogram provides a record by reading the input file and processing the record until it is ready to write to the intermediate file, at which stage the computer returns to the main routine. All references to writing to the intermediate file in the subprogram and reading the intermediate file in the main program are deleted.

If program 1 is chosen as the main routine then all references to writing to the intermediate file are replaced by calls to program 2 as a subprogram. The subprogram writes a record to the output file and performs further processing until a reference is made to reading the intermediate file, at this point the computer returns to the main program. All references to reading the intermediate file in the subprogram and writing to the intermediate file in the main program are deleted.

Whichever program is chosen as a subprogram the following modifications must be made to it in addition to the modifications already mentioned. All references to opening and closing the intermediate file must be deleted. Amendments to the schematic logic of the subprogram must be made to provide the correct entry to and exit from the subprogram each time it is called. This is because several calls from the main program to the subprogram will be necessary in the execution of the main program. The following diagram illustrates the technique.

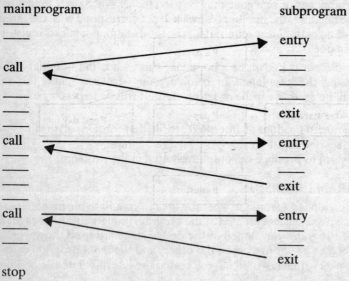

When independent routines are processed in *parallel* as illustrated they are known as *co-routines*.

15.4 WORKED EXAMPLE

The problem defined in 15.2.2 will be solved in the following stages. Two programs will be designed, the first to create an intermediate file and the second to read the intermediate file and output the required report. The second program will be chosen as the main routine and the first program will become the subprogram. The appropriate modifications will be made to the schematic logic for each program.

15.4.1 Detailed Program Structure for Program 1.

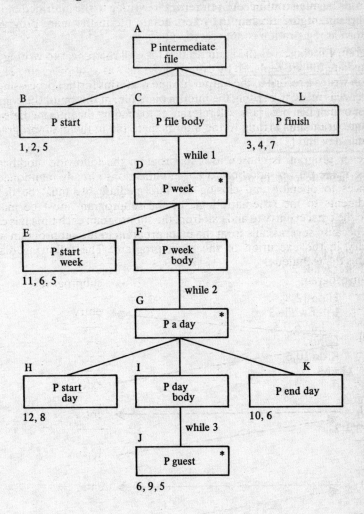

Functions List.
1. Open register file.
2. Open intermediate file.
3. Close register file.
4. Close intermediate file.
5. Read register file.
6. Write record to intermediate file.
7. Stop.
8. Initialise registration count to zero.
9. Increase registration count by 1.
10. Format registration count record.
11. Store date.
12. Store day number.

Conditions List.
1. Not end of file.
2. Same week and (1).
3. Same day and (2).

15.4.2 Schematic logic for program 1.

```
A-seq
  B do 1,2,5
  C-iter while 1
    D-seq
      E do 11,6,5
      F-iter while 2
        G-seq
          H do 12,8
          I-iter while 3
            J do 6,9,5
          I-end
          K do 10,6
        G-end
      F-end
    D-end
  C-end
  L do 3,4,7
A-end
```

Modifications necessary to the schematic logic if program 1 is to be used as a subprogram.

Functions 2 and 4 are deleted since they relate to opening and closing the intermediate file.

Function 7 (stop) is replaced by exit to allow control to be returned to the main program.

Function 6 is replaced by a statement for storing the entry position of the next co-routine to be executed, and a statement to exit the current co-routine. A goto depending on statement is used to control the entry position to a particular co-routine.

```
        A-seq
           goto Q1, Q2, Q3, Q4 depending on QS
Q1      B do 1,2,5
           C-iter while 1
              D-seq
                 E do 11,6, move 2 to QS goto QX
Q2                  do 5
                 F-iter while 2
                    G-seq
                       H do 12,8
                       I-iter while 3
                          J do 6, move 3 to QS goto QX
Q3                          do 9,5
                       I-end
                       K do 10,6 move 4 to QS goto QX
Q4                  G-end
                 F-end
              D-end
           C-end
           L do 3,4,7
QX      exit
        A-end
```

15.4.3 Detailed Program Structure for Program 2.

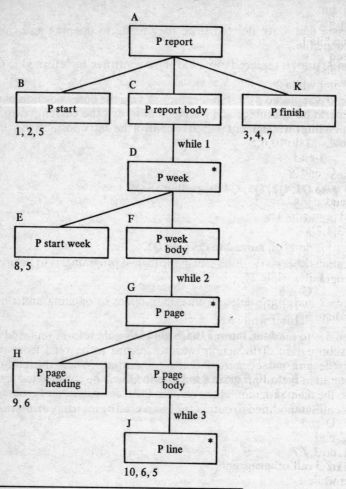

Functions List.

1. Open report file.
2. Open intermediate file.
3. Close report file.
4. Close intermediate file.
5. Read intermediate file.
6. Write record to report file with paper control.
7. Stop.
8. Store date.
9. Initialise line-count to zero.
10. Increase line-count by 1.

Conditions List.

1. Not end of file.
2. Same date and (1).
3. Line-count < 60 and (2).

Note: assume page contains
60 lines including heading.

15.4.4 Schematic Logic for Program 2.

```
A-seq
  B do 1,2,5
  C-iter while 1
    D-seq
      E do 8,5
      F-iter while 2
        G-seq
          H do 9,6
          I-iter while 3
            J do 10,6,5
          I-end
        G-end
      F-end
    D-end
  C-end
  K do 3,4,7
A-end
```

Modifications necessary to the schematic logic if program 2 is to be used as the main program.

Functions 2 and 4 are deleted since they relate to opening and closing the intermediate file.

Function 5 is to read the intermediate file and is, therefore, replaced by a call to the subprogram. This action causes a record to be read from the hotel register file and passed across ready for output. When the end-of-file is encountered in the subprogram the *total* record will be constructed and passed across to the main program. However, this final *total* will never be output unless component K is modified to output the last record by inserting an extra function 6.

```
A-seq
  B do 1,2,5 call subprogram
  C-iter while 1
    D-seq
      E do 8,5 call subprogram
      F-iter while 2
        G-seq
          H do 9,6
          I-iter while 3
            J do 10,6,5 call subprogram
          I-end
        G-end
      F-end
    D-end
  C-end
  K do 6,3,4,7
A-end
```

15.5 SUBPROGRAMS

A subprogram is a self-contained program that has been compiled independently of any other program yet can be executed from within another program. Although different programs can be compiled independently of each other they can be link-loaded together prior to run-time and executed as one suite of programs that produce the required solution to a problem. A program may be linked with one or more subprograms for the following reasons.

Subprograms have been previously written and tested and therefore are easily compiled and catalogued.

Subprograms can be used by any program in the system.

Subprograms facilitate team projects by dividing a program into smaller programs.

Subprograms can be written in another language and used by a program of another language. This is known as mixed-language programming, the implications of such an exercise go beyond the scope of this book.

When more than one program is used in the same run-time environment there will be a need to *call* one program from within another program and also to communicate data values between the programs.

15.5.1 The CALL and EXIT PROGRAM Statements.

The CALL statement causes control to be transferred from one object program to another object program, that has been link-loaded, at run-time. A simplified format of the CALL statement is:

CALL literal-1 [**USING** {data-name-1} .....]

where literal-1 is the name of the called program (subprogram). If the subprogram is another COBOL program then literal-1 is the name associated with the PROGRAM-ID statement.

In order to facilitate a return from the called program (subprogram) to the calling program every subprogram must have an EXIT PROGRAM statement. The EXIT PROGRAM statement is the only entry in a paragraph. The following skeletal COBOL code illustrates the program linkage between a calling program and a subprogram.

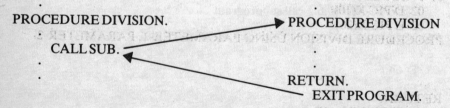

```
Calling Program                          Subprogram

ID DIVISION.                             ID DIVISION.
PROGRAM-ID. MAIN.                        PROGRAM-ID. SUB.
        .                                        .
        .                                        .
PROCEDURE DIVISION.                      PROCEDURE DIVISION
    CALL SUB.                                    .
        .                                        .
        .                                RETURN.
                                           EXIT PROGRAM.
```

Notes. The CALL statement causes the computer to branch to the **first** executable statement in the PROCEDURE DIVISION of the subprogram.

EXIT PROGRAM causes the computer to return to the **next** executable statement after CALL in the calling program. One subprogram can call another subprogram, however, it must **not** call the calling program, and since *recursion* is not allowed in the COBOL language a subprogram must **not** call itself.

15.5.2 Parameter Passing.

The communication of data values between two programs at run-time is achieved through the USING clause in the CALL statement of the calling program, the USING clause in the PROCEDURE DIVISION heading of the subprogram and the LINKAGE SECTION in the subprogram. The following skeletal COBOL code illustrates parameter passing between two programs.

Calling Program.

```
ID DIVISION.
PROGRAM-ID. MAIN.
    .
    .

WORKING-STORAGE SECTION.
01 PARAMETER-1.
    02  ALPHA PIC 9(4).
    02  BETA PIC 99.
01 PARAMETER-2.
    02  DELTA PIC X(10).
    02  EPSILON PIC X(20).
    .
    .

PROCEDURE DIVISION.
    CALL "SUB" USING PARAMETER-1, PARAMETER-2.
```

Subprogram.

```
ID DIVISION.
PROGRAM-ID. SUB.
    .
    .

WORKING-STORAGE SECTION.
    .
    .

LINKAGE SECTION.
01 PARAMETER-1.
    02  ALPHA PIC 9(4).
    02  BETA PIC 99.
01 PARAMETER-2.
    02  D PIC X(10).
    02  E PIC X(20).
PROCEDURE DIVISION USING PARAMETER-1, PARAMETER-2.
    .
    .
    .

RETURN.
    EXIT PROGRAM.
```

Notes. There must be the same number of parameters in the USING clause of the calling program as in the USING clause of the subprogram. The names of the parameters need not be identical since it is their position in the parameter list that is important.

	Parameter-1		Parameter-2	
Calling program	ALPHA	BETA	DELTA	EPSILON
Subprogram	ALPHA	BETA	D	E

The PICTURE clauses for the respective parameters between the calling program and subprogram must be the same. The subprogram contains a LINKAGE SECTION, coded after the WORKING-STORAGE SECTION, where all the identifiers specified in the USING clause of the subprogram are defined. Only level 01 and level 77 entries are permitted in this section, however, level 01 entries can contain subordinate entries. The purpose of the LINKAGE SECTION is to provide addresses in memory where the parameters defined in the calling program are stored. The parameters defined in the subprogram are **not** stored in the WORKING-STORAGE area of the subprogram.

If there are no data values to pass between programs then the USING clauses and LINKAGE SECTION can be omitted.

15.5.3 Worked Example.

The design of the programs given in 15.4 are now coded into two COBOL programs.

Program 2 – Calling (or main) routine.

```
(0001)          IDENTIFICATION DIVISION.
(0002)          PROGRAM-ID. PROG2.
(0003)          ENVIRONMENT DIVISION.
(0004)          INPUT-OUTPUT SECTION.
(0005)          FILE-CONTROL.
(0006)             SELECT HOTEL-REPORT ASSIGN TO PFMS.
(0007)          DATA DIVISION.
(0008)          FILE SECTION.
(0009)          FD HOTEL-REPORT
(0010)             LABEL RECORDS ARE STANDARD VALUE OF FILE-ID IS "OUTPUT".
(0011)          01 REPORT-OUT.
(0012)             02 FILLER PIC X.
(0013)             02 LINE-IMAGE PIC X(119).
(0014)          WORKING-STORAGE SECTION.
(0015)          01 FILE-END.
(0016)             02 EOF PIC 9.
(0017)               88 END-OF-FILE VALUE 1.
(0018)          01 RECORD-1-WS.
(0019)             02 RECORD-DATE-WS PIC 9(6).
(0020)             02 DAY-NUMBER-WS PIC 9.
(0021)             02 GUEST-DETAILS-WS PIC X(73).
(0022)          01 RECORD-2-WS.
(0023)             02 FILLER PIC X(12) VALUE IS "WEEK ENDING".
(0024)             02 HEADER-DATE PIC 99B99B99.
(0025)          01 RECORD-3-WS.
(0026)             02 DAY-NAME PIC X(4).
(0027)             02 GUEST-DETAILS-WS-1 PIC X(73).
(0028)          01 RECORD-4-WS.
(0029)             02 FILLER PIC X(21) VALUE IS "SUNMONTUEWEDTHUFRISAT".
(0030)          01 RECORD-5-WS REDEFINES RECORD-4-WS.
(0031)             02 NAME-OF-DAY PIC X(3) OCCURS 7 TIMES.
```

(program continued)

```
(0032)          01 PARAMETERS.
(0033)             02 LINE-COUNT PIC 99.
(0034)             02 HEADER-STORE PIC 9(6).
(0035)          PROCEDURE DIVISION.
(0036)          A-SEQ.
(0037)          B.
(0038)             OPEN OUTPUT HOTEL-REPORT.
(0039)             CALL "PROG1" USING RECORD-1-WS, FILE-END.
(0040)          C-ITER.
(0041)             IF END-OF-FILE GO TO C-END.
(0042)          D-SEQ.
(0043)          E.
(0044)                MOVE RECORD-DATE-WS TO HEADER-STORE.
(0045)                CALL "PROG1" USING RECORD-1-WS, FILE-END.
(0046)          F-ITER.
(0047)             IF RECORD-DATE-WS NOT = HEADER-STORE OR END-OF-FILE
(0048)                GO TO F-END.
(0049)          G-SEQ.
(0050)          H.
(0051)                MOVE ZERO TO LINE-COUNT.
(0052)                MOVE HEADER-STORE TO HEADER-DATE.
(0053)                MOVE RECORD-2-WS TO LINE-IMAGE.
(0054)                WRITE REPORT-OUT AFTER ADVANCING PAGE.
(0055)          I-ITER.
(0056)             IF LINE-COUNT NOT < 60 OR
(0057)             RECORD-DATE-WS NOT = HEADER-STORE OR END-OF-FILE
(0058)                GO TO I-END.
(0059)          J.
(0060)                ADD 1 TO LINE-COUNT.
(0061)                MOVE NAME-OF-DAY (DAY-NUMBER-WS) TO DAY-NAME.
(0062)                MOVE GUEST-DETAILS-WS TO GUEST-DETAILS-WS-1.
(0063)                MOVE RECORD-3-WS TO LINE-IMAGE.
(0064)                WRITE REPORT-OUT AFTER ADVANCING 1 LINE.
(0065)                CALL "PROG1" USING RECORD-1-WS, FILE-END.
(0066)                GO TO I-ITER.
(0067)          I-END.
(0068)          G-END.
(0069)                GO TO F-ITER.
(0070)          F-END.
(0071)          D-END.
(0072)                GO TO C-ITER.
(0073)          C-END.
(0074)          K.
(0075)             MOVE NAME-OF-DAY (DAY-NUMBER-WS) TO DAY-NAME.
(0076)             MOVE GUEST-DETAILS-WS TO GUEST-DETAILS-WS-1.
(0077)             MOVE RECORD-3-WS TO LINE-IMAGE.
(0078)             WRITE REPORT-OUT AFTER ADVANCING 1 LINE.
(0079)             CLOSE HOTEL-REPORT.
(0080)             STOP RUN.
(0081)          A-END.
```

Program 1 – Subprogram (Inverted program)

```
(0001)          IDENTIFICATION DIVISION.
(0002)          PROGRAM-ID. PROG1.
(0003)          ENVIRONMENT DIVISION.
(0004)          INPUT-OUTPUT SECTION.
(0005)          FILE-CONTROL.
(0006)             SELECT REGISTER ASSIGN TO PFMS.
(0007)          DATA DIVISION.
(0008)          FILE SECTION.
(0009)          FD REGISTER
(0010)             LABEL RECORDS ARE STANDARD VALUE OF FILE-ID IS "HOTEL".
(0011)          01 RECORD-1.
(0012)             02 RECORD-DATE PIC 9(6).
(0013)             02 DAY-NUMBER PIC 9.
(0014)             02 GUEST-DETAILS PIC X(73).
(0015)          WORKING-STORAGE SECTION.
(0016)          01 PARAMETERS.
(0017)             02 E-O-F PIC 9 VALUE IS ZERO.
(0018)                88 END-OF-FILE VALUE 1.
```

(program continued)

```
(0019)                    32 QS PIC 9 VALUE IS 1.
(0020)                    02 HEADER-DATE PIC 9(6).
(0021)                    02 DAY-STORE PIC 9.
(0022)                    32 REGISTRATION-COUNT PIC 99.
(0023)                01 REGISTRATION-LINE.
(0024)                    02 FILLER PIC X(6) VALUE IS " TOTAL".
(0025)                    32 REG-COUNT PIC Z9.
(0026)                LINKAGE SECTION.
(0027)                01 RECORD-1-LS.
(0028)                    32 RECORD-DATE-LS PIC 9(6).
(0029)                    02 DAY-NUMBER-LS PIC 9.
(0030)                    02 GUEST-DETAILS-LS PIC X(73).
(0031)                01 FILE-END.
(0032)                    02 EOF PIC 9.
(0033)                PROCEDURE DIVISION USING RECORD-1-LS, FILE-END.
(0034)                A-SEQ.
(0035)                    GO TO Q1, Q2, Q3, Q4 DEPENDING ON QS.
(0036)                Q1.
(0037)                B.
(0038)                    OPEN INPUT REGISTER.
(0039)                    READ REGISTER INTO RECORD-1-LS
(0040)                    AT END MOVE 1 TO E-O-F, EOF.
(0041)                C-ITER.
(0042)                    IF END-OF-FILE GO TO C-END.
(0043)                D-SEQ.
(0044)                E.
(0045)                    MOVE RECORD-DATE TO HEADER-DATE.
(0046)                    MOVE 2 TO QS, GO TO QX.
(0047)                Q2.
(0048)                    READ REGISTER INTO RECORD-1-LS
(0049)                    AT END MOVE 1 TO E-O-F, EOF.
(0050)                F-ITER.
(0051)                    IF RECORD-DATE NOT = HEADER-DATE OR END-OF-FILE
(0052)                    GO TO F-END.
(0053)                G-SEQ.
(0054)                H.
(0055)                    MOVE DAY-NUMBER TO DAY-STORE.
(0056)                    MOVE ZERO TO REGISTRATION-COUNT.
(0057)                I-ITER.
(0058)                    IF DAY-NUMBER NOT = DAY-STORE
(0059)                    OR RECORD-DATE NOT = HEADER-DATE OR END-OF-FILE
(0060)                    GO TO I-END.
(0061)                J.
(0062)                    MOVE 3 TO QS GO TO QX.
(0063)                Q3.
(0064)                    ADD 1 TO REGISTRATION-COUNT.
(0065)                    READ REGISTER INTO RECORD-1-LS
(0066)                    AT END MOVE 1 TO E-O-F, EOF.
(0067)                    GO TO I-ITER.
(0068)                I-END.
(0069)                K.
(0070)                    MOVE HEADER-DATE TO RECORD-DATE-LS.
(0071)                    MOVE DAY-STORE TO DAY-NUMBER-LS.
(0072)                    MOVE REGISTRATION-COUNT TO REG-COUNT.
(0073)                    MOVE REGISTRATION-LINE TO GUEST-DETAILS-LS.
(0074)                    MOVE 4 TO QS GO TO QX.
(0075)                Q4.
(0076)                    MOVE RECORD-1 TO RECORD-1-LS.
(0077)                G-END.
(0078)                    GO TO F-ITER.
(0079)                F-END.
(0080)                D-END.
(0081)                    GO TO C-ITER.
(0082)                C-END.
(0083)                L.
(0084)                    CLOSE REGISTER.
(0085)                QX.
(0086)                    EXIT PROGRAM.
(0087)                A-END.
```

Note. Since RECORD-1-LS is used to pass records to RECORD-1-WS, the contents of RECORD-1-LS will be overwritten by the *total* record. RECORD-1-LS is restored to its value prior to the output of the *total* line by modifying Q4.

Contents of test data file.

```
311283
3112831MR P JONES      136 WELSH WAY     WATFORD     BRITISH  45
3112831MRS E SMYTHE    24 ANVIL CR       LUTON       BRITISH  23
3112832REV S EVANS     7 CHURCH RD       TRING       BRITISH  13
070184
0701841MR S DAVIES     36 BLACK ST       COVENTRY    BRITISH  16
0701841MISS P JONES    23 WEST WAY       WATFORD     BRITISH  30
0701841MR S SPENCER    109 HIGH ST       POOLE       BRITISH  31
0701845MR P ALLEN      2 CHURCH GREEN    WITNEY      FRENCH   32
```

Results of test run (details for each week on new page).

```
WEEK ENDING 31 12 83
SUN MR P JONES      136 WELSH WAY     WATFORD     BRITISH  45
SUN MRS E SMYTHE    24 ANVIL CR       LUTON       BRITISH  23
SUN   TOTAL 2
MON REV S EVANS     7 CHURCH RD       TRING       BRITISH  13
MON   TOTAL 1

WEEK ENDING 07 01 84
SUN MR S DAVIES     36 BLACK ST       COVENTRY    BRITISH  16
SUN MISS P JONES    23 WEST WAY       WATFORD     BRITISH  30
SUN MR S SPENCER    109 HIGH ST       POOLE       BRITISH  31
SUN   TOTAL 3
THU MR P ALLEN      2 CHURCH GREEN    WITNEY      FRENCH   32
THU   TOTAL 1
```

15.6 RECOGNITION PROBLEMS.

At the time of executing a condition associated with either a selection or an iteration there may not be enough information available to be assured that the outcome of the condition is correct. This is a recognition problem. There are four techniques available for solving recognition problems and these will be discussed in this section.

15.6.1 Backtracking.

With a recognition problem it is not possible to always make the correct decision as to which path, in the case of a selection, or loop, in the case of an iteration, to execute in the absence of further information. The program designer must reason the course of action to be taken and incorporate this hypothesis into the design of the program. During program execution the hypothesis will either be proved right or wrong. If the hypothesis is right processing continues, however, if the hypothesis is proved to be wrong the computer must be directed to go back, or **backtrack,** to the point in the program where the decision was made and continue processing on the basis of the alternative decision.

If the hypothesis is proved to be wrong then data might have been processed that should **not** have been processed. The effects of processing this data on the predicted results would be regarded as being **harmful,** and it would be necessary to restore the data to its state prior to the wrong decision being made. However, if the hypothesis is proved to be wrong and data has been processed prior to backtracking then the effect might be **beneficial** if the data is required regardless of the outcome, or the effect might be **neutral** if it does not matter whether the data is processed or not.

When backtracking is used to solve recognition problems the technique is developed in two stages. The first stage is to consider the implications of backtracking on the expected results, this implies investigating the possible side effects that can occur and making a hypothesis on the basis of the least harmful side effects that are generated. The second stage is to amend the schematic logic based on the decisions made in the first stage.

15.6.2 Worked Example.

In the problem defined in 15.2.2 the hotel register file is to be validated for correct batches of records. A good batch of records is defined as every record in the batch having the same end of week date as the header record to the batch. For every good batch of records the end of week date and number of registrations in that week will be output, otherwise every error record in each error batch will be output.

Detailed Program Structure.

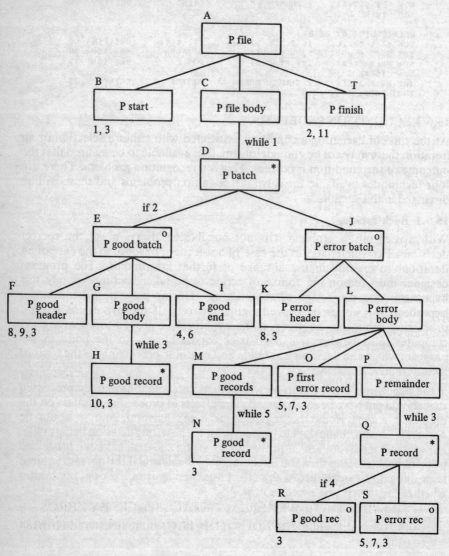

Functions List.
1. Open files.
2. Close files.
3. Read register file.
4. Format good record for output.
5. Format error record for ouput.
6. Write record to good report.
7. Write record to error report.
8. Store date.
9. Initialise number of registrations to zero.
10. Increase registrations by 1.
11. Stop.

Conditions List.
1. Not end of file.
2. All records in batch have same header date.
3. Guest details not = all spaces or (1).
4. Header date = record date.
5. Guest details not = all spaces and (4) or (1).

Schematic logic.

```
A-seq
  B do 1,3
  C-iter while 1
    D-sel if 2
      E-seq
        F do 8,9,3
        G-iter while 3
          H do 10,3
        G-end
        I do 4,6
      E-end
    D-or
      J-seq
        K do 8,3
        L-seq
          M-iter while 5
            N do 3
          M-end
          O do 5,7,3
          P-iter while 3
            Q-sel if 4
              R do 3
            Q-or
              S do 5,7,3
            Q-end
          P-end
        L-end
      J-end
    D-end
  C-end
  T do 2,11
A-end
```

If we assume that all records are good then discover an error record functions (8,9,3) and (10,3) will have been executed. These functions will cause the following side-effects.

Function 8 – beneficial, since the date is required on both paths.
Function 9 – neutral, since the registration is not required on the error path.
Function 3 – beneficial, since a record is required regardless of the path taken.
Function 10 – neutral, for the same reason as function 9.

If we assume that every batch is in error and then discover that some batches are good functions (8,3) and (3) will have been executed. These functions will cause the following side-effects.

Function 8,3 – beneficial, for the same reason given earlier.
Function 3 – harmful, since all the records in the good batch would be *flushed* through without recording the number of registrations.

The side-effects when opting for the good batch are beneficial and neutral, whereas those for the error batch are beneficial and harmful. The path chosen with the least harmful side effects will determine the hypothesis, therefore, we shall assume that all the records in the hotel registration file belong to good batches.

Amendments to the schematic logic.

The component at which the recognition problem occurs has **sel** and **or** replaced by **posit** and **admit** respectively. To **posit** is to lay down a hypothesis: we are laying down the hypothesis that all the records form good batches; if it turns out that the hypothesis is wrong, we will **admit** that the record is in error.

In processing records from a good batch if an error record is discovered then it will be necessary to **quit** the good path and backtrack and **admit** that the hypothesis was wrong.

In backtracking to the error batch it may be discovered that functions have already been executed that also occur on the error path. These duplicate functions must be deleted.

The schematic logic now becomes:

```
A-seq
  B do 1,3
  C-iter while 1
    D-posit
      E-seq
        F do 8,9,3 quit D-posit if error record
        G-iter while 3
          H do 10,3 quit D-posit if error record
        G-end
        I do 4,6
      E-end
    D-admit
      J-seq
        K do 8,3          (duplicate functions are deleted)
        L-seq
          .
          .
```

The following segment of COBOL code illustrates how backtracking is implemented in the PROCEDURE DIVISION.

Notice that condition 2 (all records in batch have the same header date) cannot be coded since not all the records in the batch have been read at that point in the program. The amendment to **quit D-posit** has been implemented by using a conditional statement and a GO TO statement.

```
       PROCEDURE DIVISION.
            _____
            _____
            _____

       D-POSIT.
       E-SEQ.
       F.
            MOVE RECORD-DATE TO HEADER-DATE.
            MOVE ZERO TO REGISTRATIONS.
            READ REGISTER AT END MOVE 1 TO E-O-F.
   *    quit D-posit if error record
            IF HEADER-DATE NOT = RECORD-DATE
            AND GUEST-DETAILS NOT = ALL SPACES
            GO TO D-ADMIT.
       G-ITER.
            IF GUEST-DETAILS = ALL SPACES
            OR END-OF-FILE GO TO G-END.
       H.       ADD 1 TO REGISTRATIONS.
            READ REGISTER AT END MOVE 1 TO E-O-F.
   *    quit D-posit if error record
            IF HEADER-DATE NOT = RECORD-DATE
            AND GUEST-DETAILS NOT = ALL SPACES
            GO TO D-ADMIT.
            GO TO G-ITER.
       G-END.
            _____
            _____
            _____

       D-ADMIT.
       J-SEQ.
       L-SEQ.
```

15.6.3 Multiple Read-Ahead.

Multiple read-ahead implies reading several records from a file prior to the evaluation of a condition that would in a single read-ahead situation cause a recognition problem. Multiple read-ahead can provide a better solution to a recognition problem than backtracking if either several physical records make up a single logical record and all parts are needed for processing together or where each record is processed in its own right but information from the record(s) that follow is required in order to evaluate some condition.

The following worked example serves to illustrate the technique of multiple read-ahead.

An insurance company specialising in motor insurance keeps a file on all its policy holders. There may be one or more logical records relating to each policy holder. The first record for each policy holder contains personal details about the insured person, however, subsequent records (if applicable) contain details of all driving convictions against the policy holder. There is a separate record for each conviction. The file is to be split into two new files, one file containing the details of policy holders with no previous convictions and the other file containing the details of convicted motorists. Design a program structure to solve this problem. Assume that two record areas R1 and R2 are used for reading two records ahead in the file.

Detailed Program Structure.

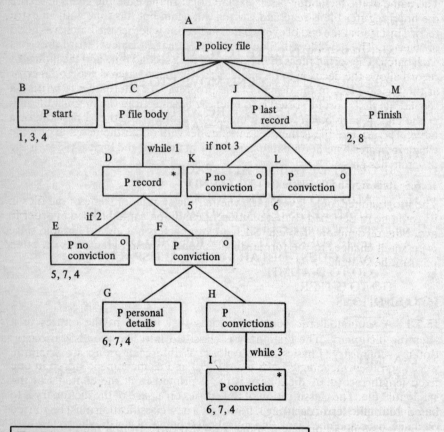

Functions List.
1. Open files.
2. Close files.
3. Read policy file into area R1.
4. Read policy file into area R2.
5. Write record R1 to non-convicted motorists file.
6. Write record R1 to convicted motorists file.
7. Move record area R2 to record area R1.
8. Stop.

314

> Conditions List.
> 1. Not end of file.
> 2. Policy holder in R1 not = policy holder in R2.
> 3. Record area R1 contains a conviction record.

Note: In the implementation of this design assume that a conviction record is coded to distinguish it from a record containing the personal details of a policy holder.

15.6.4 Processing the file twice.

The name of the technique is self-explanatory. In the example given in 15.6.2 the hotel register file is read and written out again but this time with an extra record inserted at the end of every batch indicating whether the batch was good or in error. The new file will then be sorted so that each new record precedes each batch. The sorted file is then processed for a second time and the indicator record allows the decision to be made as to whether a batch is good or in error at the logical place in the design of the program. An alternative to writing a second file that must be sorted is to read the batches from the original file and at the end of each batch write an indicator record into either a new file or a table. The original file is then read in parallel with either the new file or table which indicates whether a batch is good or in error at the logical place in the program design.

15.6.5 Redesigning the system.

The programmer could investigate whether the system, or some of the files in it, could be re-designed so that a different condition could be used in order to avoid the recognition problem. Such an approach is not always feasible since even small changes to the format of files could have repercussions on other parts of the system.

15.7 QUESTIONS

† **15.7.1** A sequential file contains records that represent the entries in a scientific dictionary. The dictionary is classified into five groups – Biology, Botany, Chemistry, Physics and Zoology. Within each group are scientific words and their meanings. Each word (key) and its meaning is stored in one fixed length record. A dictionary is to be printed from the contents of the sequential file. The classification of the entries on a page of the dictionary is to be printed at the top of each page, however, a new classification must be started on a new page and one blank line must be left between words which start with a different letter of the alphabet. The format of a record is:

    Classification code – 1 character.
    Scientific word – 20 characters.
    Meaning of word – 80 characters.

Design and write a program to print the dictionary.

† **15.7.2** Fixed length records in a serial file have the following format:

Account number (including modulus-11 check digit) – 5 characters.
Department code – 2 alphabetic chars.
Sales assistant code – 4 alphabetic characters.
Item code – 3 digits
            4 alphabetic chars.
Cost – 7 digits inc 2 dec.pl.

Design and write a data validation routine to check each field of a record, however, as soon as an error is discovered no further checking on that record is required and the record is written to an error file. Records that contain no errors are written to a good records file.

† **15.7.3** Invent a suitable test data file for the example given in 15.6.3 and write a program from the design given to split your test data file into two files, one file for motorists with no convictions and the other file for motorists with convictions.

16 Miscellaneous Features

16.1 INTRODUCTION

This final chapter introduces the reader to an assortment of features found in COBOL that can either improve program execution or improve program coding facilities.

16.2 INTERNAL STORAGE OF NUMBERS

16.2.1 Display Mode.

In every example program in this book the way in which numbers have been stored in the main memory of the computer has been using the DISPLAY mode. This has been done for simplicity of coding only, since this mode of storage is used by default.

In the DISPLAY mode each character (digit) is stored in one byte of memory using either the ASCII (7 bit) or EBCDIC (8 bit) code for that character. For example if an item of data is described in WORKING-STORAGE as:

    02 DATUM PIC 999

and the value of DATUM was 138 the number would occupy three bytes of memory. The computer, however, **cannot** perform arithmetic on an item of data stored in the DISPLAY mode. The computer must first convert the number to a mode of storage suitable for arithmetic use, in practice this means the number would either be converted to a pure binary representation or a packed decimal representation. Once the arithmetic operation on the number is complete the computer converts the number back to a DISPLAY format.

This conversion to a *computational* mode and back to a DISPLAY mode can waste time when the program is being executed. The reason being that the compiler has had to generate more machine code for the conversion process to take place and consequently program execution time will be slower. Furthermore, the amount of memory required to store a number in a DISPLAY mode is generally greater than in a *computational* mode.

A USAGE clause can be appended to an elementary or group item to specify the mode in which numbers are to be stored. The format of the USAGE clause is:

    [USAGE IS]   ⎧ COMPUTATIONAL ⎫
                  ⎪ COMP   ⎪
                  ⎨ DISPLAY   ⎬
                  ⎩ INDEX   ⎭

Computer manufacturers have the option to specify different COMPUTATIONAL modes. For example the common modes are:

    COMPUTATIONAL as a pure binary representation, and
    COMPUTATIONAL-3 as a packed decimal representation,

manufacturers such as IBM and PR1ME also include

COMPUTATIONAL-1 as a single precision floating point representation and

COMPUTATIONAL-2 as a double precision floating point representation

in addition to COMPUTATIONAL and COMPUTATIONAL-3.

16.2.2 Computational Mode.

The COMPUTATIONAL mode uses a fixed number of bytes to store integers in a pure binary format. For example, PR1ME use two bytes (16 bits) to store numbers described as COMPUTATIONAL. The least significant bit represents 2^0 (1) and the most significant bit represents 2^{15} (32,768) and is also used as the sign bit (0 – positive, 1 – negative, using the two's complement representation of negative numbers).

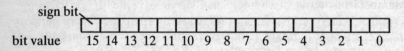

The range of integers that can be represented in this format is 32,767 to $-32,768$.

Since a fixed number of bytes is always used when a datum is described as COMPUTATIONAL there is no need to specify a PICTURE clause for that datum.

e.g.   01 PARAMETERS USAGE IS COMP.
           02 DATUM-1.
           02 DATUM-2.

e.g.   02 DATUM-3 USAGE IS COMP.

The INDEX mode of storage is the same as for storing positive integers using the COMPUTATIONAL Mode. An index does **not** have to be defined using a level number entry, however, if it is defined by such an entry then no PICTURE clause is required.

e.g.   02 DIV USAGE IS INDEX.

16.2.3 Computational-3 Mode.

The COMPUTATIONAL-3 mode is used to store *real* numbers (numbers containing a decimal fraction). Each digit is represented using Binary Coded Decimal (BCD) coding. The following table illustrates how each decimal digit is represented using a four bit binary code.

Decimal digit	BCD code
0	0000
1	0001
2	0010
3	0011
4	0100
5	0101
6	0110
7	0111
8	1000
9	1001

If a PICTURE clause contains n 9's in describing a datum, then $\frac{n}{2}+1$ bytes of storage are required for that datum. Four bits are always set aside for the sign of the number irrespective of whether S has been used in the PICTURE string.

For example, if -142.76 is to be stored using a PICTURE string of S9(4)V99 then four bytes of storage will be used.

representation of sign stored
in least significant 4 bits

Note: unless the number of 9's in the PICTURE string is odd there will be four bits wasted. The position of the decimal point is given in the PICTURE string and therefore, is not stored as part of the number.

COMPUTATIONAL-1 and COMPUTATIONAL-2 modes will not be considered here since they are seldom used in commercial applications.

Never use COMPUTATIONAL or COMPUTATIONAL-3 on data that is being input or output, only use these modes on data that is to be processed using arithmetic. Generally, the result of displaying a datum, defined as COMP or COMP-3, on the screen of a V.D.U. will result in meaningless characters being output. The datum must first be moved to a field described as being DISPLAY before any attempt is made to output the information.

16.2.4 Synchronized Clause.

The efficiency of program execution can also be improved if a datum is stored in its own multiple word area of memory and is not allowed to share words with another datum. The SYNCHRONIZED clause specifies the alignment of an elementary item on a natural memory boundary. The general format is:

$$\left\{ \begin{array}{l} \text{SYNCHRONIZED} \\ \text{SYNC} \end{array} \right\} \quad \left[\begin{array}{l} \text{LEFT} \\ \text{RIGHT} \end{array} \right]$$

e.g. 01 RECORD-1.
    02 A PIC 9 VALUE IS 1.
    02 B PIC 9 VALUE IS 12.
    02 C PIC 9 VALUE IS 123.

Assuming a natural boundary of two bytes the values of A,B and C would be stored over boundaries as:

1	1	2	1	2	3

However, if each PICTURE clause has SYNCHRONIZED RIGHT appended to it the effect is:

	1	1	2		1	2	3

alternatively SYNCHRONIZED LEFT would have the effect:

1		1	2	1	2	3

SYNCHRONIZED without the RIGHT/LEFT option specifies that the elementary item is to be positioned between memory boundaries in such a way as to effect efficient utilization of the elementary data item.

16.3 DUPLICATE IDENTIFIERS

In every example program in this book duplicate identifiers have not been used in order to avoid confusion. However, duplicate variable names and paragraph names are permitted in COBOL programs provided they are *qualified*.

16.3.1 Qualification.

An identifier that is not unique, when used in the PROCEDURE DIVISION, must be followed by either IN or OF and the higher order name to which it belongs.

For example two records may be described as:

```
01 RECORD-1.
    02 NAME.
        03 SURNAME PIC X(20).
        03 INITIALS PIC AA.
    02 ADDRESS PIC X(50)
01 RECORD-2.
    02 NAME.
        03 SURNAME PIC X(20).
        03 INITIALS PIC AA.
    02 ADDRESS PIC X(50).
```

If ADDRESS is to be moved from RECORD-1 to RECORD-2 the statement

MOVE ADDRESS IN RECORD-1 TO ADDRESS IN RECORD-2

must be used.

If SURNAME was to be moved from RECORD-1 TO RECORD-2 the statement

MOVE SURNAME IN NAME IN RECORD-1 TO SURNAME IN NAME IN RECORD-2

would be used, alternatively if SURNAME and INITIALS are to be moved from RECORD-1 to RECORD-2

MOVE NAME IN RECORD-1 TO NAME IN RECORD-2

would be used.

Paragraph names can be duplicated between section names as long as the paragraph name is qualified by the section name.

e.g.   PROCEDURE DIVISION.
        FIRST SECTION.
        A-ITER.

           ————
           ————
           ————

        SECOND SECTION.
        A-ITER.

           ————
           ————
           ————

           GO TO A-ITER OF SECOND.

16.3.2 Corresponding Option.

Fields that have the same names between two records can have the contents of these fields either moved, added or subtracted by including a CORRESPONDING option. If one record is defined as:

        01 RECORD-1.
           02 TAX PIC 9(4)V99.
           02 ALLOWANCE PIC 9(4)V99.
           02 GROSS-SALARY PIC 9(5)V99.

and a second record as:

        01 RECORD-2.
           02 GROSS-SALARY PIC 9(5).
           02 FILLER PIC X(10) VALUE IS SPACES.
           02 ALLOWANCE PIC 9(4)V99.
           02 FILLER PIC X(10) VALUE IS SPACES.
           02 TAX PIC 9(4)V99.

then MOVE CORRESPONDING RECORD-1 TO RECORD-2 has the same effect as:

    MOVE TAX IN RECORD-1 TO TAX IN RECORD-2.
    MOVE ALLOWANCE IN RECORD-1 TO ALLOWANCE IN RECORD-2.
    MOVE GROSS-SALARY IN RECORD-1 TO GROSS-SALARY IN RECORD-2.

If GROSS-SALARY, ALLOWANCE and TAX had edited PICTURE fields in RECORD-2 then the data would be edited as a result of the MOVE.

If the values in RECORD-1 are to be either added to or subtracted from the values in RECORD-2 then

    ADD CORRESPONDING RECORD-1 TO RECORD-2

or

    SUBTRACT CORRESPONDING RECORD-1 FROM RECORD-2

would be used respectively. Both the ROUNDED and ON SIZE ERROR options can be appended to these statements.

For example, if RECORD-1 and RECORD-2 contain the following values:

	TAX	ALLOWANCE	GROSS-SALARY
RECORD-1	085050	120000	0945095
RECORD-2	915050	130000	08500

then the execution of the statement

> ADD CORRESPONDING RECORD-1 TO RECORD-2 ROUNDED ON SIZE ERROR DISPLAY "DATA ERROR ABORT RUN".

will result in the following changes to the data.

	TAX	ALLOWANCE	GROSS-SALARY
RECORD-1	085050	120000	0945095
RECORD-2	915050	250000	17951

and the message DATA ERROR ABORT RUN being displayed since the value of TAX was computed as 1000100 and has overflowed the PICTURE 9(4)V99. The original value for TAX in RECORD-2 has not been changed.

The PICTURE for GROSS-SALARY in RECORD-2 is 9(5), therefore, the ROUNDED option has been used to give an answer of 17951 and not 1795095.

16.4 STRING PROCESSING

The STRING statement concatenates (joins together) two or more strings to form one string. The following example uses a simplified format of the STRING statement compared with the format given in Appendix III.

Example. The format of a record on a file is described as:

```
01 RECORD-1.
    02 SURNAME PIC X(20).
    02 INITIALS.
        03 FIRST PIC A.
        03 SECOND PIC A.
    02 TELE-NUMBER.
        03 EXCHANGE PIC X(20).
        03 NUMBER PIC 9(7).
```

If these PICTURE strings were used to output the information then a large number of spaces between the SURNAME and INITIALS, and EXCHANGE and NUMBER would occur, and there would be a lack of separation between INITIALS and EXCHANGE.

e.g. BLOGGSbbbbbbbbbbbbbbHCOXFORDbbbbbbbbbbbbbb2198764

The format of this output for, say, a telephone directory would not be acceptable. A much improved output would be:

> BLOGGSbH.CbbbbbbbbbbbbbbbOXFORDb2198764bbbbbbbbbbbbbb

This format is achieved if the output record is changed to:

```
01 RECORD-1.
    02 SUBSCRIBER PIC X(25).
    02 TELE-NUMBER PIC X(28).
```

and the following PROCEDURE DIVISION code is used.

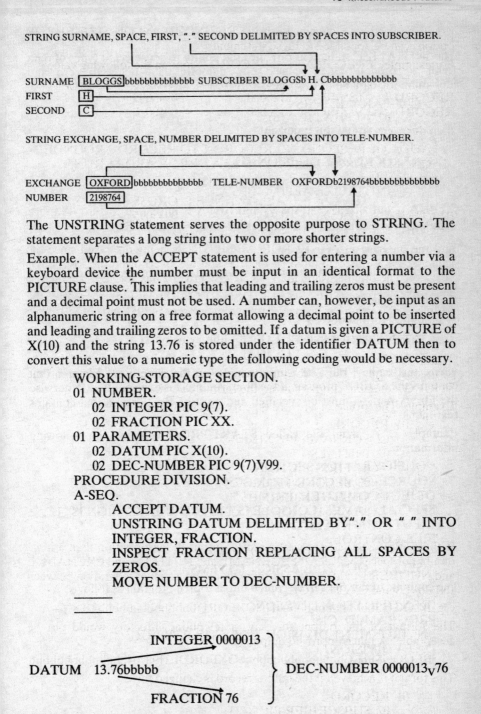

STRING SURNAME, SPACE, FIRST, "." SECOND DELIMITED BY SPACES INTO SUBSCRIBER.

SURNAME BLOGGS bbbbbbbbbbbbb SUBSCRIBER BLOGGSb H. Cbbbbbbbbbbbbbb
FIRST   H
SECOND   C

STRING EXCHANGE, SPACE, NUMBER DELIMITED BY SPACES INTO TELE-NUMBER.

EXCHANGE OXFORD bbbbbbbbbbbbb TELE-NUMBER OXFORDb2198764bbbbbbbbbbbbbb
NUMBER   2198764

The UNSTRING statement serves the opposite purpose to STRING. The statement separates a long string into two or more shorter strings.

Example. When the ACCEPT statement is used for entering a number via a keyboard device the number must be input in an identical format to the PICTURE clause. This implies that leading and trailing zeros must be present and a decimal point must not be used. A number can, however, be input as an alphanumeric string on a free format allowing a decimal point to be inserted and leading and trailing zeros to be omitted. If a datum is given a PICTURE of X(10) and the string 13.76 is stored under the identifier DATUM then to convert this value to a numeric type the following coding would be necessary.

```
        WORKING-STORAGE SECTION.
        01 NUMBER.
            02  INTEGER PIC 9(7).
            02  FRACTION PIC XX.
        01 PARAMETERS.
            02  DATUM PIC X(10).
            02  DEC-NUMBER PIC 9(7)V99.
        PROCEDURE DIVISION.
        A-SEQ.
            ACCEPT DATUM.
            UNSTRING DATUM DELIMITED BY"." OR " " INTO
            INTEGER, FRACTION.
            INSPECT FRACTION REPLACING ALL SPACES BY
            ZEROS.
            MOVE NUMBER TO DEC-NUMBER.
```

                INTEGER 0000013

DATUM   13.76bbbbb   DEC-NUMBER 0000013ᵥ76

                FRACTION 76

16.5 THE INITIALIZE STATEMENT

The INITIALIZE statement provides the ability to set selected types of data fields to predetermined values, e.g. numeric data fields to zero and alphanumeric data fields to spaces.

```
e.g.    01 PARAMETERS.
           02  ALPHA PIC A(6).
           02  BETA PIC 999V99.


        PROCEDURE DIVISION.
        A-SEQ.
           INITIALIZE ALPHA, BETA.
```

ALPHA is initialised to all spaces and BETA is initialised to zero. A more detailed description of INITIALIZE is given in Appendix III.

16.6 THE COPY STATEMENT

The COPY statement is a *compiler directing* statement and provides a means of including pre-written COBOL source code anywhere in a source program at the time of compilation.

A simplified format of COPY is:

$$\textbf{COPY} \quad \text{text-name-1} \left[\left\{ \begin{matrix} \textbf{OF} \\ \textbf{IN} \end{matrix} \right\} \quad \text{library-name-1} \right]$$

where text-name-1 must be a unique name on the same user's file area that contains the COBOL program if the library-name-1 is to be omitted, otherwise the library-name-1 must be specified and must be the file area that contains text-name-1.

Example 1. A serial file called START-PROG contains the following information.

```
CONFIGURATION SECTION.
SOURCE-COMPUTER. PR1ME 750.
OBJECT-COMPUTER. PR1ME 750.
SPECIAL-NAMES. CONSOLE IS TTY, CURRENCY SIGN IS "L".
INPUT-OUTPUT SECTION.
FILE-CONTROL.
    SELECT IN-FILE ASSIGN TO PFMS.
    SELECT OUT-FILE ASSIGN TO PFMS.
```

The contents of this file can be copied into a source program as follows.

```
IDENTIFICATION DIVISION.
PROGRAM-ID. C166.
ENVIRONMENT DIVISION. COPY START-PROG.
DATA DIVISION.
FILE SECTION.
```

The compiled source listing reveals the copied code thus:

```
(0001)          IDENTIFICATION DIVISION.
(0002)          PROGRAM-ID. C166.
(0003)          ENVIRONMENT DIVISION. COPY START-PROG.
[0001]          CONFIGURATION SECTION.
[0002]          SOURCE-COMPUTER. PRIME 750.
[0003]          OBJECT-COMPUTER. PRIME 750.
[0004]          SPECIAL-NAMES. CONSOLE IS TTY, CURRENCY SIGN IS "L".
[0005]          INPUT-OUTPUT SECTION.
[0006]          FILE-CONTROL.
[0007]              SELECT IN-FILE ASSIGN TO PFMS.
[0008]              SELECT OUT-FILE ASSIGN TO PFMS.
(0003)          ENVIRONMENT DIVISION. COPY START-PROG.
(0004)          DATA DIVISION.
(0005)          FILE SECTION.
```

16.7 DECLARATIVES SECTION

The DECLARATIVES SECTION when included in the PROCEDURE DIVISION must be written directly after the Division heading and before any procedural sections or paragraphs. The format of the DECLARATIVES SECTION is:

> **PROCEDURE DIVISION.**
> **[DECLARARTIVES.**
> {section-name **SECTION.**
>   **USE** statement.
> [paragraph-name.
>   [sentence] ...] ... }...
>   **END DECLARATIVES.]**
> {section-name **SECTION**
> [paragraph-name.
>   [sentence] ...] ... } ...

The USE statement is a compiler-directing sentence that causes the compiler to take a specific action during compilation. USE covers three areas:

> specific procedures for input and output errors handling,
> USE FOR DEBUGGING (only applicable when the *debug* module is present),
> USE BEFORE REPORTING (only applicable when the *report writer* module is present).

The latter two areas are beyond the scope of this book.

16.7.1 Input and Output error handling.

The sections under the DECLARATIVES header provide a method for including procedures which are invoked when a condition occurs which cannot be tested by the programmer. Although the system automatically handles checking and creation of standard labels, and execution error recovery in the case of input and output errors, additional procedures may be specified here by the programmer. Since such procedures are executed only at the time an error in reading or writing occurs, they cannot appear in the regular sequence of procedural statements. Instead, they must appear in the DECLARATIVES SECTION. Related procedures are preceded by a USE sentence.

16.7.2 USE Statement.

The USE statement specifies procedures for input and output error handling which are in addition to the standard procedures provided by the input and output control systems. The format of the USE statement is:

USE AFTER STANDARD $\left\{\begin{matrix} \textbf{EXCEPTION} \\ \textbf{ERROR} \end{matrix}\right\}$ **PROCEDURE** ON $\left\{\begin{matrix} \text{file-name} \\ \textbf{INPUT} \\ \textbf{OUTPUT} \\ \textbf{I-O} \end{matrix}\right\}$

The DECLARATIVES SECTION is executed by the same mechanism that executes a PERFORM statement, after the standard I-O recovery procedures for the files designated, or after the invalid key condition arises on a statement lacking the INVALID KEY clause. After the execution of the USE procedure, control is returned to the invoking routine.

The following example illustrates the use of a DECLARATIVES SECTION for detecting an empty serial file. The execution of the initial READ statement causes the end-of-file record to be read, however, the READ statement does not have the AT END option appended to it, therefore, control is directed to the DECLARATIVES SECTION where the operator is informed of the error, and the end-of-file flag is set to allow for the termination of the program.

```
WORKING-STORAGE SECTION.
01 PARAMETERS.
    02 E-O-F PIC 9 VALUE IS ZERO.
       88 END-OF-FILE VALUE IS 1.
_____
_____
_____

PROCEDURE DIVISION.
DECLARATIVES.
EMPTY-FILE SECTION.
    USE AFTER STANDARD ERROR PROCEDURE ON INPUT.
E-F.
    DISPLAY "**FILE EMPTY**"
    MOVE 1 to E-O-F.
END DECLARATIVES.
A-SEQ.
    OPEN INPUT DATAFILE.
    READ DATAFILE.
_____
_____

C-ITER.
    IF END-OF-FILE GO TO C-END.
_____
_____
_____

    READ DATAFILE AT END MOVE 1 TO E-O-F.
    GO TO C-ITER.
C-END.
    CLOSE DATAFILE.
    STOP RUN.
A-END.
```

Appendix I.
Answers to selected questions

1.6.1 False – the IDENTIFICATION and PROCEDURE DIVISIONS are the minimum under certain circumstances. However, even if the ENVIRONMENT DIVISION was not present the DATA DIVISION would almost certainly have to be included.

False – the order must be preserved.

True

False – variable names must begin with an alphabetic character.

True – both, and ; can be used as separators provided each character is followed by a space.

True

False – a sequence of instructions could be written in a PROCEDURE DIVISION that contains one paragraph without a paragraph name, however, this is not recommended since it will probably cause strange errors to be generated by the compiler. You should always start a procedure with a paragraph name.

1.6.2 + * / < A

1.6.3

WAGE/3	*PARA1
23	COUNT
DATA	247.34
	TAX ALLOWANCE

See 1.3.4 for the reasons why these variables are illegal.

1.6.4

PARA 1	*BEGIN
DATA DIVISION	START
C END	MAX VAL OUT
	"A-SEQ"

See 1.3.1 for the reasons why these paragraph names are illegal.

1.6.5 Taken in the order presented.

numeric	non-numeric	non-numeric
numeric	figurative	numeric
numeric	figurative	figurative

1.6.6 Taken in the order presented.

comma illegal	space illegal	delimiters do not match
space illegal	space illegal	not a reserved word
missing delimiter	spaces illegal	non-figurative reserved word

1.6.7 THIRTY-TWO
1234
ZERO – this would normally be used for initialisation or comparison.

1.6.8   True – the first character of the paragraph name must be in zone A.

False – statements can be split over several lines within zone B without the use of a hyphen. However, a hyphen will be used to split a non-numeric literal between two lines (or more) within zone B, provided the first character in zone B of the continuation line is a matching delimiter.

True.

False – the asterisk must be in column 7.

False – columns 1 to 6 can be used for sequence numbers, columns 73 to 80 for identification, however, this is normally confined to the program being transferred to punched cards.

2.8.1   Taken in the order presented.

Destination numeric literal. Correct version ADD 3.5 TO A.

Two destination identifiers. Correct version SUBTRACT X FROM Y.
SUBTRACT X FROM Z.

TO is not defined in this context in older versions of COBOL. Correct version (1974 Standard) ADD A B GIVING C.

TIMES not reserved word. Correct version MULTIPLY X BY Y.

Destination numeric literal. Correct version DIVIDE 5 INTO X.

Identifier missing. Correct version COMPUTE TEMP = 3.4 * A * B

Illegal identifiers. Correct version COMPUTE A = B + C

2.8.2   Taken in the order presented.

A	B	C	D
36	36	36	36

A	B	C	D
10	14	29	89

A	B	C
24	98	122

X	Y
17	15

U	V	W	X
29	32	84	−67

A	B
16	13

X	Y	Z
18	3	54

A	B
6	7

A	B
12	9

U	V	W	X
37	13	6	4

R	A	B	C
0	2	4	2

2.8.3 Taken in the order presented.

8

1

¾

1

648

2.8.4 Taken in the order presented.

Illegal multiplication symbol. Correct version A * B

Two operators together. Correct version X * (− Y)

Two operators together. Correct version (64 + B) / (−6)

Missing closing parenthesis.

Operator missing.

2.8.5 Taken in the order presented.

$x + y^3$

$x + \dfrac{2}{y} + 4$

$\dfrac{a \cdot b}{c + 2}$

$\dfrac{a}{b} + \dfrac{c.d}{f.g.h}$

$\dfrac{1}{(x + y)^2}$

$\dfrac{a}{b} + \dfrac{c}{d} + \dfrac{e}{f}$

2.8.6 Taken in the order presented.

Three identifiers ALPHA, BETA, GAMMA illegal. Must be split into three separate ACCEPT statements.

PRINT illegal, should be DISPLAY.

PROCEDURE DIVISION are reserved words paragraph name used in this context must be unique.

NEXT SENTENCE is used in the wrong context.

GOTO should be GO   TO or just GO since TO is optional.

Condition not in correct sequence. This is an in-line PERFORM as indicated in the Draft Proposal.

2.8.7

A	B		A	B
34	55		5	0

2.8.8

```
    ACCEPT X.
    PARA1.
        IF X < 0 GO TO PARA2.
            ACCEPT X.
        GO TO PARA1.
    PARA2.
```

2.8.9   IF A NOT > B GO TO PARA-OR.
      MOVE C TO D.
    GO TO PARA-END.
  PARA-OR.
      MOVE E TO D.
  PARA-END.

2.8.10   A
256

2.8.11

EVALUATE MUSIC-CODE
WHEN "A" MOVE "POPULAR" TO MUSIC-TYPE
WHEN "B" MOVE "JAZZ" TO MUSIC-TYPE
WHEN OTHER MOVE "CLASSICAL" TO MUSIC-TYPE
END-EVALUATE

3.5.1

```
PROCEDURE DIVISION.
GARDEN-SEQ.
    ACCEPT L-SIDE.
    ACCEPT S-SIDE.
    COMPUTE TURF = L-SIDE * S-SIDE * 0.5.
    COMPUTE FENCE = 2.0 * (2.0 * L-SIDE + S-SIDE).
    DISPLAY TURF
    DISPLAY FENCE
    STOP RUN.
GARDEN-END.
```

3.5.2

```
PROCEDURE DIVISION.
MEAN-SEQ.
    MOVE ZERO TO TOTAL, COUNTER
    ACCEPT NUMB.
CALC-ITER.
    IF NUMB = 0 GO TO CALC-END.
    ADD NUMB TO TOTAL
    ADD 1 TO COUNTER
    ACCEPT NUMB.
    GO TO CALC-ITER.
CALC-END.
    COMPUTE MEAN = TOTAL / COUNTER.
    DISPLAY MEAN.
    STOP RUN.
MEAN-END.
```

3.5.3

```
PROCEDURE DIVISION.
MAX-SEQ.
    ACCEPT NUMB.
    MOVE 1 TO COUNTER.
    MOVE NUMB TO MAXNUMB.
COMP-ITER.
    IF COUNTER = 10 GO TO COMP-END.
    ACCEPT NUMB.
    ADD 1 TO COUNTER.
LARGEST-SEL.
    IF NUMB NOT > MAXNUMB GO TO LARGEST-END.
    MOVE NUMB TO MAXNUMB.
LARGEST-END.
    GO TO COMP-ITER.
COMP-END.
    DISPLAY MAXNUMB.
    STOP RUN.
MAX-END.
```

3.5.4

```
PROCEDURE DIVISION.
MONEY-SEG.
     MOVE ZERO TO TOT-10, TOT-5.
     ACCEPT MONEY.
TEN-ITER.
     IF MONEY < 10 GO TO TEN-END.
     SUBTRACT 10 FROM MONEY.
     ADD 1 TO TOT-10.
     GO TO TEN-ITER.
TEN-END.
FIVE-SEL.
     IF MONEY < 5 GO TO FIVE-END.
     SUBTRACT 5 FROM MONEY.
     ADD 1 TO TOT-5.
FIVE-END.
     DISPLAY TOT-10
     DISPLAY TOT-5
     DISPLAY MONEY
     STOP RUN.
MONEY-END.
```

3.5.5

```
Functions List.
1. Input sale.
2. Output commission.
3. Calculate 10% of sale.
4. Calculate 5% of sale.
5. Calculate 1% of sale.
6. Stop.
```

```
Conditions List.
1. Sale not = 0.
2. Sale < 1000.
3. Sale < 10000.
```

```
PROCEDURE DIVISION.
SALES-SEG.
     ACCEPT SALES.
SALESMAN-ITER.
     IF SALES = 0 GO TO SALESMAN-END.
COMM-SEL.
     IF SALES NOT < 1000 GO TO COMM-OR-2.
     MULTIPLY 0.01 BY SALES GIVING COMMISSION.
     GO TO COMM-END.
COMM-OR-2.
     IF SALES NOT < 10000 GO TO COMM-OR-3.
     MULTIPLY 0.05 BY SALES GIVING COMMISSION.
     GO TO COMM-END.
COMM-OR-3.
     MULTIPLY 0.1 BY SALES GIVING COMMISSION.
COMM-END.
     DISPLAY COMMISSION.
     ACCEPT SALES.
     GO TO SALESMAN-ITER.
SALESMAN-END.
     STOP RUN.
SALES-END.
```

3.5.6

```
Functions List.
1. Input surname.
2. Input age.
3. Input weight.
4. Input height.
5. Output name.
6. Stop.
7. Initialise count to zero.
8. Increase count by 1.
```

```
Conditions List.
1. Count not = 10.
2. 18 ≤ age ≤ 23.
3. 80 ≤ weight ≤ 180.
4. 152 ≤ height ≤ 182.
```

```
PROCEDURE DIVISION.
DETAILS-SEQ.
    MOVE ZERO TO COUNTER.
PERSON-ITER.
    IF COUNTER = 10 GO TO PERSON-END.
        ACCEPT SURNAME.
        ACCEPT AGE.
        ACCEPT WEIGHT.
        ACCEPT HEIGHT.
        ADD 1 TO COUNTER.
AGE-SEL.
    IF AGE < 18 OR AGE > 23 GO TO AGE-END.
WEIGHT-SEL.
        IF WEIGHT < 80 OR WEIGHT > 180 GO TO WEIGHT-END.
HEIGHT-SEL.
            IF HEIGHT < 152 OR HEIGHT > 182 GO TO HEIGHT-END.
                DISPLAY SURNAME.
HEIGHT-END.
WEIGHT-END.
AGE-END.
    GO TO PERSON-ITER.
PERSON-END.
    STOP RUN.
DETAILS-END.
```

3.5.7

Functions List.
1. Input gross salary.
2. Input tax-status.
3. Input number of children.
4. Assign single allowance.
5. Assign married allowance.
6. Calculate child allowance.
7. Calculate total allowances.
8. Calculate taxable income.
9. Calculate income tax on £4000 and above.
10. Calculate tax on £2000 and above.
11. Calculate tax on £1000 and above.
12. Income tax = 0.
13. Output income tax.
14. Stop.

Conditions List.
1. Gross salary not = 0.
2. Tax status = M.
3. Number of children > 0.
4. Taxable income ≤ 1000.
5. Taxable income ≤ 2000.
6. Taxable income ≤ 4000.

```
PROCEDURE DIVISION.
INC-SEQ.
    ACCEPT G-SALARY.
TAX-ITER.
    IF G-SALARY = 0 GO TO TAX-END.
    ACCEPT TAX-STATUS.
    ACCEPT CHILDREN.
STATUS-SEL.
    IF TAX-STATUS NOT = "M" GO TO STATUS-OR.
        MOVE 2300 TO ALLOWANCE.
CHILD-SEL.
    IF CHILDREN = 0 GO TO CHILD-END.
        MULTIPLY 100 BY CHILDREN GIVING CHILD-ALLOWANCE.
        ADD CHILD-ALLOWANCE TO ALLOWANCE.
CHILD-END.
    GO TO STATUS-END.
STATUS-OR.
    MOVE 1200 TO ALLOWANCE.
STATUS-END.
    SUBTRACT ALLOWANCE FROM G-SALARY GIVING TAX-INCOME.
CALC-SEL.
    IF TAX-INCOME > 1000 GO TO CALC-OR-2.
        MOVE ZERO TO TAX.
    GO TO CALC-END.
CALC-OR-2.
    IF TAX-INCOME > 2000 GO TO CALC-OR-3.
        COMPUTE TAX = 0.2 * (TAX-INCOME - 1000).
    GO TO CALC-END.
CALC-OR-3.
    IF TAX-INCOME > 4000 GO TO CALC-OR-4.
        COMPUTE TAX = 0.3 * (TAX-INCOME - 2000) + 200.
    GO TO CALC-END.
```

(program continued)

```
CALC-OR-4.
        COMPUTE TAX = 0.4 * (TAX-INCOME - 4000) + 800.
CALC-END.
    DISPLAY TAX.
    ACCEPT G-SALARY.
    GO TO TAX-ITER.
TAX-END.
    STOP RUN.
INC-END.
```

3.5.8

Functions List.

1. Input mark.
2. Output grade.
3. Initialise totals for grades to zero.
4. Increase F total by 1.
5. Increase D total by 1.
6. Increase C total by 1.
7. Increase B total by 1.
8. Increase A total by 1.
9. Output A total.
10. Output B total.
11. Output C total.
12. Output D total.
13. Output F total.
14. Stop.
15. Assign appropriate grade.

Conditions List.

1. Mark not = 999.
2. Mark < 40.
3. Mark < 50.
4. Mark < 60.
5. Mark < 70.

```
PROCEDURE DIVISION.
MARKS-SEQ.
    MOVE ZERO TO TOTAL-A, TOTAL-B, TOTAL-C, TOTAL-D, TOTAL-F.
    ACCEPT MARK.
STUDENT-ITER.
    IF MARK = 999 GO TO STUDENT-END.
GRADE-SEL.
    IF MARK NOT < 40 GO TO GRADE-OR-2.
        ADD 1 TO TOTAL-F, MOVE "F" TO GRADE.
        GO TO GRADE-END.
GRADE-OR-2.
    IF MARK NOT < 50 GO TO GRADE-OR-3.
        ADD 1 TO TOTAL-D, MOVE "D" TO GRADE.
        GO TO GRADE-END.
GRADE-OR-3.
    IF MARK NOT < 60 GO TO GRADE-OR-4.
        ADD 1 TO TOTAL-C, MOVE "C" TO GRADE.
        GO TO GRADE-END.
GRADE-OR-4.
    IF MARK NOT < 70 GO TO GRADE-OR-5.
        ADD 1 TO TOTAL-B, MOVE "B" TO GRADE.
        GO TO GRADE-END.
```

(program continued)

```
               GRADE-OR-5.
                   ADD 1 TO TOTAL-A, MOVE "A" TO GRADE.
               GRADE-END.
                   DISPLAY GRADE
                   ACCEPT MARK.
                   GO TO STUDENT-ITER.
               STUDENT-END.
                   DISPLAY TOTAL-A
                   DISPLAY TOTAL-B
                   DISPLAY TOTAL-C
                   DISPLAY TOTAL-D
                   DISPLAY TOTAL-F
                   STOP RUN.
               MARKS-END.
```

4.10.1

```
(0001)         IDENTIFICATION DIVISION.
(0002)         PROGRAM-ID. C4101.
(0003)         DATA DIVISION.
(0004)         WORKING-STORAGE SECTION.
(0005)         77 L-SIDE PIC 99.
(0006)         77 S-SIDE PIC 99.
(0007)         77 TURF PIC 9999V99.
(0008)         77 FENCE PIC 999.
(0009)         PROCEDURE DIVISION.
(0010)         GARDEN-SEQ.
(0011)             DISPLAY "INPUT LONG SIDE (2 DIGITS)".
(0012)             ACCEPT L-SIDE.
(0013)             DISPLAY "INPUT SHORT SIDE (2 DIGITS)".
(0014)             ACCEPT S-SIDE.
(0015)             COMPUTE TURF = L-SIDE * S-SIDE * 0.5.
(0016)             COMPUTE FENCE = 2.0 * (2.0 * L-SIDE + S-SIDE).
(0017)             DISPLAY "COST OF TURF " TURF.
(0018)             DISPLAY "COST OF FENCE " FENCE.
(0019)             STOP RUN.
(0020)         GARDEN-END.
```

4.10.2

```
(0001)         IDENTIFICATION DIVISION.
(0002)         PROGRAM-ID. C4102.
(0003)         DATA DIVISION.
(0004)         WORKING-STORAGE SECTION.
(0005)         77 TOTAL PIC 9(4).
(0006)         77 COUNTER PIC 99.
(0007)         77 NUMB PIC 99.
(0008)         77 MEAN PIC 99.
(0009)         PROCEDURE DIVISION.
(0010)         MEAN-SEQ.
(0011)             MOVE ZERO TO TOTAL, COUNTER
(0012)             DISPLAY "INPUT NUMBER (2 DIGITS) TYPE ZERO TO EXIT".
(0013)             ACCEPT NUMB.
(0014)         CALC-ITER.
(0015)             IF NUMB = 0 GO TO CALC-END.
(0016)                 ADD NUMB TO TOTAL
(0017)                 ADD 1 TO COUNTER
(0018)                 DISPLAY "INPUT NUMBER (2 DIGITS) TYPE ZERO TO EXIT".
(0019)                 ACCEPT NUMB.
(0020)                 GO TO CALC-ITER.
(0021)         CALC-END.
(0022)             COMPUTE MEAN = TOTAL / COUNTER.
(0023)             DISPLAY "MEAN " MEAN.
(0024)             STOP RUN.
(0025)         MEAN-END.
```

4.10.3

```
(0001)              IDENTIFICATION DIVISION.
(0002)              PROGRAM-ID. C4103.
(0003)              DATA DIVISION.
(0004)              WORKING-STORAGE SECTION.
(0005)              77 NUMB PIC 99.
(0006)              77 MAXNUMB PIC 99.
(0007)              77 COUNTER PIC 99.
(0008)              PROCEDURE DIVISION.
(0009)              MAX-SEQ.
(0010)                  DISPLAY "INPUT NUMBER (2 DIGITS)".
(0011)                  ACCEPT NUMB.
(0012)                  MOVE 1 TO COUNTER.
(0013)                  MOVE NUMB TO MAXNUMB.
(0014)              COMP-ITER.
(0015)                  IF COUNTER = 10 GO TO COMP-END.
(0016)                  DISPLAY "INPUT NUMBER (2 DIGITS)".
(0017)                  ACCEPT NUMB.
(0018)                  ADD 1 TO COUNTER.
(0019)              LARGEST-SEL.
(0020)                  IF NUMB NOT > MAXNUMB GO TO LARGEST-END.
(0021)                  MOVE NUMB TO MAXNUMB.
(0022)              LARGEST-END.
(0023)                  GO TO COMP-ITER.
(0024)              COMP-END.
(0025)                  DISPLAY "MAXIMUM NUMBER " MAXNUMB.
(0026)                  STOP RUN.
(0027)              MAX-END.
```

4.10.4

```
(0001)              IDENTIFICATION DIVISION.
(0002)              PROGRAM-ID. C4104.
(0003)              DATA DIVISION.
(0004)              WORKING-STORAGE SECTION.
(0005)              77 MONEY PIC 999.
(0006)              77 TOT-10 PIC 99.
(0007)              77 TOT-5 PIC 9.
(0008)              PROCEDURE DIVISION.
(0009)              MONEY-SEQ.
(0010)                  MOVE ZERO TO TOT-10, TOT-5.
(0011)                  DISPLAY "INPUT SUM OF MONEY (3 DIGITS)".
(0012)                  ACCEPT MONEY.
(0013)              TEN-ITER.
(0014)                  IF MONEY < 10 GO TO TEN-END.
(0015)                  SUBTRACT 10 FROM MONEY.
(0016)                  ADD 1 TO TOT-10.
(0017)                  GO TO TEN-ITER.
(0018)              TEN-END.
(0019)              FIVE-SEL.
(0020)                  IF MONEY < 5 GO TO FIVE-END.
(0021)                  SUBTRACT 5 FROM MONEY.
(0022)                  ADD 1 TO TOT-5.
(0023)              FIVE-END.
(0024)                  DISPLAY "TEN POUND NOTES " TOT-10
(0025)                  DISPLAY "FIVE POUND NOTES " TOT-5.
(0026)                  DISPLAY "ONE POUND NOTES " MONEY.
(0027)                  STOP RUN.
(0028)              MONEY-END.
```

4.10.5

```
(0001)          IDENTIFICATION DIVISION.
(0002)          PROGRAM-ID. C4105.
(0003)          DATA DIVISION.
(0004)          WORKING-STORAGE SECTION.
(0005)          77 SALES PIC 9(5).
(0006)          77 COMMISSION PIC 9999V99.
(0007)          PROCEDURE DIVISION.
(0008)          SALES-SEQ.
(0009)              DISPLAY "INPUT SALE VALUE (5 DIGITS)".
(0010)              DISPLAY "TYPE ZERO TO EXIT".
(0011)              ACCEPT SALES.
(0012)          SALESMAN-ITER.
(0013)              IF SALES = 0 GO TO SALESMAN-END.
(0014)          COMM-SEL.
(0015)              IF SALES NOT < 1000 GO TO COMM-OR-2.
(0016)                  MULTIPLY 0.01 BY SALES GIVING COMMISSION.
(0017)              GO TO COMM-END.
(0018)          COMM-OR-2.
(0019)              IF SALES NOT < 10000 GO TO COMM-OR-3.
(0020)                  MULTIPLY 0.05 BY SALES GIVING COMMISSION.
(0021)              GO TO COMM-END.
(0022)          COMM-OR-3.
(0023)                  MULTIPLY 0.1 BY SALES GIVING COMMISSION.
(0024)          COMM-END.
(0025)              DISPLAY "COMMISSION " COMMISSION.
(0026)              DISPLAY "INPUT SALE VALUE (5 DIGITS)".
(0027)              DISPLAY "TYPE ZERO TO EXIT".
(0028)              ACCEPT SALES.
(0029)              GO TO SALESMAN-ITER.
(0030)          SALESMAN-END.
(0031)              STOP RUN.
(0032)          SALES-END.
```

4.10.6

```
(0001)          IDENTIFICATION DIVISION.
(0002)          PROGRAM-ID. C4106.
(0003)          DATA DIVISION.
(0004)          WORKING-STORAGE SECTION.
(0005)          77 SURNAME PIC X(15).
(0006)          77 AGE PIC 99.
(0007)          77 WEIGHT PIC 999.
(0008)          77 HEIGHT PIC 999.
(0009)          77 COUNTER PIC 99.
(0010)          PROCEDURE DIVISION.
(0011)          DETAILS-SEQ.
(0012)              MOVE ZERO TO COUNTER.
(0013)          PERSON-ITER.
(0014)              IF COUNTER = 10 GO TO PERSON-END.
(0015)              DISPLAY "INPUT SURNAME (15 CHARS MAX)".
(0016)              ACCEPT SURNAME.
(0017)              DISPLAY "INPUT AGE YEARS (2 DIGITS)".
(0018)              ACCEPT AGE.
(0019)              DISPLAY "INPUT WEIGHT KG (3 DIGITS)".
(0020)              ACCEPT WEIGHT.
(0021)              DISPLAY "INPUT HEIGHT CM (3 DIGITS)".
(0022)              ACCEPT HEIGHT.
(0023)              ADD 1 TO COUNTER.
(0024)          AGE-SEL.
(0025)              IF AGE < 18 OR AGE > 23 GO TO AGE-END.
(0026)          WEIGHT-SEL.
(0027)              IF WEIGHT < 80 OR WEIGHT > 180 GO TO WEIGHT-END.
(0028)          HEIGHT-SEL.
(0029)              IF HEIGHT < 152 OR HEIGHT > 182 GO TO HEIGHT-END.
(0030)                  DISPLAY "SURNAME " SURNAME.
(0031)          HEIGHT-END.
(0032)          WEIGHT-END.
(0033)          AGE-END.
(0034)              GO TO PERSON-ITER.
(0035)          PERSON-END.
(0036)              STOP RUN.
(0037)          DETAILS-END.
```

4.10.7

```
(0001)              IDENTIFICATION DIVISION.
(0002)              PROGRAM-ID. C4107.
(0003)              DATA DIVISION.
(0004)              WORKING-STORAGE SECTION.
(0005)              77 G-SALARY PIC 9(5).
(0006)              77 TAX-STATUS PIC A.
(0007)              77 CHILDREN PIC 9.
(0008)              77 ALLOWANCE PIC 9999.
(0009)              77 CHILD-ALLOWANCE PIC 999.
(0010)              77 TAX-INCOME PIC S9(5).
(0011)              77 TAX PIC 9(5).
(0012)              PROCEDURE DIVISION.
(0013)              INC-SEQ.
(0014)                  DISPLAY "INPUT GROSS SALARY (5 DIGITS)".
(0015)                  DISPLAY "TYPE ZERO TO EXIT".
(0016)                  ACCEPT G-SALARY.
(0017)              TAX-ITER.
(0018)                  IF G-SALARY = 0 GO TO TAX-END.
(0019)                  DISPLAY "INPUT TAX STATUS M OR S".
(0020)                  ACCEPT TAX-STATUS.
(0021)                  DISPLAY "INPUT NUMBER OF CHILDREN (1 DIGIT)".
(0022)                  ACCEPT CHILDREN.
(0023)              STATUS-SEL.
(0024)                  IF TAX-STATUS NOT = "M" GO TO STATUS-OR.
(0025)                      MOVE 2300 TO ALLOWANCE.
(0026)              CHILD-SEL.
(0027)                      IF CHILDREN = 0 GO TO CHILD-END.
(0028)                          MULTIPLY 100 BY CHILDREN GIVING CHILD-ALLOWANCE.
(0029)                          ADD CHILD-ALLOWANCE TO ALLOWANCE.
(0030)              CHILD-END.
(0031)                  GO TO STATUS-END.
(0032)              STATUS-OR.
(0033)                  MOVE 1200 TO ALLOWANCE.
(0034)              STATUS-END.
(0035)                  SUBTRACT ALLOWANCE FROM G-SALARY GIVING TAX-INCOME.
(0036)              CALC-SEL.
(0037)                  IF TAX-INCOME > 1000 GO TO CALC-OR-2.
(0038)                      MOVE ZERO TO TAX.
(0039)                      GO TO CALC-END.
(0040)              CALC-OR-2.
(0041)                  IF TAX-INCOME > 2000 GO TO CALC-OR-3.
(0042)                      COMPUTE TAX = 0.2 * (TAX-INCOME - 1000).
(0043)                      GO TO CALC-END.
(0044)              CALC-OR-3.
(0045)                  IF TAX-INCOME > 4000 GO TO CALC-OR-4.
(0046)                      COMPUTE TAX = 0.3 * (TAX-INCOME - 2000) + 200.
(0047)                      GO TO CALC-END.
(0048)              CALC-OR-4.
(0049)                  COMPUTE TAX = 0.4 * (TAX-INCOME - 4000) + 800.
(0050)              CALC-END.
(0051)                  DISPLAY "INCOME TAX " TAX.
(0052)                  DISPLAY "INPUT GROSS SALARY (5 DIGITS)".
(0053)                  DISPLAY "TYPE ZERO TO EXIT".
(0054)                  ACCEPT G-SALARY.
(0055)                  GO TO TAX-ITER.
(0056)              TAX-END.
(0057)                  STOP RUN.
(0058)              INC-END.
```

338

4.10.8

```
(0001)          IDENTIFICATION DIVISION.
(0002)          PROGRAM-ID. C4108.
(0003)          DATA DIVISION.
(0004)          WORKING-STORAGE SECTION.
(0005)          77 MARK PIC 999.
(0006)          77 GRADE PIC A.
(0007)          77 TOTAL-A PIC 99.
(0008)          77 TOTAL-B PIC 99.
(0009)          77 TOTAL-C PIC 99.
(0010)          77 TOTAL-D PIC 99.
(0011)          77 TOTAL-F PIC 99.
(0012)          PROCEDURE DIVISION.
(0013)          MARKS-SEQ.
(0014)              MOVE ZERO TO TOTAL-A, TOTAL-B, TOTAL-C, TOTAL-D, TOTAL-F.
(0015)              DISPLAY "INPUT MARK (3 DIGITS)".
(0016)              ACCEPT MARK.
(0017)          STUDENT-ITER.
(0018)              IF MARK = 999 GO TO STUDENT-END.
(0019)          GRADE-SEL.
(0020)              IF MARK NOT < 40 GO TO GRADE-OR-2.
(0021)                  ADD 1 TO TOTAL-F, MOVE "F" TO GRADE.
(0022)              GO TO GRADE-END.
(0023)          GRADE-OR-2.
(0024)              IF MARK NOT < 50 GO TO GRADE-OR-3.
(0025)                  ADD 1 TO TOTAL-D, MOVE "D" TO GRADE.
(0026)              GO TO GRADE-END.
(0027)          GRADE-OR-3.
(0028)              IF MARK NOT < 60 GO TO GRADE-OR-4.
(0029)                  ADD 1 TO TOTAL-C, MOVE "C" TO GRADE.
(0030)              GO TO GRADE-END.
(0031)          GRADE-OR-4.
(0032)              IF MARK NOT < 70 GO TO GRADE-OR-5.
(0033)                  ADD 1 TO TOTAL-B, MOVE "B" TO GRADE.
(0034)                  GO TO GRADE-END.
(0035)          GRADE-OR-5.
(0036)              ADD 1 TO TOTAL-A, MOVE "A" TO GRADE.
(0037)          GRADE-END.
(0038)              DISPLAY "GRADE " GRADE.
(0039)              DISPLAY "INPUT MARK (3 DIGITS)".
(0040)              ACCEPT MARK.
(0041)          GO TO STUDENT-ITER.
(0042)          STUDENT-END.
(0043)              DISPLAY "GRADE A " TOTAL-A
(0044)              DISPLAY "GRADE B " TOTAL-B
(0045)              DISPLAY "GRADE C " TOTAL-C
(0046)              DISPLAY "GRADE D " TOTAL-D
(0047)              DISPLAY "GRADE F " TOTAL-F
(0048)              STOP RUN.
(0049)          MARKS-END.
```

4.10.9

IDENTIFICATION DIVISION full-stop missing.
PROGRAM ID. hyphen missing.
DATA DIVISION full-stop missing.
No WORKING-STORAGE SECTION.
PIC X20 parenthesis missing.
ITEM COST hyphen missing.
999V99 PIC missing.
PROCEDURE-DIVISION hyphen not required.
BILL-SEQ full-stop missing.
MOVE starts in wrong zone.
INPUT ITEM-DESC wrong verb, should be ACCEPT.
INPUT ITEM-COST wrong verb, should be ACCEPT, full-stop missing at end
    of sentence.
GOTO INPUT-END GOTO is two words GO   TO, INPUT-END does not exist.
INPUT ITER hyphen missing.
CALCULATE VAT = 0.15 X TOTAL use COMPUTE not CALCULATE
and * not X.
OUTPUT TOTAL verb should be DISPLAY.
STOP-RUN hyphen not required.
BILL-END full-stop missing.

Correct version.

IDENTIFICATION DIVISION.
PROGRAM-ID. QUEST09.
DATA DIVISION.
WORKING-STORAGE SECTION.
77 ITEM-DESC PIC X(20).
77 ITEM-COST PIC 999V99.
77 VAT PIC 999V99.
77 TOTAL PIC 9999V99.
PROCEDURE DIVISION.
BILL-SEQ.
    MOVE 0 TO TOTAL
    ACCEPT ITEM-DESC
    ACCEPT ITEM-COST.
INPUT-ITER.
    IF ITEM-COST = 0 GO TO INPUT-END.
        ADD ITEM-COST TO TOTAL
        ACCEPT ITEM-DESC
        ACCEPT ITEM-COST
    GO TO INPUT-ITER.
INPUT-END.
    COMPUTE VAT = 0.15 * TOTAL
    ADD VAT TO TOTAL
    DISPLAY TOTAL
    STOP RUN.
BILL-END.

4.10.10

Desk Check.

WEIGHT	TOT-WEIGHT	PARCEL-COUNT
	0	0.0
1.3000	1.3000	1.0
3.5000	4.8000	2.0
(1)2.6000		

note: PIC clause for WEIGHT is not large enough

| | 7.4000 | 3.0 |

note: since the weight of 12.6 cannot be represented the value for TOT-WEIGHT is now incorrect.

| 2.1000 | 9.5000 | 4.0 |
| 5.9000 | (1)5.4000 | 5.0 |

note: PIC clause for TOT-WEIGHT not large enough

.	.	.
.	.	.
5.5		10.0

note: PIC clause for PARCEL-COUNT not large enough

0

note: any value calculated for AVER-WEIGHT would be incorrect since the values stored in the other three identifiers are also incorrect.

Assumptions.

WEIGHT should represent the size of the test data i.e. PIC 99V9.
TOT-WEIGHT is too small to the sum of the weights, PIC 999V9 is better.

PARCEL-COUNT need not be a real number, PIC 99 would be better.

AVER-WEIGHT will truncate the average weight to a 1 digit value, thus giving an inaccurate answer. The answer should be the accuracy of the test data, therefore, a PIC 99V9 would be better.

WORKING-STORAGE SECTION.
77 WEIGHT PIC 99V9.
77 TOT-WEIGHT PIC 999V9.
77 PARCEL-COUNT PIC 99.
77 AVER-WEIGHT PIC 99V9.

5.6.1

Note: in the following answers the character b represents a space.

bbbb67
bbb45,277.45
254.89
bb$457.34
$***,*95.89
bb$294.56CR
835bb
4573−
bb528
bb67+
bbb−23
bbbb−45.78
267,845.90
bbbb1456bb23
bbbb345.00

6.8.2

FILE SECTION.
FD STOCK
    BLOCK CONTAINS 64 RECORDS.
    LABEL RECORDS ARE STANDARD.
01 STOCK-REC.
    02 STOCK-NOS PIC 9(8).
    02 DESC PIC X(20).
    02 QUANT PIC 999.
    02 RE-ORD PIC 999.
    02 COST PIC 99V99.
    02 LOCATION.
        03 FAC-CODE PIC A.
        03 BIN-CODE PIC 99.

6.8.4

WORKING-STORAGE SECTION.
01 RECORD-1-WS.
  02 FILLER PIC X(31) VALUE IS "SALES OF CARS (SOUTHERN REGION)".
01 RECORD-2-WS.
  02 FILLER PIC X(8) VALUE IS "COUNTY:b".
  02 COUNTY-WS PIC A(15).
01 RECORD-3-WS.
  02 FILLER PIC X(16) VALUE IS "TOWN:b".
  02 TOWN-WS PIC A(15).
01 RECORD-4-WS.
  02 MODEL-WS PIC A(8).
  02 FILLER PIC X(9) VALUE IS SPACES.
  02 SALE-WS PIC $$,$$$,$$9.

6.8.6

```
WORKING-STORAGE SECTION.
01 RECORD-1-WS.
   02 FILLER PIC X(18) VALUE IS "THE UNIVERSAL BANK".
01 RECORD-2-WS.
   02 FILLER PIC X(22) VALUE IS "STATEMENT OF ACCOUNT:b".
   02 ACCOUNT-NO-WS PIC 9(8)B9(7).
01 RECORD-3-WS.
   02 FILLER PIC X(51) VALUE IS "DATEbbDESCRIPTIONbbbbbDEBITbbbb
   "bCREDITbbbbbbBALANCE".
01 RECORD-4-WS.
   02 DATE-WS PIC X(6).
   02 DESCRIPTION-WS PIC X(12).
   02 DEBIT-WS PIC ZZ,ZZ9.99  BLANK WHEN ZERO.
   02 FILLER PIC XX VALUE IS SPACES.
   02 CREDIT-WS PIC ZZ,ZZ9.99  BLANK WHEN ZERO.
   02 FILLER PIC X(4) VALUE IS SPACES.
   02 BALANCE-WS PIC ZZ,ZZ9.99.
01 RECORD-5-WS.
   02 FILLER PIC X(25) VALUE IS SPACES.
   02 FILLER PIC X(16) VALUE IS "FINAL BALANCE".
   02 FINAL-BALANCE-WS PIC £££,££9.99DB.
```

6.8.8

```
ENVIRONMENT DIVISION.
CONFIGURATION SECTION.
SOURCE-COMPUTER. PR1ME 750.
OBJECT-COMPUTER. PR1ME 550.
SPECIAL-NAMES.
    CONSOLE IS TTY.
    PRINTER IS PRT.
    CURRENCY SIGN IS "F".
    DECIMAL-POINT IS COMMA.
INPUT-OUTPUT SECTION.
FILE-CONTROL.
    SELECT ALPHA ASSIGN TO CR0.
    SELECT BETA ASSIGN TO LP0.
    SELECT DELTA ASSIGN TO MT1,
    ORGANIZATION IS SEQUENTIAL.
    SELECT EPSILON ASSIGN TO MD1,
    ORGANIZATION IS SEQUENTIAL.
```

7.6.1   OPEN statements can be combined into one statement,

OPEN INPUT FILE-X, OUTPUT FILE-Y.

In reading a serial or sequential file it is necessary to **read ahead** so that a record is always available for processing. No read ahead in this program segment!

FILE-Y is opened for OUTPUT (i.e. writing), therefore, cannot be READ. Records can be moved from one file to another but files **cannot** be moved.

FILE-X is opened for INPUT (i.e. reading), therefore, cannot be written to. Never write a file always write a record.

No IF test at the beginning of the paragraph P2 as a means of an exit from this paragraph.

7.6.2   The statement IF RECORD-1 = "END" GO TO P3 assumes that RECORD-1 is only three characters in length. If RECORD-1 was larger than three characters then the condition would never be true.

The statement WRITE RECORD-1 AFTER ADVANCING 2 LINES assumes that the file being created is a report. If the first character of RECORD-1 is used for line-printer paper control then the first character of each record will not appear in each line of the report.

The structure of paragraph P2 is incorrect, the IF statement should be at the beginning of the paragraph.

In paragraph P3 the file cannot be read since it was previously created as a report file with paper control characters.

7.6.3   Sorting the file on the primary key FULL-NAME would order the file on the first names or initials of each employee. This would not be a very convenient way of ordering the file if it was to be searched on the key of surname which is a common practice. Sorting the file on the secondary key SEX would be pointless since it would not improve the classification of the records.

Sorting the file on the primary key DATE-OF-BIRTH only is not practical since the date of birth is organised as DDMMYY, which would result in the following ordering.

      010148
      010236
      010352
      010434
      .
      .
      .

Although these dates are in numerical sequence they are not in chronological sequence, therefore, sorting dates organised as DDMMYY is impractical. However, if the key is changed to YYMMDD then the data would be ordered as follows.

      340401
      360201
      480101
      520301
      .
      .
      .

Clearly this makes more sense since the oldest employee will be at the beginning of the file and the youngest employee at the end of the file.

7.6.6

```
(0001)        IDENTIFICATION DIVISION.
(0002)        PROGRAM-ID. C766.
(0003)        ENVIRONMENT DIVISION.
(0004)        INPUT-OUTPUT SECTION.
(0005)        FILE-CONTROL.
(0006)            SELECT SUBSCRIBERS ASSIGN TO PFMS.
(0007)        DATA DIVISION.
(0008)        FILE SECTION.
(0009)        FD SUBSCRIBERS
(0010)            LABEL RECORDS ARE STANDARD VALUE OF FILE-ID IS "SUBS".
(0011)        01 RECORD-1.
(0012)            02 FULL-NAME.
(0013)                03 SURNAME PIC X(19).
(0014)                03 INITIALS.
(0015)                    04 INIT-1 PIC A.
(0016)                    04 INIT-2 PIC A.
(0017)                03 TITLE PIC A(4).
(0018)            02 ADDRESS.
(0019)                03 ROAD PIC X(20).
(0020)                03 TOWN PIC X(20).
(0021)                03 POSTCODE PIC X(8).
(0022)            02 TELE-NUMBER PIC X(20).
(0023)            02 PREV-READ PIC 9(6).
(0024)            02 PRES-READ PIC 9(6).
(0025)        WORKING-STORAGE SECTION.
(0026)        01 END-STORE PIC XXX.
(0027)        PROCEDURE DIVISION.
(0028)        FILE-SEQ.
(0029)            OPEN OUTPUT SUBSCRIBERS.
(0030)            DISPLAY "INPUT SURNAME (MAX 19 CHARS) TYPE XXX TO STOP"
(0031)            ACCEPT SURNAME
(0032)            MOVE SURNAME TO END-STORE.
(0033)        INPUT-ITER.
(0034)            IF END-STORE = "XXX" GO TO INPUT-END.
(0035)                DISPLAY "INPUT INITIALS (MAX 2 CHARS)"
(0036)                ACCEPT INITIALS.
(0037)                DISPLAY "INPUT TITLE (MAX 4 CHARS)"
(0038)                ACCEPT TITLE.
(0039)                DISPLAY "INPUT ADDRESS"
(0040)                DISPLAY "ROAD (MAX 20 CHARS)"
(0041)                ACCEPT ROAD.
(0042)                DISPLAY "TOWN (MAX 20 CHARS)"
(0043)                ACCEPT TOWN.
(0044)                DISPLAY "POSTCODE (MAX 8 CHARS)"
(0045)                ACCEPT POSTCODE
(0046)                DISPLAY "INPUT TELEPHONE NUMBER (MAX 20 CHARS)".
(0047)                ACCEPT TELE-NUMBER.
(0048)                DISPLAY "INPUT PREVIOUS METER READING (6 DIGITS)"
(0049)                ACCEPT PREV-READ.
(0050)                DISPLAY "INPUT PRESENT METRE READING (6 DIGITS)"
(0051)                ACCEPT PRES-READ.
(0052)                WRITE RECORD-1.
(0053)                DISPLAY "INPUT SURNAME (MAX 19 CHARS) TYPE XXX TO STOP"
(0054)                ACCEPT SURNAME
(0055)                MOVE SURNAME TO END-STORE.
(0056)            GO TO INPUT-ITER.
(0057)        INPUT-END.
(0058)            CLOSE SUBSCRIBERS.
(0059)            STOP RUN.
(0060)        FILE-END.
```

7.6.7

```
(0001)              IDENTIFICATION DIVISION.
(0002)              PROGRAM-ID. C767.
(0003)              ENVIRONMENT DIVISION.
(0004)              INPUT-OUTPUT SECTION.
(0005)              FILE-CONTROL.
(0006)                  SELECT SUBSCRIBER ASSIGN TO PFMS.
(0007)                  SELECT SUB-REPORT ASSIGN TO PFMS.
(0008)                  SELECT SUB-WORK ASSIGN TO PFMS.
(0009)                  SELECT SUB-SORT ASSIGN TO PFMS.
(0010)              DATA DIVISION.
(0011)              FILE SECTION.
(0012)              SD SUB-WORK.
(0013)              01 RECORD-1.
(0014)                  02 SURNAME PIC X(19).
(0015)                  02 FILLER PIC X(26).
(0016)                  02 TOWN PIC X(20).
(0017)                  02 FILLER PIC X(40).
(0018)              FD SUBSCRIBER
(0019)                  LABEL RECORDS ARE STANDARD VALUE OF FILE-ID IS "SUBS".
(0020)              01 RECORD-2.
(0021)                  02 FILLER PIC X(105).
(0022)              FD SUB-SORT
(0023)                  LABEL RECORDS ARE STANDARD VALUE OF FILE-ID IS "SUBS1".
(0024)              01 RECORD-3.
(0025)                  02 FULL-NAME.
(0026)                      03 SURNAME-3 PIC X(19).
(0027)                      03 INIT-1 PIC A.
(0028)                      03 INIT-2 PIC A.
(0029)                      03 TITLE PIC A(4).
(0030)                  02 FILLER PIC X(48).
(0031)                  02 TELE-NUMBER PIC X(20).
(0032)                  02 PREV-READ PIC 9(6).
(0033)                  02 PRES-READ PIC 9(6).
(0034)              FD SUB-REPORT
(0035)                  LABEL RECORDS ARE STANDARD VALUE OF FILE-ID IS "SUB2".
(0036)              01 REPORT-OUT.
(0037)                  02 FILLER PIC X.
(0038)                  02 LINE-IMAGE PIC X(119).
(0039)
(0040)
(0041)              WORKING-STORAGE SECTION.
(0042)              01 RECORD-1-WS.
(0043)                  02 FILLER PIC X(24) VALUE IS SPACES.
(0044)                  02 FILLER PIC X(11) VALUE IS "SUBSCRIBERS".
(0045)              01 RECORD-2-WS.
(0046)                  02 FILLER PIC X(4) VALUE IS "NAME".
(0047)                  02 FILLER PIC X(25) VALUE IS SPACES.
(0048)                  02 FILLER PIC X(33) VALUE IS "TELEPHONE NUMBER          UNITS US
(0049)       -        "ED".
(0050)              01 RECORD-3-WS.
(0051)                  02 TITLE-WS PIC X(5).
(0052)                  02 INIT-1-WS PIC A.
(0053)                  02 FILLER PIC X VALUE IS ".".
(0054)                  02 INIT-2-WS PIC AA.
(0055)                  02 SURNAME-WS PIC X(20).
(0056)                  02 TELE-NUMBER-WS PIC X(22).
(0057)                  02 UNITS-USED-WS PIC ZZZ,ZZ9.
(0058)              01 PARAMETERS.
(0059)                  02 UNITS-USED PIC S9(6).
(0060)                  02 E-O-F PIC 9 VALUE IS ZERO.
(0061)
(0062)              PROCEDURE DIVISION.
(0063)              FILE-SEQ.
(0064)                  SORT SUB-WORK ON ASCENDING KEY TOWN, SURNAME
(0065)                                  USING SUBSCRIBER
(0066)                                  GIVING SUB-SORT.
(0067)                  OPEN INPUT SUB-SORT
(0068)                       OUTPUT SUB-REPORT.
(0069)                  READ SUB-SORT.
```

(program continued)

```
(0070)          MOVE RECORD-1-WS TO LINE-IMAGE.
(0071)          WRITE REPORT-OUT AFTER ADVANCING PAGE.
(0072)          MOVE RECORD-2-WS TO LINE-IMAGE.
(0073)          WRITE REPORT-OUT AFTER ADVANCING 2 LINES.
(0074)          MOVE SPACES TO LINE-IMAGE.
(0075)          WRITE REPORT-OUT AFTER ADVANCING 1 LINE.
(0076)      INPUT-ITER.
(0077)          IF E-O-F NOT = 0 GO TO INPUT-END.
(0078)            MOVE TITLE TO TITLE-WS.
(0079)            MOVE INIT-1 TO INIT-1-WS.
(0080)            MOVE INIT-2 TO INIT-2-WS.
(0081)            MOVE SURNAME-3 TO SURNAME-WS.
(0082)            MOVE TELE-NUMBER TO TELE-NUMBER-WS.
(0083)            SUBTRACT PREV-READ FROM PRES-READ GIVING UNITS-USED-WS.
(0084)            MOVE RECORD-3-WS TO LINE-IMAGE.
(0085)            WRITE REPORT-OUT AFTER ADVANCING 1 LINE.
(0086)            READ SUB-SORT AT END MOVE 1 TO E-O-F.
(0087)          GO TO INPUT-ITER.
(0088)      INPUT-END.
(0089)          CLOSE SUB-SORT
(0090)              SUB-REPORT.
(0091)          STOP RUN.
(0092)      FILE-END.
```

8.5.1

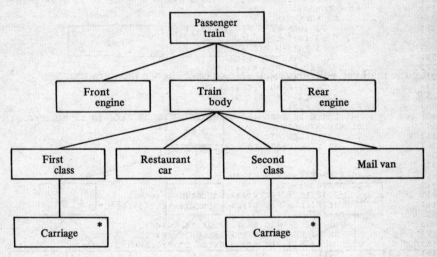

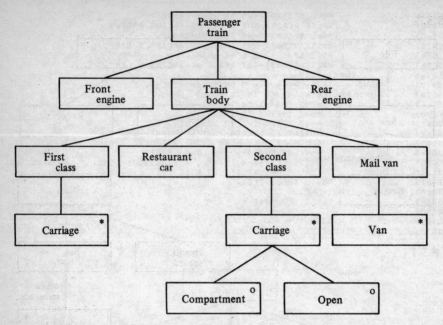

Note: the mail van will be present zero or once, hence the iteration.

8.5.2

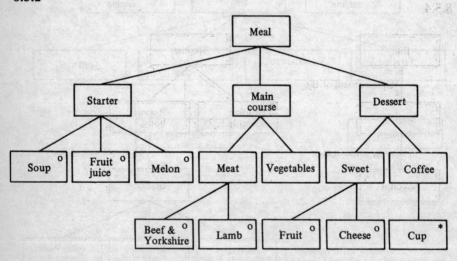

8.5.3

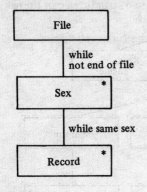
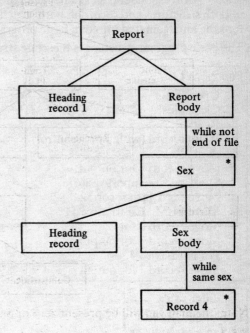

8.5.4

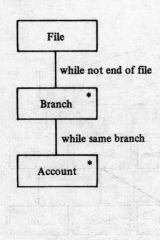
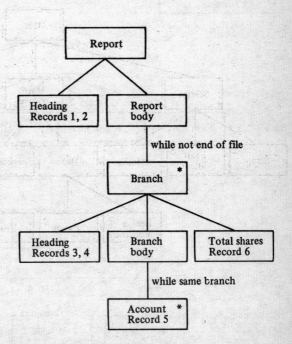

8.5.5   Correspondences exist between file and report at the highest level, sex in both structures and record in both structures. The two structures can therefore, be amalgamated into one basic program structure.

The basic program structure is the same structure as the report structure.

Functions List.

1. Open files.
2. Close files.
3. Read file.
4. Write record (with paper control)
5. Stop.
6. Move record 1 for output.
7. Store sex in temporary store.
8. Move MALE to record 2.
9. Move FEMALE to record 2.
10. Move record 2 for output.
11. Move record 3 for output.
12. Format record 4.
13. Move record 4 for output.

Conditions List

1. Not end of file.
2. Same sex and (1).
3. Sex female.

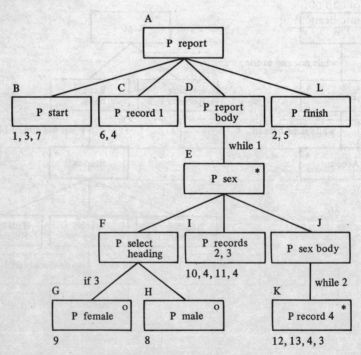

Detailed program structure (8.5.5)

8.5.6 Correspondences exist between the file and the report at the highest level, branch in both structures and account in both structures. The two structures can therefore, be amalgamated into one basic program structure.

The basic program structure is the same structure as the report structure.

Functions List.
1. Open files.
2. Close files.
3. Read file.
4. Write record (with paper control).
5. Stop.
6. Move record 1 for output.
7. Move record 2 for output.
8. Store branch code in record 3.
9. Move record 3 for output.
10. Move record 4 for output.
11. Format record 5.
12. Move record 5 for output.
13. Format record 6.
14. Move record 6 for output.
15. Initialise total shares to zero.
16. Increase total shares by number of shares for account holder.

Conditions List.
1. Not end of file.
2. Same branch.

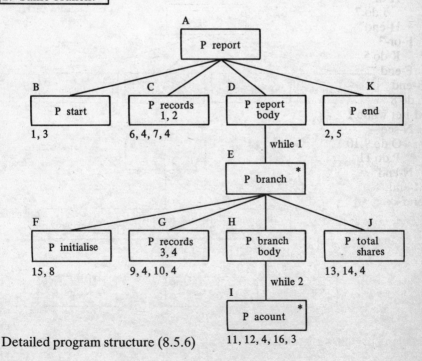

Detailed program structure (8.5.6)

8.5.7   **I**

A-seq
  B-sel if 2
    C do 1
  B-or
    D-iter while 1
      E do 6
    D-end
  B-end
  F do 3,4
  G do 2,5
A-end

8.5.7   **II**

A-seq
  B-seq
    C-iter while 1
      D-iter while 2
        E do 4,5
      D-end
    C-end
    F-sel if 4
      G do 1,2
    F-or-2 if 5
      H-sel if 3
        I do 3,6
      H-or
        J do 7
      H-end
    F-or-3
      K do 5
    F-end
  B-end
  L do 8
  M-iter while 1
    N-seq
      O do 9,10
      P do 11
    N-end
  M-end
A-end

8.5.8   Schematic logic for 8.5.5.

A-seq
  B do 1,3,7
  C do 6,4
  D-iter while 1
    E-seq
      F-sel if 3
        G do 9
      F-or
        H do 8
      F-end
      I do 10,4,11,4
      J-iter while 2
        K do 12,13,4,3
      J-end
    E-end
  D-end
  L do 2,5
A-end

Schematic logic for 8.5.6.

A-seq
  B do 1,3
  C do 6,4,7,4
  D-iter while 1
    E-seq
      F do 15,8
      G do 9,4,10,4
      H-iter while 2
        I do 11,12,4,16,3
      H-end
      J do 13,14,4
    E-end
  D-end
  K do 2,5
A-end

9.4.1

```
(0001)          IDENTIFICATION DIVISION.
(0002)          PROGRAM-ID. C941.
(0003)          ENVIRONMENT DIVISION.
(0004)          INPUT-OUTPUT SECTION.
(0005)          FILE-CONTROL.
(0006)              SELECT EMPLOYEE ASSIGN TO PFMS.
(0007)              SELECT AGE-REPORT ASSIGN TO PFMS.
(0008)          DATA DIVISION.
(0009)          FILE SECTION.
(0010)          FD EMPLOYEE
(0011)              LABEL RECORDS ARE STANDARD, VALUE OF FILE-ID IS "EMPLO".
(0012)          01 RECORD-1.
(0013)              02 NAME PIC X(20).
(0014)              02 SEX PIC A.
(0015)              02 Y-O-B PIC 99.
```

(program continued)

```
(0016)          FD AGE-REPORT
(0017)            LABEL RECORDS ARE STANDARD, VALUE OF FILE-ID IS "OUTPUT".
(0018)          01 REPORT-OUT.
(0019)            02 FILLER PIC X.
(0020)            02 LINE-IMAGE PIC X(119).
(0021)          WORKING-STORAGE SECTION.
(0022)          01 RECORD-1-WS.
(0023)            02 FILLER PIC X(25) VALUE IS "AGE DISTRIBUTION OF STAFF".
(0024)          01 RECORD-2-WS.
(0025)            02 FILLER PIC X(5) VALUE IS "SEX: ".
(0026)            02 SEX-STATUS PIC X(6).
(0027)          01 RECORD-3-WS.
(0028)            02 FILLER PIC X(24) VALUE IS "YEAR OF BIRTH       NAME".
(0029)          01 RECORD-4-WS.
(0030)            02 FILLER PIC 99 VALUE IS 19.
(0031)            02 Y-O-B-WS PIC 99.
(0032)            02 FILLER PIC X(16) VALUE IS SPACES.
(0033)            02 NAME-WS PIC X(20).
(0034)          01 PARAMETERS.
(0035)            02 E-O-F PIC 9 VALUE IS ZERO.
(0036)            02 TEMP-STORE PIC A.
(0037)          PROCEDURE DIVISION.
(0038)          A-SEQ.
(0039)          B.
(0040)            OPEN INPUT EMPLOYEE, OUTPUT AGE-REPORT.
(0041)            READ EMPLOYEE.
(0042)          C.
(0043)            MOVE RECORD-1-WS TO LINE-IMAGE.
(0044)            WRITE REPORT-OUT AFTER ADVANCING PAGE.
(0045)          D-ITER.
(0046)            IF E-O-F NOT = 0 GO TO D-END.
(0047)          E-SEQ.
(0048)          F-SEL.
(0049)            IF SEX NOT = "F" GO TO F-OR.
(0050)          G.
(0051)            MOVE "FEMALE" TO SEX-STATUS.
(0052)            GO TO F-END.
(0053)          F-OR.
(0054)            MOVE "MALE" TO SEX-STATUS.
(0055)          F-END.
(0056)          I.
(0057)            MOVE SEX TO TEMP-STORE.
(0058)            MOVE RECORD-2-WS TO LINE-IMAGE.
(0059)            WRITE REPORT-OUT AFTER ADVANCING 1 LINE.
(0060)            MOVE RECORD-3-WS TO LINE-IMAGE.
(0061)            WRITE REPORT-OUT AFTER ADVANCING 1 LINE.
(0062)          J-ITER.
(0063)            IF SEX NOT = TEMP-STORE OR E-O-F NOT = 0 GO TO J-END.
(0064)          K.
(0065)            MOVE Y-O-B TO Y-O-B-WS.
(0066)            MOVE NAME TO NAME-WS.
(0067)            MOVE RECORD-4-WS TO LINE-IMAGE.
(0068)            WRITE REPORT-OUT AFTER ADVANCING 1 LINE.
(0069)            READ EMPLOYEE AT END MOVE 1 TO E-O-F.
(0070)            GO TO J-ITER.
(0071)          J-END.
(0072)          E-END.
(0073)            GO TO D-ITER.
(0074)          D-END.
(0075)          L.
(0076)            CLOSE EMPLOYEE, AGE-REPORT.
(0077)            STOP RUN.
(0078)          A-END.
```

9.4.2

```
(0001)          IDENTIFICATION DIVISION.
(0002)          PROGRAM-ID. C942.
(0003)          ENVIRONMENT DIVISION.
(0004)          INPUT-OUTPUT SECTION.
(0005)          FILE-CONTROL.
(0006)              SELECT ACCOUNTS ASSIGN TO PFMS.
(0007)              SELECT SHARE-REPORT ASSIGN TO PFMS.
(0008)          DATA DIVISION.
(0009)          FILE SECTION.
(0010)          FD ACCOUNTS
(0011)              LABEL RECORDS ARE STANDARD, VALUE OF FILE-ID IS "SHARES".
(0012)          01 RECORD-1.
(0013)              02 BRANCH PIC X(5).
(0014)              02 ACCOUNT-NO PIC 9(6).
(0015)              02 SHARES PIC 9(5).
(0016)          FD SHARE-REPORT
(0017)              LABEL RECORDS ARE STANDARD, VALUE OF FILE-ID IS "OUTPUT".
(0018)          01 REPORT-OUT.
(0019)              02 FILLER PIC X.
(0020)              02 LINE-IMAGE PIC X(119).
(0021)
(0022)          WORKING-STORAGE SECTION.
(0023)          01 RECORD-1-WS.
(0024)              02 FILLER PIC X(33) VALUE IS "THE HAPPY HOMES BUILDING SOCIET
(0025)     -        "Y.".
(0026)          01 RECORD-2-WS.
(0027)              02 FILLER PIC X(44) VALUE IS "DETAILS OF ORDINARY SHARE ACCOU
(0028)     -        "NT CUSTOMERS.".
(0029)          01 RECORD-3-WS.
(0030)              02 FILLER PIC X(13) VALUE IS "BRANCH CODE: ".
(0031)              02 BRANCH-CODE PIC X(5).
(0032)          01 RECORD-4-WS.
(0033)              02 FILLER PIC X(40) VALUE IS "ACCOUNT NUMBER
(0034)     -        "£1 SHARES".
(0035)          01 RECORD-5-WS.
(0036)              02 ACCOUNT-NO-WS PIC 9(6).
(0037)              02 FILLER PIC X(25) VALUE IS SPACES.
(0038)              02 SHARE-WS PIC ZZ,ZZ9.
(0039)          01 RECORD-6-WS.
(0040)              02 FILLER PIC X(21) VALUE IS SPACES.
(0041)              02 FILLER PIC X(6) VALUE IS "TOTAL ".
(0042)              02 TOTAL-SHARES-ED PIC ££,£££,££9.
(0043)          01 PARAMETERS.
(0044)              02 E-O-F PIC 9 VALUE IS ZERO.
(0045)              02 TOTAL-SHARES PIC 9(7).
(0046)          PROCEDURE DIVISION.
(0047)          A-SEQ.
(0048)              PERFORM B.
(0049)              PERFORM C.
(0050)              PERFORM D-ITER UNTIL E-O-F NOT = 0.
(0051)              PERFORM K.
(0052)          B.
(0053)              OPEN INPUT ACCOUNTS
(0054)                   OUTPUT SHARE-REPORT.
(0055)              READ ACCOUNTS.
(0056)          C.
(0057)              MOVE RECORD-1-WS TO LINE-IMAGE.
(0058)              WRITE REPORT-OUT AFTER ADVANCING PAGE.
(0059)              MOVE RECORD-2-WS TO LINE-IMAGE.
(0060)              WRITE REPORT-OUT AFTER ADVANCING 1 LINE.
(0061)          D-ITER.
(0062)              PERFORM E-SEQ.
(0063)          K.
(0064)              CLOSE ACCOUNTS, SHARE-REPORT.
(0065)              STOP RUN.
(0066)          E-SEQ.
(0067)              PERFORM F.
(0068)              PERFORM G.
(0069)              PERFORM H-ITER UNTIL BRANCH NOT = BRANCH-CODE
(0070)                              OR E-O-F NOT = 0.
(0071)              PERFORM J.
```

(program continued)

```
(0072)          F.
(0073)               MOVE ZERO TO TOTAL-SHARES.
(0074)               MOVE BRANCH TO BRANCH-CODE.
(0075)          G.
(0076)               MOVE RECORD-3-WS TO LINE-IMAGE.
(0077)               WRITE REPORT-OUT AFTER ADVANCING 1 LINE.
(0078)               MOVE RECORD-4-WS TO LINE-IMAGE.
(0079)               WRITE REPORT-OUT AFTER ADVANCING 1 LINE.
(0080)          H-ITER.
(0081)               PERFORM I.
(0082)          J.
(0083)               MOVE TOTAL-SHARES TO TOTAL-SHARES-ED.
(0084)               MOVE RECORD-6-WS TO LINE-IMAGE.
(0085)               WRITE REPORT-OUT AFTER ADVANCING 1 LINE.
(0086)          I.
(0087)               MOVE ACCOUNT-NO TO ACCOUNT-NO-WS.
(0088)               MOVE SHARES TO SHARE-WS.
(0089)               MOVE RECORD-5-WS TO LINE-IMAGE.
(0090)               WRITE REPORT-OUT AFTER ADVANCING 1 LINE.
(0091)               ADD SHARES TO TOTAL-SHARES.
(0092)               READ ACCOUNTS AT END MOVE 1 TO E-O-F.
```

11.7.1   OCCURS should not be used at level 01.

OCCURS and VALUE should not be present in the same statement.

DATA-X should not have a PICTURE clause since the identifier represents the *rows* of the two-dimensional table and not the individual elements.

OCCURS should not be used at level 77.

REDEFINES should not be used in the FILE SECTION since it is enough to use different 01 entries to describe the records of a file in a different format.

REDEFINES should only be used to redefine an identifier of the same level.

Use REDEFINES immediately after the description of the identifier to be redefined.

11.7.2

01 TABLE-1.
   02 ALPHA PIC 999 OCCURS 50 TIMES.

01 TABLE-2.
   02 ALPHA OCCURS 10 TIMES.
      03 BETA PIC 9(5)V99 OCCURS 3 TIMES.

01 TABLE-2.
   02 ALPHA OCCURS 10 TIMES.
      03 BETA OCCURS 50 TIMES.
         04 GAMMA PIC X(20).
         04 DELTA PIC 999.

01 TABLE-3.
   02 TABLE-2 OCCURS 5 TIMES.
      03 TABLE-1 OCCURS 10 TIMES.
         04 EPSILON PIC 999 OCCURS 8 TIMES.

11.7.3

01 COUNTY-STRING.
  02 FILLER PIC X(27) VALUE IS "CORNWALLbDORSETbbbHAMPSHIRE".
01 COUNTY-TABLE REDEFINES COUNTY-STRING.
  02 COUNTY PIC X(9) OCCURS 3 TIMES.

```
01 TOWN-STRING.
   02 FILLER PIC X(33) VALUE IS "PENZANCEbbbTRUORObbbbbbNEWQUAYbbbb".
   02 FILLER PIC X(33) VALUE IS "POOLEbbbbbbbDORCHESTERbSHAFTESBURY".
   02 FILLER PIC X(33) VALUE IS "SOUTHAMPTONBASINGSTOKEWINCHESTERb".

01 TOWN-TABLE REDEFINES TOWN-STRING.
   02 COUNTIES OCCURS 3 TIMES.
      03 TOWNS PIC X(11) OCCURS 3 TIMES.

01 POPULATION-STRING.
   02 FILLER PIC X(54) VALUE IS "019360015690013890118922013880
 —   "04180204406060910031620".

01 TOWN-POPULATION REDEFINES POPULATION-STRING.
   02 COUNTY-POPULATION OCCURS 3 TIMES.
      03 POPULATION PIC 9(6) OCCURS 3 TIMES.
```

11.7.4

```
PROCEDURE DIVISION.
A-SEQ.
    PERFORM B.
    PERFORM C VARYING SUB FROM 1 BY 1 UNTIL SUB > 3.
    PERFORM D VARYING SUB FROM 1 BY 1 UNTIL SUB > 3.
    PERFORM E.
    PERFORM F.
    PERFORM C VARYING SUB FROM 1 BY 1 UNTIL SUB > 3.
    PERFORM G.
    PERFORM H VARYING SUB FROM 1 BY 1 UNTIL SUB > 3.
    PERFORM I VARYING ROW-SUB FROM 1 BY 1 UNTIL
      ROW-SUB > 3 AFTER COL-SUB FROM 1 BY 1 UNTIL
      COL-SUB > 3.
    PERFORM J.
B.
    ACCEPT COUNTY-NAME.
    ACCEPT TOWN-NAME.
C.
    IF COUNTY-NAME = COUNTY (SUB) MOVE SUB TO ROW-SUB.
D.
    IF TOWN-NAME = TOWNS (ROW-SUB, SUB) MOVE SUB TO COL-
    SUB.
E.
    DISPLAY "POPULATION OF " TOWN-NAME " IS "
    POPULATION (ROW-SUB, COL-SUB).
F.
    ACCEPT COUNTY-NAME.
G.
    MOVE ZERO TO COUNTY-POP, TOTAL-POP.
H.
    ADD POPULATION (ROW-SUB, SUB) TO COUNTY-POP.
I.
    ADD POPULATION (ROW-SUB, COL-SUB) TO TOTAL-POP.
```

J.

  COMPUTE PERCENTAGE-POPULATION = COUNTY-POP / TOTAL-POP * 100
  DISPLAY "PERCENTAGE POPULATION FOR " COUNTY-NAME " IS " PERCENTAGE-POPULATION.
  STOP RUN.

11.7.5

  PERFORM A VARYING SUB1 FROM 1 BY 1 UNTIL SUB1 > 50.

A. MOVE ZERO TO ALPHA (SUB1).

  PERFORM B VARYING SUB1 FROM 1 BY 1 UNTIL SUB1 > 10
        AFTER SUB2 FROM 1 BY 1 UNTIL SUB2 > 3.

B. MOVE ZERO TO BETA (SUB1, SUB2).

  PERFORM C VARYING SUB1 FROM 1 BY 1 UNTIL SUB1 > 10
        AFTER SUB2 FROM 1 BY 1 UNTIL SUB2 > 50.

C. MOVE SPACES TO GAMMA (SUB1, SUB2)
  MOVE ZERO TO DELTA (SUB1, SUB2).

  PERFORM D VARYING SUB1 FROM 1 BY 1 UNTIL SUB1 > 5
        AFTER SUB2 FROM 1 BY 1 UNTIL SUB2 > 10
        AFTER SUB3 FROM 1 BY 1 UNTIL SUB3 > 8.

D. MOVE ZERO TO EPSILON (SUB1, SUB2, SUB3).

11.7.6 02 RECORD OCCURS 50 TIMES INDEXED BY I.

Reserved word RECORD should not be used, and the statement does not need a full-stop.

ASCENDING-KEY IS NAME (I).

Hyphen not required in ASCENDING KEY, and NAME should not contain a parenthesised index.

04 TELE-NUMBER PIC 9(12).

Incorrect level number, should be 03 since this is part of the record. The PIC clause is also incorrect.

77 I PIC 99.

Since I is an index it does not need to be declared using a level number entry.

MOVE 1 TO I.

This is an illegal statement for an index.

INPUT-NAME (I).

This is an illegal identifier since no table using INPUT-NAME has been declared.

SEARCH ALL TELE-TABLE CHANGING NAME.

SEARCH ALL should be SEARCH since the contents of the table is not ordered into key sequence, TELE-TABLE should be RECORD, and CHANGING should be VARYING.

```
WORKING-STORAGE SECTION.
01 TELE-TABLE.
     02 RECORD-1 OCCURS 50 TIMES INDEXED BY I.
         03 NAME PIC X(12).
         03 TELE-NUMBER PIC X(12).
PROCEDURE DIVISION.
     SET I TO 1.
     ACCEPT INPUT-NAME.
     SEARCH RECORD-1 VARYING I
             AT END DISPLAY "NAME NOT FOUND"
     WHEN INPUT-NAME = NAME (I)
     DISPLAY TELE-NUMBER (I).
```

14.7.1 ALPHA-TEST values are the wrong type and format.

BETA-TEST must immediately follow BETA.

DELTA-TEST is either true or false, therefore, the type test NOT NUMERIC has no meaning. The statement should be: IF DELTA NOT NUMERIC GO TO ......

DELTA does not have the values true or false, therefore, the statement IF DELTA GO TO H-OR has no meaning.

14.7.2 The statements should have been written as:

INSPECT ALPHA TALLYING COUNTER FOR ALL SPACES AFTER INITIAL "."

where COUNTER is used to store the number of occurrences of spaces after the full-stop.

INSPECT BETA REPLACING CHARACTERS BY "0" BEFORE INITIAL "."

IF GAMMA PERFORM .....
assuming GAMMA is a condition name.

14.7.3

```
01 TIME-OF-DAY.
     02 HOURS-WS PIC 99.
         88 HOUR-TEST VALUES 0 THRU 23.
     02 MINS-WS PIC 99.
         88 MINS-TEST VALUES 0 THRU 59.
PROCEDURE DIVISION.
     IF TIME-OF-DAY NOT NUMERIC GO TO .....
         IF NOT HOUR-TEST OR NOT MINS-TEST GO TO .....
```

Appendix II.
Procedure Division coding based on the Draft Proposed Revised X3.23 American National Standard Programming Language COBOL.

This appendix is included to illustrate to readers how the COBOL language has been enhanced to meet the requirements of structure programming. A selection of the computer programs used in chapters 3,9 and 10 have been re-written and are included here. Only the Procedure Divisions are represented since this is where the changes are made to the coding, the other Divisions remain unchanged. The method uses in-line (or flat) code and is based on the following rules.

The code is written directly from the schematic logic.

All schematic logic labels (e.g. A-seq, B, C-iter, D-seq, etc) are coded as comments, unless they represent a procedure to be performed out-of-line.

All iterations, unless otherwise stated in the design, are coded using the in-line PERFORM....END-PERFORM statement, using a negated condition.

All binary selections are coded using the IF....ELSE....END-IF statement.

All multiple selections are coded using the EVALUATE.....END-EVALUATE statement.

The functions of these three statements has already been described in chapter two.

Coding a sequence (3.2.3).

```
      PROCEDURE DIVISION.
    *wages-seq
         ACCEPT HOURLY-RATE.
         ACCEPT HOURS-WORKED.
         MULTIPLY HOURS-WORKED BY HOURLY-RATE GIVING GROSS-WAGE.
         DISPLAY GROSS-WAGE.
         STOP RUN.
    *wages-end
```

Coding a binary selection (3.2.6).

```
      PROCEDURE DIVISION.
    *wages-seq
         ACCEPT HOURLY-RATE.
         ACCEPT HOURS-WORKED.
    *overtime-sel
         IF HOURS-WORKED > 40
            COMPUTE GROSS-WAGE
            = HOURLY-RATE * (1.5 * HOURS-WORKED - 20)
         ELSE
            MULTIPLY HOURS-WORKED BY HOURLY-RATE GIVING GROSS-WAGE
         END-IF
    *overtime-end
         DISPLAY GROSS-WAGE.
         STOP RUN.
    *wages-end
```

360

Coding a repetition (3.2.9)

```
    PROCEDURE DIVISION.
*wages-sec
        ACCEPT HOURLY-RATE.
        ACCEPT HOURS-WORKED.
*payroll-iter
        PERFORM UNTIL HOURS-WORKED < 0
*overtime-sel
            IF HOURS-WORKED > 40
                COMPUTE GROSS-WAGE
                = HOURLY-RATE * (1.5 * HOURS-WORKED - 20)
*overtime-or
            ELSE
                MULTIPLY HOURS-WORKED BY HOURLY-RATE GIVING GROSS-WAGE
            END-IF
*overtime-end
            DISPLAY GROSS-WAGE
            ACCEPT HOURS-WORKED
        END-PERFORM
*payroll-end
        STOP RUN.
*wages-end
```

Coding a multiple selection (3.3.3).

```
    PROCEDURE DIVISION.
*sales-sec
        ACCEPT PRODUCT-CODE.
        ACCEPT SALE-VALUE.
*comm-sel
        EVALUATE PRODUCT-CODE
        WHEN "A"
            MULTIPLY 0.005 BY SALE-VALUE GIVING COMMISSION
*comm-or-2
        WHEN "B"
            MULTIPLY 0.01 BY SALE-VALUE GIVING COMMISSION
*comm-or-3
        WHEN "C"
            MULTIPLY 0.02 BY SALE-VALUE GIVING COMMISSION
*comm-or-4
        WHEN "D"
            MULTIPLY 0.025 BY SALE-VALUE GIVING COMMISSION
        END-EVALUATE
*comm-end
        DISPLAY COMMISSION.
        STOP RUN.
*sales-end
```

Worked Example (3.4.3).

```
    PROCEDURE DIVISION.
*sales-sec
        MOVE ZERO TO TOTAL-COMMISSION.
        ACCEPT SALE-VALUE.
*total-sales-iter
        PERFORM UNTIL SALE-VALUE = 0
            ACCEPT PRODUCT-CODE
*comm-sel
        EVALUATE PRODUCT-CODE
        WHEN "A"
            MULTIPLY 0.005 BY SALE-VALUE GIVING COMMISSION
*comm-or-2
        WHEN "B"
            MULTIPLY 0.01 BY SALE-VALUE GIVING COMMISSION
*comm-or-3
        WHEN "C"
            MULTIPLY 0.02 BY SALE-VALUE GIVING COMMISSION
```

(program continued)

361

```
*comm-or-4
    WHEN "D"
        MULTIPLY 0.025 BY SALE-VALUE GIVING COMMISSION
    END-EVALUATE
*comm-end
        DISPLAY COMMISSION
        ADD COMMISSION TO TOTAL-COMMISSION
        ACCEPT SALE-VALUE
    END-PERFORM
*total-sales-end
        DISPLAY TOTAL-COMMISSION.
        STOP RUN.
*sales-end
```

Worked Example (9.2.2).

```
PROCEDURE DIVISION.
*A-seq
*B
    OPEN INPUT SALES-DATA
              OUTPUT REPORT-OUT.
    READ SALES-DATA.
    MOVE COUNTY TO COUNTY-STORE.
    MOVE TOWN TO TOWN-STORE.
*C
    MOVE RECORD-1-WS TO LINE-IMAGE.
    WRITE REPORT-OUT AFTER ADVANCING PAGE.
*D-iter
    PERFORM UNTIL E-O-F NOT = 0
*E-seq
*F
        MOVE COUNTY TO COUNTY-WS
        MOVE RECORD-2-WS TO LINE-IMAGE
        WRITE REPORT-OUT AFTER ADVANCING 2 LINES
*G-iter
        PERFORM UNTIL E-O-F NOT = 0
                OR COUNTY NOT = COUNTY-STORE
*H-seq
*I
            MOVE TOWN TO TOWN-WS
            MOVE RECORD-3-WS TO LINE-IMAGE
            WRITE REPORT-OUT AFTER ADVANCING 2 LINES
            MOVE SPACES TO LINE-IMAGE
            WRITE REPORT-OUT AFTER ADVANCING 1 LINE
*J-iter
            PERFORM UNTIL E-O-F NOT = 0
                    OR COUNTY NOT = COUNTY-STORE
                    OR TOWN NOT = TOWN-STORE
*K
                MOVE MODEL TO MODEL-WS
                MOVE SALE TO SALE-WS
                MOVE RECORD-4-WS TO LINE-IMAGE
                WRITE REPORT-OUT AFTER ADVANCING 1 LINE
                READ SALES-DATA AT END MOVE 1 TO E-O-F END-READ
            END-PERFORM
*J-end
*L
            MOVE TOWN TO TOWN-STORE
            MOVE SPACES TO LINE-IMAGE
            WRITE REPORT-OUT AFTER ADVANCING 2 LINES
*H-end
        END-PERFORM
*G-end
*M
        MOVE COUNTY TO COUNTY-STORE
        MOVE SPACES TO LINE-IMAGE
        WRITE REPORT-OUT AFTER ADVANCING 2 LINES
*E-end
    END-PERFORM
*D-end
*N
    CLOSE SALES-DATA
          REPORT-OUT.
    STOP RUN.
*A-end
```

Worked Example (9.3.2).

```
PROCEDURE DIVISION.
*A-seq
*B
     OPEN INPUT MUSIC-DATA
          OUTPUT REPORT-OUT.
     READ MUSIC-DATA.
     MOVE MUSIC-CODE TO MUSIC-CODE-STORE.
     MOVE STOCK-NUMBER TO STOCK-NUMBER-STORE.
*C
     MOVE RECORD-1-WS TO LINE-IMAGE.
     WRITE REPORT-OUT AFTER ADVANCING PAGE.
     MOVE ALL "-" TO TITLE-1.
     MOVE RECORD-1-WS TO LINE-IMAGE.
     WRITE REPORT-OUT AFTER ADVANCING 1 LINE.
*D-iter
     PERFORM UNTIL E-O-F NOT = 0
*E-seq
*F-sel
     EVALUATE MUSIC-CODE
     WHEN "A"
*G
          MOVE "POPULAR" TO TITLE-2
*F-or-2
     WHEN "B"
*H
          MOVE "JAZZ" TO TITLE-2
*F-or-3
     WHEN "C"
*I
          MOVE "CLASSICAL" TO TITLE-2
     END-EVALUATE
*F-end
*J
     MOVE RECORD-2-WS TO LINE-IMAGE
     WRITE REPORT-OUT AFTER ADVANCING 2 LINES
     MOVE RECORD-3-WS TO LINE-IMAGE
     WRITE REPORT-OUT AFTER ADVANCING 2 LINES
*K-iter
     PERFORM UNTIL E-O-F NOT = 0
            OR MUSIC-CODE NOT = MUSIC-CODE-STORE
*L-seq
*M-iter
     PERFORM UNTIL E-O-F NOT = 0
            OR MUSIC-CODE NOT = MUSIC-CODE-STORE
            OR STOCK-NUMBER NOT = STOCK-NUMBER-STORE
*N
          ADD QUANTITY TO TOTAL-QUANTITY
          READ MUSIC-DATA AT END MOVE 1 TO E-O-F END-READ
     END-PERFORM
*M-end
*O
          MOVE STOCK-NUMBER-STORE TO STOCK-NUMBER-WS
          MOVE TOTAL-QUANTITY TO QUANTITY-WS
          MOVE RECORD-4-WS TO LINE-IMAGE
          WRITE REPORT-OUT AFTER ADVANCING 1 LINE
          MOVE STOCK-NUMBER TO STOCK-NUMBER-STORE
          MOVE ZERO TO TOTAL-QUANTITY
*L-end
     END-PERFORM
*K-end
*P
          MOVE MUSIC-CODE TO MUSIC-CODE-STORE
*E-end
     END-PERFORM
*D-end
*Q
     CLOSE MUSIC-DATA
           REPORT-OUT.
     STOP RUN.
*A-end
```

Worked Example (10.9.1)

```
         PROCEDURE DIVISION.
         *A-seq
         *B
             OPEN INPUT FILE-A, FILE-B, OUTPUT FILE-C.
             READ FILE-A.
             READ FILE-B.
         *C-iter
             PERFORM UNTIL E-O-FA = 1 AND E-O-FB = 1
         *D-sel
                 IF KEYA < KEYB
         *E-sel
                     IF TCODE NOT = 3
         *EA-iter
                         PERFORM UNTIL TCODE = 3 OR KEYA NOT < KEYB
         *EB
                             DISPLAY "ERROR-ATEMPT TO AMEND/DELETE.NON-EXISTENT"
                                     " RECORD" RECORD-A
                             READ FILE-A AT END MOVE 1 TO E-O-FA, MOVE HIGH-VALUES
                             TO KEYA
                             END-READ
                         END-PERFORM
         *EA-end
                     ELSE
         *E-or
         *EC-seq
         *ED
                         MOVE KEYA TO STOREY
         *EE
                         MOVE KEYA TO KEYX
                         MOVE NAME-A TO NAME-X
                         MOVE ADDRESS-A TO ADDRESS-X
                         MOVE AMOUNT-A TO AMOUNT-X
                         READ FILE-A AT END MOVE 1 TO E-O-FA, MOVE HIGH-VALUES
                         TO KEYA
                         END-READ
         *EF-iter
                         PERFORM UNTIL TCODE NOT = 1 OR KEYA NOT = STOREY
         *EG
                             PERFORM SR-A-SEQ THRU SR-A-END
                         END-PERFORM
         *EF-end
         *EH-sel
                         IF TCODE = 2 AND KEYA = STOREY
         *EI
                             READ FILE-A AT END MOVE 1 TO E-O-FA, MOVE HIGH-VALUES
                             TO KEYA
                             END-READ
                         ELSE
         *EH-or
         *EJ
                             MOVE RECORD-X TO RECORD-C
                             WRITE RECORD-C
                         END-IF
         *EH-end
         *EC-end
                     END-IF
         *E-end
                 ELSE
         *D-or-2
                 IF KEYA = KEYB
         *F-sel
                     IF TCODE = 3
         *FA-iter
                         PERFORM UNTIL TCODE NOT = 3 OR KEYA NOT = KEYB
         *FB
                             DISPLAY "ERROR-ATTEMPT TO INSERT A RECORD THAT"
                                     " EXISTS" RECORD-A
                             READ FILE-A AT END MOVE 1 TO E-O-FA,
                             MOVE HIGH-VALUES TO KEYA
                             END-READ
                         END-PERFORM
```

(program continued)

```
*FA-end
            ELSE
*F-or
*FC-seq
*FE
                MOVE KEYA TO STOREY, KEYX
                MOVE NAME-B TO NAME-X
                MOVE ADDRESS-B TO ADDRESS-X
                MOVE AMOUNT-B TO AMOUNT-X
*FF-iter
                PERFORM UNTIL TCODE NOT = 1 OR KEYA NOT = STOREY
*FG
                    PERFORM SR-A-SEQ THRU SR-A-END
                END-PERFORM
*FF-end
*FH-sel
                IF TCODE = 2 AND KEYA = STOREY
*FI
                    READ FILE-A AT END MOVE 1 TO E-O-FA,
                    MOVE HIGH-VALUES TO KEYA
                    END-READ
                    READ FILE-B AT END MOVE 1 TO E-O-FB,
                    MOVE HIGH-VALUES TO KEYB
                    END-READ
                ELSE
*FH-or
*FJ
                    MOVE RECORD-X TO RECORD-C
                    WRITE RECORD-C
                    READ FILE-B AT END MOVE 1 TO E-O-FB,
                    MOVE HIGH-VALUES TO KEYB
                    END-READ
*FH-end
                END-IF
*FC-end
                END-IF
*F-end
            ELSE
*D-or-3
*G
                MOVE RECORD-B TO RECORD-C
                WRITE RECORD-C
                READ FILE-B AT END MOVE 1 TO E-O-FB,
                MOVE HIGH-VALUES TO KEYB
                END-READ
*D-end
            END-IF
          END-IF
        END-PERFORM
*C-end
*H
        CLOSE FILE-A, FILE-B, FILE-C.
        STOP RUN.
*A-end

 SR-A-SEQ.
*sr-aa-sel
        IF NAME-A NOT = ALL SPACES
*SR-ab
            MOVE NAME-A TO NAME-X
        END-IF
*SR-aa-end
*SR-ac-sel
        IF ADDRESS-A NOT = ALL SPACES
*SR-ad
            MOVE ADDRESS-A TO ADDRESS-X
        END-IF
*SR-ac-end
*SR-ae
        ADD AMOUNT TO AMOUNT-X
*SR-af
        READ FILE-A AT END MOVE 1 TO E-O-FA,
        MOVE HIGH-VALUES TO KEYA
        END-READ
 SR-A-END.
```

Appendix III.
Procedure Division verbs from the Nucleus module as defined in the Draft Proposed Revised X3.23 American National Standard Programming Language COBOL

The organisation of COBOL specifications in the Draft Proposed Standard are based on a functional processing module concept. The Standard defines eleven functional processing modules of which the Nucleus is one. The Nucleus module contains the language elements for internal processing of data within the basic structure of the four Divisions of a program. The purpose of this appendix is to provide the reader with the function, general format and rules of syntax of the Procedure Division verbs defined in the Nucleus so as to illustrate the compatibility between the Draft Proposed Standard and the 1974 Standard.

THE ACCEPT STATEMENT

Function

The ACCEPT statement causes low volume data to be made available to the specified data item.

General Format

Format 1:

ACCEPT identifier-1   [**FROM** mnemonic-name-1]

Format 2:

$$\text{ACCEPT identifier-2 FROM} \left\{ \begin{array}{l} \textbf{DATE} \\ \textbf{DAY} \\ \textbf{DAY-OF-WEEK} \\ \textbf{TIME} \end{array} \right\}$$

Syntax Rules

(1) Mnemonic-name-1 in format 1 must also be specified in the SPECIAL-NAMES paragraph of the Environment Division and must be associated with a hardware device.

THE ADD STATEMENT

Function

The ADD statement causes two or more numeric operands to be summed and the result to be stored.

General Format

Format 1:

$$\text{ADD} \left\{ \begin{array}{l} \text{identifier-1} \\ \text{literal-1} \end{array} \right\} \dots \text{ TO } \{\text{identifier-2 [ROUNDED]}\} \dots$$

[ON **SIZE ERROR** imperative-statement-1 [**END-ADD**]]

Format 2:

ADD $\begin{Bmatrix} \text{identifier-1} \\ \text{literal-1} \end{Bmatrix}$ ... TO $\begin{Bmatrix} \text{identifier-2} \\ \text{literal-2} \end{Bmatrix}$

    GIVING {identifier-3 [**ROUNDED**]} ...

    [ON **SIZE ERROR** imperative-statement-1 [**END-ADD**]]

Format 3:

ADD $\begin{Bmatrix} \textbf{CORRESPONDING} \\ \textbf{CORR} \end{Bmatrix}$ identifier-1 **TO** identifier-2 [**ROUNDED**]

    [ON **SIZE ERROR** imperative-statement-1 [**END-ADD**]]

Syntax Rules

(1) In formats 1 and 2, each identifier must refer to an elementary numeric item, except that in format 2 each identifier following the word GIVING must refer to either an elementary numeric item or an elementary numeric edited item. In format 3, each identifier must refer to a group item.

(2) Each literal must be a numeric literal.

(3) The composite of operands must not contain more than 18 digits.

    a. In format 1 the composite of operands is determined by using all of the operands in a given statement.

    b. In format 2 the composite of operands is determined by using all of the operands in a given statement excluding the data items that follow the word GIVING.

    c. In format 3 the composite of operands is determined separately for each pair of corresponding data items.

(4) CORR is an abbreviation for CORRESPONDING.

THE COMPUTE STATEMENT

Function

The COMPUTE statement assigns to one or more data items the value of an arithmetic expression.

General Format

COMPUTE {identifier-1 [**ROUNDED**]} ... = arithmetic-expression-1

    [ON **SIZE ERROR** imperative-statement-1 [**END-COMPUTE**]]

Syntax Rules

(1) Identifier-1 must reference either an elementary numeric item or an elementary numeric edited item.

THE CONTINUE STATEMENT

Function

The CONTINUE statement is a no operation statement. It indicates that no executable statement is present.

General Format

CONTINUE

Syntax Rules

(1) The CONTINUE statement may be used anywhere a conditional statement or an imperative-statement may be used.

THE DISPLAY STATEMENT

Function

The DISPLAY statement causes low volume data to be transferred to an appropriate hardware device.

General Format

DISPLAY $\left\{ \begin{array}{l} \text{identifier-1} \\ \text{literal-1} \end{array} \right\}$ ... [UPON mnemonic-name-1] [WITH NO ADVANCING]

Syntax Rules

(1) Mnemonic-name-1 is associated with a hardware device in the SPECIAL-NAMES paragraph in the Environment Division.

(2) Literal-1 may be any figurative constant, except ALL literal.

(3) If literal-1 is numeric, then it must be an unsigned integer.

THE DIVIDE STATEMENT

Function

The DIVIDE statement divides one numeric data item into others and sets the values of data items equal to the quotient and remainder.

General Format

Format 1:

DIVIDE $\left\{ \begin{array}{l} \text{identifier-1} \\ \text{literal-1} \end{array} \right\}$ INTO {identifier-2 [ROUNDED]} ...

[ON SIZE ERROR imperative-statement-1 [END-DIVIDE]]

Format 2:

DIVIDE $\left\{ \begin{array}{l} \text{identifier-1} \\ \text{literal-1} \end{array} \right\}$ INTO $\left\{ \begin{array}{l} \text{identifier-2} \\ \text{literal-2} \end{array} \right\}$

GIVING {identifier-3 [ROUNDED]} ...

[ON SIZE ERROR imperative-statement-1 [END-DIVIDE]]

Format 3:

DIVIDE $\left\{ \begin{array}{l} \text{identifier-1} \\ \text{literal-1} \end{array} \right\}$ BY $\left\{ \begin{array}{l} \text{identifier-2} \\ \text{literal-2} \end{array} \right\}$

GIVING {identifier-3 [ROUNDED]} ...

[ON SIZE ERROR imperative-statement-1 [END-DIVIDE]]

Format 4:

DIVIDE $\left\{ \begin{array}{l} \text{identifier-1} \\ \text{literal-1} \end{array} \right\}$ INTO $\left\{ \begin{array}{l} \text{identifer-2} \\ \text{literal-2} \end{array} \right\}$ GIVING identifier-3 [ROUNDED]

REMAINDER identifier-4

[ON SIZE ERROR imperative-statement-1 [END-DIVIDE]]

Format 5:

DIVIDE $\left\{ \begin{array}{c} \text{identifier-1} \\ \text{literal-1} \end{array} \right\}$ **BY** $\left\{ \begin{array}{c} \text{identifier-2} \\ \text{literal-2} \end{array} \right\}$ **GIVING** identifier-3 [**ROUNDED**]

REMAINDER identifier-4

[ON **SIZE ERROR** imperative-statement-1 [**END-DIVIDE**]]

Syntax Rules

(1) Each identifier must refer to an elementary numeric item, except that any identifier associated with the GIVING or REMAINDER phrase must refer to either an elementary numeric item or an elementary numeric edited item.

(2) Each literal must be a numeric literal.

(3) The composite of operands, which is the hypothetical data item resulting from the superimposition of all receiving data items (except the REMAINDER data item) of a given statement aligned on their decimal points, must not contain more than 18 digits.

THE EVALUATE STATEMENT

Function

The EVALUATE statement describes a multi-branch, multi-join structure. It can cause multiple conditions to be evaluated. The subsequent action of the object program depends on the results of these evaluations.

General Format

EVALUATE $\left\{ \begin{array}{l} \text{identifier-1} \\ \text{literal-1} \\ \text{expression-1} \\ \textbf{TRUE} \\ \textbf{FALSE} \end{array} \right\}$ ...

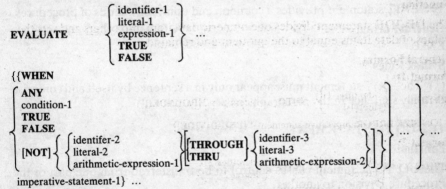

imperative-statement-1} ...

[**WHEN OTHER** imperative-statement-2]

[**END-EVALUATE**]

Syntax Rules

(1) The operands or the words TRUE and FALSE which appear before the first WHEN phrase of the EVALUATE statement are referred to individually as selection subjects and collectively, for all those specified, as the set of selection subjects.

(2) The operands or the words TRUE, FALSE, and ANY which appear in a WHEN phrase of an EVALUATE statement are referred to individually as selection objects and collectively, for all those specified in a single WHEN phrase, as the set of selection objects.

(3) Literal-1 cannot be the figurative constant ZERO.

(4) The words THROUGH and THRU are equivalent.

(5) Two operands connected by a THROUGH phrase must be of the same class. The two operands thus connected constitute a single selection object.

(6) The number of selection objects within each set of selection objects must be equal to the number of selection subjects.

(7) Each selection object within a set of selection objects must correspond to the selection subject having the same ordinal position within the set of selection subjects according to the following rules:

    a. Identifier, literals, or arithmetic expressions appearing within a selection object must be valid operands for comparison to the corresponding operand in the set of selection subjects.

    b. Condition-1 or the words TRUE or FALSE appearing as a selection object must correspond to a conditional expression or the words TRUE or FALSE in the set of selection subjects.

    c. The word ANY may correspond to a selection subject of any type.

(8) Conditional expressions may be simple or complex conditions but may consist only of the relation conditions or condition-name condition.

THE EXIT STATEMENT

Function

The EXIT statement provides a common end point for a series of procedures.

General Format

EXIT.

Syntax Rules

(1) The EXIT statement must appear only in a sentence by itself and comprise the only sentence in the paragraph.

THE GO TO STATEMENT

Function

The GO TO statement causes control to be transferred from one part of the Procedure Division to another.

General Format

Format 1:

GO TO procedure-name-1

Format 2:

GO TO {procedure-name-1} ...   **DEPENDING** ON identifier-1

Syntax Rules

(1) Identifier-1 must reference a numeric elementary data item which is an integer.

(2) If a GO TO statement represented by format 1 appears in a consecutive sequence of imperative statements within a sentence, it must appear as the last statement in that sequence.

THE IF STATEMENT

Function

The IF statement causes a condition to be evaluated. The subsequent action of the object program depends on whether the value of the condition is true or false.

General Format

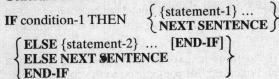

IF condition-1 THEN $\left\{ \begin{array}{l} \text{\{statement-1\} ...} \\ \textbf{NEXT SENTENCE} \end{array} \right\}$

$\left\{ \begin{array}{l} \textbf{ELSE \{statement-2\} ...} \quad \textbf{[END-IF]} \\ \textbf{ELSE NEXT SENTENCE} \\ \textbf{END-IF} \end{array} \right\}$

Syntax Rules

(1) Statement-1 and statement-2 represent either an imperative statement or a conditional statement optionally preceded by an imperative statement.

(2) The ELSE NEXT SENTENCE phrase may be omitted if it immediately precedes the terminal period of the sentence.

(3) If the END-IF phrase is specified, the NEXT SENTENCE phrase must not be specified.

THE INITIALIZE STATEMENT

Function

The INITIALIZE statement provides the ability to set selected types of data fields to predetermined values, e.g., numeric data to zeros or alphanumeric data to spaces.

General Format

INITIALIZE {identifier-1} ...

$\left[\text{REPLACING} \left\{ \begin{array}{l} \textbf{ALPHABETIC} \\ \textbf{ALPHANUMERIC} \\ \textbf{NUMERIC} \\ \textbf{ALPHANUMERIC-EDITED} \\ \textbf{NUMERIC-EDITED} \end{array} \right\} \textbf{DATA BY} \left\{ \begin{array}{l} \text{identifier-2} \\ \text{literal-1} \end{array} \right\} \right]$

Syntax Rules

(1) Literal-1 and the data item referenced by identifier-2 represent the sending area; the data item referenced by identifier-1 represents the receiving area.

(2) The category of the data item referred to by identifier-2 or literal-1 must be consistent with the category indicated by the phrase following the word REPLACING as defined in the appropriate paragraph such that a legal MOVE can be executed.

(3) If identifier-1 references an elementary item, its category must be identical to the category indicated by the phrase following the word REPLACING.

(4) The description of the data item referenced by identifier-1 or any items subordinate to identifier-1 may not contain the DEPENDING phrase of the OCCURS clause.

(5) An index data item may not appear as an operand of an INITIALIZE statement.

THE INSPECT STATEMENT

Function

The INSPECT statement provides the ability to tally or replace occurrences of single characters or groups of characters in a data item. Format 3 of the INSPECT statement is a transitional element in this revision of American National Standard COBOL because it is currently planned for deletion in a subsequent revision of American National Standard COBOL.

General Format

Format 1:

```
INSPECT identifier-1 TALLYING

{                   {  CHARACTERS  [ {BEFORE} INITIAL {identifier-4} ] ...                                                       }  }
{ identifier-2 FOR  {             [ {AFTER }         {literal-2  }     }                                                         }  } ...
{                   { {ALL    }  { {identifier-3} }  [ {BEFORE} INITIAL {identifier-4} ] ...                                      }  }
                      {LEADING}  { {literal-1  } }    {AFTER }         {literal-2  }
```

Format 2:

```
INSPECT identifier-1 REPLACING

{ CHARACTERS BY  { identifier-5 }  [ {BEFORE} INITIAL {identifier-4} ] ...                                                                           }
{                { literal-5   }     {AFTER }         {literal-2  }                                                                                  }
{ {ALL    }                                                                                                                                         } ...
{ {LEADING}  { identifier-3 }  BY { identifier-5 }  [ {BEFORE} INITIAL {identifier-4} ] ...                                                          }
{ {FIRST  }  { literal-1   }      { literal-3   }     {AFTER }         {literal-2  }                                                                 }
```

Format 3:

```
INSPECT identifier-1 TALLYING

{                   {  CHARACTERS  [ {BEFORE} INITIAL {identifier-4} ] ...                                    }  }
{ identifier-2 FOR  {             [ {AFTER }         {literal-2  }     }                                      }  } ...
{                   { {ALL    }  { {identifier-3} }  [ {BEFORE} INITIAL {identifier-4} ] ...                   }  }
  REPLACING           {LEADING}  { {literal-1  } }    {AFTER }         {literal-2  }

{ CHARACTERS BY  { identifier-5 }  [ {BEFORE} INITIAL {identifier-4} ] ...                                    }
{                { literal-5   }     {AFTER }         {literal-2  }                                           }
{ {ALL    }                                                                                                  } ...
{ {LEADING}  { identifier-3 }  BY { identifier-5 }  [ {BEFORE} INITIAL {identifier-4} ] ...                   }
{ {FIRST  }  { literal-1   }      { literal-3   }     {AFTER }         {literal-2  }                          }
```

Format 4:

```
INSPECT identifier-1 CONVERTING  { identifier-6 }  to  { identifier-7 }
                                 { literal-4    }      { literal-5    }

[ {BEFORE} INITIAL { identifier-4 } ] ...
  {AFTER }         { literal-2   }
```

Syntax Rules

ALL FORMATS:

(1) Identifier-1 must reference either a group item or any category of elementary item described, implicitly or explicitly, as USAGE IS DISPLAY.

(2) Identifier-3, ... , identifier-n must reference an elementary item described, implicitly or explicitly, as USAGE IS DISPLAY.

(3) Each literal must be nonnumeric and may be any figurative constant, except ALL literal. If literal-1, literal-2, or literal-4 is a figurative constant, it refers to an implicit one character data item.

(4) No more than one BEFORE phrase and one AFTER phrase can be specified for any one ALL, LEADING, CHARACTERS, FIRST, or CONVERTING phrase.

FORMATS 1 AND 3:

(5) Identifier-2 must reference an elementary numeric data item.

FORMATS 2 AND 3:

(6) The size of literal-3 or the data item referenced by identifier-5 must be equal to the size of literal-1 or the data item referenced by identifier-3. When a figurative constant is used as literal-3, the size of the figurative constant is equal to the size of literal-1 or the size of the data item referenced by identifier-3.

(7) When the CHARACTERS phrase is used, literal-2, literal-3, or the size of the data item referenced by identifier-4, identifier-5 must be one character in length.

FORMAT 4:

(8) The size of literal-5 or the data item referenced by identifier-7 must be equal to the size of literal-4 or the data item referenced by identifier-6. When a figurative constant is used as literal-5, the size of the figurative constant is equal to the size of literal-4 or the size of the data item referenced by identifier-6.

(9) The same character must not appear more than once either in literal-4 or in the data item referenced by identifier-6.

THE MOVE STATEMENT

Function

The MOVE statement transfers data, in accordance with the rules of editing, to one or more data areas.

General Format

Format 1:

MOVE $\left\{ \begin{array}{l} \text{identifier-1} \\ \text{literal-1} \end{array} \right\}$ TO {identifer-2} ...

Format 2:

MOVE $\left\{ \begin{array}{l} \text{CORRESPONDING} \\ \text{CORR} \end{array} \right\}$ identifier-1 **TO** identifier-2

Syntax Rules

(1) Literal-1 or the data item referenced by identifier-1 represents the sending area. The data item referenced by identifier-2 represents the receiving area.

(2) CORR is an abbreviation for CORRESPONDING.

(3) When the CORRESPONDING phrase is used, all identifiers must be group items.

(4) An index data item must not appear as an operand of a MOVE statement.

THE MULTIPLY STATEMENT

Function

The MULTIPLY statement causes numeric data items to be multiplied and sets the values of data items equal to the results.

General Format
Format 1:

MULTIPLY $\left\{ \begin{array}{l} \text{identifier-1} \\ \text{literal-1} \end{array} \right\}$ **BY** {identifier-2 [**ROUNDED**]} ...

[ON **SIZE ERROR** imperative-statement-1 [**END-MULTIPLY**]]

Format 2:

MULTIPLY $\left\{ \begin{array}{l} \text{identifier-1} \\ \text{literal-1} \end{array} \right\}$ **BY** $\left\{ \begin{array}{l} \text{identifier-2} \\ \text{literal-2} \end{array} \right\}$

GIVING {identifier-3 [**ROUNDED**]} ...

[ON **SIZE ERROR** imperative-statement-1 [**END-MULTIPLY**]]

Syntax Rules

(1) Each identifier must refer to a numeric elementary item, except, that in format 2 each identifier following the word GIVING must refer to either an elementary numeric item or an elementary numeric edited item.

(2) Each literal must be a numeric literal.

(3) The composite of operands, which is that hypothetical data item resulting from the superimposition of all receiving data items of a given statement aligned on their decimal points, must not contain more than 18 digits.

THE PERFORM STATEMENT

Function

The PERFORM statement is used to transfer control explicitly to one or more procedures and to return control implicitly whenever execution of the specified procedure is complete. The PERFORM statement is also used to control execution of one or more imperative statements which are within the scope of that PERFORM statement.

General Format
Format 1:

PERFORM $\left[\text{procedure-name-1} \left[\left\{ \begin{array}{l} \textbf{THROUGH} \\ \textbf{THRU} \end{array} \right\} \text{procedure-name-2} \right] \right]$

[imperative-statement-1 **END-PERFORM**]

Format 2:

PERFORM $\left[\text{procedure-name-1} \left[\left\{ \begin{array}{l} \textbf{THROUGH} \\ \textbf{THRU} \end{array} \right\} \text{procedure-name-2} \right] \right]$

$\left\{ \begin{array}{l} \text{identifier-1} \\ \text{integer-1} \end{array} \right\}$ **TIMES** [imperative-statement-1 **END-PERFORM**]

Format 3:

PERFORM $\left[\right.$ procedure-name-1 $\left[\left\{\begin{array}{l}\textbf{THROUGH} \\ \textbf{THRU}\end{array}\right\}\right.$ procedure-name-2 $\left.\left.\right]\right]$

$\left[\textbf{WITH TEST}\left\{\begin{array}{l}\textbf{BEFORE} \\ \textbf{AFTER}\end{array}\right\}\right]$ **UNTIL** condition-1

[imperative-statement-1 **END-PERFORM**]

Format 4:

PERFORM $\left[\right.$ procedure-name-1 $\left[\left\{\begin{array}{l}\textbf{THROUGH} \\ \textbf{THRU}\end{array}\right\}\right.$ procedure-name-2 $\left.\left.\right]\right]$

$\left[\textbf{WITH TEST}\left\{\begin{array}{l}\textbf{BEFORE} \\ \textbf{AFTER}\end{array}\right\}\right]$

VARYING $\left\{\begin{array}{l}\text{identifier-2} \\ \text{index-name-1}\end{array}\right\}$ **FROM** $\left\{\begin{array}{l}\text{identifier-3} \\ \text{index-name-2} \\ \text{literal-1}\end{array}\right\}$

BY $\left\{\begin{array}{l}\text{identifier-4} \\ \text{literal-2}\end{array}\right\}$ **UNTIL** condition-1

$\left[\textbf{AFTER}\left\{\begin{array}{l}\text{identifier-5} \\ \text{index-name-3}\end{array}\right\}\textbf{FROM}\left\{\begin{array}{l}\text{identifier-6} \\ \text{index-name-4} \\ \text{literal-3}\end{array}\right\}\right.$

$\textbf{BY}\left\{\begin{array}{l}\text{identifier-7} \\ \text{literal-4}\end{array}\right\}\textbf{UNTIL} \text{condition-2} \left.\right] \cdots$

[imperative-statement-1 **END-PERFORM**]

Syntax Rules

(1) If procedure-name-1 is omitted, imperative-statement-1 and the END-PERFORM phrase must be specified; if procedure-name-1 is specified, imperative-statement-1 and the END-PERFORM phrase must not be specified.

(2) In format 4, if procedure-name-1 is omitted, the AFTER phrase must not be specified.

(3) If neither the TEST BEFORE nor the TEST AFTER phrase is specified, the TEST BEFORE phrase is assumed.

(4) Each identifier represents a numeric elementary item described in the Data Division. In format 2, identifier-1 must be described as a numeric integer.

(5) Each literal represents a numeric literal.

(6) The words THROUGH and THRU are equivalent.

(7) If an index-name is specified in the VARYING or AFTER phrase, then:

    a. The identifier in the associated FROM and BY phrases must reference an integer data item.

    b. The literal in the associated FROM phrase must be a positive integer.

    c. The literal in the associated BY phrase must be a nonzero integer.

(8) If an index-name is specified in the FROM phrase, then:

    a. The identifier in the associated VARYING or AFTER phrase must reference an integer data item.

b. The identifier in the associated BY phrase must reference an integer data item.

c. The literal in the associated BY phrase must be an integer.

(9) Literal in the BY phrase must not be zero.

(10) Condition-1, condition-2, ... , may be any conditional expression.

(11) Where procedure-name-1 and procedure-name-2 are both specified and either is the name of a procedure in the declaratives portion of the Procedure Division, both must be procedure-names in the same declarative section.

THE SEARCH STATEMENT

Function

The SEARCH statement is used to search a table for a table element that satisfies the specified condition and to adjust the value of the associated index to indicate that table element.

General Format

Format 1:

SEARCH identifier-1 $\left[\text{VARYING} \quad \left\{ \begin{array}{l} \text{identifier-2} \\ \text{index-name-1} \end{array} \right\} \right]$

[AT END imperative-statement-1]

$\left\{ \text{WHEN condition-1} \quad \left\{ \begin{array}{l} \text{imperative-statement-2} \\ \text{NEXT SENTENCE} \end{array} \right\} \right\}$ ...

[END-SEARCH]

Format 2:

SEARCH ALL identifier-1 [AT END imperative-statement-1]

$\text{WHEN} \left\{ \begin{array}{l} \text{data-name-1} \left\{ \begin{array}{l} \text{IS EQUAL TO} \\ \text{IS} = \end{array} \right\} \left\{ \begin{array}{l} \text{identifier-3} \\ \text{literal 1} \\ \text{arithmetic-expression-1} \end{array} \right\} \\ \text{condition-name-1} \end{array} \right\}$

$\left[\text{AND} \left\{ \begin{array}{l} \text{data-name-2} \left\{ \begin{array}{l} \text{IS EQUAL TO} \\ \text{IS} = \end{array} \right\} \left\{ \begin{array}{l} \text{identifier-4} \\ \text{literal-2} \\ \text{arithemtic-expression-2} \end{array} \right\} \\ \text{condition-name-2} \end{array} \right\} \right]$ ...

$\left\{ \begin{array}{l} \text{imperative-statement-2} \\ \text{NEXT SENTENCE} \end{array} \right\}$

[END-SEARCH]

Syntax Rules

(1) In both formats 1 and 2, identifier-1 must not be subscripted or reference modified, but its description must contain an OCCURS clause including an INDEXED BY phrase. The description of identifier-1 in format 2 must also contain the KEY IS phrase in its OCCURS clause.

(2) Identifier-2 must reference a data item described as USAGE IS INDEX or as a numeric elementary data item without any positions to the right of the assumed decimal point. Identifier-2 may not be subscripted by the first (or only) index-name specified in the INDEXED BY phrase in the OCCURS clause associated with identifier-1.

(3) In format 1, condition-1 may be any conditional expression.

(4) In format 2, all referenced condition-names must be defined as having only a single value. The data-name associated with a condition-name must appear in the KEY IS phrase in the OCCURS clause referenced by identifier-1. Each data-name-1, data-name-2 may be qualified. Each data-name-1, data-name-2 must be subscripted by the first index-name associated with identifier-1 along with other indices or literals as required, and must be referenced in the KEY IS phrase in the OCCURS clause referenced by identifier-1. Indentifier-3, indentifier-4, or identifiers specified in arithmetic-expression-1, arithmetic-expression-2 must not be referenced in the KEY IS phrase in the OCCURS clause referenced by identifier-1 or be subscripted by the first index-name associated with identifier-1.

In format 2, when a data-name in the KEY IS Phrase in the OCCURS clause referenced by identifier-1 is referenced, or when a condition-name associated with a data-name in the KEY IS phrase in the OCCURS clause referenced by identifier-1 is referenced, all preceding data-names in the KEY IS phrase in the OCCURS clause referenced by identifier-1 or their associated condition-names must also be referenced.

(5) If the END-SEARCH phrase is specified, the NEXT SENTENCE phrase must not be specified.

THE SET STATEMENT

Function

(1) The SET statement establishes reference points for table handling operations by setting indices associated with table elements.

(2) The SET statement is also used to alter the status of external switches.

(3) The SET statement is also used to alter the value of conditional variables.

General Format

Format 1:

$$\text{SET} \quad \left\{ \begin{array}{l} \text{index-name-1} \\ \text{identifier-1} \end{array} \right\} \quad \cdots \quad \text{TO} \left\{ \begin{array}{l} \text{index-name-2} \\ \text{identifier-2} \\ \text{integer-1} \end{array} \right\}$$

Format 2:

$$\text{SET} \quad \{\text{index-name-3}\} \quad \cdots \quad \left\{ \begin{array}{l} \textbf{UP BY} \\ \textbf{DOWN BY} \end{array} \right\} \left\{ \begin{array}{l} \text{identifier-3} \\ \text{integer-2} \end{array} \right\}$$

Format 3:

$$\text{SET} \quad \left\{ \{\text{mnemonic-name-1}\} \right\} \quad \cdots \quad \text{TO} \left\{ \begin{array}{l} \textbf{ON} \\ \textbf{OFF} \end{array} \right\} \cdots$$

Format 4:

SET {condition-name-1} ... **TO TRUE**

Syntax Rules

(1) All references to index-name-1, identifier-1, and index-name-3 apply equally to all recursions thereof.

(2) Identifier-1 and identifier-2 must each reference an index data item or an elementary item described as an integer.

(3) Identifier-3 must reference an elementary numeric integer.

(4) Integer-1 and integer-2 may be signed. Integer-1 must be positive.

(5) Mnemonic-name-1 must be associated with an external switch, the status of which can be altered. The implementor defines which external switches can be referenced by the SET statement.

(6) Condition-name-1 must be associated with a conditional variable.

THE STOP STATEMENT

Function

The STOP statement causes a permanent or temporary suspension of the execution of the run unit. The literal variation of the STOP statement is a transitional element in this revision of American National Standard COBOL because it is currently planned for deletion in a subsequent revision of American National Standard COBOL.

General Format

$$\text{STOP} \begin{Bmatrix} \text{RUN} \\ \text{literal-1} \end{Bmatrix}$$

Syntax Rules

(1) Literal-1 may be any figurative constant, expect ALL literal.

(2) If a STOP RUN statement appears in a consecutive sequence of imperative statements within a sentence, it must appear as the last statement in that sequence.

(3) If literal-1 is numeric, then it must be an unsigned integer.

THE STRING STATEMENT

Function

The STRING statement provides juxtaposition of the partial or complete contents of two or more data items into a single data item.

General Format

$$\text{STRING} \begin{Bmatrix} \begin{Bmatrix} \text{identifier-1} \\ \text{literal-1} \end{Bmatrix} \end{Bmatrix} \dots \text{DELIMITED BY} \begin{Bmatrix} \text{identifier-2} \\ \text{literal-2} \\ \text{SIZE} \end{Bmatrix} \end{Bmatrix} \dots$$

    INTO identifier-3

    [WITH **POINTER** identifier-4]

       [ON **OVERFLOW** imperative-statement-1 [**END-STRING**]]

Syntax Rules

(1) Each literal may be any figurative constant, except ALL literal.

(2) All literals must be described as nonnumeric literals, and all identifiers, except identifier-4, must be described implicitly or explicitly as USAGE IS DISPLAY.

(3) Identifier-3 must not be reference modified.

(4) Identifier-3 must not represent an edited data item and must not be described with the JUSTIFIED clause.

(5) Identifier-4 must be described as an elementary numeric integer data item of sufficient size to contain a value equal to 1 plus the size of the data item referenced by identifier-3. The symbol 'P' may not be used in the PICTURE character-string of identifier-4.

(6) Where identifier-1 or identifier-2 is an elementary numeric data item, it must be described as an integer without the symbol 'P' in its PICTURE character-string.

THE SUBTRACT STATEMENT

Function

The SUBTRACT statement is used to subtract one, or the sum of two or more, numeric data items from one or more items, and set the values of one or more items equal to the results.

General Format
Format 1:

SUBTRACT $\left\{ \begin{array}{l} \text{identifier-1} \\ \text{literal-1} \end{array} \right\}$ ... **FROM** {identifier-2 **[ROUNDED]**} ...

   [ON **SIZE ERROR** imperative-statement-1 **[END-SUBTRACT]**]

Format 2:

SUBTRACT $\left\{ \begin{array}{l} \text{identifier-1} \\ \text{literal-1} \end{array} \right\}$ ... **FROM** $\left\{ \begin{array}{l} \text{identifier-2} \\ \text{literal-2} \end{array} \right\}$

   [ON **SIZE ERROR** imperative-statement-1 **[END-SUBTRACT]**]

Format 3:

SUBTRACT $\left\{ \begin{array}{l} \text{CORRESPONDING} \\ \text{CORR} \end{array} \right\}$ identifier-1 **FROM** identifier-2 **[ROUNDED]**

   [ON **SIZE ERROR** imperative-statement-1 **[END-SUBTRACT]**]

Syntax Rules

(1) Each identifier must refer to a numeric elementary item except that:

    a. In format 2, each identifier following the word GIVING must refer to either an elementary numeric item or an elementary numeric edited item.

    b. In format 3, each identifier must refer to a group item.

(2) Each literal must be a numeric literal.

(3) The composite of operands must not contain more than 18 digits.

    a. In format 1 the composite of operands is determined by using all of the operands in a given statement.

    b. In format 2 the composite of operands is determined by using all of the operands in a given statement excluding the data items that follow the word GIVING.

    c. In format 3 the composite of operands is determined separately for each pair of corresponding data items.

(4) CORR is an abbreviation for CORRESPONDING.

THE UNSTRING STATEMENT

Function

The UNSTRING statement causes contiguous data in a sending field to be separated and placed into multiple receiving fields.

General Format

UNSTRING identifier-1

$$\left[\textbf{DELIMITED BY} [\textbf{ALL}] \begin{Bmatrix} \text{identifier-2} \\ \text{literal-1} \end{Bmatrix} \left[\textbf{OR} [\textbf{ALL}] \begin{Bmatrix} \text{identifier-3} \\ \text{literal-2} \end{Bmatrix} \right] \dots \right]$$

INTO {identifier-4 [**DELIMITER** IN identifier-5] [**COUNT** IN identifier-6]} ...

[WITH **POINTER** identifier-7]

[**TALLYING** IN identifier-8]

[ON **OVERFLOW** imperative-statement-1 [**END-UNSTRING**]]

Syntax Rules

(1) Each literal must be a nonnumeric literal. In addition, each literal may be any figurative constant, except ALL literal.

(2) Identifier-1, identifier-2, identifier-3, and identifier-5 must reference data items described, implicitly or explicitly, as category alphanumeric.

(3) Identifier-4 may be described as either the category alphabetic, alphanumeric, or numeric (except that the symbol 'P' may not be used in the PICTURE character-string), and must be described implicitly or explicitly, as USAGE IS DISPLAY.

(4) Identifier-6 and identifier-8 must reference integer data items (except that the symbol 'P' may not be used in the PICTURE character-string).

(5) Identifier-7 must be described as an elementary numeric integer data item of sufficient size to contain a value equal to 1 plus the size of the data item referenced by identifier-1. The symbol 'P' may not be used in the PICTURE character-string of identifier-7.

(6) The DELIMITER IN phrase and the COUNT IN phrase may be specified only if the DELIMITED BY phrase is specified.

(7) Identifier-1 must not be reference modified.

Index

A margin – see zone A 7
ACCEPT 15, 62, 84, 95, 366
ACCESS 84, 236, 264
ADD 12, 321, 366, 367
AFTER 99
ALL 154
ALPHABETIC 278
ALPHABETIC – LOWER 278
ALPHABETIC – UPPER 278
ALTERNATE RECORD
 KEY 236, 264
AND 17
ASCENDING 107, 108, 193
ASCII 7, 317
AT END 97, 237
AUTHOR 46
Alphabetic 44
Alphanumeric 44
Array – see table 190

B margin – see zone B 7
BCD 318, 319
BEFORE 99
BLANK WHEN ZERO 69
BLOCK clause 83
Backtracking 309
Basic program structure 126
Binary search 205
Bit 318
Blocking factor 83
Boundary alignment 319
Boundary clash 295
Braces 10
Brackets 10
Buffer 83, 96, 98
Byte 189, 318

CALL 304
CLOSE 96, 237
COBOL Character set 7
COBOL Standards 10
COBOL program sheet 7, 8
COMPUTATIONAL 317, 318
COMPUTATIONAL – 1 318
COMPUTATIONAL – 2 318
COMPUTATIONAL – 3 317, 318

COMPUTE 14, 367
CONFIGURATION
 SECTION 84, 85
CONTINUE 367, 368
COPY 324
CORRESPONDING 321
CURRENCY 84, 85
Carriage control on printer 99
Character edit $ 67
Character edit + – 68
Character edit , B O 68
Character edit · 67
Character edit CR DB 69
Check digit 277, 290
Co-routines 298
Coding a multiple section 35
Coding a repetition 33
Coding a report 82
Coding a selection 30, 31
Coding a sequence 28
Columns 190
Comment 7
Compilation 51
Complication diagnostics 53
Condition names 278
Conditional statement 5
Conditions 16
Conditions list 25, 28, 31, 34, 128, 136
Continuation line 7
Correspondence 126

DATA DIVISION 1, 2, 46
DATA RECORD clause 82, 83
DATE 271, 272
DATE – COMPILED 46
DATE – WRITTEN 46
DECIMAL-POINT 84
DECLARATIVE 3, 325
DELETE 240, 241
DELIMITED 323
DESCENDING 107, 108, 193
DISPLAY 15, 62, 84, 95, 368
DIVIDE 14, 368
DOS 51
DUPLICATES 236
DYNAMIC 236, 241, 264

Data movement 69
Data structures 125, 135
Debugging 52
Decimal point 67
Defining fields 78
Desk check 27, 29, 32, 35
Detailed program structure 129, 137
Direct access 234
Divisions 1
Duplicate identifiers 320

EBCDIC 7, 317
ENVIRONMENT
 DIVISION 1, 2, 84, 86
ERROR 326
EVALUATE 18, 369
EXCEPTION 326
EXIT 28, 370
EXIT PROGRAM 304
Editing 54, 66
Editor 54
Elementary component 126, 128
Elementary item 77
Ellipsis 10
Empty file 326
End of file 96, 97, 98, 105, 326
Error data 276
Error listing 53
Error loading 54
Error logical 54
Error run-time 56

FD 83
FILE SECTION 1, 2, 82, 89
FILE-CONTROL 84, 86
FILLER 79, 101, 195
FROM 99, 240
Feasibility error 277
Field 76
Figurative constant 7
File 76
File maintenance 172, 242, 264
Floating sign 68
Format error 276
Functions
 list 25, 26, 29, 31, 34, 128, 136

GIVING 107, 108
GO TO 19, 370
GO TO DEPENDING ON 19
Good data 276

HIGH-VALUES 7, 164
Hierarchical code 148, 155

I-O 237, 326
IDENTIFICATION
 DIVISION 1, 2, 46
IF . . . ELSE . . . 16, 371
IN 320
INDEXED 193, 202, 204, 205, 318
INITIALIZE 324, 371
INPUT 96, 237, 326
INPUT-OUTPUT SECTION 84, 86
INSPECT 279, 372
INSTALLATION 46
INTO 97, 237
INVALID KEY 237, 238, 240
Imperative statement 5
In-line code 148
Indentation 18, 131
Index 202
Index area 234
Indexed sequential access 234
Indexed sequential files 234
Internal sort 230
Invalid data 276
Inversion 297, 298, 301

JCL 51
JUSTIFIED 70

Key words 5

LABEL clause 83
LEADING 187
LINKAGE-SECTION 1, 2, 305
Labels 83
Level 01-49 77, 101, 306
Level 66 274
Level 77 46, 101, 306
Level 88 278
Library 95, 324
Lineprinter control 89, 98
Literals 5, 6
Loading and running a program 54
Logical record 76, 83, 97, 98

MOVE 11, 320, 373
MULTIPLY 13, 374
Main program 297, 303, 306
Main storage area 234
Master file 164

Merging	160
Modular programming	224
Modules	224
Multiple Selection	34
Multiple read ahead	313
NEXT RECORD	237
NEXT SENTENCE	18
NOT	17
NUMERIC	44, 278
Non-numeric literal	6
Numeric Literal	6
OBJECT-COMPUTER	84
OCCURS	192
OCCURS DEPENDING ON	194
OF	320
ON SIZE ERROR	15, 61
OPEN	96, 237
OR	17
ORGANIZATION	84, 236, 264
OUTPUT	96, 237, 326
Operators	14
Optimisation	171
Optional words	5
Ordering clash	294
Overflow area	234
PAGE	99
PERFORM VARYING	198, 200
PERFORM in-line	20, 374, 375
PERFORM	
out-of-line	21, 148, 149, 374, 375
PICTURE	45
PROCEDURE	
DIVISION	1, 3, 10, 25
PROGRAM-ID	46
Paragraphs	3, 5
Parameter passing	305
Period	5
Physical record	83
Picture edit	66
Primary key	77
Processing file twice	315
Pure binary	318
Qualifications	320
RANDOM	236, 241, 264
READ	96, 237, 241

RECORD KEY	236
RECORD clause	83
REDEFINES	194, 195
RELATIVE	264
RELATIVE KEY	264
RENAMES	274
REWRITE	240, 241
ROUNDED	15, 61
Random access	234
Range error	277
Real-time	267
Recognition	309
Redesigning system	315
Relationship error	277
Relative Indexing	203
Relative access	234
Relative files	263
Repetition	31, 119
Report layout form	78
Report writer	103
Reserved words	5
Rows	190
SD	107, 108
SEARCH	204, 225, 228, 376
SEARCH ALL	204, 205, 225, 228, 376
SECURITY	46
SELECT	84, 86, 236, 364
SEPARATE	187
SEQUENTAL	236, 241, 264
SET	203, 377
SET DOWN	203
SET UP	203
SIGN IS	187
SORT	107, 108
SOURCE-COMPUTER	84
SPECIAL-NAMES	84
START	237, 238, 239, 241
STATUS	84, 236, 264
STOP	19, 378
STRING	323, 378
SUBTRACT	12, 321, 379
SYNCHRONIZED	319
Schematic logic	25, 27, 29, 31, 32, 35, 130, 131, 132, 138
Secondary key	107
Sections	1, 3
Selection	28, 118
Sentences	3, 5

Sequence 26, 117
Sequential file 77
Serial file 77
Side effects 309, 312
Sign bit 318
Sorting 107, 230
Source listing 52
Spooling 106
Statement 3, 5
Storing a program 51
String processing 322
Structure clash 294
Structure diagram 1, 107
Subprogram 297, 301, 304, 307
Subroutine 171
Subscript 190, 193
Symbols 5

TALLYING 280, 372
TIME 51
TIMES 192
TRAILING 187
Tables one-dimensional 190, 192, 202
Tables three-dimensional 191, 193, 202
Tables two-dimensional 190, 193, 202
Tertiary key 107
Test data 27
Transaction file 164
Transcription 277
Type error 276

UNSTRING 323, 380
USAGE 317
USE 325
USING 107, 108

V decimal point specifier 45
VALUE Clause 79
VALUE OF clause 83
Valid data 276
Variable length tables 194
Variables 5, 6
Visual display unit 15

WORKING-STORAGE
 SECTION 1, 2, 46, 79, 82
WRITE 98, 240, 241

ZERO 154
Zero supression 67
Zone A 7
Zone B 7